Acclaim for

ELLEN ALDERMAN AND
CAROLINE KENNEDY'S

The Right to Privacy

"A fascinating book that contains a wealth of information about everyday, ordinary citizens and what they should know about the law and their rights.... Eye-opening." —Ann Landers

"[Alderman and Kennedy] have a flair for telling human detail, making each case a riveting drama.... *The Right to Privacy* ... will open your eyes to the countless ways in which the most sacrosanct corners of our lives may be invaded." —*Chicago Tribune*

"These are the cases brought by individuals with whom we can all empathize. In this, Kennedy and Alderman bring home how intense and distressing is the pain from invasions of privacy.... By concentrating ... on the victims of physical intrusions, press coverage, biotechnology and videotaping, Kennedy and Alderman have found their niche." —*Boston Globe*

"One of the many virtues of *The Right to Privacy* ... is that it makes us feel in our gut the downside of the view that loss of privacy builds a stronger community.... [Alderman and Kennedy] persuade one that, on the whole, privacy is losing ground against public access, and we, as a society, should reexamine the balance.... Their book stands tall as a thought-provoking rebuke to all who view intrusion on others too casually." —*Newsday*

"With its vivid case studies and accessible legal explanations, [*The Right to Privacy*] is a powerful indictment of a Peeping Tom society.... The real-life stories at the heart of the book are gripping.... Fast-paced and engaging." —*Vogue*

ELLEN ALDERMAN AND
CAROLINE KENNEDY

The Right to Privacy

Ellen Alderman and Caroline Kennedy are attorneys who met at the Columbia University
School of Law. Ellen Alderman lives in Maine
and Caroline Kennedy lives in New York City.
This is their second book.

ELLEN ALDERMAN AND
CAROLINE KENNEDY

The Right to Privacy

VINTAGE BOOKS
A Division of Random House, Inc.
New York

FIRST VINTAGE BOOKS EDITION, FEBRUARY 1997

The Library of Congress has cataloged the Knopf edition as follows:

Alderman, Ellen, and Kennedy, Caroline, [date]
The right to privacy / by Ellen Alderman and Caroline Kennedy.
p. cm.
ISBN 0-679-41986-1
1. Privacy, Right of—United States.
I. Alderman, Ellen. II. Title.
KF1262.K46 1995
323.44′8′0973—dc20   95-14286
CIP

Vintage ISBN: 0-679-74434-7

Book design by Cassandra Pappas
Author photograph © Arthur L. Cohen

Random House Web address: http://www.randomhouse.com/

Printed in the United States of America
10 9 8 7 6 5

To William

To Ed

Contents

Acknowledgments   *ix*

Authors' Note   *xi*

Introduction   *xiii*

PRIVACY V. LAW ENFORCEMENT

Joan W. v. City of Chicago: The Strip Search Cases   3

People of New York v. Hollman: The Drug
Interdiction Cases   31

New Jersey v. T.L.O.: The School Search Cases   36

PRIVACY AND YOUR SELF

From Griswold to Casey: The Contraception and
Abortion Cases   55

Davis v. Davis: The Frozen Embryos Case   71

In re A.C.: The Forced Cesarean Case   95

Quill v. Koppell: The Right-to-Die Cases   127

Doe v. City of New York: The Other Constitutional
Right to Privacy   140

PRIVACY V. THE PRESS

   The Right to Be Let Alone   154

   Hall v. Post: The Case of an Adoption Revealed
     (Private Facts)   158

   Miller v. NBC: The Case of the Televised Death
     (Intrusion)   176

   Braun v. Flynt: The Case of the Swimming Pig
     (False Light)   191

   Arrington v. The New York Times Company:
     The Case of the Cover Photo (Appropriation)   209

PRIVACY V. THE VOYEUR

   Cooper v. Anderson: The Sex Tape Case   227

   McCall v. The Sherwood Inn: The Peephole Cases   249

PRIVACY IN THE WORKPLACE

   Soroka v. Dayton Hudson Corp.: Psychological
     Testing   277

   Shahar v. Bowers: Lifestyle Monitoring   294

   Shoars v. Epson America, Inc.: High-Tech
     Monitoring   310

PRIVACY AND INFORMATION   321

   Afterword to the Vintage Edition   335

   An Update   339

   Notes   343

   Bibliography   399

   Index   401

Acknowledgments

THERE ARE many people we would like to thank. Most importantly, we are indebted to those who were gracious enough to speak with us about their experiences, especially those who did so in spite of the personal pain it caused them to retell their stories. We would also like to thank their attorneys for their time and assistance.

Along the way, many people helped us at various stages, particularly our endnote researcher, Mindy Meade, and our editorial assistant, Svenja Soldovieri. We are also grateful to Maxine Rosenthal, Ilse Thielmann, and Aitken Thompson.

For crucial back-up support, we are indebted to Elaine Kennelly, Marta Sgubin, and Kristen Robinson. As they always do, our friends Arthur Cohen, Nicole Seligman, and Mark Geistfeld once again came through.

We feel particularly fortunate to have had the intelligence, judgment, and support of our editor, Peter Gethers, and our agent, Esther Newberg.

Finally, we would like to thank LEXIS/NEXIS for their generous support.

The following people were kind enough to speak with us:

Privacy v. Law Enforcement

Mark Beem, Richard Brzeczek, Peter Carey, Ted Choplick, Carol D., Lois DeJulio, Linda Fairstein, Frank Farfalla, Diane H., Harold Haley, John Klein, Lois Lipton, James McCarthy, Alan Nodes, Jody P.,

Linda P., Lisa P., Paul Schectman, Ted Stein, Mary T., Bruce Viania, Joan W., Jim Wheeler

Privacy and Your Self

Catherine Albisa, Mark Barnes, Vincent Burke, Sidney Callahan, Jay Christenberry, Charles Clifford, Brenda Davis, J. R. Davis, Marla Hassner, Mitchell Holtzman, Nan Hunter, Dr. I. Ray King, Madeleine McDowell, Barbara Mishkin, Leslie Moore, Lynn Paltrow, Timothy Quill, William Rubenstein, Mark Scherzer, Dan Stoner, Nettie Stoner, Sherri Stoner, Mary Stowe, Dr. Alan Weingold, Judge W. Dale Young

Privacy v. The Press

Clarence Arrington, Floyd Abrams, Marlene Belloni, Tom Belloni, Steve Bouser, Ed Braun, Jeannie Braun, Tom Capra, Ann Edgerton, Mitch Ezer, Larry Flynt, George Freeman, Mary Hall, Susie Hall, Alan Isaacman, Edward Klein, Ken Kulzick, Joe Millsaps, Ruben Norte, Rose Post, Jack Price, Hugh Stevens

Privacy v. The Voyeur

Debbie Anderson, Faye Anderson, Ken Burch, Barry Chasnoff, Jeff Cooper, Ron Krist, Peter McCall, Richard Morrison, Terry Nelson, Tom Riley, Keith Stapleton

Privacy in the Workplace

Judy Bain, Gail Dorn, Mica England, Karen Grabow, Ruth Harlow, Dorothy Kirkley, Bill Kirkpatrick, Rick Kranz, Lewis Maltby, Mike Lindsay, Jim Martin, King Rogers, Brad Seligman, Fran Shahar, Robin Shahar, Noel Shipman, Alana Shoars, Ann Smith, Sibi Soroka, Arthur Spitzer, Sheilah Stewart, Bob Sykes, Evan Wolfson

Privacy and Information

John Perry Barlow, Jerry Berman, Ira Glasser, Jan Lori Goldman, Evan Hendricks, Gary Marx, Eli Noam, Marc Rotenberg, Harvey Silverglate, Robert Ellis Smith

Authors' Note

ALTHOUGH the names of the people whose cases appear in this book are part of the public record, we have chosen to alter or delete some of them to protect the individuals' privacy. Because our primary goal was to explain the principles of law underlying the various aspects of the right to privacy, we offered to change the names of people with whom we spoke. In the few instances when they accepted, we have done so. We have also deleted or changed the names of some people we did not speak with, particularly those who had filed suit for invasion of privacy.

Introduction

THE WORD "privacy" does not appear in the United States Constitution. Yet ask anyone and they will tell you that they have a fundamental right to privacy. They will also tell you that privacy is under siege. We wrote this book to explore why people believe so strongly in the right to privacy, and what the legal system does to protect it, even though the right is not mentioned in our charter of freedom.

The issues are especially vital today as more and more of our privacy is stripped away. Private individuals join public figures in decrying "tabloid journalism" and complaining that the press can invade lives with impunity. Pro-choice advocates argue that a woman's right to make fundamental decisions is threatened by a hostile and intrusive government. Increasing concern about crime and terrorism, and calls for stricter law enforcement, have led to measures expanding the authority of police to enter our homes, search our belongings, and intercept our communications. And the notion that information can be kept secret to any degree may simply vanish in cyberspace.

Why we as Americans so cherish our privacy is not easy to explain. Privacy covers many things. It protects the solitude necessary for creative thought. It allows us the independence that is part of raising a family. It protects our right to be secure in our own homes and possessions, assured that the government cannot come barging in. Privacy also encompasses our right to self-determination and to define who we are. Although we live in a world of noisy self-confession, privacy allows us to keep certain facts to ourselves if we so choose. The right to privacy, it seems, is what makes us civilized.

Our own views on the subject evolved considerably during the time we worked on this book. As authors, we came to the subject with very different experiences, though with similar legal training as attorneys. One of us is a public figure who grew up with little privacy. The other is like the people in this book who, until recently, had taken the right to privacy for granted.

We began our research with the same gut reaction that most people have: there is less privacy than there used to be. As we immersed ourselves further in the topic, reading privacy cases and talking with people who had tried (and often failed) to vindicate their loss of privacy through the legal system, we concluded that things were worse than we originally thought. We came to realize that the general erosion of privacy is no longer affecting only well-known public personalities. Now, private individuals face a similar loss of privacy, and it is these people who are shaping the law. Whether it be the disclosure of intimate details about a person's life or interference with private decisions, there is a growing sense that all of us, well known and unknown, are losing control.

One hundred years ago, Justice Louis D. Brandeis called the right to privacy "the right to be let alone." Eloquent in its simplicity, Brandeis' phrase seems to sum up what most Americans have in mind when they think of privacy. However, legally, it offers no guidance at all. Coveting an indefinable right is one thing; enforcing it in a court of law is another.

Whether you have a recognized right to privacy, and whether that right has been violated so that you can vindicate yourself in court, depends on what area of privacy you are talking about. There are different legal sources for the right to privacy: the federal Constitution, state constitutions, federal and state statutes, and judicial decisions. Different legal doctrines govern the resolution of a given conflict, depending on the area of privacy involved.

Equally important to an understanding of the legal right to privacy (and the crucial element missing from the debate thus far) is an understanding of other interests that may override it. Whenever an invasion of privacy is claimed, there are usually competing values at stake. Privacy may seem paramount to a person who has lost it, but that right often clashes with other rights and responsibilities that we as a society deem important. Our right to be secure in our own homes often collides with a police officer's need to investigate a crime. A woman's right to terminate a pregnancy or refuse medical treatment often conflicts with the state's interest in protecting life and potential life. Our right to keep facts about ourselves secret often clashes with a free press, an employer's right to run a business, and the free flow of information for us all. The tradeoffs between privacy and competing social values or legal rights are different in each area.

Thus in researching this book, we concluded that the best way to understand our right to privacy was to break it down. We have chosen categories that reflect areas of our lives in which the law has distinctly recognized a privacy interest: Privacy v. Law Enforcement; Privacy and Your Self; Privacy v. The Press; Privacy v. The Voyeur; Privacy in the Workplace; and Privacy and Information.

Each topic could fill a book on its own. But in order to fully grasp the threat to privacy today, we must view the assault from all sides. Then, to understand what we can do about it, we need to take privacy apart and analyze the competing legal principles and societal interests.

Because privacy is by definition a personal right, it seemed that the best way to illustrate the legal principles involved was to tell the stories of people who have struggled to exercise that right. There is an inherent irony in asking people to reveal their private lives in a book on privacy, but we found that individuals who had suffered what they considered to be invasions of privacy, particularly when they also withstood legal battles to prove it, became committed to the cause. For the most part, they were more than willing to share their experiences and eager to prevent the same thing from happening to others.

Through the people we talked to, we learned that as much as we cherish our privacy, it does not always triumph. There are many intrusions which cause great personal pain but are not legally actionable. Not all betrayals rise to the level at which society, through the legal system, becomes involved. Some are just gossip or the acts of faithless friends, which the law can do nothing about. Other intrusions are deemed justifiable in order to let the press, police, employers, or others do their jobs. Even when the law does provide a remedy, the injuries caused by invasions of privacy are notoriously difficult to quantify. How much, in dollars, did it hurt when you were spied on in your hotel room? Or when you were strip-searched by police?

This book begins with a discussion of the Fourth Amendment. It is a good starting point because although the word "privacy" is not specifically mentioned in the Constitution, our right to be free from unreasonable searches and seizures is. The Fourth Amendment has been interpreted as protecting our privacy at least against government officials, and as such it is the most direct constitutional safeguard for privacy. The central question in this area is one that carries throughout the book: What can we reasonably expect to keep private?

The Constitution has also been interpreted to protect another form of privacy: the right to make decisions involving family life and procreation, including contraception and abortion. However, this form of privacy is not explicitly set out in the Constitution, but is derived from the broader concept of "liberty," and is therefore somewhat harder to define and more controversial. These conflicts we have grouped under the heading Privacy and Your Self.

In addition to our constitutional right, state laws also protect our privacy. Such laws cover what we commonly think of first when we hear the term "invasion of privacy": revelations about someone's private life or intrusions into his or her private space. Often these conflicts involve the press. But here there is a twist, for the Constitution is now on the other side. The press is specifically protected by the First Amendment, and in the battle over privacy that is a truly powerful shield.

The same state laws may be involved when one's privacy is compromised in an intimate manner. In Privacy v. The Voyeur we consider the area in which we are perhaps most vulnerable to invasions of privacy, but also, legally, most likely to prevail.

In Privacy in the Workplace we outline new privacy conflicts which are arising on the job. Employers, facing liability, rising health insurance costs, and more intense competition, are demanding more information about their workers and often obtaining it through new and more intrusive technology. Here, privacy interests often collide with an employer's right to run a business and earn a profit.

Finally, we look to the future and the privacy issues looming in the high-tech world of cyberspace. The law is lagging far behind in this area and we are making up the rules as we go along. So on the eve of the twenty-first century, we will have to decide anew: What can we as Americans reasonably expect to keep private?

Privacy v. Law Enforcement

The right of the people to be secure in their persons, houses, papers, and effects, against unreasonable searches and seizures, shall not be violated, and no Warrants shall issue, but upon probable cause, supported by Oath or affirmation, and particularly describing the place to be searched, and the persons or things to be seized.

—*The Fourth Amendment to the United States Constitution*

JOAN W. v. CITY OF CHICAGO

The Strip Search Cases

J OAN W. REMEMBERS exactly what she was wearing in Chicago on January 28, 1978. "I remember very distinctly," she says, "because when they made me undress, I had a whole lot of stuff to take off." Joan, age thirty-two, is the daughter of a midwestern college professor and a homemaker. She had recently graduated from medical school and moved to Chicago to take a job as an intern at the local VA hospital. On a rare Saturday off, she and her sister were headed to the Art Institute.

Joan dressed warmly for a windy, wintry day, all in her favorite color, purple. She wore panty hose, slacks, a turtleneck, a silk blouse with a tie, a sweater, and some inexpensive jewelry. She says, "I was really dolled up. You know, to go looking 'artsy' to the Art Institute." Joan picked up her sister in the hand-me-down car she had received from her father.

The two women were nearing the museum when a Chicago police officer stopped them. Joan had no idea what she had done wrong. The officer explained that the two-way street they were driving on had turned one-way—something Joan, unfamiliar with the city, had not known. She expected the officer to write her a ticket, but instead he directed her to follow him to the police station. Joan thought that was odd, but dutifully followed along.

At the station, she was informed that she had several outstanding parking tickets. Joan offered to pay the fines, but was told she had to be taken to the women's lockup across town. She asked if her sister could come along and was told no. Joan asked if she could make a

phone call, and was told no. She asked where, specifically, she was being taken, and was told nothing.

"They put me in a paddy wagon—one of those police wagons they
take the criminals to jail in," she says. The wagon had a small window
with bars, little steel shelves for seats, and nothing to hold on to. This
was of particular significance to Joan who, since she was a teenager,
had suffered from a form of rheumatoid arthritis affecting her spine,
hips, and joints. The ride in the paddy wagon took nearly half an
hour, and by the time they reached the police station, Joan was hob-
bling and angry.

Walking with a stiff limp, she followed the officers through a loading dock area and up an elevator to a floor of jail cells. She kept asking
where they were going, but got no response. "They put me in a
cell—a regular jail cell—and locked it. It was amazing," she says.
The cell was cold, gray, and empty, except for a toilet with a plywood
cover. For a moment, Joan was simply stunned that she was there.

Within minutes, two matrons entered the cell and demanded that
Joan take off all of her clothes. "Excuse me?" Joan responded.

"Take off all of your clothes," one of the matrons repeated. As
Joan recalls, the woman spit out the words.

"I'm in here for parking tickets," Joan explained. She assumed
there had to be some kind of mix-up or misunderstanding.

Several more matrons entered the cell and told Joan, "You better
start taking off your clothes now or you're in for big trouble."

Joan continued to protest. She said that she had not known it was
a one-way street and that she was ready to write a check for the parking tickets. The matrons again ordered her to strip. "They were clearly
delighted that I was kind of putting up a fight," Joan says. "It gave
them an excuse to be even more menacing."

The matrons moved in closer and Joan began to feel afraid. So she
started taking articles of clothing off, very slowly, one piece at a time.
"I was trying to see what was going to happen," she says. "I was very
modest. That is just the way I was. Even back in the sixties, in college,
I wouldn't take a shower or get undressed in front of anybody. My
mother is kind of Victorian. Actually, she is very very Victorian. And,
well, it was just *inconceivable* to me that I was going to be in a jail cell
taking my clothes off."

Joan removed her shoes, socks, sweater, and jewelry, then could
go no further. "Look," she said, "I'm a doctor. I don't even do this

to my patients! They have sheets and gowns and everything. AND–
I–AM–ONLY–HERE–FOR–PARKING–TICKETS!"

At the mention of Joan's profession, she says the matrons hooted.
They clearly did not believe her and began mocking the "doctor" in
their midst. An older matron approached the cell and Joan thought she
had come to stop the harassment. Instead, Joan says the woman told
Joan to strip "if you know what's good for you." The four other matrons moved in, forcing Joan to the back of the cell. By now she was
extremely frightened. Trembling, she removed her blouse, turtleneck,
and panty hose. The matrons told her to keep going. Joan took off her
underwear. "And then I just stood there," she says.

"Raise your left breast," one of the matrons ordered. Joan did.
"Now raise your right breast." Joan did as she was told. She was no
longer protesting. She wasn't saying a word. Then the matrons told
Joan to "spread your lips."

"I swear to God," Joan says, "I really wasn't sure what they wanted
me to do. I'm more familiar with that kind of language now, but then
I didn't know." Joan opened her mouth.

The matrons were yelling now. "Spread your lips!" Joan opened
her mouth wider. "Your lips, lady, your pussy!"

Finally, Joan understood and she spread the lips of her vagina. The
matrons ordered her to squat, which she did. The matrons taunted the
"doctor" and told her she was not doing anything right. "Get the hell
up in there and spread it," they said. Joan was spreading and squatting,
all at once, each time they told her to. "Now turn around and bend
over," they ordered. "Spread your cheeks." Joan turned around, bent
over, and pulled her buttocks apart so they could look inside.

"I felt like an animal," Joan says. "I felt like I had no control. I felt
like I was going through some—some kind of deportation or kind of
a—a—I felt like what I thought people I had seen in films of Nazis. I
felt like one of those people."

MARY T. AND Lillian, secretarial students, were in a car, pulling away
from a drugstore, when Chicago police stopped them for not having
the proper registration stickers. Mary, the driver, protested that it was
a borrowed car, and a male friend in the car began arguing with the
officers. Mary, Lillian, and their friend were arrested for disorderly conduct and taken to the city lockup.

Mary T. is a strong, outspoken woman, and for that, she says, she was treated particularly harshly. "[The matron] snatched Lillian's clothes off. Lillian is a little bitty something and [the matron] snatched Lillian's clothes down and shoved her. Then this lady put her hand all the way up inside Lillian. She didn't even wear a glove. I kept telling her she didn't have to do that and to stop. The more I yelled, the more [the matron] kept saying, 'You just better shut up, because your turn is coming.' She told me she was going to do the same thing to me, and she was going to let the men watch, the policemen watch, if I didn't cooperate.

"Well, of course, I *didn't* cooperate with her. I called her every name under the sun and my girlfriend just kept telling me to shut up and do as they say. But I just kept resisting. I'm not going to let this lady touch me like that. We were just students on our way home from school. I fought her and fought her and it didn't make any difference. She took her nightstick and she literally forced me with that stick. She did the same thing to me that she did to Lillian—she took her whole hand—and I don't know what she was doing, but she was using it as if it were a screwdriver or something, and there was nothing anybody could do. Those policemen over there heard us screaming in there, but they—I don't know if they watched or not.

"For her to be so brutal . . . I would never do that to a dog. I would never treat a dog the way that lady treated us."

WHAT HAPPENED to Joan W. and Mary T. was not unusual. It was not the result of a miscommunication or the fault of a few arrogant officers. What happened to them was the result of Chicago Police Department policy dating back to 1952. It was policy to take people to the lockup for even trivial traffic violations in order to run a background check or hold them until they could post bond, usually around thirty dollars. It was also policy that any woman in a Chicago lockup, no matter the reason for her arrest, be strip-searched. So since 1952, women had been plucked off the streets of Chicago for minor traffic offenses, taken to jail cells, and stripped.

The blanket strip-search policy did not discriminate on the basis of race, age, or class. White, black, Asian, and Hispanic women, teenagers and grandmothers, doctors, housewives, and college students—all were strip-searched. No exceptions were made. Menstruating women were simply told to remove tampons or drop sanitary napkins.

The only distinction was that of gender. Men taken to a city lock-up were subjected to a "pat-down" search instead.

Making matters worse, according to Richard Brzeczek, who at the time was executive assistant and chief legal counsel to the superintendent of police (and later was himself appointed superintendent), was that during this period there was only one lockup for women in the entire city. Thus, women, unlike men, had to be transported, often great distances, in handcuffs and paddy wagons, to be locked up. Brzeczek says, "We would ship them downtown and strip-search them and body-cavity-search them down there."

CAROL D. AND Diane H. lived next door to each other in Chicago. They also worked at Walgreen's together—Carol as the head cashier and Diane at the front register. Carol is tall and strong-willed; Diane is smaller and more timid. They were with Carol's husband, Diane's boyfriend, and two or three other men at a friend's apartment for a dinner party when, sometime after midnight, police came to the door. Diane and Carol did not know it, but the police had been there earlier in the evening responding to complaints about loud music. Now the police were back to arrest all of them for disorderly conduct.

At the police station, a woman in uniform approached them. "I thought she was a crossing guard," Carol says. The woman led Diane into another room, but no one knew why. She was gone for perhaps fifteen minutes, then Diane returned to the room where her friends were being detained. As Carol recalls, "[Diane's] blouse was raised. She was kind of tucking it back in her skirt, and she looked scared." The policewoman called for Carol, and her husband began to object. But Carol stood up, confident she could handle the situation, and followed the officer. When she came back, Carol was shaking. She, like Diane, had been strip-searched.

Before they could say anything, Carol and Diane were handcuffed together and led, by the cuffs, outside. They were taken in a paddy wagon to the women's lockup across town. They walked past several male police officers, through a door, and into a cell. There was another woman already in the cell. Carol and Diane were told to strip again.

"And then I objected strongly," Carol says. "My mouth was going. I remember telling her, 'This is ridiculous. They've already done this. We haven't been out of anyone's sight. What could you possibly gain? I don't want this done.' And she told me, 'Either you do it, honey, or we do it for you.' "

Carol and Diane submitted to the second strip search, removing their clothes, squatting, spreading, and bending over for inspection.

They were then kept in the cell for several hours. "I didn't sit at all in there," Carol says. "I just paced back and forth. And it dawned on me, as I looked toward the door we came in, that there were police officers walking around. I thought, my God, they were watching, they could see us." Carol says she also looked up and noticed a video monitor pointed at the cell.

When they were released, Carol's husband and the other men from the party came to pick them up. The men had been "patted down" once.

Unlike many of the other women who had been searched, Carol did not keep quiet. She called friends who worked with the police department and was told that this was simply how things were done. She called the police department herself to file a complaint and was told someone would come out to talk with her. When no one came, Carol called again, but again no one came. Then she gave up.

Carol D. was one of the very few who at least *tried* to speak out. The search policy had been in place for more than twenty-five years, during which time thousands of Chicago women had been strip-searched. Some told one or two close confidants, but most said nothing at all. They were frightened and felt humiliated, and tried to act as if the incident had never occurred. Some said that although they knew better, they could not shake the feeling that what had happened to them was somehow their fault. "The whole situation left me feeling like I had done something very wrong, like I was kind of a dirty person," Joan W. says. "They really were very effective in making you feel like they had every right to do this to you."

Those who did confide in someone were discouraged from speaking up. Mary T., who is black, told her sister and a girlfriend. She recalls: "My girlfriend says, 'Well, black people are not supposed to be lingering over anything like that.' And my sister said, 'You're not supposed to be thinking about things like that. . . . We black people forget, just like that. We pick up and carry on.' "

Even within the police department, it is unclear to what extent the policy was known. Richard Brzeczek says that he had not been aware of the policy until the story broke in the media and that he was "appalled" when he found out. According to Brzeczek, it is not unusual for a standard police practice to go on for years, even a practice such as strip searches which had gotten out of control, without others in the department knowing or caring. Brzeczek had come up through the ranks, working several years on the streets, and says, "If I ever, as a police officer, arrested a woman, after I had filled out all the paperwork and I took her to the detention area where she was going to be taken over by a female officer, I had no idea what went on. I mean, it's like the right hand not knowing what the left hand is doing." Apparently, once the women were placed in the detention cells, the matrons called the shots.

"Another thing in police departments," Brzeczek says, "if you ever question a policy—'Why do we do this?'—you know what the answer is? 'We've *always* done it that way.'"

However, by late 1979 the shroud of secrecy and indifference around the strip search policy began to unravel. A local civil rights and criminal defense attorney, Ted Stein, was asked to speak with a group of city social workers about their rights in an upcoming dispute with the city. "I went to someone's house," he says, "and toward the end of the evening there was a commotion and somebody came over and said there was a woman who wanted to speak with me. I went into the bedroom. There were several people and one of the women was hysterical."

It was a woman named MaryAnn T., one of the social workers who had attended the meeting. Not long before, during a snowstorm, she had illegally parked in front of the mental health center where she was employed. When she saw police officers ticketing her car, she ran out and argued with them. MaryAnn T. was arrested for disorderly conduct, taken to jail, and strip-searched. She told Ted Stein everything that had happened to her.

Stein says, "I thought it was shocking. I thought it was outrageous." He also thought it was an isolated incident. Stein filed a lawsuit on behalf of MaryAnn T., claiming, among other things, that the Chicago police had violated her Fourth Amendment rights.

At about the same time, the American Civil Liberties Union of Illinois also received a complaint about a strip search and had heard rumors of others. ACLU attorneys began to suspect a more widespread problem. They tipped off an investigative reporter at Channel 5, the local NBC station. Channel 5 ran a special segment on strip searches by the Chicago police, disguising the identities of several women who had agreed to tell their stories. The television report included the tele-

phone number of the ACLU and encouraged women with similar experiences to call.

"I *flew* off that couch," says Carol D. "I couldn't get to my phone
fast enough. I kept on saying the number over and over and over."
Mary T. also heard about the segment. It was as though a dam had
burst. The ACLU had expected a handful of calls; they received hundreds. "Something broke loose," Carol says. "Somebody finally said
something. Somebody finally did something."

After the television exposé, things began to happen quickly. The
ACLU filed a class action suit on behalf of all of the women, asserting
that the city's strip search policy violated the Fourth Amendment's
prohibition against unreasonable searches and seizures. The complaint
also charged that because the policy applied only to women, it violated the Equal Protection Clause of the Fourteenth Amendment. Public officials expressed outrage and called for a change. The Illinois
legislature passed a law prohibiting strip searches of people arrested for
misdemeanors without a reasonable belief that they were concealing a
weapon or contraband.

The city of Chicago agreed to change the police department policy. But it did not agree that the policy was unconstitutional in the first
place. The city defended itself against the charges in the women's
lawsuit, claiming that the strip searches were "reasonable" under the
Fourth Amendment.

THE FOURTH AMENDMENT is the most direct constitutional protection of our right to privacy. The amendment declares, in part, that
"the right of the people to be secure in their persons, houses, papers,
and effects, against unreasonable searches and seizures, shall not be violated." Although the word "privacy" does not appear in the Fourth
Amendment (or anywhere else in the Constitution), the Supreme
Court has interpreted the amendment as protecting an individual's
"reasonable expectation of privacy."

The Fourth Amendment grew out of opposition to the infamous
"writs of assistance" used by officers of the Crown against the colonists in the New World. The writs were, in essence, general warrants
allowing officers to enter private property and conduct a dragnet
search for "smuggled goods." Because they did not have to declare exactly what they were looking for and why, the British officers had full
power to act as they saw fit. Such unlimited discretion led to terrible

abuses. James Otis, Jr., said at the time that use of the writs "places the liberty of every man in the hands of every petty officer."

The Fourth Amendment was drafted to curb that power. After stating that all Americans have a right of protection against "unreasonable searches and seizures," the Founders declared that a warrant to conduct a search must be based upon "probable cause . . . particularly describing the place to be searched, and the persons or things to be seized." In other words, a police officer has to convince a judge or magistrate that he has good reason to believe he will find evidence of a crime, and then must specifically state where he is going to search and what he is looking for before he can get a warrant.

As with most rules, there are exceptions. In recent years, the Supreme Court has determined that the split-second demands of law enforcement often make obtaining a warrant impractical. For example, if a police officer witnesses a bank robbery and takes off in "hot pursuit" of the suspected felon, the officer does not have to stop off and get a warrant along the way. Or if a police officer enters a home with a warrant to look for drugs and sees a bomb in "plain view" on a desktop, the officer is not required to ignore the bomb simply because he does not have a warrant to search for it.

Most relevant to the Chicago strip search case, the Supreme Court has upheld certain exceptions to the warrant rule regarding people who are placed under arrest. The Court has recognized that such individuals may attempt to destroy evidence or conceal a weapon that could be used to escape or to harm the arresting officer. Therefore, if the police have lawfully arrested someone, they can search that person without a warrant.

But under the Fourth Amendment all searches, whether conducted with or without a warrant, must be "reasonable." The Court has stated that "reasonableness" is measured by balancing the need to search against the invasion that the search entails. The more intrusive the search, the greater the justification for it must be.

The city of Chicago argued that its strip search policy was constitutional under the well-established right to search people who have been placed under arrest. The city conceded that stripping individuals is an extreme form of search, but, the city's attorneys asserted, at the women's lockup a mere "pat-down" search would not suffice. Security at a lockup is always a serious concern, and women had been known to hide weapons and contraband in their body cavities. Thus, the city said, given the potential danger as well as the great number of women brought in for a variety of reasons, a blanket strip-search policy was needed to maintain the security of the lockup.

The city relied heavily on a recent Supreme Court decision regarding individuals who had been held in jail while awaiting trial on federal charges. In that case, the Supreme Court declared that in order to maintain security, all detainees could be strip-searched after contact visits with people from the outside.

The city of Chicago said that its own policy regarding female "detainees" was to require each woman to:

> (1) lift her blouse or sweater and to unhook and lift her brassiere to allow a visual inspection of the breast area, to replace these articles of clothing and then

> (2) pull up her skirt or dress or to lower her pants and pull down any undergarments, to squat two or three times facing the detention aide and to bend over at the waist to permit visual inspection of the vaginal and anal area.

The city said the matrons had no authority to physically probe female detainees, strip them naked, or conduct the search in front of other personnel.

A federal district court decided that, even in the form described by the city, the strip search policy was unconstitutional. (So the court did not have to consider that several women who had been subjected to the procedure contradicted the city's description of its policy.) First, the court said the city could not rely on the recent Supreme Court decision. That case had dealt with individuals charged with serious federal crimes who had failed to make bail. In contrast, the court pointed out, the Chicago women had been arrested for misdemeanors and were being detained only a few hours before paying minimal bail.

The court then declared that the few instances in which women had secreted weapons on their bodies in Chicago jails did not justify a strip search of every woman, regardless of why she was being detained. Furthermore, the court said, if dangerous weapons were the concern, the police could use handheld metal detectors, which would be just as effective and much less intrusive.

The court *did* say that a strip search may be justified if there were reasonable grounds to believe that a woman was hiding contraband in a body cavity (if she had been arrested on drug charges, for example).

But a strip search of a woman arrested for a traffic violation or other misdemeanor, without any reason to believe she was concealing contraband, was an "unreasonable" search under the Fourth Amendment.

With respect to the Equal Protection claim, the court found no justification for having different search procedures for men and women at a lockup. The court was unimpressed by the city's assertion that women were known to hide weapons and contraband in their brassieres, noting that it was just as easy for men to secrete items in *their* clothing. The court also pointed out that there was no reason to treat the rectal cavities of women differently from those of men. Finally, the court declared that the incremental risk posed by women having one more body cavity than men did not justify the grossly different, and far more intrusive, treatment.

In an attempt at damage control, the city of Chicago still maintained that the policy was constitutional, and appealed to the United States Court of Appeals for the Seventh Circuit. Meanwhile, under the district court opinion the women were entitled to receive monetary damages compensating them for any harm they had suffered as a result of the strip search.

Assessing damages is never easy, but compensation for privacy invasions is particularly difficult. The harm is almost always emotional rather than physical. The reasons we value our privacy are often hard to articulate. And by definition, the invasion is personal to the individual. In the strip search cases, each woman's experience, and her reaction to it, were different. So the district court ordered that each case be tried separately to determine the amount of damages to be awarded. Thus, the question became: When government officials invade your privacy in this way, how much is it worth?

There seems to be a qualitative difference between an invasion of privacy by your government and an invasion by a stranger. The women spoke of an abuse of a basic trust. They felt they had been violated by the very people who were supposed to be their protectors and expressed a sense of betrayal and vulnerability. All of them said they dreaded any future contact with the police.

Each of the women said the strip search had other lasting effects on their lives as well. Mary T. and others said that relationships had broken up over the incident, as some men did not understand the women's anger, humiliation, and fear of intimacy after the search. Joan W. said that for years afterward she undressed in a closet. Many women testified that jobs or schoolwork had suffered and that they had experienced nightmares and depression, as well as episodes of panic, shame, and rage.

Surprisingly, it was the strongest women who seemed most unnerved by their ordeal. Women like Joan, who had overcome great disabilities to become successful, or who, like Mary and Carol, had always kept going by keeping matters under tight control, were within minutes stripped of their defenses and their dignity. They were, as Mary T. said, "totally dismantled." It was these strong women who surprised themselves when, recalling the incident fifteen years later, they broke down and cried—their anguish and anger palpable.

In seeking compensation for the pain they had suffered, all of the women ran up against one of the ironies of privacy law. By bringing a lawsuit, they were ensuring that their private sphere would be breached again. They would have to testify in open court, as well as tell their story to several attorneys in preparation for trial. Even though they would be doing so voluntarily, many felt as if they were suffering a second intrusion.

Because of the sensitive nature of the claims, as well as the sheer number of them, the ACLU assigned many of the individual damages cases to outside attorneys. Ted Stein took on more than a dozen, including Mary T's. The victims' attorneys were certain that if their clients could go through with a trial, each would receive hundreds of thousands of dollars in damages. The city of Chicago was thinking more in terms of hundreds—period.

Thus, one day in 1982 Joan W. returned home from work and found a letter from the ACLU in her mailbox. The letter described the lawsuit, informed Joan that under the district court decision she was entitled to damages, and said the city was willing to settle with her for $800. Joan was surprised, to say the least. She had not seen the television exposé on the strip searches, nor any of the subsequent publicity. "I was working as a resident," she explains. "And I was totally out of it."

She did not know how the ACLU got her name. But for several years she had been trying to forget her ordeal with the police, and now she was not sure what the letter meant for her. "I didn't envision anything," she says. "I just knew that I didn't want $800 [for what happened]." Joan checked the appropriate box rejecting a settlement and returned the form.

Not long after, Joan again received word from the ACLU. They had found an attorney, Peter Carey, who was willing to bring her case to trial. At first, Joan was uneasy. She says, "I didn't want my name in the papers because I had just started a career, a private practice. I guess [I was afraid] that people were going to think that I was at fault. It was that same sort of feeling of shame that I had when I went through this." Peter Carey assured Joan that they could keep her identity confidential—as in the other cases, only her last initial would be used.

But Joan was still reluctant to discuss the incident at all, let alone with lawyers and in front of a jury. She said she would tell her story only once, at trial. Peter agreed. He says he wasn't worried. "I thought she was probably going to be an outstanding witness. She really had not been able to put [the strip search] behind her in any meaningful sense. So, telling it was, in effect, reliving it for her." In January of 1983, Peter Carey filed suit on behalf of "Joan W."

In the meantime, other women had been going to trial solely on the issue of damages. With each jury verdict, the victims' attorneys became more dismayed. MaryAnn T. was one of the first—a jury awarded her $30,000. MaryBeth G. and Sharon N., who had had experiences similar to Joan W.'s, each received $25,000. Hinda H., who had not been able to produce her driver's license when stopped for making an illegal left turn—and says she was then strip-searched in front of two men and eight to ten women—received the highest amount, $60,000. One woman received as little as $3,300.

Other women decided that they did not want to go to trial at all. Carol D. says, "I had had enough of them and they had had enough of me." She and Diane H. settled with the city for approximately $23,000 apiece. For Diane, that put an end to it. "I just try to let it go," she says. "It's done." But settling did not allow Carol to put the episode fully behind her. "The humiliation is still there. The anger is still there, and probably always will be," she says. "Unfortunately, I don't think they were punished enough. . . . What they had to pay was nothing for what we went through."

In contrast, Mary T. pushed ahead to trial. A jury awarded her $45,000 (when the city appealed, she accepted $39,000). Yet she, too, remains angry. "No amount of money that they could have awarded me could give me back my dignity—what they took away from me in that jail," she says. "I was angry because I wanted to beat her [the matron] up myself. . . . I wish they would have just fired that woman and the policeman [who arrested me]. I would have been happy with that. But I took the money and ran." Her attorney, Ted Stein, says that all of the jury awards were smaller than he had expected.

On the other hand, the damages were far larger than the city of Chicago thought the women deserved. The city now had another issue to appeal to the Seventh Circuit. First, city officials still did not agree that the strip searches had violated the Fourth Amendment and the Equal Protection Clause to begin with. Second, the city argued that even if there was a constitutional violation, the damage awards were excessive and should be reduced.

The Seventh Circuit disagreed. The appellate court affirmed the district court's decision that the policy was unconstitutional. The court said that the city's claim that the women had posed a dangerous threat did not make sense in light of the circumstances of the arrests. None of the women had been searched immediately, and some had even been permitted to follow the police to the station house in their own cars.

The court also found that the city's own evidence belied the threat of any real danger. To justify the searches, the city had supplied evidence stating that over one thirty-five-day period, eighteen hundred women were searched and nine items were found in body cavities. The court considered nine out of eighteen hundred to be a small amount and, most important, pointed out that the items came from women who had been arrested for prostitution or drugs, not parking tickets. In effect, the blanket strip searches were like the general searches conducted two hundred years ago under the notorious writs of assistance—the liberty of each woman had been placed in the hands of the police matrons.

The court also considered the nature of the search, declaring that a strip search is "one of the more humiliating invasions of privacy imaginable . . . dehumanizing, terrifying, repulsive . . . signifying degradation and submission." The court said: "Balanced against the [women's] privacy interests, such searches cannot be considered 'reasonable.'" The Seventh Circuit also agreed that the search policy violated the women's right to Equal Protection under the Fourteenth Amendment. With respect to the damage awards, the court indicated that it had "misgivings" about some of the higher awards, but said it would let the amounts stand.

Soon after the Seventh Circuit decision, in 1984, Joan W. went to trial to determine the amount of damages she should receive. She was one of the last women in the strip search cases to do so. Joan took the stand and told how she had been stopped for going the wrong way on a one-way street. She described her surprise, and mounting terror, as she realized that she was completely under the matrons' control. She explained the humiliation and degradation she had felt, and still feels, about submitting to the search. Friends, relatives, and her former supervisor testified about the changes they noticed in Joan after the incident.

Some of the matrons who had searched Joan testified for the city. But in contrast to Joan, who, as much as she tried, could not forget the uniformed women in that cell, none of the matrons really remembered Joan. She was just one of the hundreds of women they had processed.

The jury awarded Joan W. $112,000 in damages. Her attorney, Peter Carey, thought the amount should have been higher. But the city thought that an award almost twice that of any other was far too much. City attorneys immediately asked the trial judge to reduce the amount.

Judge Susan Getzendanner turned them down. She declared that the emotional distress Joan had suffered "amply justified the amount." Judge Getzendanner wrote: "The matrons had a single goal: to force the doctor to . . . weep and bend to their will." She also noted that even during their testimony at the trial, the matrons had been "aggressive and hostile."

Furthermore, the judge pointed out, the city's attorneys had cross-examined Joan in a "highly insulting and antagonistic manner." While such aggressive trial tactics can sometimes work, Judge Getzendanner wrote, "they run an enormous risk of focusing the jury's sympathy on the plaintiff. That happened in this case. It would be a mistake to reduce the plaintiff's verdict under these circumstances. A reduction would allow the city's attorneys to continue their use of very aggressive trial tactics in an effort to get low verdicts, without risking a high verdict when those tactics backfire."

Despite this rebuke, the city of Chicago appealed to the Seventh Circuit to reduce the amount of damages awarded to Joan W. This time, the appellate court agreed. Considering the amounts awarded in the other strip search cases (ranging from $3,300 to $60,000), the court declared an award of $112,000 to be "flagrantly extravagant." The court reduced Joan's damages to $75,000.

Joan W. did not mind. She says, "The joy I felt in that verdict was not so much the money, although that was pretty exciting, but that the jury really believed me and was mad for me." Unlike some of the other women who remain angry, Joan felt that the trial liberated her and finally allowed her to put the incident behind her. "You wouldn't think you would need to have someone say, 'You are a good person. You didn't do anything wrong.' But sometimes in our lives we really do need that, you know. And the trial did that for me. It really did." Most important, Joan was certain that her case would prevent others from being violated in the same way. "The jurors took the power that they had," she says, "and used it for all of those people that get stomped on. That's what I felt happy about."

DESPITE THE public outcry generated by the Chicago strip search trials, they did not put an end to this particular violation of the Fourth Amendment in the state of Illinois. In 1990, a district court judge expressed his disbelief and distress that Chicago's neighbor, Calumet City, was still conducting strip searches under a policy almost identical to the Chicago policy declared unconstitutional nearly a decade before. In Calumet City, women arrested for misdemeanors (such as driving with a suspended license or being underage in a tavern) were routinely strip-searched. At least twenty-seven women had been searched by *male* police officers. After ordering the women to strip and squat, the male officers lifted the women's breasts and inserted their fingers in the women's genitals. As in Chicago, only women were routinely searched in this manner. Men were strip-searched only if there was reason to believe that they were concealing contraband.

The district court judge who heard the Calumet City case noted that in spite of the widespread publicity about the unconstitutional Chicago policy, Calumet City had not altered its own procedures until the women there filed suit. He declared that not only constitutional law but also common sense dictated that such searches were an invasion of privacy.

Passing Judgments

*One of the most remarkable things about the Chicago (and Calumet City)
strip search policies is that they were not unique.*

A DENVER man on his way to work was stopped by police for
having an expired inspection sticker on his car. A routine check
turned up a warrant for failing to appear in court regarding a
speeding ticket. (The warrant was actually a mistake—the man
had appeared and paid the $18 fine.) Police took the man to
the police station. There, in a lobby area with ten or twelve
people milling about, he was ordered to remove his clothes,
face a wall, and allow officers to visually inspect him. He was
released when his wife arrived with bail. A few days later, the
man was notified that a mistake had been made and he could
come and claim his bail money.

The man sued for violation of his right to privacy under
the Fourth Amendment. Denver's policy was similar to Chicago's—all persons at the lockup, regardless of why they were
there and without regard to any suspicion that they were concealing contraband, were strip-searched. The policy applied to
men as well as women.

A District Court upheld the policy as "reasonable" under
the Fourth Amendment. In 1984, the Tenth Circuit Court of
Appeals reversed that decision and declared the strip search
policy a violation of the Fourth Amendment.

Hill v. Bogans, Colorado 1984

IN A 1985 case, several people in Hastings, Minnesota, male
and female, sued the county for its policy of indiscriminately
strip-searching all people booked at the county jail, even those
brought in for traffic violations and other misdemeanors. The

county claimed an "overwhelming need for security" at the
jail. A district court judge pointed out that over an eleven-year
period more than twenty thousand people had been strip-
searched at the county jail and only thirteen items had been
discovered. Furthermore, all of the items were found in clothing, not body cavities, and could have been discovered with a
"pat-down" search.

The judge declared: "The Court is appalled that at this
stage of civilized society citizens accused of minor infractions
of the law should be forced to undergo such treatment by their
government." He struck down the blanket strip searches as unconstitutional invasions of privacy.

Doe v. Boyd, Minnesota 1985

———

AN UPSTATE New York couple attended their daughter's wedding and reception, then hosted a party at their home for
some of the guests. The couple's son left the party to buy cigarettes and was attacked by a man wielding a baseball bat. The
son escaped serious injury, came home, and related the assault.
His mother called the police. Soon after, the son and other
family members left in search of the attacker.

The mother called the police again and was told that her
first call had been recorded as an episode of "malicious mis-
chief." She asked what she needed to do to get immediate
police assistance. The dispatcher allegedly told her that she
would have to report a shooting. She complied. The dispatcher
then informed the police that the woman had falsely reported
a shooting.

The police arrived at the the woman's home and placed
her under arrest. Her husband "exchanged words" with the
police. More officers arrived, and, according to the court, "the
officers eventually carried the woman out of her house and
transported her, still protesting, still dressed in formal wedding attire, now encumbered with handcuffs, to the Monroe
County Jail." There, she was charged with filing a false report
and resisting arrest (both misdemeanors). She was booked,
photographed, fingerprinted, and strip-searched. The police

barely had time to complete their procedure because within half an hour the couple's newlywed daughter arrived with bail money and sprang her mother from jail.

The woman was acquitted on all charges and filed suit claiming that the indiscriminate strip-search policy was unconstitutional. Although several such policies had been struck down by various courts, the District Court declared the strip search in this case "reasonable" under the Fourth Amendment.

The Second Circuit Court of Appeals reversed the decision. The appellate court said that a local sheriff's off-the-cuff "estimate" that 70 percent of arrestees conceal contraband was not enough to justify strip-searching every person brought in for any reason. The indiscriminate strip searches were invasions of privacy under the Fourth Amendment.

Weber v. Dell, New York 1986

———

IN THE 1980s, a Maryland woman was arrested at her suburban home at 10 p.m., transported to the Montgomery County Detention Center (MCDC), and charged with failing to appear in court regarding child support payments. Pursuant to policy, she was strip-searched and placed in a cell overnight. The charges were dismissed the next day. A district court ruled that the MCDC's blanket strip-search procedures were unconstitutional.

Nonetheless, the MCDC apparently did not discontinue its practice. In the 1990s, another Maryland woman suffered a similar fate. JLR's ex-husband swore under oath that she was not making required child support payments. Two deputies went to JLR's workplace, arrested her, put her against a wall, kicked her legs apart, and patted her down. They brought JLR to the squad car, where she says she was patted down again. JLR says that she was patted down a third time, upon arrival at the police station, then a fourth time, when they left for the Montgomery County Detention Center. She says a fifth pat-down occurred upon arrival at the MCDC, and a sixth and final pat-down before she was taken to a jail cell. Then JLR was strip-searched. It turned out that she had been making the required child support payments all along.

A Maryland district court stated that the MCDC's blanket strip-search policy was still unconstitutional. The court also held that if JLR could prove that the six pat-down searches had occurred, they would be considered an invasion of privacy as well.

Smith v. Montgomery County, Maryland 1986;
Roth v. Parries et al., Maryland 1995

———

LATE ONE AFTERNOON in 1992, a man registering voters at a New Jersey mall was approached by a security officer. The officer wanted to know whether the man had permission from mall management to be there. The man said he did not think that he needed permission, as he had done the same thing the week before with no problem. Police arrived and ordered the man to leave. When he refused, he was arrested, handcuffed, and taken in a squad car to the police station. At the station, the man was told to disrobe and an officer conducted a visual body-cavity search.

The man sued the town and police for unlawfully strip-searching him. The case was settled, with the police department agreeing to abide by New Jersey laws prohibiting suspicionless strip searches. In addition, the police department agreed to provide special training for officers, specifying when a strip search is permitted.

Moctezuma v. Township of Montclair, New Jersey 1993

Is It a Search?

FOURTH AMENDMENT protection is triggered only when the government conducts a "search." Stripping someone obviously falls under that category. So does looking in someone's pockets or rummaging through someone's desk drawers. But what of the many other, more modern ways the government can gather information about you? What of taking blood or voice samples, surveilling property from an airplane, or placing a wiretap on a telephone line? Are those actions considered searches under the Fourth Amendment?

In the 1960s, a case involving a wiretap prompted the Supreme Court to recognize that the notion of what constitutes a search under the Fourth Amendment must evolve to keep pace with new technology. Police, without a warrant, had placed a wiretap on a public phone booth. In holding that the wiretap was indeed a search, the Court declared that Fourth Amendment protection was not limited to instances when police rummage through pockets or drawers. Instead, the High Court declared, the Fourth Amendment "protects people, not places." Most important, the amendment protects a person's *reasonable expectation of privacy*.

So in order to determine what is protected by the Fourth Amendment, courts must consider the question: What can we, as Americans, legitimately expect to keep to ourselves? The analysis entails reliance on legal precedent, basic common sense, and some pretty fine hairsplitting.

PERSONS

The High Court began the inquiry into what constitutes a search of our "persons" in 1966, after one Mr. Schmerber left a bowling alley and ran his car into a tree. Schmerber was taken to a hospital, where he was arrested for driving while intoxicated. Over Schmerber's protests, the arresting officer directed a doctor to take a sample of Schmerber's blood. Was he "searched"? The Supreme Court said yes. The Court decided that extracting a person's blood for analysis clearly implicated privacy interests that the Fourth Amendment was designed to protect.

In the 1970s, the Court had to decide whether taking a voice sample (recording someone's voice) constituted a Fourth Amendment search. It set forth a test for determining what we can reasonably expect to keep private. The Court declared that there was *no* expectation of privacy in what "a person knowingly exposes to the public, even in his own home or office." Thus, taking a voice sample was ruled not to be a search. The Court wrote: "No person can have a reasonable expectation that others will not know the sound of his voice, any more than he can reasonably expect that his face will be a mystery to the world."

Likewise, taking a handwriting sample is not a search. According to the Court, "Handwriting, like speech, is repeatedly shown to the public." By the same reasoning, taking a fingerprint would not be a Fourth Amendment search. We leave our fingerprints everywhere, every day.

But finger *scrapings* are a different matter entirely. A finger scraping involves the material that can be scraped out from underneath your fingernail (and, if you have committed a crime, may contain microscopic evidence that can be used against you). Whereas your fingerprints are routinely left behind wherever you go, finger scrapings have to be physically removed. Therein lies a difference of constitutional dimension. Taking someone's finger scrapings is the kind of "severe, though brief, intrusion upon cherished personal security" that demands Fourth Amendment protection.

If digging under a fingernail is a search, then it seems that digging around in someone's body would be as well. This was the case when the Commonwealth of Virginia wanted to retrieve a bullet that was fired during a robbery, but the bullet happened to be lodged in the robbery suspect's chest. When state officials requested court-ordered surgery to remove the bullet, a federal court said that the state was asking to "drug this citizen—not yet convicted of a criminal offense—with narcotics and barbiturates into a state of unconsciousness, and then search beneath his skin for evidence of a crime." Somewhat less evocatively, the Supreme Court declared that the intrusion on privacy was "severe" and therefore triggered Fourth Amendment protection.

In the late 1980s, in response to a national drug crisis, the Federal Railroad Administration (FRA) managed to raise three Fourth Amendment questions with one testing program. The FRA wanted to subject railway employees to blood, breath, and urine tests for drugs and alcohol. A blood test had already been deemed to be a search, but what about Breathalyzers and urinalysis?

The High Court found breath testing, in which "deep-lung" breath is produced for chemical analysis, to be similar enough to blood–alcohol testing that it, too, should be deemed a search. While urinalysis appears at first glance to test only material already eliminated from a person's body, the Court found that this test also intruded upon a reasonable expectation of privacy. Chemical analysis of urine could reveal much private medical information about a person. In addition, the manner of collecting the urine in itself could constitute an invasion of privacy.

Therefore, breath and urine tests joined blood tests, fingernail scraping, and surgery as bodily intrusions deemed to be searches under the Fourth Amendment. On the other hand, we can have no reasonable expectation that our physical appearance, voice, handwriting, or fingerprints will remain private.

HOUSES

The home is sacrosanct under American law and has long been protected against unwarranted government intrusions. It was the general searches of colonists' houses that prompted the Framers to draft the Fourth Amendment two hundred years ago. In the 1990s, courts are still quoting William Pitt's impassioned plea for the inviolability of the home. "The poorest man may in his cottage bid defiance to all the forces of the Crown. It may be frail—its roof may shake—the wind may blow through it—the storm may enter—the rain may enter—but the King of England cannot enter!"

Indeed, the law even recognizes a certain zone of privacy *around* the home that we can reasonably expect to reserve for ourselves. That space, along with our house, is protected by the Fourth Amendment. Under the law, this area is known as the "curtilage." To most of us, it is known as our yard.

But what if we have a really *big* yard—say, a farm with hundreds of acres? Is all of it protected by the Fourth Amendment?

A Kentucky man had a farm with a locked gate and "No Trespassing" signs posted along the perimeter. A mile from the farmhouse, bounded on all sides by fences and woods, was an open field not visible from any public road. In the field, the man was growing a crop of marijuana. Police officers walked along a footpath on the property and observed the marijuana. Was that a Fourth Amendment search?

The Supreme Court said no. The Court held that although the open field was on the man's property, it was not within the curtilage, or protected area of the house. "An individual may not legitimately demand privacy for activities conducted out of doors in fields," the Court wrote, "except in the area immediately surrounding the home."

How "immediately surrounding" would the field have to be? In another case, the Supreme Court held that a barn on a field sixty yards from a farmhouse was not within the curtilage.

Even if an area is deemed to be protected by the Fourth Amendment, it does not mean that all police observation of that area is prohibited. For example, police received a tip that marijuana was growing in a California man's backyard. The yard was surrounded by two high fences and, by design, could not be observed from street level. So the police hired a plane, flew over the house, and from the air spotted the marijuana in the yard. The Supreme Court held that the aerial surveillance (at least from this altitude) did not constitute a Fourth Amendment search.

If anyone walking by your house can clearly see a marijuana plant growing in your yard, it does not become a search when a police officer sees it as he passes by. In the California case, the Court said it did not matter that the police were passing by in a plane. The Court wrote: "Any member of the public flying in this airspace who glanced down could have seen everything that these officers observed." The Court said that an expectation that one's garden is protected from such observation is "unreasonable and is not an expectation that society is prepared to honor." Police traveling on public airways, just like police traveling along a public street, do not need warrants to view something "visible to the naked eye."

Of course, it was only a matter of time before government agents began using high-tech devices to detect things *not* visible to the naked eye. EPA investigators flew over a chemical plant and took photographs with a "precision aerial mapping camera" that was able to capture objects as small as one-half inch in diameter. The Court decided that although the camera recorded more than a person could see on his own, such observation did not constitute a search under the Fourth Amendment. "The mere fact that human vision is enhanced somewhat, *at least to the degree here*, does not give rise to constitutional problems," the court declared, leaving open the possibility that some other high-tech intrusions could indeed be prohibited under the Fourth Amendment.

PAPERS

When the Fourth Amendment was drafted, one's "papers" were likely to comprise a record of one's life. They were also likely to be stored in a desk drawer, closet, or trunk—someplace in the house. Today, our papers are just as likely to comprise a record of our lives. But instead of a stack of papers on a desk, we have a paper trail that leads right out the door and into a multitude of offices and institutions. Are those papers still protected by the Fourth Amendment? For some of them, at least, the answer is no. What's more, they are not, surprisingly, even considered to be ours.

When a fire broke out in M. Miller's Georgia warehouse, firefighters discovered a 7,500-gallon-capacity distillery and 175 gallons of "non-tax-paid" whiskey. Government agents then issued subpoenas to two banks in which Miller maintained accounts. Without telling Miller, the banks turned over to the agents his records, checks, and deposit slips. When Miller was indicted for possessing a still and defrauding the government of whiskey taxes, he claimed that his Fourth Amendment rights had been violated when the government obtained his bank records.

The Supreme Court, however, held that Miller's bank records were *not* protected by the Fourth Amendment. The Court said that Miller did not have a legitimate expectation of privacy in the contents of his bank records. He did not own or possess the records. "All of the documents obtained, including financial statements and deposit slips, contain only information voluntarily conveyed to the banks and exposed to their employees in the ordinary course of business," the Court wrote. "The depositer takes the risk, in revealing his affairs to another, that the information will be conveyed by that person to the Government."

In a later case, police suspected M. L. Smith of making threatening phone calls. Without first obtaining a warrant, police directed the phone company to use a "pen register" to record the numbers dialed from the telephone in Smith's home. A pen register is installed at the company's central offices and records only the numbers dialed from a certain telephone, not any actual conversations. Smith claimed that the use of the pen register violated his Fourth Amendment rights.

The Supreme Court disagreed. The Court wrote: "We doubt that people in general entertain any actual expectation of privacy in the numbers they dial." Like Miller, who had turned his records over to the bank, Smith "voluntarily conveyed numerical information to the telephone company" each time he dialed his phone. Therefore, he "assumed the risk that the company would reveal to police the numbers he dialed."

EFFECTS

Garbage, of all things, has been thoughtfully considered and discussed by the United States Supreme Court. Of all of our personal "effects," our trash presents the greatest paradox. On the one hand, our garbage can reveal the most intimate facts about our lives, including sexual practices, personal relationships, medical conditions, political affiliations, and financial status. On the other hand, trash, by definition, has been discarded. Do we have any legitimate expectation that something we've deliberately thrown away will remain private?

Every week for two months, police combed through a California man's trash without first obtaining a warrant. When the man was arrested on drug charges, he claimed that he had a reasonable expectation of privacy in his trash and that his Fourth Amendment rights had been violated. He conceded that he had placed his garbage out for collection, but said that he had used a sealed container with the expectation that it would be collected, combined with everyone else's trash, and taken to the dump, not singled out by police for inspection.

The Supreme Court decided that trash placed out for collection is *not* protected by the Fourth Amendment. Instead, we "knowingly expose it to the public" and "voluntarily turn it over to third parties." Whether we like it or not, when we put out the trash, it is open to all comers, including the police.

So is there anything you can do to protect the contents of your garbage can? A Massachusetts man tried to do so by shredding his documents into strips 5/32 of an inch wide. IRS agents picking through his trash retrieved the tiny strands of paper and painstakingly pieced them together to produce evidence of tax fraud. A federal district court held that by shredding his trash, the man had created a reasonable expectation of privacy in it. An appellate court disagreed and reversed that decision. The court said that the man had not created any expectation of privacy that society was prepared to recognize. He had simply underestimated the resourcefulness, not to mention patience, of the IRS. For constitutional purposes, the court said, trash is trash.

A Warrantless Search: Is It Reasonable?

EVEN IF a police officer's action is considered a search under the Fourth Amendment, it does not follow that such action is forbidden. It just means that the officer must comply with the Fourth Amendment. While the first half of the amendment—declaring our right against unreasonable searches and seizures—is expanding to recognize more modern means of searching, the second half of the amendment—requiring a warrant based upon probable cause—is disappearing.

As we have noted, the Supreme Court has carved out exceptions to the rule that police must obtain a warrant before they may conduct a search. Indeed, there are now so many exceptions, they are threatening to swallow the rule. Even the Supreme Court speaks of a warrant as a constitutional "preference" rather than a requirement.

Hence, sometimes it is sufficient that the officers simply have "probable cause" (or enough information "to warrant a man of reasonable caution" to believe that a crime has occurred), and they do not need to get a warrant. For example, when Mr. Schmerber slammed his car into a tree and police directed a doctor to extract Schmerber's blood, the Supreme Court said that the blood test was a "search." But the Court also went on to say that the search was constitutional. The police had probable cause to believe that Schmerber had been driving drunk, and had they taken the time to obtain a warrant, Schmerber's blood–alcohol level would naturally have diminished. Under these circumstances, the Court said, the warrantless search was reasonable.

For the same reasons, the Court upheld a warrantless search in the fingernail scrapings case. The police had probable cause to believe that the man had committed murder, and when they asked to examine his fingernails, the man began rubbing them. Again, because of the evanescent nature of the evidence, the Court held that the police were justified in conducting the search (scraping the suspect's fingernails) without a warrant.

A warrantless search may also be conducted upon "reasonable suspicion"—a standard no more precisely defined than "probable cause" but recognized as a lesser level of suspicion. A police officer needs only a "reasonable suspicion" that a person has violated the law in order to stop the individual and frisk him.

Finally, in some instances under the Fourth Amendment, people can be searched even if they are not suspected of having done anything wrong. This was the case in the drug and alcohol tests of railway employees. Although the Court held that blood, breath, and urine tests constituted searches, the Court also held that they could be carried out on certain railway employees without any reason to believe that the workers were under the influence. Given the grave threat to public safety posed by impaired railway workers, the Court said that the relatively minor intrusion on the workers' privacy was reasonable under the Fourth Amendment.

As always under the Fourth Amendment, "reasonableness" is determined by balancing an individual's right to privacy against society's interest in conducting the search. In the context of law enforcement, privacy rights often come up short. As much as we value our privacy, it often seems to pale in the face of violent crime. Many say they are willing to forgo a right, even a constitutional one, in exchange for simply feeling safe.

Others say that we should not be "balancing away" our rights, and that the proper balance was struck two hundred years ago—when the Founders declared in the Fourth Amendment that a warrant to conduct a search must be based upon probable cause. In this view, the true threat to freedom is the overwhelming power of the government, and a Fourth Amendment enfeebled by exceptions is no match for that power.

But there is another line of defense. In reaction to the more relaxed standards set out by the Supreme Court, states have developed rules of their own. States may not afford citizens *less* protection than the Constitution does, but they can provide *more*.

For example, New York courts have carved out two more levels of suspicion that police must meet if they so much as ask someone a question. These two additional levels, like "probable cause" and "reasonable suspicion," cannot be defined with any degree of scientific accuracy. New York's highest court concedes that the distinctions among them are "subtle ones." Caught in the middle of all of these exceptions, distinctions, and shades of gray are police officers themselves. They not only have to know the details of these rather vague laws, they have to know the practical applications—and they often have to act on those applications instantaneously. If the strip search cases from Chicago and elsewhere show the need for the protection that comes with the Fourth Amendment, the following New York cases show the difficulty that the police sometimes encounter in trying to do their day-to-day jobs within the often confusing confines of the Fourth Amendment and state law.

PEOPLE OF NEW YORK v. HOLLMAN

The Drug Interdiction Cases

N EW YORK's Port Authority Bus Terminal is located near Times Square in midtown Manhattan. One of the nation's biggest and busiest bus terminals, it covers almost two square city blocks and operates twenty-four hours a day, seven days a week. On a typical weekday, the terminal services 6,700 buses carrying 171,000 passengers. Three levels of gate areas are capable of loading 223 buses at the same time.

Patrolling this behemoth are officers of the Port Authority of New York and New Jersey. The officers at the terminal encounter mostly "street-level" crimes—robbery, assault, rape, and (making up almost three-quarters of their work) drugs. Detective Lieutenant Frank Farfalla of the Port Authority police says that New York is a "source city." Couriers enter the city with money and leave with drugs, often on a bus. It is the job of Detective Farfalla and his colleagues to stop the couriers before they spread their booty throughout the country. The question then becomes: How do the officers know who among the 171,000 daily passengers is carrying drugs?

Farfalla says that in deciding whom to approach, the police rely on a combination of tips and their experience in knowing what to look for. Informants may lead them to a particular courier or shipment. Police in other cities also alert the Port Authority when their town is considered "hot" so the Port Authority police can pay particular attention to buses arriving from and departing for that city.

In addition, there are general signs which the officers say they learn to recognize. For example, couriers are likely to appear nervous, run up to pay for their ticket in cash, and hop on the bus at the last minute. Passengers who try to disassociate themselves from their luggage—standing apart from a bag or placing the bag at a distance from them on the bus—are also considered suspicious. The officers may also look for someone who disembarks from a three-hour bus trip and then reappears to board a return bus only an hour later. In the end, Detective Farfalla says, deciding whom to approach comes from "that sixth sense, that feeling you get as a cop on the street."

Governing all of these tips, clues, and hunches are laws designed to protect the privacy of the 50 million passengers who pass through the Port Authority each year. The Fourth Amendment applies, of course, to any search and seizure. In addition, New York's highest court has set forth what it calls "a four-tiered method for evaluating the propriety of encounters initiated by police officers in their criminal law enforcement capacity." Here are the steps that the Port Authority police, and all New York police officers, are supposed to follow when they want to approach a citizen:

(1) If a police officer seeks simply to request information from an individual, that request must be supported by an objective, credible reason, not necessarily indicative of criminality;

(2) The common-law right of inquiry, a wholly separate level of contact, is activated by a founded suspicion that criminal activity is afoot and permits a somewhat greater intrusion;

(3) Where a police officer has reasonable suspicion that a particular person was involved in a felony or misdemeanor, the officer is authorized to forcibly stop and detain that person;

(4) Where the officer has probable cause to believe that a person has committed a crime, an arrest is authorized.

At the Port Authority, the police often must distinguish among "credible reason," "founded suspicion," "reasonable suspicion," and "probable cause" between the moment they spot someone boarding a bus and the moment the bus pulls away from the platform. Indeed, the New York rules arose out of a pair of cases from the Port Authority Bus Terminal.

In one case, an undercover police officer noticed a man in a boarding area who stood out in the crowd. In contrast to the other passengers, who were milling about in a casual manner, G. Saunders appeared nervous, scanning the area in an agitated manner and giving up his place in line as it moved toward the bus. Just before the bus was to depart, Saunders rejoined the line and the undercover officer approached him. Identifying himself, the officer asked Saunders if he could speak to him. Saunders agreed and stepped off the line. The officer asked him where he was going and why. Looking around rapidly and speaking in a broken voice, Saunders answered that he was headed for Baltimore to visit family. The officer then asked if he could look in the man's bag. Saunders said yes. The officer asked a second time to be sure, and again Saunders clearly said yes. In the bag, inside a sneaker, the police found thirty-eight vials of cocaine.

In the second case, the same undercover officer observed T. Hollman coming down an escalator carrying an orange bag. When he reached the bottom, Hollman looked around and then went back up the escalator. A few minutes later, the officer saw Hollman coming back down the escalator, this time with another man, who was carrying a black knapsack. The two spoke briefly, then stood roughly ten feet apart with the orange bag on the ground between them. After about twenty minutes, Hollman picked up the orange bag and entered the men's room with his companion. When they left the restroom, the two men resumed their earlier positions for about fifteen minutes, then boarded a bus. They placed their bags in the overhead rack two or three seats up from the seats they took for themselves.

At this point, the officer boarded the bus, identified himself, and requested permission to ask the men a few questions. The men agreed. The officer asked if they were traveling together and the men said they had just met. The officer asked where they were headed; Hollman said Virginia and the other man said Carolina. Finally, the officer asked about their luggage and the men said they did not have any. The officer persisted, inquiring about the orange bag and black knapsack. When the two men (and everyone else on the bus) denied owning the bags, the officer opened them and found crack cocaine.

Both G. Saunders and T. Hollman claimed that their right to privacy had been violated. In one case, the New York court agreed. The court said that when Hollman and his companion denied owning the orange bag and black knapsack, the officer had a "founded suspicion that criminality was afoot." Thus, the officer was permitted to continue asking about the bags and ultimately to open them. On the other hand, the court said that even though Saunders had expressly consented to the officer searching his bag, the search was unlawful. The court said the officer had enough suspicion to ask general questions, but not to request permission to search. "No matter how calm the tone of narcotics officers may be, or how polite their phrasing, a request to search a bag is intrusive and intimidating," the court wrote. Therefore, the court decided, Saunders could not really be deemed to have consented to his bag being searched.

In contrast, the United States Supreme Court has rejected the notion that an encounter with police is so inherently intimidating that people cannot be expected to walk away. The Supreme Court has long held that a refusal to cooperate with the police does not justify detaining or arresting someone. Furthermore, the Court assumes that we know this. Therefore, the Court has declared that under the Fourth Amendment, police officers may approach an individual without any suspicion whatsoever, ask potentially incriminating questions, and request to search the individual's luggage "so long as the officers do not convey a message that compliance with their requests is required." It is up to the individual to simply walk away if he does not want his bags searched.

In the Supreme Court case, two officers with badges, one of them holding a recognizable zipper pouch containing a pistol, boarded a bus during a stopover in Fort Lauderdale. The officers, without any particular suspicion, picked out one man and asked to see his ticket and identification. The man's papers were found to be in order and returned to him. Then the police officers explained that they were looking for drugs, asked if they could search the man's bag, and told him he could refuse. The man consented to the search and the police found cocaine in his suitcase. The Supreme Court held that the officers' actions were not necessarily unreasonable—the man could have disregarded the police and gotten off the bus.

In dissent, Justice Thurgood Marshall said he agreed that the appropriate question was whether the passenger felt free to disregard the police. But, Justice Marshall wrote, "What I cannot understand is how the majority can possibly suggest an affirmative answer to this question." To Justice Marshall, the fact that an individual's refusal to cooperate cannot be used against him or her is "utterly beside the point," because most people do not even know they have a right to refuse. Nonetheless, Justice Marshall was in dissent and the law under the Fourth Amendment remains that police officers may stop people at random and request permission to search their bags as long as the police do not "convey a message that compliance with their requests is required."

"Federally, they're beautiful," says Detective Farfalla. New York police officers are well aware that their state has stricter rules regarding searches. "Sure, it makes it harder," says Farfalla. "But you adapt." He and his colleagues say they always walk alongside someone they are questioning, never block the way, and always assume a low-key manner. And, as counterintuitive as it may seem, none of the officers *want* someone to tell them they can search a bag. Despite the search based on consent that was upheld by the Supreme Court, they say that in New York a search based on consent will rarely stand up because the court is not likely to conclude that the consent was given freely. So sometimes you just have to let the person walk away.

"There are times when you *know* the guy is dirty, you know it," says Farfalla, "and you've got to let him go." But Farfalla doesn't mind. He says that there is so much drug traffic, they will just find someone else. The "mules," or couriers, are considered expendable, and dealers will send out a group of them assuming that some will get through and some will get caught.

Even a number of those who are caught will be freed rather quickly when a judge does not agree with the officer that there were adequate grounds for a search. "I don't get upset about that either," Farfalla says. "That's the system." The thirty-five-year veteran says that it is the junior members of the police force who get frustrated. "The younger guys haven't been around long enough," he says. "They don't understand the system."

Farfalla's colleague, Lieutenant Harold Haley, has a different take. "You know the guy is dirty, you *know* he's carrying, and you have to walk away. That's what hurts inside. There are more and more restrictions that make it harder to do our jobs. That's why there's so much chaos out there."

NEW JERSEY v. T.L.O.

The School Search Cases

SOME OF the chaos from the streets has spilled over into the nation's schools as well. In some areas, "schoolteacher" is now considered a high-risk job. Schools everywhere, not just in urban centers, have been trying to cope with increased disciplinary problems, rising drug use, and the potential for violence. To enter their schools, some children walk through metal detectors like those set up at airports to foil terrorist attacks. Many more students customarily have their lockers or desks searched by school officials. And some administrators have considered routine drug testing of all of their students.

Yet as widespread as these measures are, it is not clear that they are always constitutional. In general, the use of metal detectors and drug tests is considered a search under the Fourth Amendment. But as late as the mid-1980s, the United States Supreme Court had not even ruled on whether the Fourth Amendment applied to public school officials, much less on the specific standards to be followed in a school setting. Ironically, the case that finally got the Court's attention in 1985 did not involve violence or weapons or any high-tech searches. Instead, the incident that sparked the landmark lawsuit was so old and familiar that in light of today's problems, it almost seems quaint.

A NEW JERSEY high school teacher opened the door to the girls' lavatory between class periods and walked into a cloud of smoke. Through the acrid haze, she saw two freshman girls lounging on the sinks and windowsill, smoking cigarettes. At this particular high school, smoking was allowed, but only in designated areas—which most definitely did not include the rest rooms. The teacher promptly led the two girls to the principal's office.

At the office, the students were confronted by Theodore Choplick, vice principal. At a public school, the vice principal is the disciplinarian, responsible for ferreting out wrongdoing and meting out punishment. Choplick has been in education for more than twenty years, mostly as a vice principal. He views his role as something approaching that of a surrogate parent. "We are responsible for them," he says of the students. "I treat them like they are my children. It's as simple as that." But times have changed and Choplick's job has changed with them.

In a measure of how dire the situation has become in some schools, Choplick says that his own suburban school, with a student population of twenty-six hundred, is "not totally out of control"—by which he means: "I have never feared for my life." Instead, Choplick says his New Jersey high school has "typical" problems, ranging from fistfights and truancy to teen pregnancy, alcohol, and, more recently, drugs. Choplick says his students are involved mostly with marijuana and, less frequently, cocaine and LSD. Though he sees himself as a stand-in for parents, when the vice principal describes his job, he sounds more like a cop walking his beat.

"You have an idea who is dealing and you always keep your eye out," he says. "You position yourself in certain places in the hallway where you can get a vantage point. Or you suddenly walk in a different direction so you can sneak up on something." If Choplick finds students with contraband, he walks them down to his office. He says that one of the rules he learned early is never to discipline a student in front of others. "But," he continues, "when you walk the students, you always make sure they stay in front of you. You never lead the way because they will drop things off. If they're in front of you, you're able to see if they drop things along the way."

However, none of this was on Choplick's mind when the two freshman girls were brought to the office for smoking in the lavatory. Neither of the students was known to be a troublemaker or a drug user. "They were not ones I was watching," the vice principal says. "The ones we watched, we caught." Standing at a counter in the waiting area, he simply asked the girls if they had been smoking in the rest room. One of them said yes right away, and Choplick gave her the punishment mandated by the Board of Education: three days' suspension. However, when he turned to the second student, fourteen-year-old "T.L.O.," she denied that she had been smoking in the rest room. Indeed, she denied that she smoked at all.

Choplick did not want to confront T.L.O. in front of her friend, so he asked her to step into his office. There, he again asked her if she had been smoking, and T.L.O. again denied it. So Choplick asked to see the girl's purse. It was something he had done dozens, maybe even hundreds, of times. "I had asked boys or girls before to empty their purses or give me their wallets. If they had book bags, we looked in the book bags. We did all of that," he says. In other words, Choplick never would have guessed that his actions over the next two minutes would be scrutinized by four separate state courts and, ultimately, nine justices of the United States Supreme Court.

Choplick opened T.L.O.'s purse and saw a pack of Marlboro cigarettes "sitting right on top there." He held the cigarettes in front of T.L.O. and accused her of lying. But as he did so, Choplick looked down into the purse again and this time saw a package of E-Z Widers. He says, "If you're a school administrator, you know E-Z Widers are rolling papers used for marijuana."

At that point, Choplick began to empty T.L.O.'s pocketbook. He found a pipe, several empty plastic bags, and one bag containing a tobacco-like substance. "You take the plastic bag and take a smell," Choplick says, "and you smell marijuana. And now you say, 'Whoa, whoa, whoa.'" He opened T.L.O.'s wallet, which contained $40 in singles. Then, opening a separate compartment, he found an index card with the heading "People Who Owe Me Money," followed by a list of names and amounts of $1.00 or $1.50. Finally, Choplick found two letters apparently concerning marijuana sales.

He was surprised because T.L.O. had never been in trouble before. Nonetheless, he was certain, given what was now arrayed before him, that the fourteen-year-old was in the business of selling marijuana. Following board policy, Choplick notified T.L.O.'s parents first, then called the police. With her mother present, T.L.O. was given "Miranda" warnings and questioned by police officers. She first told them that the $40 was from her paper route. ("Give me a break" was Choplick's response.) Then the girl admitted that she had been selling marijuana in school and on that day had sold eighteen to twenty joints for $1.00 apiece. In accordance with board policy, T.L.O. was suspended from school for ten days—three days for smoking cigarettes in the girls' room and seven days for selling marijuana at school.

But the matter did not end there. The police turned the case over to the local prosecutor's office, which filed a complaint against T.L.O. in juvenile court. She was charged with delinquency based on possession of marijuana with intent to distribute.

T.L.O.'s parents hired an attorney and fought the charges on two fronts. They defended against the delinquency charge in juvenile court, and they went to civil court to contest T.L.O.'s suspension from school. In both courts, T.L.O.'s argument was the same: The vice principal's search of T.L.O.'s purse had violated her Fourth Amendment rights. Therefore, the evidence seized could not be used against her. Without the evidence of drug dealing, there would be no delinquency case against T.L.O., nor would there be any grounds for suspending her from school.

It all seemed perfectly straightforward. But it was nothing of the kind.

The United States Supreme Court had never ruled on whether the Fourth Amendment applied to school officials such as Vice Principal Choplick. Although the Court had long ago declared that students do not "shed their Constitutional rights . . . at the schoolhouse gate," there was an equally long tradition of deferring to school officials in recognition of their unique responsibilities. For Fourth Amendment purposes, the singular context of the public schools cuts both ways.

School officials are charged with the crucial task of educating our children. They are also charged with what today has become an equally awesome responsibility: that of keeping our children safe. Teachers and administrators need to be able to act swiftly and surely to maintain an environment where students can not just grow intellectually but also be assured of getting through the day in one piece.

There are also more subtle but equally important forces at work. One of the most essential lessons a public school teaches is that of citizenship. As early as 1943, the Supreme Court declared that that was reason enough "for scrupulous protection of Constitutional freedoms of the individual, if we are not to strangle the free mind at its source and teach youth to discount important principles of our government as mere platitudes." The lesson is taught not only in civics class but also by example. How school officials treat students suspected of wrongdoing—when and why they search—may be one of the most lasting lessons a child will learn.

Without a ruling from the Supreme Court, state and federal courts were, as one attorney put it, "all over the place." At one extreme, schoolteachers and administrators were considered to be *in loco pa-*

rentis—that is, "in the place of a parent." Under this view, school officials were not bound by the Fourth Amendment and could search students and their belongings as freely as a parent could. At the other extreme, school officials were held to the strictest standards under the Fourth Amendment. Before they could search a student, they had to obtain a warrant based upon "probable cause" that a crime had been committed.

Taking a middle position, many courts held that public school officials were bound by the Fourth Amendment but that a less strict standard was appropriate. Under this compromise view, a search merely had to be "reasonable under all of the circumstances" to be considered constitutional.

Yet deciding that the Fourth Amendment does indeed apply to school officials raises still another question. If a search of a student is found to violate the Fourth Amendment, can the evidence seized in the search be turned over to the police, or must it be excluded from any criminal or even disciplinary proceedings? Does the so-called exclusionary rule apply in the school setting?

The exclusionary rule is one of the most controversial aspects of the Fourth Amendment. The rule is not specifically set out in the text of the amendment. Rather, in the criminal context the Supreme Court has decided that if a search violates the Fourth Amendment, then the evidence seized in that search cannot be used in court. Otherwise, the Court reasoned, there would be a right without a remedy. Law enforcement officials could not be counted on to follow the rules unless there was a penalty for violating them. Critics say that the exclusionary rule allows an obviously guilty person to "get off on a technicality." Or, as Justice Benjamin Cardozo put it more colorfully, "The criminal is to go free because the constable has blundered."

Perhaps in the school setting, where courts often defer to school officials, the rule need not apply. On the other hand, it seems especially unfair to allow school officials to search students under a lesser standard than that which applies to suspected criminals, and also be able to use the evidence seized against students in disciplinary or even criminal proceedings. The Supreme Court had not ruled on these issues either.

Thus, T.L.O.'s "smoking in the girls' room" case began a roller-coaster ride through the courts. Three lower courts in New Jersey reached different conclusions regarding the legality of Choplick's search. Then it was the New Jersey Supreme Court's turn to scrutinize Vice Principal Choplick's actions. The court held that the Fourth Amendment applied to public schools, and that searches by school officials need only be "reasonable." But the New Jersey Supreme Court held that Choplick's search was *not* reasonable.

The court said that there had been no reasonable basis for opening T.L.O.'s purse in the first place. No one had furnished any information to Choplick indicating that the purse contained cigarettes. Furthermore, the mere presence of cigarettes in the bag did not prove that T.L.O. had been smoking them in the girls' room. And possessing cigarettes at school was not in itself an infraction, because smoking was allowed in certain areas. Even if opening the purse had been reasonable, the court continued, Choplick's "wholesale rummaging" was not. The court then declared that the exclusionary rule applied in the school setting. Therefore, the evidence found in T.L.O.'s purse should be suppressed.

Immediately, the state of New Jersey, represented by attorney Alan Nodes, asked the United States Supreme Court to review the case. However, Nodes did not ask the Court to reverse the state court's holding in its entirety. New Jersey was willing to accept that the Fourth Amendment applied to school officials with the lesser standard of "reasonableness." The state was even willing to accept the Court's decision that Choplick's search was not reasonable. But New Jersey did not want the exclusionary rule to be used for school searches. "We felt more comfortable asking for a modification of a judge-made rule, like the exclusionary rule, than asking for a modification of the Fourth Amendment," Nodes says.

When the Supreme Court agreed to hear the case, T.L.O.'s court-appointed attorney, Lois DeJulio, was not pleased. Noting recent cases in which the Supreme Court had cut back on Fourth Amendment protections, she says, "I was really kind of dreading what was going to happen next. . . . I was really very afraid that this would be the end of the Fourth Amendment for juveniles."

The person who was most unhappy about the case being reviewed by the High Court was the one who had started it all, T.L.O. "This was not a case where she set out to test constitutional rights," says DeJulio. Indeed, T.L.O.'s goal had simply been to get back in school. By the time the case reached the Supreme Court, T.L.O. not only had been readmitted to high school but had graduated and moved on with her life. Nonetheless, she was forever frozen in court papers as the fourteen-year-old caught smoking in the girls' room. Now that girl was going to become a part of constitutional history.

In March of 1984, the Supreme Court heard oral arguments concerning whether the exclusionary rule should apply in the school setting. In June of 1984, the Court told the parties to back up and address a constitutional issue that they had not even raised. The Court wanted to use T.L.O.'s case to decide what role, if any, the Fourth Amendment should play in public schools.

In October of 1984, the parties were back before the Court, this time arguing about whether school officials were bound by the Fourth Amendment in the first place. On January 15, 1985, the Supreme Court finally issued its opinion.

The Court noted what anyone with a school-age child already knows. "In recent years, school disorder has often taken particularly ugly forms: drug use and violent crime in the schools have become major social problems." Nonetheless, the Court said that "the situation is not so dire that students in schools may claim no legitimate expectations of privacy." From this day forward, public school teachers and administrators would be bound by the Fourth Amendment.

However, the Court also held that because of the special circumstances relating to the school context, some "modification" of the usual Fourth Amendment rules would be necessary. Teachers would not be expected to obtain warrants before conducting a search in school. Nor would they be expected to train themselves in the "niceties" of the "probable cause" standard used by police officers. The search should simply be "reasonable under all of the circumstances." By this the Court meant two things. First, there must be reasonable grounds for suspecting that the search will turn up evidence that the student has violated either the law or school rules. Second, the search must not be excessively intrusive in light of the student's age and sex and the nature of the infraction.

Turning to T.L.O. and Mr. Choplick, the Court held that the search was "in no sense unreasonable." The Court agreed that the presence of cigarettes in T.L.O.'s purse did not prove conclusively that she had been smoking in the rest room. However, the Court held that conclusive proof was not necessary. It was enough that the cigarettes would corroborate the charge and undermine T.L.O.'s defense that she did not smoke at all. Addressing the New Jersey court's concern that no one had specifically told Choplick that there were cigarettes in T.L.O.'s purse, the Court stated, "If she did have cigarettes, her purse was the obvious place in which to find them." Once the purse was opened and Choplick saw the E-Z Wider cigarette papers in plain view, he was justified in looking further. From start to finish, the Court concluded, the vice principal's search was reasonable. Therefore, it was not necessary to resolve the question of whether the exclusionary rule should apply.

In dissent, Justices William Brennan and Thurgood Marshall declared: "Vice Principal Choplick's thorough excavation of T.L.O.'s purse was undoubtedly a serious intrusion on her privacy." The dissent decried the Court's creation of yet another exception to the clear command of the Fourth Amendment. According to the dissent, the new standard of "reasonable under all of the circumstances" not only watered down the privacy rights of students but also posed a practical problem for administrators. The dissent found the new standard to be ambiguous, stating that the only thing definite about it was that "it is *not* the same test as the 'probable cause' standard found in the text of the Fourth Amendment." The dissent predicted that after *T.L.O.*, school students' privacy rights would be trampled and school administrators "would be hopelessly adrift as to when a search may be permissible."

Passing Judgments

THE DEAN at a Los Angeles high school found two students in the boys' room without a pass. He thought the boys appeared to be nervous. He also knew that students sometimes smoked marijuana in the rest rooms. So the dean asked the boys to empty their pockets. The students produced nothing incriminating. Then the dean looked through the wallet that one of the boys had taken out and found two marijuana cigarettes and one gram of cocaine.

A California court found that the search was reasonable under *T.L.O.* The court said the search was justified at its inception—it was enough that the boys were in the rest room without a pass. The court also said the search was reasonably related in scope—looking through pockets, and even a wallet, was not much of an intrusion.

In re Bobby B., California 1985

IN ARIZONA, a teacher found a high school student outside by the school bleachers during class hours and brought him to the principal's office. The principal knew that students often went to the bleachers to smoke cigarettes or marijuana. In addition, an assistant principal had mentioned this student's name "in connection with discussions about student drug use and sales." The principal instructed the boy to empty his pockets and the boy produced a small bag of cocaine.

An Arizona court held that the search was unreasonable under *T.L.O.* The court said that simply seeing the boy out by the bleachers, as well as hearing the boy's name mentioned in connection with drugs, was not enough to justify even the minor intrusion of emptying his pockets.

In re Appeal in Pima County Juvenile Action No. 80484-1, Arizona 1987

———

DURING A class test, an Ohio high school teacher noticed a strong odor of marijuana coming from one student. The teacher alerted a security guard, who took the student to the principal's office. Both the guard and the principal detected the odor of marijuana and also thought that the student appeared sluggish. Another security guard was summoned. They requested and received the boy's permission to search his bag and jacket (which he was not wearing). The guards also "patted down" the student under his arms. Finally, the boy emptied his pockets. None of the searches turned up evidence of drug use.

Then the principal (female) left the office so that the two security guards (male) could search the boy further. The guards had the boy remove his shoes and socks, lift his shirt, lower his pants, and pull his underwear tight around his genitals to permit the guards to observe his crotch. Again, no evidence of drugs was found.

An Ohio district court found that the search was reasonable both at its inception and in its scope. The court said the odor of marijuana and the boy's lethargic appearance were enough to justify the search and that the strip search had been carried out in a reasonable manner. The fact that the boy was, "quite understandably, embarrassed to some degree" did not make the search unreasonable.

Widener v. Frye, Ohio 1992

———

A TEACHER at an Alaska high school reported that a student in the library appeared intoxicated. The school security guard took the student to a storage room to talk. The guard said the student appeared flushed and glassy-eyed, smelled like alcohol, and "bounced into large objects" as he walked. In the storage room, the guard asked where the boy had been during lunch and told him to turn over his car keys. The boy refused and was brought to the assistant principal's office. The student surrendered his keys to the assistant principal, who gave the boy a search consent form and told him to sign it. The boy complied. School officials searched the car (parked improperly on school property) and found two Baggies of cocaine.

An Alaska court said that under the circumstances, the boy had not freely consented to the search of his car. Nonetheless, the court still upheld the search because the school officials had had enough reasonable suspicion to search the boy's car even without his consent.

Shamberg v. State, Alaska 1988

———

AN ASSISTANT PRINCIPAL at a Texas high school heard that a male student had tried to sell drugs to another student. The assistant principal questioned and "patted down" the boy, had him turn his pockets inside out, remove his shoes and socks, and pull down his pants. The search, which the assistant principal said was "standard," did not produce any drugs. However, the assistant principal did find $300 in the boy's wallet, and when he asked the boy, "Do you sell drugs?" the student replied, "Not on campus."

A week later, the same student attempted to leave the school under false pretenses. (He claimed that he had to attend his grandfather's funeral, but a call to relatives revealed that his grandfather had not died.) The assistant principal summoned the boy to his office, patted him down, but found only keys and a wallet with $197. He then had the boy pull down his pants, but again found no contraband. The assistant principal next searched the student's locker and, finding nothing, took the boy out to his car and told him to open it. In the trunk, school officials found bags of white powder, a triple-beam scale, and what appeared to be marijuana.

A Texas court declared that the search of the student's car was unconstitutional under *T.L.O.* The court said that information from the week before indicating that the student was selling drugs could not be used to justify the search. Acting only on the suspicion that the boy was skipping school, the assistant principal had been justified in patting him down. But the progressively intrusive searches, including searching the student's car, were not reasonably related in scope to the original infraction of skipping school. Therefore, the drugs found in the car could not be used as evidence against the boy.

Coronado v. State, Texas 1992

T.L.O. Revisited

IN *New Jersey v. T.L.O.*, the Supreme Court declared for the first time that the Fourth Amendment applied to public school officials. But the case is also notable for the issues it did *not* resolve.

In *T.L.O.*, the Court went out of its way to list all of the questions that remained unanswered. Do schoolchildren have any legitimate expectation of privacy in their lockers, desks, and other property supplied by the school? Does the same "reasonableness" standard apply if police participate in the search, along with school officials? Is it reasonable to conduct blanket searches of all students without any reason to believe a particular student has done anything wrong? It would be ten years before a small Oregon logging community would prompt the Court to answer even one of these questions.

In the late 1980s drug and alcohol use, and therefore disciplinary problems, rose sharply among schoolchildren in Vernonia, Oregon. Student athletes were identified as the "leaders of the drug culture." School authorities first responded by stepping up drug educational programs and bringing in drug-sniffing dogs, but the problem only got worse.

So the school district began a drug testing program. All students who want to participate in interscholastic sports must consent to the program. Each student athlete is tested at the start of the season. Then once a week, the names of ten percent of the student athletes are selected at random for testing. The student to be tested must disclose any prescription drugs he is taking and provide a copy of the prescription. The student then enters an empty rest room accompanied by an adult monitor of the same sex. Boys produce a specimen at a urinal with their backs to the monitor and girls use an enclosed bathroom stall with the monitor outside in a position to hear but not observe. Monitors for both boys and girls listen for normal sounds of urination, then check the sample provided for temperature and tampering.

The samples are sent to an independent laboratory which does not know the identities of the students. Results are mailed to the school superintendent. Only the superintendent, principals, vice principals, and athletic directors have access to the test results. If a sample tests positive, a second test is done. If the second test is positive, then the student's parents are notified and the student is given the option of six weeks of drug counseling with weekly testing, or suspension from athletics for two seasons.

Twelve-year-old James Acton wanted to play football at his grade school in Vernonia, but he and his parents refused to consent to the testing program. They said James should not be subjected to an intrusive bodily search when there was no reason to believe he was taking drugs. They filed suit claiming that the blanket drug-testing policy violated the Fourth Amendment.

A district court dismissed Acton's claim. The Ninth Circuit reversed, holding that the testing program violated the Fourth Amendment. In June of 1995, by a vote of six to three, the United States Supreme Court reversed that decision and declared that the blanket drug-testing program was reasonable under the Fourth Amendment.

Justice Scalia, writing for the Court, emphasized that while students do have Fourth Amendment rights, they are significantly weaker than those of an adult. Student athletes have even less of an expectation of privacy, the justice wrote, noting that such students usually change clothes and shower in communal locker rooms. Given the lowered expectation of privacy and the careful manner in which the urine samples are collected, the Court declared that the intrusion upon the students' privacy was "negligible."

On the other hand, the crisis of drug use in the Vernonia schools was obvious and immediate. The Court said that it was "self-evident" that the drug problem was "largely fueled by the 'role model' effect of athletes' drug use," therefore testing the athletes was an effective way of dealing with the problem. The Court did, however, caution against the assumption that such dragnet searches could be conducted in other contexts.

Sandra Day O'Connor, writing for the three dissenters, accused the majority of casting aside the most fundamental principle of the Fourth Amendment. If the Fourth Amendment means anything, she said, it means that before government officials can conduct a search, they must have at least some reason to believe that the individual has done something wrong. Indeed, the Fourth Amendment had been drafted to prevent blanket suspicionless searches.

Justice O'Connor acknowledged that the Court had upheld some blanket searches in the past, but, she said, that was only when the search was minimally intrusive and individualized suspicion would not work. The dissent strongly disagreed with the majority's conclusion that the invasion of privacy was "negligible." Instead, the dissent found state-compelled and monitored collection of urine to be "particularly destructive of privacy and offensive to personal dignity."

Furthermore, dragnet testing of *all* student athletes for drugs was not necessary to combat the problem. Justice O'Connor pointed out that because students are under day-to-day supervision, effective programs could be designed based on *individualized* suspicion. She said that the "great irony" of the case was that most of the evidence used to justify the suspicionless testing consisted of stories of particular students acting in ways that clearly gave rise to reasonable suspicion of drug use (dancing and singing at the top of one's voice during class, for example) and would have justified a search of that particular student.

Noting James Acton's explanation of why he did not want to submit to the testing—"Because I feel that they have no reason to think I was taking drugs"—Justice O'Connor wrote, "It is hard to think of [an] explanation that resonates more intensely in our Fourth Amendment tradition than this." Instead, she said, many of the nation's 18 million public-school children may now be forced to submit to an intrusive bodily search, even though they have given school officials no reason whatsoever to suspect they have done anything wrong.

Privacy and Your Self

THE FRAMERS protected our privacy in the Fourth Amendment. But that safeguard pertains to "searches and seizures" only. The question of whether or not there is any other protection of privacy provided for in the Constitution is at the heart of the *legal* debate over abortion.

On this issue the Supreme Court is as bitterly divided as the nation—but for a different reason. The argument among the justices is not about whether abortion is "right" or "wrong," but whether the Court should be involved at all. The abortion cases—indeed, the whole line of privacy cases—rest on a method of constitutional interpretation that some say is essential to a free society and others say undermines the entire democratic process. In one view, since the word "privacy" does not appear anywhere in the Constitution, that is the end of the matter. In the opposing view, the concept of "liberty" in the Constitution necessarily includes a right as fundamental as the right to privacy.

The constitutional conflict over privacy involves matters of reproductive choice other than abortion. Even if the Supreme Court continues to uphold a woman's right to terminate a pregnancy, important issues remain unresolved. As in other areas of privacy law, technology is raising new questions. For example, the abortion cases have focused on the woman's right to control her own body. But what if conception occurs in a laboratory? Does the man then have a protected privacy interest as well? Or, what happens when the interests of the mother and fetus collide?

The constitutional right to privacy also protects our right to make fundamental decisions concerning other areas of family life. The Supreme Court long ago upheld our right to marry whom we choose, and the right of parents to make decisions concerning their children's education. In the 1980s, some argued that other forms of intimate association—such as homosexual behavior between consenting adults—should also be constitutionally protected. But the Supreme Court rejected that claim.

In this decade, the looming privacy battle has to do with decisions at the end of life—the right to refuse medical treatment, the right to die, the right to assisted suicide. Can a competent person refuse medical treatment in order to end his life? Can people seek help in hastening their deaths? If they are incompetent, who decides for them?

In addition, the Constitution protects a second, lesser-known aspect of privacy in certain personal information, notably our medical records. In the age of AIDS, such protection has encouraged people to seek testing and has helped combat discrimination. But when others may be at risk, do public health interests outweigh the right to privacy?

From the beginning of life to its end, the right to privacy often protects our most fundamental decisions. But courts struggle to balance new technology and old values, societal interests and individual freedom.

FROM GRISWOLD TO CASEY

The Contraception and Abortion Cases

OVER THE past twenty years, abortion has become the most heavily litigated, fiercely political, and socially divisive issue involving the right to privacy. In addition to its religious and moral dimensions, the controversy has raised, answered, and raised again profound legal and constitutional questions. Whereas the Fourth Amendment's protection against unreasonable searches and seizures *explicitly* protects the privacy of our homes, our persons, and our possessions, the constitutional right to reproductive freedom is *implicit*.

Constitutional protection of a woman's decision to end a pregnancy is based in the Due Process Clause of the Fourteenth Amendment. That clause declares that no person will be denied "life, liberty, or property, without due process of law." Beginning nearly a hundred years ago, the Supreme Court interpreted "liberty" as encompassing certain fundamental rights not specifically listed in the Bill of Rights. Giving substance to the term "liberty" in this way is known as "substantive due process." In this view, rights "deeply rooted in this Nation's history and tradition" and "implicit in the concept of ordered liberty such that neither liberty nor justice would exist if they were sacrificed," are protected.

How did "liberty" come to be viewed as "privacy"? In the earliest cases, beginning in the 1920s, the Supreme Court held that "liberty" encompasses a parent's right to make certain decisions about his or her child's education without state interference, such as the right to send a child to private school, and a right to have the child study a foreign language. And in 1967, in striking down a law forbidding interracial marriage, the Court said that "liberty" includes the right to marry whom one chooses, and cannot be infringed by the state.

In the 1960s and 1970s, the Court, building on these cases, declared that the Constitution also protected the right to privacy, which in turn protected the right to use contraceptives or have an abortion. It was the contraceptive and abortion cases that set off the national controversy, but the debate over the legal underpinnings of those rulings had been under way on the Court for a long time.

At one end of the spectrum, opponents of substantive due process and a constitutionally protected right to privacy say that both diverge from the plain text of the Constitution and invest judges with more power than they were intended to have. In this view, the Due Process Clause addresses only the *process* by which one can be deprived of life, liberty, or property (for example, the question of whether a person has received proper notice and a fair hearing). And under the strictest form of this argument, the "liberty" protected by the clause includes only those rights specifically listed in the Bill of Rights.

The Bill of Rights, the argument goes, may provide the most complete protection of individual rights in the world, but it does not cover everything. The argument suggests that the proper way to constitutionally protect rights not mentioned in the Bill of Rights is for Americans to amend the Constitution, not for judges to simply interpret them into existence. Otherwise, in deciding what is protected by "liberty," we run the risk that judges, no matter how well-intentioned, will inject their own values. Under our system of government, such value judgments are properly left to the democratic process. State legislatures, duly elected by the people, have the power to make these decisions. It is undemocratic—indeed, contrary to our country's explicit balance of governmental powers—to invest this authority in a handful of individuals who are not elected by the people and who enjoy life tenure on the Supreme Court. Under the Constitution, a judge's job is to interpret the law, not to make it.

On the other hand, those who support substantive due process and a constitutional right to privacy counter that the justices *are* interpreting the text—they are interpreting "liberty." It is true that many important issues are left to state legislatures and the democratic process. But it is also true that in America certain fundamental liberties are beyond the reach of the ballot box. It is precisely because the justices do serve for life and are not seeking reelection that they are able to resist popular pressure and to safeguard these crucial individual rights.

While it sounds good to say that the concept of "liberty" is too open-ended, such an argument ignores the reality of constitutional interpretation. Interpreting "liberty" in the Fourteenth Amendment is no more freewheeling than determining what is "unreasonable" under the Fourth Amendment. Judges will not "roam at large in the constitutional field," but rather will look to history and precedent and apply reasoned judgment to come to a conclusion, just as they always have.

Furthermore, the argument goes, the Supreme Court has been doing just that for nearly a century. Unless one is prepared to uproot a hundred years of constitutional jurisprudence, the concept of "substantive due process" will stand. If "liberty" protects a parent's right to send his or her child to a particular school or to have the child study a particular language, then it must surely encompass a person's right to decide whether to have children in the first place.

It was against this backdrop that in 1965 the Supreme Court decided the landmark case *Griswold v. Connecticut*, the precursor of *Roe v. Wade* and subsequent abortion cases. In *Griswold*, the Supreme Court struck down a Connecticut statute making it a crime to use or counsel anyone in the use of contraceptives. A New Haven doctor and the executive director of the local Planned Parenthood affiliate had been arrested, and each fined $100, for counseling married couples regarding birth control.

The arguments on both sides in *Griswold* foreshadowed not only the central debate in the abortion cases but also the division among the justices, who issued six different opinions. Nonetheless, a majority of the Court did conclude that the Constitution protects a fundamental right to privacy, which in turn includes the right to make the intimate decision as to whether to use contraceptives. To a majority of the Court, it was inconceivable that the government could regulate family size without violating the Constitution. "We deal with a right to privacy older than the Bill of Rights," Justice William O. Douglas wrote for the Court. However, the justices disagreed about where in the Constitution such a right was located.

Justice Douglas pointed out that many rights which are not specifically mentioned in the Constitution but are derived from specific provisions have long been protected by the Court. For example, freedom of association is an extension of the guarantees of freedom of speech and assembly. Justice Douglas found that the spirit, structure, and specific provisions of the Bill of Rights created "zones of privacy" which are broad enough to protect aspects of personal and family life—in this case, marital privacy. The opposite conclusion was almost surreal. "Would we allow the police to search the sacred precincts of marital bedrooms for telltale signs of the use of contraceptives?" he asked.

Two justices dissented. "I like my privacy as well as the next one," wrote Justice Hugo Black, "but I am nevertheless compelled to admit that the government has a right to invade it unless prohibited by some specific constitutional provision." Justice Potter Stewart agreed. Of the Connecticut ban on contraceptives, he wrote, "I think this is an uncommonly silly law. . . . But we are not asked, in this case, to say whether we think this law is unwise, or even asinine. We are asked to hold that it violates the United States Constitution. And that I cannot do." Justice Stewart suggested that if the law did not represent the views of Connecticut's citizens, the state legislature should simply repeal it. "I can find no such general right of privacy in the Bill of Rights, in any other part of the Constitution, or in any case ever before decided by this Court," Justice Stewart wrote.

With rhetorical swords drawn, both sides headed into the battle over abortion. On the way to *Roe v. Wade*, the Court passed an important stepping stone. In 1972, in *Eisenstadt v. Baird*, the Court held that a ban on contraception violated the rights of *unmarried* persons under the Equal Protection Clause and was therefore unconstitutional. In language expanding the right to privacy, Justice William Brennan wrote for the Court, "If the right to privacy means anything, it is the right of the *individual*, married or single, to be free from unwarranted governmental intrusion into matters so fundamentally affecting a person as the decision whether to bear or beget a child."

Exactly ten months later, on January 22, 1973, the Court decided *Roe v. Wade*. By a vote of 7 to 2, the Supreme Court held that a Texas law criminalizing all abortions except those necessary to save the mother's life violated the constitutional right to privacy.

The Court went out of its way to declare, "We need not resolve the difficult question of when life begins." The Court noted the diversity of medical, philosophical, and religious opinion on the issue and confined its discussion to the legal treatment of the unborn. The Court concluded that as used in the Constitution, the word "persons" had never been interpreted to include the unborn. Similarly, under state laws a fetus must generally be born alive in order to inherit or to recover damages, even for injuries sustained in the womb. Therefore, the Court concluded, "The unborn have never been recognized in the law as persons in the whole sense."

In an opinion by Justice Harry Blackmun, the Court first surveyed the laws regarding abortion from ancient times to the present. The Court concluded that, perhaps surprisingly, laws prohibiting abortion, particularly in the earlier stages of pregnancy, were relatively new. Looking back to antiquity and up through English and American common law and statute, the Court determined that abortion had been widely practiced throughout history and had not always been illegal. It was only in the late nineteenth century that most American states had outlawed abortion.

In fact, as the majority saw it, the trend was toward greater liberalization of abortion laws. Twentieth-century advances in medicine had made abortion a safer medical procedure than it had been in the past and, at least in the early stages of pregnancy, women were less likely to die in abortion than in childbirth. By 1970, about one-third of the states had loosened some of the restrictions on abortion, or adopted less stringent laws. The medical and legal professions also recommended liberalization.

The majority acknowledged that the right to privacy was not explicitly mentioned in the Constitution, yet pointed out that it had been recognized by the Court for many years. The right to privacy was not unlimited but included only those personal rights that were "fundamental" or "implicit in the concept of ordered liberty": rights pertaining to marriage, procreation, contraception, family relationships, child rearing, and education. In a now famous declaration, the Court added abortion to the list. "This right of privacy . . . is broad enough to encompass a woman's decision whether or not to terminate her pregnancy."

However, the opinion next made clear that the right, although fundamental, was not absolute. The state has important interests in protecting the woman's health and the "potential for life" within her. These state interests limit the woman's right to end a pregnancy. Each of these state interests exists on a continuum and grows in strength during the course of the pregnancy. The state interest in maternal health allows the state to regulate the safety of the procedures used to perform abortions, and it becomes compelling around the end of the first trimester of pregnancy, after which time abortion is no longer statistically safer than childbirth. The state interest in protecting prenatal life becomes compelling at the point at which the fetus becomes viable—that is, capable of meaningful life outside the mother's womb. Out of the tension between the woman's right and the state's in-

terests, Justice Blackmun's opinion constructed the trimester framework that would come under criticism in later years. During the first
trimester of pregnancy, when abortion is medically safer than childbirth, the decision to have an abortion is to be made by the woman
and her physician, free of state interference. During the second trimester, until the crucial point of "viability," the state may still regulate
abortion to protect maternal health. But after viability, which occurs
around the end of the second trimester, the state's interest in potential
life becomes compelling and the state may regulate, and even prohibit,
abortion, except if necessary to save the life or health of the mother.

Justice William Rehnquist, in dissent, attacked both the decision
and its reasoning. Like the majority, Justice Rehnquist also reviewed
the history of laws restricting abortion. However, he concluded that
for the purposes of interpreting the Fourteenth Amendment, the relevant period was not antiquity or English common law, but the time
when the amendment was drafted, after the Civil War. At that point,
at least thirty-six states or territories limited and often criminalized
abortion. Twenty-one of those laws remained on the books at the time
of the Court's decision. Thus, Justice Rehnquist wrote, the right to
abortion could hardly be "so rooted in the traditions and conscience of
our people as to be ranked as fundamental."

Justice Rehnquist also attacked the trimester framework set out by
the Court as "judicial legislation." The framework was so detailed and
specific that it read more like a law passed by a legislature than a
sound piece of constitutional interpretation in which lofty principles
are construed to give general guidance to courts below. The end result, Justice Rehnquist predicted, was that "the Court's opinion will accomplish the seemingly impossible feat of leaving this area of the law
more confused than it found it."

IN THE years following *Roe*, the Court decided a major abortion case
just about every other year. The justices struck down many of the provisions that came before them, including the requirements that a
woman obtain the consent of her husband before having an abortion,
that she wait twenty-four hours between her initial consultation with
a health care provider and the abortion procedure itself, and that all
second-trimester abortions be performed in a hospital.

The Court upheld other restrictions, including the withdrawal of
federal funding for abortion, a rule that all second-trimester abortions

be performed in a licensed clinic, and that a second physician be present during abortions performed after viability.

In 1976, the Court also struck down a requirement that both parents of a minor must consent before their daughter can have an abortion. (As with spousal consent, the Court has refused to grant veto power over a woman's decision to another person.) However, in 1981, it upheld a law providing that parents must be notified, "if possible." And in 1983, the Court upheld a parental consent law which contained an alternative whereby a judge could waive the consent requirement if the minor could show she was sufficiently mature to make the decision on her own, or that notifying her parents would not be in her best interest (for example, if the pregnancy was the result of incest). This process is known as a judicial bypass.

By the late 1980s, abortion had become an enormous, and enormously divisive, political issue. The Court was also divided, and bitterly so. The presence of several new justices, including Antonin Scalia, Sandra Day O'Connor, and Anthony Kennedy, fueled speculation that the Court was preparing to overrule *Roe*.

In 1989, in *Webster v. Reproductive Health Services*, the Supreme Court almost did so, upholding the most severe restrictions on abortion until that time. Missouri had passed a law designed to "encourage childbirth over abortion." The law banned the use of public facilities or staff to perform abortions except to save the mother's life. The law also required a physician to perform tests on a woman twenty or more weeks pregnant to determine whether the fetus was "viable." (Viability itself was estimated at twenty-four weeks. The earlier starting date was intended to compensate for errors in estimating gestational age.)

In upholding the Missouri regulations, the nine justices issued six opinions. One justice, Antonin Scalia, called on the Court to overrule *Roe* outright. Three more justices—Chief Justice William Rehnquist and Justices Byron White and Anthony Kennedy—called for doing away with *Roe*'s trimester framework. Justice Sandra Day O'Connor provided the swing vote, in favor of the restrictions, but against revisiting *Roe*. (She also expressed dissatisfaction with the trimester framework, but concluded that *Webster* was not the proper case in which to reexamine it.)

Chief Justice Rehnquist wrote the 5-to-4 decision for the Court. Harking back to his dissent in *Roe*, Justice Rehnquist criticized the trimester framework as judicial legislation that had turned the Court into the country's "ex officio medical board." In addition, he said, the framework's reliance on the crucial point of "viability" did not make sense. If the state has an interest in protecting potential human life, then that interest must exist throughout pregnancy, not just after "viability." Thus, states should be able to regulate abortion in the early stages of pregnancy as well. Once again, Rehnquist claimed that abortion was not a fundamental right but could be regulated as the states saw fit, as long as it was not outlawed altogether.

Justice Blackmun led the dissenters. Over the years, the author of *Roe* had seen a 7-to-2 majority shrink to a 5-to-4 defeat. He accused the plurality of "winks, nods, and knowing glances to those who would do away with *Roe* explicitly" and criticized those justices for avoiding a discussion on the crucial issue: the right to privacy. Questions about the existence and extent of the right to privacy, Blackmun said, "[are] of unsurpassed significance in this Court's interpretation of the Constitution."

Justice Blackmun maintained that the Constitution recognizes a sphere of individual liberty which includes the right to make personal decisions of the greatest importance without government interference. If that liberty is to be truly meaningful, it must include the right of a woman to exercise some control over her role in procreation. The Constitution must respect the "moral fact that a person belongs to himself and not others nor to society as a whole."

Justice Blackmun defended the trimester framework and the viability standard as a fair, sensible, and effective way of safeguarding the freedom of women while accommodating the state's interest in potential human life. That the trimester framework does not appear in the Constitution was not a true concern, Blackmun argued. The distinctions made in the abortion context were no more intricate than those in other areas, such as the First Amendment's "actual malice" standard, or the determination of reasonableness under the Fourth Amendment. Their intricacy was not a result of judicial overreaching, Blackmun argued, but rather a sign of the Court's conscientiousness and care in the execution of its duty. Such care is especially important when fundamental rights are at stake.

In a last-ditch defense of the decision that made his career, Blackmun wrote, "In a Nation that cherishes liberty, the ability of a woman to control the biological operation of her body . . . must fall within that limited sphere of individual autonomy that lies beyond the will or power of any transient majority. . . . This Court stands as the ultimate guarantor of that zone of privacy, regardless of the bitter disputes to which our decisions may give rise. In *Roe*, . . . we did no more than discharge our constitutional duty."

By 1992, the only thing that all nine members of the Court seemed to agree upon was that the law in this area had become extremely confused. So the Court took on *Planned Parenthood v. Casey*, a case challenging Pennsylvania's abortion regulations. This time, the Court squarely faced the privacy issue—and again the nine justices produced five opinions, with only three justices writing a joint opinion for the Court.

Declaring that "liberty finds no refuge in a jurisprudence of doubt," the Court reaffirmed what it considered the "essential holding" of *Roe v. Wade*. Justice O'Connor once again provided the swing vote, and wrote the joint opinion. She stated the law as follows: A woman has a right to choose abortion before viability and to obtain it without undue interference from the state; the state has the power to restrict abortion after viability (with exceptions for cases in which the woman's health is endangered); and the state has legitimate interests from the outset of pregnancy in protecting the health of the woman and the life of the fetus.

Justice O'Connor then defended substantive due process and, in turn, the right to privacy. She concluded that the Court was not limited by practices current at the time the Bill of Rights was written or the Fourteenth Amendment adopted. Rather, as it had concluded in *Griswold* and *Roe*, the Court found that its responsibility was to balance individual liberty against the demands of organized society through an exercise of reasoned judgment. "It is a promise of the Constitution that there is a realm of personal liberty which the government may not enter. . . . At the heart of liberty is the right to define one's own concept of existence, of meaning, of the universe, and of the mystery of human life. Beliefs about these matters could not define the attributes of personhood were they formed under compulsion of the State," the Court declared.

The Court also relied heavily on the legal doctrine of *stare decisis*, the obligation to follow the rule of law in prior cases. First, Justice O'Connor balanced the effect of *Roe* against the human cost of overruling it. The Court pointed out that millions of people had organized their intimate relationships, as well as their professional and social lives, depending upon the availability of abortion. Furthermore, *Roe* had not, as the dissent claimed, proved to be unworkable or anachronistic. No new facts had emerged to justify overruling it. Even those advances in medical technology that had fixed viability at an earlier date did not change the central principle that viability was the earliest point at which the state could completely ban nontherapeutic abortions. The Court considered the costs of overruling *Roe* in legal terms as well, and found that doing so without the highest and most convincing need would amount to nothing more than capitulating to political pressure. Such a surrender would profoundly damage the Court's integrity and the nation's commitment to the rule of law.

However, the Court did overrule *Roe*'s trimester framework. The Court found that the framework, in particular the ban on all regulations before viability, undervalued the state's interest in potential life. Instead, the Court announced a new legal standard under which restrictions on abortion would now be evaluated, a standard that Justice O'Connor had proposed before. Any law that placed an *undue burden* on a woman's right to obtain an abortion before viability would be unconstitutional. Under the new standard, a law will not be found unconstitutional if it merely makes abortion more difficult or more expensive to obtain. Only if a law places a "substantial obstacle" in the path of a woman seeking an abortion before viability will it be struck down.

Turning to the Pennsylvania law at issue in the case, the Court found that only the requirement that a woman notify her spouse before an abortion was an "undue burden." Spousal notification would not merely make abortions more difficult or expensive, it would effectively enable a husband to veto his wife's decision. For the majority of women who voluntarily notify their partners, the law would have no effect. But spousal notification, the Court found, is likely to prevent a significant number of women from obtaining an abortion, particularly those who are victims of physical, psychological, or sexual abuse, or who fear for their safety and the safety of their children.

The Court recognized that a man and a woman have an equal interest in their living children. But before a child's birth, the impact of any state regulation will be greater on a woman's liberty and bodily integrity than on a man's. Therefore, the woman must have the ultimate decisional authority. Any other conclusion would return women to their common-law status as subordinate to their husbands, with no independent legal existence. The Court called this view "repugnant to our present understanding of marriage and of the nature of the rights secured by the Constitution."

The Court upheld all of the other provisions of the Pennsylvania law, including an informed-consent provision requiring that at least twenty-four hours before an abortion, a physician must inform the woman of the nature of abortion, and of the health risks involved. A doctor must also describe the developing fetus, and the availability of alternatives to abortion. The law also provided that the woman must wait twenty-four hours between this initial consultation and the abortion procedure. All facilities performing abortions must then file reports identifying the physicians and referring physician, the woman's age, marital status, prior pregnancies, and abortions, the date and type of abortion, medical complications, weight of aborted fetus, and number of abortions performed per trimester.

In a concurring opinion, Justice Blackmun argued that the trimester framework should be retained and all of the Pennsylvania regulations struck down as unconstitutional. Still, he hailed the decision by Justices O'Connor, Kennedy, and David Souter to reaffirm the holding of *Roe*, as "an act of personal courage and constitutional principle." He criticized the dissent's "stunted conception of individual liberty" and disregard for the long line of cases "grounded in a more general right to privacy."

In stark contrast, the dissent declared that *Roe* had been wrongly decided from the outset and should be overruled. Justices White, Scalia, and Clarence Thomas joined an opinion written by Chief Justice Rehnquist. They acknowledged that the Court had long protected liberties such as the right to procreate, to marry, and to use contraceptives. But the dissent said these rights were simply separate protected liberties and did not create a more general constitutionally protected right to privacy. Furthermore, abortion was different from these other protected rights because it "involves the purposeful termination of potential life."

Finally, the dissent criticized the "undue burden" standard as unworkable. Chief Justice Rehnquist said it "will do nothing to prevent 'judges from roaming at large in the constitutional field' guided only by their personal views."

Justice Scalia also found the "undue burden" standard to be hopelessly ambiguous. He wrote a separate dissent to address what he called "a few of the more outrageous arguments in today's opinion." Repeating the majority's statement—"liberty finds no refuge in a jurisprudence of doubt"—Justice Scalia said that to come across that statement in an opinion that set forth the hazy "undue burden" standard

was "really more than one should have to bear." He said the Court
was merely continuing its "wanderings in this forsaken wilderness,"
and with the rest of the dissenters predicted only more confusion and
divisiveness to come.

So where does all of this leave the right to privacy? Justice Scalia
exhorted his colleagues, "We should get out of this area, where we
have no right to be, and where we do neither ourselves nor the country any good by remaining." Justice Blackmun, the original author of
Roe, responded, "I fear for the darkness as four justices anxiously await
the single vote necessary to extinguish the light."

SINCE *Casey*, Justices Blackmun and White have retired. Two new justices, Ruth Bader Ginsberg and Stephen Breyer, have joined the Court.
Neither has ruled on the central privacy questions underlying the right
to terminate a pregnancy. It is too early to tell whether one of them
will be the single vote that Justice Blackmun feared.

Passing Judgments

A MISSISSIPPI statute requires a minor to obtain the *consent* of *both* her parents before an abortion. The statute contains a judicial bypass mechanism. Consent is not required if the girl can demonstrate to a judge that: she is mature and well informed enough to make the decision on her own; one or both of her parents have abused her; or notification would otherwise not be in her best interest. The law was challenged as an undue burden because it gave her parents a veto over the minor's decision and involved too much judicial intrusiveness into a family's private decision.

The U.S. Court of Appeals for the Fifth Circuit upheld the statute, finding that it did not place an undue burden on the right to obtain an abortion. The U.S. Supreme Court refused to take the case.

Barnes v. Mississippi, Mississippi 1993

A NORTH DAKOTA statute requires women seeking abortions to certify in writing that they have received information concerning the medical risks of abortion and pregnancy, the probable gestational age of the fetus, and the possibility of medical-assistance benefits and child support. Then the women must wait twenty-four hours before undergoing the procedure.

The U.S. Court of Appeals for the Eighth Circuit upheld the statute. In reaching its decision, the court noted that nothing in the statute prevented the information from being given over the telephone. A telephone call and a single trip to the medical facility did not create an undue burden, the court concluded.

Fargo Women's Health Organization v. Schafer, North Dakota 1994

IN JUNE 1991, Louisiana enacted an abortion statute. The law made it a crime to "administer or prescribe any drug, potion, or any other substance to a female" or to "use any instrumental or external force whatsoever on a female" with the specific intent of terminating a pregnancy. Exceptions were made for abortions carried out in order to save the life of the mother, or when the pregnancy resulted from rape or incest, provided the rape or incest had been reported to the police and the abortion was performed within the first thirteen weeks of pregnancy.

In September 1992, the U.S. Court of Appeals for the Fifth Circuit found the Louisiana statute clearly unconstitutional under *Casey*. The court held that the law imposed an undue burden on women seeking abortion before viability. The U.S. Supreme Court refused to hear the case.

Sojourner T. v. Edwards, Louisiana 1992

Some cases involve more than one aspect of the right to privacy. This is particularly true when antiabortion protesters picket the homes of doctors who perform abortions. The doctors say their residential privacy is invaded because they help women exercise their constitutional right to reproductive privacy. Yet in these cases, another constitutional right—the right to free speech—is on the other side.

ON AT LEAST six occasions between April 20, 1985, and May 20, 1985, groups of up to forty picketers assembled in front of a Wisconsin doctor's home. The demonstrators were peaceful but shouted slogans and told neighborhood children that the doctor was a "baby killer." In response to numerous complaints, the town passed an ordinance prohibiting all picketing "before or about the residence or dwelling of any individual." The purpose of the ban was to protect and preserve the feelings of "well-being, tranquillity and privacy" that people enjoy in their homes.

The picketers challenged the ordinance as an unconstitutional restriction on their right to free speech. They argued that public streets have traditionally been open to all and that picketing on an issue of public concern is at the core of First Amendment protection.

The United States Supreme Court upheld the ban. The Court found that residential privacy was an interest that the government could protect and that the ban was limited to picketing in front of a particular residence. "There is simply no right to force speech into the home of an unwilling listener," the Court wrote. The Court also found that the picketers had other ways to get their message across, such as proselytizing door to door, using the mail or telephone, or marching through an entire neighborhood, rather than targeting one house.

Frisby v. Schultz, Wisconsin 1988

IN SEPTEMBER 1992, a Florida court prohibited antiabortion demonstrators from blocking the entrances to a Melbourne clinic that performed abortions or from physically abusing people entering or leaving the premises. Six months later, the clinic was back in court claiming that groups of up to four hundred shouting, chanting protesters with bullhorns were still blocking access to the clinic. The homes of clinic workers were also targeted.

The trial court then established a thirty-six-foot buffer zone around the clinic and the adjoining, privately owned lots. From 7:30 a.m. until noon on Mondays through Saturdays during surgery and recovery periods, no singing, shouting, yelling, use of bullhorns, car horns, or other sounds or images observable within the clinic were allowed. The court also established a three-hundred-foot no-approach zone around the clinic, in which protesters were not allowed to physically approach anyone entering the clinic without that person's consent. A three-hundred-foot buffer zone was also established around the homes of clinic workers, and protesters were prohibited from trying to gain access to workers' homes.

The protesters challenged the restrictions as a violation of their First Amendment right to free speech. They claimed that the ban discriminated against them on the basis of their views and was unnecessarily restrictive.

In June 1994, the U.S. Supreme Court upheld the thirty-six-foot buffer zone around the clinic as well as the noise restrictions. "The First Amendment does not demand that patients at a medical facility undertake Herculean efforts to escape the cacophony of political protests," the Court wrote.

However, the Court struck down the thirty-six-foot buffer zone around the adjoining private property, the three-hundred-foot no-approach zone, and the three-hundred-foot zone around the homes of clinic staff. The Court also struck down the ban on observable images (finding that the clinic could simply draw the curtains). Regarding the residential picketing, the Court found that a limitation on the time, duration, and number of pickets outside a smaller zone could have achieved the desired result. With respect to the noise restrictions, whether around the clinic or in residential neighborhoods, the Court noted that the government could require the protesters to turn down the volume "if the protests overwhelm the neighborhood."

Madsden v. Women's Health Center, Florida 1994

DAVIS v. DAVIS

The Frozen Embryos Case

T HE SECOND of six children, Mary Sue Easterly of Massillon, Ohio, grew up wanting a big family of her own. In the spring of 1979, she had completed basic training in the U.S. Army and was stationed in Würzburg, West Germany, when she met Junior Lewis Davis of Knoxville, Tennessee. Junior—or J.R., as he prefers to be called—was in signal maintenance, working in the electronics shop. They soon began courting, and after about a year they visited Mary Sue's hometown on leave and announced their plans to get married. The ceremony took place three days later, on April 26, 1980. J.R. was twenty-one years old at the time. Mary Sue was twenty.

Six months later, back in Würzburg, Mary Sue felt terrible abdominal pain and started hemorrhaging. Emergency surgery revealed that a tubal pregnancy had caused her right fallopian tube to rupture, requiring its removal.

After Mary Sue had recovered from the surgery, she and J.R. decided to try again. By this time, the couple had returned to the U.S. and settled in Seymour, Tennessee, near Knoxville. J.R. was working at Seymour Heating and Air Conditioning; Mary Sue was a secretary at Magnavox.

Over the next three years, Mary Sue had three more tubal pregnancies. In September of 1983, she was referred to Dr. I. Ray King, a Knoxville obstetrician and gynecologist specializing in infertility. Dr. King performed surgery to repair Mary Sue's damaged fallopian tube. On December 28, 1983, she and J.R. received good news: a positive pregnancy test. But a few days later, when Mary Sue went in for an ultrasound, her hopes were dashed again. Another tubular pregnancy—her fifth.

As Dr. King puts it, "That's enough for any person. Apparently, the tubes were not going to work right." He recommended that her remaining fallopian tube be ligated (tied). Mary Sue confronted the disappointing reality that she would never be able to conceive in the usual way. But she and J.R. refused to give up.

In the fall of 1985, after counseling and a physical exam, they entered Dr. King's in vitro fertilization program. In vitro fertilization and embryo transfer, commonly known as IVF, is the process used to produce a "test-tube baby." In IVF, eggs are removed from the woman's ovaries and inseminated with sperm in a petri dish; then the fertilized eggs are returned to the woman's uterus. If all goes well, at least one fertilized egg will attach to the uterine wall and a "normal" pregnancy and delivery will result. But that description is deceptively simple. In fact, the process can be a grueling ordeal, as Mary Sue and J.R. would discover.

On the third day of her menstrual cycle, Mary Sue began daily injections to suppress her body's own hormone production. Midway through her cycle, she underwent another series of injections designed to stimulate egg production. All her life, Mary Sue had been terrified of needles. She couldn't bring herself to administer the shots, so J.R.'s mother came over to help. The IVF process also required constant contact with Dr. King and his nurse, frequent blood and ultrasound tests to determine exact hormone levels and follicle growth, and precise timing.

On the day Dr. King determined that Mary Sue's eggs were mature, an injection was given at around 10 p.m. Ovulation would occur thirty-six to thirty-eight hours after the injection, so surgery to remove the eggs was scheduled for thirty-five hours later, to allow the eggs to develop inside Mary Sue's body for as long as possible.

To remove the eggs, Dr. King performed a surgical procedure known as a "laparoscopy." Three incisions were made into Mary Sue's abdomen, allowing a miniature telescope and an instrument to hold the ovary in place to be inserted through her belly button. Dr. King then punctured a follicle on the ovary and drew fluid containing the eggs into a tube. He then handed the tube, which resembles a tiny straw, to Dr. Charles Shivers, the zoology professor and embryology specialist who assisted him. The procedure took about thirty minutes per follicle, and, in the case of Mary Sue, yielded an average of three to four eggs.

Once the eggs were retrieved, Dr. Shivers placed them in a petri dish in an incubator for four to eight hours. He then returned with J.R.'s semen sample to inseminate the eggs. As Dr. Shivers is careful to point out, "insemination" refers merely to the process of mixing the sperm and egg together in the petri dish. "Fertilization" is defined as the union of the sperm and the egg and the fusion of their nuclei. Fertilization is entirely up to the cells themselves. After placing the sperm and egg together in the petri dish, Dr. Shivers said good night and left them alone until the following morning.

Once an egg has been fertilized, it becomes known as a zygote. The next morning, Dr. Shivers checked on the fertilization process and determined how many eggs had become zygotes. Then he put them back in the incubator for another twelve hours, and checked them again in the late afternoon. Twenty-four hours after fertilization, a zygote begins to cleave into two cells. Once cell division has occurred, the zygote becomes known as a pre-embryo.

The next step in the process is referred to as a "transfer"—placing the pre-embryos in Mary Sue's uterus. According to Dr. Shivers, the highest success rate occurs if the pre-embryos are transferred between the two- and eight-cell stage of development—roughly on the afternoon of the second day after fertilization has been identified. On that day, Mary Sue was brought into a patient room next to the laboratory and prepared. The pre-embryos were then drawn into a transfer catheter and inserted into her uterus by Dr. King. After that, J.R. recalls, he and Mary Sue hung around the hospital for a few hours, until they were told Mary Sue could go home. She then had to take it easy for the rest of the day.

Back on the biological level, once the pre-embryo has been transferred, it develops into a ball of identical cells which is the same size as the original single cell. Over the next six to eight days, it grows to number several hundred cells and attaches itself to the uterine wall. This process is known as "implantation." A few hours before implantation, a process of cell differentiation begins: Some of the cells begin to form the inner cell mass, which will develop into the placenta; others form the embryo itself.

Over the next three years, Mary Sue began this process six times and completed the cycle five times. None led to a pregnancy. But the couple remained determined to become parents. J.R. signed up to be a Big Brother. The Davises also attended classes and became eligible for the state adoption program. They were hoping for two children: one from the IVF program and the other adopted.

However, the adoption process did not work out for Mary Sue and J.R. (In one instance, the birth mother changed her mind at the last minute.) And the IVF process did not seem to be working, either. With each failed attempt to become pregnant, the disappointment and heartbreak seemed greater, and it took longer for Mary Sue to regain the emotional strength to begin again. Finally, in 1988, Mary Sue and J.R. got what sounded like good news. A new technique, called "cryopreservation," had become available.

Cryopreservation is the process by which pre-embryos are frozen to preserve them for future use. Its primary advantage is that it increases the chances of pregnancy by allowing fertilized egg cells to be saved and then transferred back into the woman during a natural menstrual cycle rather than an artificially stimulated one. With cryopreservation, the ovaries can be stimulated to produce additional eggs during one cycle, as previously but, rather than having to transfer them all back into the patient (as the Davises had been doing), Dr. King could return only two pre-embryos and save the rest for transfer at a later date.

After the eggs have been fertilized, each pre-embryo is placed in a French straw—"like a soda straw except much smaller," says Dr. Shivers. Somewhere around the two- to sixteen-cell stage, or about the same time they would be transferred, a process of gradual freezing begins. To prevent the formation of ice crystals, the pre-embryos are mixed with cryoprotective agents and are then placed in a series of progressively more concentrated freezing solutions. At -10 degrees centigrade, the straw is grasped by a cold metal instrument which instantly turns the contents from liquid to solid (ice). This is known as "seeding." The temperature is further lowered to -50 to -60 degrees centigrade. During the final step, the straw is plunged into liquid nitrogen, lowering the temperature to -160 to -190 degrees centigrade, where it is kept until thawing for transfer.

According to Dr. King, the "tricky" parts of the process are freezing and thawing. "It's a bit like flying a plane," he says. "It's the takeoff and landing that are the problem." No one knows for certain how long pre-embryos can be successfully stored. As of 1988, two years seemed the maximum, and 20 to 30 percent would not make it at all. The only way to tell if pre-embryos have survived the process is to thaw them out one at a time.

By November 1988, Mary Sue and J.R. were ready to try the new technique. They had agreed with Dr. King that if they got three or four eggs as usual, they would transfer them all, as usual. If they were lucky enough to get more, the additional pre-embryos would be frozen for future use.

Mary Sue underwent the cycle of injections in late November. On December 8, at 6:30 a.m., J.R. and Mary Sue arrived at Fort Sanders Hospital. J.R. brought his sperm donation from home and gave it to the nurse, Debbie McCarter. He got a cup of coffee and sat around the waiting room looking at magazines while Mary Sue was taken down for surgery. About two or three hours later, Nurse McCarter returned with exciting news. Dr. King and Dr. Shivers had retrieved *nine* eggs— six more than they had gotten in any of their previous attempts.

Two days later, in the afternoon of December 10, 1988, the Davises returned to the hospital for transfer. They looked under the microscope at the pre-embryos. Mary Sue recalls her excitement: "After everything you go through, and there they are, especially nine of them. We got to see seven. It was just exciting. . . . It was something we had both produced. . . . You're hoping they're going to become children. . . . [You feel] an attachment to them."

Everyone was thrilled by the success of the retrieval. Based on Dr. King's recommendation, they decided to transfer two of the pre-embryos and freeze the remaining seven. J.R. stayed with Mary Sue while the pre-embryos were inserted. They went home hoping for a baby.

About two weeks later, they got the news. The transfer had not worked. The pregnancy test was negative. Two months after that, in February 1989, J.R. filed for divorce.

J.R. says the marriage had been "rocky" for a year and a half, and he had entered the last round of IVF with Mary Sue in the misguided belief that a child would save their relationship. Mary Sue says she had no idea that the marriage was in trouble. In fact, she said later, had she known they were heading for divorce, she doubts she would have tried again.

At first, it seemed like a typical divorce. They agreed to sell their house and split the proceeds, and they divided up their other property. But what about the seven frozen pre-embryos? Who would get them?

"I am the mother of those embryos. They are the beginning of life. They are a part of me," said Mary Sue. "When we put them in frozen storage, it was only temporary, until they were ready to be returned to my body. I believe that is where they belong."

J.R. saw it differently. "This is half me and half Mary. This is part of me as much as it is her, and I should have control, as well as herself." After their marriage broke up, J.R. did not think that he wanted Mary to have their child. J.R. was not sure what he wanted to do with the pre-embryos, but he did not feel the middle of a divorce was the time to decide. "I have to agree that Mary went through a lot," he says. "No one knows that better than Mary or myself. I was right there with her, all the time. And during the course of this, it wasn't just the physical, there was a lot of emotional pain on both sides. But . . . I can't throw my feelings aside just to accommodate hers."

As is usual when two people have a seemingly unresolvable dispute, they get lawyers. J.R.'s attorney, Charles Clifford, describes his first meeting with his client: "In February 1989, I was standing in my office and my secretary told me that there was a man on the phone who wanted to come in and see me about a no-fault divorce. And I looked at her and said, 'So what's the big deal?' She said, 'He wants to come in at night.' I didn't particularly feel like staying late, so I was about to tell her to tell this guy to rearrange his life when she reminded me that we advertised some evening times in the yellow pages. So I said okay. He came in at seven o'clock. I'm in a big hurry. I want out of here. I have a checklist I'm going down. Real simple case until we get to the last question, which is, 'Is there anything else?' "

When Clifford realized that J.R. and Mary Sue could not agree on what to do with the pre-embryos, he acted fast. He filed for divorce on behalf of J.R. and got a preliminary injunction against Mary Sue and Dr. King to prevent either of them from proceeding with a transfer. Shortly after that, the headlines began.

Clifford knew an explosive constitutional issue when he saw one. He admits, "I told J.R. real early on, 'This is horrible for you, you hate this, but I'm not going to kid you. For me this is like seventh heaven.' "

Mary Sue's lawyer, Jay Christenberry, had a different reaction. "Probably the worst day of my life," he recalls. Christenberry received a phone call from a neighbor asking him to see a lady who needed a divorce. The woman had been "experimenting with human reproduction," he was told. On a Friday afternoon at about 4 p.m., Mary Sue walked into Christenberry's Knoxville law office. "She told me that a reporter from one of these wild magazines had broken through her fence and jimmied her kitchen door, and shoved money in her face and said, 'Take this, we need to interview you.' They had a copy of the pleadings. She had tried to call the sheriff. She said, 'I've got to have some help.' "

Christenberry says he and Mary Sue talked about the situation, and his reaction was, "Quite frankly, I'm probably not the lawyer who should handle this." But, he continued, "I don't think you'll find any lawyer that's been to school on this one. The only thing I can say is, 'You are the lady. You're the female. As far as I know, a man has never been successful in preventing a woman from terminating a pregnancy. Nor has a man ever been successful in telling her that she has to continue a pregnancy.' And I said, 'The only distinction we have in this case is that the embryos are not in you.' " Christenberry didn't regard the distinction as all that important.

Not only did Christenberry agree to take up Mary Sue's cause, he believed he was also fighting for the pre-embryos themselves. "I saw them as having rights on their own," he says.

For the next seven months, it was all anyone in town could talk about. The battle over the "frozen embryos" was the front-page story in local newspapers every day, and of course it was perfect for talk radio, tabloid TV, and late-night comedians.

"Q: What's Junior going to get the kids for Christmas this year? A: Pink and blue ice cube trays"; "Q: Did you hear Junior was picked up for child abuse? A: He left his kids out of the freezer" are two jokes that J.R. recalls particularly upset him.

"The media terrorized me," says Mary Sue. She believes that members of the press broke into her house and tapped her phone. She says they constantly harassed her for interviews.

J.R. did not fare any better. It was difficult not only to deal with the constant publicity but also with the distorted impressions it produced. J.R. explains, "I've heard so many times, 'Oh, you're going to be rich'; 'Oh, you're making money hand over fist'; or 'You're going to be famous out there.' But I wasn't doing this to get famous. That's the last thing I wanted. I'd rather never have been involved in this than to be known for what I am today."

On August 7, 1989, *Davis v. Davis* went to trial in the Maryville, Tennessee, courtroom of Judge William Dale Young. Outside the courthouse, the Chamber of Commerce had pitched a tent to serve refreshments to the international press, T-shirts were hawked all over town, and crowds gathered. Not since the Scopes monkey trial had a Tennessee case caused such a commotion. The comparisons were easy: a sleepy country courthouse and a groundbreaking constitutional issue. The issue itself was a futuristic descendant of the Creation v. Evolution dispute argued by William Jennings Bryan and Clarence Darrow. *Davis v. Davis* pitted right-to-lifers against pro-choice activists, albeit with a twist. This time, the person claiming the right not to be a parent was a man.

In the quarter century of debate over abortion rights, the focus has been almost exclusively on the woman. The potential father's interest has been given little or no weight. In fact, in 1976 the Supreme Court struck down a law requiring a woman to obtain her husband's *consent* before an abortion. Similarly, in 1992 the Court would even strike down a mandatory *notification* provision as unconstitutional, on the grounds that it would effectively give the husband a veto over his wife's decision and, as such, would infringe upon her right to control her own body.

Now J.R. Davis was saying that because the pre-embryos were in a freezer rather than in his wife's body, the potential mother and father were equal before the law. He argued that just as a woman in the abortion context has a right not to become a mother against her will, a man in his situation should have a similar right not to become a father.

Inside the courtroom, the attorneys made their opening statements. On J.R.'s behalf, Charles Clifford asked for joint custody of the pre-embryos. He expressed J.R.'s desire to leave the pre-embryos in cryopreservation until J.R. and Mary Sue could agree on what should be done with them. Mary Sue's advocate, Jay Christenberry, stated his position that the pre-embryos were, in fact, "pre-born children" in need of legal protection. He asked that the court dissolve the preliminary injunction so that Mary Sue could proceed with the transfers of her children.

Judge Young would later recall his thoughts on the eve of trial. "I got to thinking about the basic question in the whole case. These frozen embryos: What do we do with them? What are they? Are they people or are they property? And that's a question I asked myself throughout the case. I've asked myself that since. I guess I always will."

If the press attention up until this point had seemed intrusive, the legal proceedings themselves were a further invasion, exposing the Davises' most intimate decisions to the courtroom and, via satellite, to the world. The first witness was Dr. King. He testified in detail about human reproduction and infertility, specifically the problems of J.R. and Mary Sue Davis. Slides were projected showing the female reproductive organs and the fertilization process. Dr. King expressed his belief that it would be wasteful to destroy the seven pre-embryos. "I favor helping people be parents," he said, adding that he hoped the pre-embryos could be donated to another childless couple.

One of the most important issues at trial was whether there had been "informed consent" and what the terms of that consent were. Had J.R. consented to the transfer of the pre-embryos merely by participating in the program? As in a normal conception, could it be said that once he donated his sperm, he had consented to become a father and could not back out? Or conversely, was written consent required at each step along the way? And did divorce change anything?

The testimony revealed that the Davises actually had not signed any consent forms before participating in the IVF process. The day Mary Sue came in for the egg retrieval, the nurse had forgotten to bring the forms with her. No one remembered to bring the consent forms on the transfer day either. Dr. King testified that although the papers were mailed to the Davises two days later, they were never returned. However, even if the Davises had signed the documents, the issue would not have been resolved. At that time, Dr. King's consent forms dealt only with consent to do the procedure. They contained no provision regarding the disposition of the pre-embryos in the event of divorce.

The next witness was John Robertson, a law professor from the University of Texas at Austin specializing in bioethics issues and a member of the American Fertility Society's ethics committee. Professor Robertson testified that a pre-embryo is a group of cells that could develop, or not, into one person, or more than one. Professor Robertson said that a pre-embryo does not become a clearly defined biologic individual until after implantation. He noted the consensus among the scientific community that a pre-embryo is not a person or entity with rights or interests of its own, but because it has the potential for life, it deserves "special respect," respect greater than that due to other human tissue.

Professor Robertson expressed his belief that a couple should be joint decision-makers with respect to the disposition of a pre-embryo; that if they have made a prior agreement between them that agreement should control; and that in the absence of such an agreement, the court should analyze the burdens on each of the parties. If the woman could create new embryos, Professor Robertson said, it would be reasonable for her to do so rather than to impose on the man the burdens of unwanted parenthood.

According to Robertson, when the act of conception takes place outside the woman's body, it brings about a fundamental change in privacy rights. The woman's interest in controlling her own body is no longer present, he said, so there is no longer any reason why she should be the primary decision-maker. Once the privacy interest in bodily integrity is removed from the equation, only the right to become or not to become a genetic parent remains. Here, the parties are on equal terms.

On the second day of trial, Dr. Shivers took the stand for a detailed explication of cryopreservation.

Then it was J.R.'s turn. J.R. testified that as far as formal consent was concerned, he had never been asked to sign a document of any kind during the entire IVF program. Furthermore, no one had discussed with him the ramifications of cryopreservation beyond its usefulness in increasing the chances of pregnancy. His intent, he explained, had always been to use the pre-embryos only within his marriage. He asked the court to leave the pre-embryos in cryopreservation. "At this time I don't feel that I could make a logical decision on the disposition of the pre-embryos other than the fact that I do not want them used at this time or in the near future. I do not ask for them to be destroyed; I just ask that they not be inserted in Mary or any donor," he said.

The lawyers pressed him to explain how he could oppose Mary Sue's wish to proceed when for the previous nine years he had joined her every step of the way. Then J.R.'s whole life story came spilling out. He told the court that he was the fifth of six children whose parents had divorced just before his sixth birthday. After his father left, J.R. said, his world was shattered. His mother had a breakdown and sent four of her sons, including J.R., to live in a boys' home. A fifth boy went to live with an aunt, and J.R.'s sister stayed with their mother. J.R. lived in the home until his eighteenth birthday, visiting his mother only once a month. His father lived locally but, J.R. said, "He didn't care to have a relationship with his children."

The home itself was "fine," J.R. testified. "We had a very religious upbringing, we were in church, in school, raised very properly. I probably had more as far as material things than I would have had with my parents." But growing up like an orphan, feeling unwanted, took a terrible toll. "The biggest problem," he says, "was being away from my parents. At that age there was no way I could understand, and I had a lot of problems with it. As I grew older I became very angry, a lot of mistrust, possible hatred for people."

J.R. explained that the pain he had suffered as a result of his parents' divorce led him to conclude that as long as he still had a choice, he did not want to father a child that would grow up in a broken home, a child that might feel abandoned or unwanted as he had. "This was such a psychological burden on [me]. This is one of the strongest reasons why I feel there is no way I want to put a child of mine in a single-parent home," he testified. "It's not just the burden it would be on the child. It would be on myself." J.R. added that if the court ruled against him and allowed Mary Sue to proceed, he would seek to have the child with him "every opportunity I could."

When asked how he felt about donating the pre-embryos anonymously to another infertile couple, J.R. answered that he would still consider the child to be his. "It would be a burden on myself, and I'm sure it would be a burden on Mary knowing that there is a child out there that should belong to us." To J.R., donating the pre-embryos to another couple would be like abandoning his children to strangers. Besides, what if the other couple ended up divorced?

J.R. told the court that if forced to choose between Mary and donation, "naturally I would choose Mary."

He continued, "I do not view them as life at this point. We are looking at potential life, but I would definitely rather see them destroyed rather than donated to another couple. That may seem cruel, but those are my feelings."

His testimony concluded with the following exchange:

Q: Have you ever felt anything more strongly in your life?
A: I don't think I can say I have. Just for the mere reason that my whole life has pretty much led me to this conclusion.

Mary Sue was next to take the stand. She described in detail her eleven surgical procedures and six IVF attempts. She explained why she believed the embryos should be awarded to her, and why she felt they represented her only chance to become a mother. "I believe I have contributed the most. I have been through so much mentally and physically. . . . I can't take any more. My body can't take any more; I just can't do it."

Toward the end of her testimony, she implored the court: "They are more than just a few little cells. . . . I do consider them my children because they are the beginning of life; they are a part of me. The only person that has a right to use them is me."

Mary Sue testified that she believed J.R. didn't really know what he wanted, while there was no doubt in her mind that she would like to have her own child. She added, "I really don't feel it abuses his rights because to me he did consent to be a father, and I'm willing to let him be a father. I have no reservations about being a single parent. Like he said, if he's willing to participate, then I don't really consider that too much of a single-parent home." She repeated her conviction that she was "the mother of the embryos," that they were intended to be transferred back to her body, and that they had been removed only temporarily.

Just before trial, Jay Christenberry had received word that an eminent geneticist would be willing to fly over from France to testify for Mary Sue. Christenberry asked that the trial be extended an extra day to accommodate Dr. Jerome LeJeune. In the early 1960s, Dr. LeJeune had discovered the chromosomal abnormality that causes Down's syndrome, a leading cause of mental retardation. Since then, he had been appointed to many illustrious committees, although to Charles Clifford he seemed "a plump Jacques Cousteau, floating around on the fame of his early years." LeJeune was treated with great deference by the court, and his reputation (and perhaps his accent) made a striking impression. He testified without interruption for most of the day, expounding a mixture of philosophical, metaphysical, scientific, and religious opinions.

After describing his own career, LeJeune was asked if he was familiar with the Davises' dilemma. LeJeune answered, "I know there are babies, there are human beings in the fridge, this is the only thing I know." He compared the process of fertilization to democracy. "The voting process is the fertilization itself, because there are a lot of proposals, many, many sperms. Only one got in; that is the voting process which enacts the new constitution of a man." He compared chromosomes to "a mini-cassette in which a symphony is written, the symphony of life."

Dr. LeJeune turned to the process of cryopreservation, which he called "the fact of putting inside a very chilly space, tiny human beings who are deprived of any liberty, of any movement, they are even deprived of time, making them survive, so to speak, in a concentration can. It's not as hospitable and prepared for life as would be the secret temple which is inside the female body that is a womb." When asked if he had any ethical concerns about cryopreservation, LeJeune answered, "Love is the contrary of chilly. Love is warmth, and life needs good temperature."

Dr. LeJeune testified that there was no such thing as a pre-embryo, only an embryo; that a unique individual was present at the three-cell stage; and that in his expert opinion "science has a very simple conception of man—as soon as he has been conceived, a man is man."

This lofty exposition was followed by Charles Clifford's cross-examination, which took LeJeune from the sublime to the ridiculous. It concluded with the following exchange:

Q: I have only one final question for you. Okay, what is this? (holding up an object)

A: Well, from here I suppose it's an egg, but I'm not sure.

Q: Let me get a little closer.

A: It looks like an egg.

Q: It's an egg?

A: It looks like.

Mr. Clifford: Thank you, Doctor. I thought you were going to tell me it was an early chicken.

The Witness: Oh.

Mr. Clifford: I have no further questions.

The Witness: Your honor—

The Court: You may respond if you wish.

The Witness: I don't know if it has been fertilized so I cannot know whether it's an early chicken.

Mr. Clifford: All right. Let's talk about the difference for a moment. If I had in this hand a live chicken, would you agree with me if I were to take it and squeeze its head that it would feel pain?

A: Oh, probably.

Q: That it will be frightened?

A: Yes.

Q: And that it would suffer psychological, if you can use that term with a chicken, stress?

A: I'm not competent in psychology you told me, and especially about chickens.

Q: But if I take this egg and assuming it is fertilized—I wouldn't really do this, Jay—but if I were to crush it in my hand, this egg would not feel pain, it would not be aware in the slightest of what was happening to it?

A: Yeah. But it would still be a chicken and only a chicken.

Q: I thought you told me it was an egg?

A: You told me it was a chicken.

Q: No further questions.

The trial ended after closing arguments, and the parties waited for Judge Young's opinion. For the judge, it would be the decision of his career. Many had compared the choice to the one that faced Solomon three thousand years ago. (In Solomon's case each of two women claimed a baby as her own. Solomon's solution was to order the baby cut in half, anticipating the true mother would give up her baby rather than allow it to be killed.) Others opined that the decision should be a scientific/medical one or a private/personal one, but that the legal system was ill-equipped for decisions of this magnitude.

Judge Young disagrees. "I don't find any fault with judges having to make hard decisions. We ask for the job. It was a terribly hard decision to make for me. I don't want to go through that process again. But if I have to, I will. I guess that's a roundabout way of saying I think it's all right for courts to have to decide whatever issues are put to them."

As it turned out, Judge Young embraced the role. In fact, he went beyond what many legal experts believed necessary. On September 21, 1989, he concluded that human life begins at the moment of conception. The eight-cell entities in frozen storage were not pre-embryos, he said, but rather "children in vitro." Judge Young then determined that it was "in the best interest of the children" to be born rather than destroyed. Thus, he awarded "custody" of the "children in vitro" to Mary Sue.

The ruling sent shock waves through the legal community. Even the United States Supreme Court, in its many decisions involving the issue of abortion, had never attempted to answer the ultimate question: When does life begin?

Judge Young viewed the reaction with equanimity. "I don't think society is ready for a judicial decision that life begins at conception. To me, it's not a religious question. It's not a question of morality. To me, it's a simple question of deciding what the facts in the case were, and applying whatever applicable law I could find to those facts." His critics point out that the decision didn't hurt Judge Young in the conservative Christian South; he won reelection as "the embryo judge" the next year.

J.R. appealed. One year later, in September 1990, an intermediate court reversed Judge Young's decision and awarded "joint control" over the pre-embryos to J.R. and Mary Sue. Relying on J.R.'s constitutional right not to beget a child when no pregnancy has taken place, the intermediate court concluded that there was no compelling state interest to justify ordering implantation against the will of either party. But it was clear by then that both sides were willing to fight all the way. Mary Sue appealed to the Tennessee Supreme Court.

By that time, only the seven pre-embryos remained where they had been at the start of the controversy—in cryopreservation at Dr. King's clinic. Mary Sue and J.R. had both moved on. J.R. had married a woman named Brenda and now lived in Maryville, Tennessee. Mary Sue was living in Florida with a new husband and a new name, Mary Stowe.

Mary had a new legal position as well. Her lawyers now argued that she did not wish to use the pre-embryos herself but wanted to donate them to another childless couple. J.R. was still adamantly opposed to donation. He asked that he be given custody of the embryos, presumably to destroy them.

New fissures had also opened up in the legal landscape. In 1989, a sharply divided and bitter U.S. Supreme Court had issued the *Webster* decision, upholding strict regulations on abortion.

The constitutional right to choose whether to terminate a pregnancy was widely perceived to be hanging by a thread. Justice Blackmun, the author of the *Roe* decision, wrote in his dissent in *Webster*, "For today, at least, the law of abortion stands undisturbed. For today, the women of this Nation still retain the liberty to control their destinies. But the signs are evident and very ominous, and a chill wind blows." With a Republican president committed to overturning *Roe* just one year into his first term, and the possibility of Supreme Court vacancies opening up, many people agreed with Justice Blackmun's assessment.

Although the Supreme Court debate centered around the point at which a fetus becomes viable outside the mother's body, a point far removed from the four-cell stage of the Davis pre-embryos, the constitutional controversy over abortion had potentially important consequences for their fate. On the one hand, the Supreme Court had consistently held that the unborn were not considered "persons" under the Constitution. And in *Roe*, the Court had written, "We need not resolve the difficult question of when life begins." On the other hand, there was no doubt that the Court had narrowed the federal constitutional right to privacy, and it was not clear exactly what protection remained.

The Supreme Court had never considered anything like the central question in the *Davis* case: What happens when the woman's right to control her bodily integrity is no longer part of the equation? What effect does that have on the decision to "bear or beget a child," a cornerstone of the constitutional right to privacy? Given the mood on the Supreme Court, what would happen if *Davis v. Davis* ended up there? This was the backdrop against which the Tennessee Supreme Court considered the case.

On June 1, 1992, the Tennessee Supreme Court found that although five thousand "test-tube" babies had been born in the United States, and approximately twenty thousand pre-embryos were currently in "storage," the questions raised by *Davis v. Davis* had never been answered before. Because of the importance of the issues at stake, and the advancing technology available in the reproductive area, the court set about fashioning a framework to guide future resolution of such issues.

First, the court summarized the facts and scientific testimony introduced at trial. It concluded that the consensus within the scientific community was that "pre-embryo" was the proper term, and that although terminology was not dispositive, "inaccuracy can lead to misanalysis such as occurred at the trial court level." It found that Dr. LeJeune's testimony "revealed a profound confusion between science and religion."

Next, the court turned to the question that had bedeviled Judge Young: Were the pre-embryos persons or property? The Tennessee Supreme Court found that under the laws of Tennessee and the federal Constitution, the unborn have never been and could not be considered "persons." Neither did the court find the pre-embryos to be "property," although it determined that the decision-making authority which Mary and J.R. had over them was similar to the power which people have over their property. Rather, the court followed the ethical guidelines of the American Fertility Society and concluded that the pre-embryos were in an interim category. They were human tissue deserving of special respect because of their potential for human life (the position Professor Robertson had introduced at trial).

The court then addressed the issues of contract and implied contract—or, in laymen's terms, consent. The court found that in the event that the couple had signed a written agreement, that agreement and any later modifications should be enforced. The Davises, of course, had signed no such agreement. The court rejected the argument that by participating in the process, and by donating his sperm, J.R. had consented to become a father and could not back out. "There is no indication in the record that . . . Junior Davis intended to pursue reproduction outside the confines of a continuing marital relationship with Mary Sue," the court wrote.

The court then turned to what it considered "the essential dispute: whether the parties will become parents." The court concluded that the answer hinged upon the right to privacy as guaranteed by the Tennessee state constitution. In our federalist system, the supreme courts of the various states have the last word on interpreting their own state laws and constitutions. While states cannot provide less protection than the federal Constitution dictates, they are free under their own constitutions to provide more. This is as true in the context of reproductive privacy as it is in that of the Fourth Amendment. Because of the uncertainty surrounding the right to privacy under the United States Constitution, the Tennessee court based its decision entirely on its own state constitution.

The court found that although the right to privacy is not specifically mentioned in the Tennessee constitution, just as it is not articulated in the federal Constitution, such a right is nonetheless protected. The court listed the various provisions of the Tennessee constitution which protect individual liberty and personal autonomy, including the freedom to worship, the right to be free from unreasonable searches, freedom of speech and the press, and the prohibition against quartering troops. It noted that Tennessee, unique among states, even provided for a right of rebellion against an oppressive government.

The court concluded: "Obviously, the drafters of the Tennessee

Constitution of 1796 could not have anticipated the need to construe that document in terms of the choices flowing from in vitro fertilization procedures. But there can be little doubt that they foresaw the need to protect individuals from unwarranted governmental intrusion into matters involving intimate questions of personal and family concern." The court then held that under the Tennessee state constitution, "The right of procreation is a vital part of the individual's right to privacy."

The court said that federal law is in agreement on this point. It noted the uncertainty caused by the United States Supreme Court's decision in *Webster*, but determined that whatever its ultimate boundaries, "the right to procreational autonomy is composed of two rights of equal significance—the right to procreate and the right not to procreate."

"The tension between the two interests is nowhere more evident than in the context of in vitro fertilization," the court continued. "None of the concerns about a woman's bodily integrity that have previously precluded men from controlling abortion provisions is applicable here." In other words, the fact that the pre-embryos were in storage, rather than in Mary Sue's body, was crucial. For the first time, men and women were equals in a reproductive decision.

The court recognized the profound impact that parenthood has on both a mother and a father. It noted that in the abortion context, the state's interest in protecting potential life is not compelling until viability (almost six months into pregnancy). Therefore, the state has even less interest in protecting pre-embryos. The decision should be left entirely to the potential mother and father. If they cannot agree, then the way to resolve the dispute is to weigh the burdens on each party.

The court determined that in light of his testimony and life experience, the burdens of unwanted parenthood on J.R. would outweigh the burden on Mary Sue of not being able to donate the pre-embryos to another couple. Allowing Mary Sue to proceed with donation would "rob [J.R.] twice—his procreational autonomy would be defeated and his relationship with his offspring would be prohibited." The court noted that if Mary Sue had stuck to her initial position and wanted to use the pre-embryos herself, it would be a closer case. Even then, the court said that although it might be grueling, it was still possible for Mary Sue to undergo another round of IVF with her present husband or to pursue parenthood through adoption. The court was careful to point out that in future cases, if no reasonable possibility of achieving parenthood existed other than by using the pre-embryos, that factor should be strongly considered.

A few months later, the U.S. Supreme Court refused to hear the case.

Although the Tennessee Supreme Court resolved the Davises' dispute, serious questions remain. What if Mary Sue had not wished merely to donate the pre-embryos but had wanted to use them herself? What if she had been older, unable to undergo another round of IVF, and the pre-embryos represented her only chance to have children? One thing is certain: Fertility clinics across the country began obtaining written consent providing for disposition of pre-embryos in case of death or divorce, and states rushed to pass legislation regulating the area.

J.R. had won. But the case was not over, for the seven pre-embryos were still in frozen storage. At the end of its opinion, the court had directed Dr. King to follow his "normal procedure in dealing with unused pre-embryos, as long as that procedure was not in conflict with the court's opinion" (i.e., no donation).

But Dr. King's usual procedure *was*, in fact, donation, if not to other couples, then for scientific research. Dr. King was opposed to simply discarding the pre-embryos and asked to be relieved of his custodial responsibilities. J.R. petitioned Judge Young to designate a person to remove the pre-embryos from the clinic. Mary, still looking for a way around the state supreme court's decision, asked the judge to allow her to proceed with implantation solely for the scientific purpose of determining whether a frozen pre-embryo could survive more than two years in storage. She also asked Judge Young to grant a six-month "cooling-off" period, during which time, she argued, J.R. might change his mind.

On May 24, 1993, Judge Young granted the cooling-off period. J.R. and Charles Clifford were furious, and filed an extraordinary appeal in the Tennessee Supreme Court. On June 7, 1993, one year after its original decision and four years after the trial, the Tennessee Supreme Court called Judge Young's decision "an abuse of discretion" and ordered Dr. King to surrender the frozen pre-embryos to J.R. within five days, which he did.

So what did J.R. do with them? J.R. and his new wife, Brenda, consider this private.

LOOKING BACK, Mary says that for her, the U.S. Supreme Court's refusal to hear the case was the biggest blow. "I was totally, totally devastated. I had to leave work for days and all I could do was sit and cry. I knew then I would never have my own children; that I would be childless and my embryos were going to be destroyed."

She deeply regrets having changed her position in the Tennessee Supreme Court to argue for donation, a switch she believes lost her the case. She says she did it for her children. "The media had terrorized me so badly that I started thinking, 'Maybe it would be better if I donated the embryos, let them live a normal life.' That was the worst decision in the world."

Mary says she still can't believe that she lost. As far as she is concerned, it should always be the woman's right to choose. "Women get to make the decision on whether they want to carry a baby to term or not. Just because the embryos were outside my body, I don't think that should have taken away my right to make that decision."

She also believes that the Tennessee Supreme Court incorrectly balanced the burdens, undervaluing her ordeal and her chances of having children while overstating the burdens on her former husband. "I have had a lot of female-type problems; I can't afford $5,000 to $6,000 a try, to try again. I have been so messed up physically, from everything I have already been through," she says. "My ex-husband can go out right now and have as many children as he wants. He does not have anything wrong with him. Whereas what has been taken away from me is my chance to ever become a mother."

J.R. grants that the nine years of trying were horrible for Mary Sue. But, he says, "It was for me also. I stood beside her, and each time there was a failure, I felt it, too." He adds that, ironically, *he* is the one who will never have children of his own. Although Brenda Davis has a child from a former marriage, she is unable to have any more. J.R. Davis knows now that he will never be a father. "That biological need to have a child is always going to be with me," he says. "But I chose. I made a decision that Brenda was more important to me. I'm in this marriage hopefully for life."

For his part, J.R. says that when the U.S. Supreme Court refused to hear the case, "It felt like the world was lifted off my shoulders."

But, he says, a lot of people still don't understand what he was fighting for. "They ask me, 'Why do you care if you have a child out there?' But it would be so detrimental to me because of my background to think that there was a child out there that I had no control over. I could not allow that to happen. One reporter said, 'What do you care, there're guys all over the place with kids out there they don't even know about.' Well, maybe so, but I'm not that guy. And I'm not going to be that guy."

Still, some people feel they have the right to an opinion on J.R.'s intimate decisions, and the right to tell him exactly what that opinion is. He gets a monthly reminder as well. Unlike Mary Sue, whose legal assistance was provided for free, J.R. went into debt to pay his attorney, and will be paying off the bills for years to come.

At one point, there was interest in making a TV movie about the case. Charles Clifford, hoping for a cameo, brought the producers to meet J.R. and Brenda. They saw it as a possible solution to some of their financial problems, at least. But the idea stalled because the producer determined that there was no happy ending. "I guess they wanted an ending where she has kids," says J.R., adding, "Get real. Life is not always what you see on TV."

Passing Judgments

IN JANUARY 1995, a New York trial judge issued a decision that directly contradicted *Davis v. Davis*. Faced with a divorce action in which the only outstanding issue was the disposition of five frozen pre-embryos, the judge ruled that those pre-embryos should become the property of the wife.

Describing the normal process of fertilization, the judge wrote, "The simple fact of the matter is that a husband's rights and control over the procreative process end with ejaculation." The judge could find no "legal, logical or ethical reason" why a husband should gain additional rights if the fertilization takes place in "the public glare of a petri dish." Unlike the Tennessee Supreme Court, the New York judge determined that a husband has no constitutional right to avoid procreation after fertilization, and awarded the wife the exclusive right to determine the fate of the zygotes.

However, the judge also concluded that the husband's potential for unwanted parenthood should not be open-ended. Therefore, he imposed a "medically reasonable" time limit on the wife's ability to implant the pre-embryos. The judge reserved the question of the husband's child support obligation.

The husband plans to appeal the decision.

Kass v. Kass, New York 1995

———

SHORTLY BEFORE committing suicide in Las Vegas on October 30, 1991, a California attorney deposited fifteen vials of his sperm at a local California sperm bank. In his will, he left the sperm to his girlfriend. But when the dead man's two grown children from a previous marriage heard about it, they sued to have the sperm destroyed. They argued that destruction of the sperm would "help guard their family unit" and "prevent additional emotional, psychological and financial stress on family members already in existence." A trial court ordered the sperm destroyed.

After the ruling, the girlfriend was described as "stunned and sobbing." Her lawyer claimed that the thirty-seven-year-old woman had a fundamental right to procreate and that her biological clock was ticking. The man's ex-wife said, "I was flabbergasted to discover there was no law on this. You could take a frozen egg of a dead woman, and the frozen sperm of a dead man, and create a child who is an orphan. Is that wise?"

In June 1993, an appellate court disagreed with the lower court's order. The appellate court found that the artificial insemination of an unmarried woman with a dead man's sperm would not violate public policy.

Hecht v. Superior Court, California 1993

———

IN 1990, after four years of marriage, a Louisiana electrical worker was diagnosed with cancer of the esophagus. Before beginning chemotherapy treatments, which would likely render him sterile, he stored one sperm sample at a fertility clinic. A few months later, he died. In fulfillment of his last request, his widow, a music teacher, used the single sample and became pregnant. She gave birth to a little girl.

But under Louisiana law, the child has no legal father because a man cannot be a "natural father" unless he is alive when his child is conceived. Therefore, the U.S. Department of Health and Human Services denied the child the $700 a month in survivor's benefits for which she would otherwise be eligible. The mother sued the federal government and the state of Louisiana. In May 1995, an administrative law judge ruled in favor of the little girl.

Hart v. Shalala, Louisiana 1995

———

IN 1981, a gay San Francisco man donated his sperm so that a lesbian couple could have a child. The man visited the child regularly from the time she was three until she was ten. When her mother and her mother's partner refused to allow him to bring the child to California to meet his family, problems developed and the visits stopped. The man then filed a paternity and visitation action.

In November 1994, a New York appellate court held that the man was the child's legal father. The women appealed and, in 1995, New York's highest court granted a stay. The man then withdrew his case.

Thomas S. v. Robin Y., New York 1995

———

IN 1992, fourteen inmates on California's death row sued for the right to preserve their sperm for artificial insemination. In July 1994, the Ninth Circuit refused to address the issue because the inmates had not followed the proper procedures. The inmates are now doing so, determined to have the option to procreate after their deaths.

Anderson v. Vasquez, California 1994

IN RE A.C.

The Forced Cesarean Case

January, 1987

Hi, My Name is Angie.

In October, 1986, I married a wonderful man, who I've known and been with for six years.

I wanted to tell you my story, and how I've beat cancer twice in my life and I feel GREAT!!

ANGELA C. began her journal in response to a request from her doctors at the National Institutes of Health (NIH) in Bethesda, Maryland, who often asked her to come in and talk to patients whose spirits were flagging during a long battle with cancer.

Angela was one of NIH's success stories. According to her mother, Nettie Stoner, "They called her their 'miracle.' " After months of enduring pain in her left thigh, she had first been diagnosed with a rare form of cancer—Ewing's sarcoma (cancer of the connective tissue)—in 1973. She was thirteen. She was referred to the National Cancer Institute (part of NIH), and enrolled in a study of Ewing's sarcoma that was taking place at the time. "They told us it was incurable," says Nettie. "With treatment it would go into remission. They didn't give us any hope." Over the next year, Angie underwent experimental chemotherapy and radiation.

I was told I would lose my hair, and the treatment would make me sick. Of course at that age, I was very upset and really didn't understand why

*or what was really wrong with me. All I knew was that the biopsy they
did showed I had a tumor on my left femur bone, and that the medicine
they gave me would help the pain and possibly save my life.*

Angie became one of the first, and few, to survive.

During the next five years, she attended regular checkups at NIH,
once a month at first, then less often. When she hit the five-year
mark without a recurrence, Angie wrote, *"I was considered cured of
cancer."*

Unfortunately, the treatment Angie received had greatly weakened
the bone in her thigh. She fractured it, and a steel rod and pins were
inserted to stabilize and strengthen the bone. They came loose, requiring additional surgery. All in all, Angie endured and recovered from
eight operations on her leg during the next four years. She was laid up
a good deal of the time and had to have a home tutor. Typically,
Angela made the best of things. *"I was constantly around adults, and actually made to grow up faster than a normal child as a result of my illness
and handicap."*

Her mother, as usual, puts it more bluntly. "The teenage years
were awful for her." The bone in her leg had become compressed,
leaving her with one leg 2¾ inches shorter than the other, and a pronounced limp. As a result, she developed curvature of the spine. She
had her shoes built up to compensate, but "she walked like a pen-
guin," says her father, Dan Stoner. "It was bad on her going through
school like that. She was a little heavy anyway, and then being kind of
handicapped." But Angie's spirit was already apparent. Although she
cried when she first found out she would lose her hair, her mother
says it was possibly the only time. After that, "She'd pull her wig off
anyplace," says her sister, Sherri. Angie tried hard to keep up and was
able to graduate with her high school class in May 1978.

That same year, another catastrophe befell the Stoner family. Nettie was involved in a tractor/lawnmower accident. She lost both her
legs and was confined to a wheelchair.

The next year, Angie underwent a bone graft.

*Lo and behold, I "lucked out" and for once, something worked!! The bone
grew, and the doctors were amazed at the bone growth after all the radiation I had undergone in the past. My life was back to normal, and I was
on my way to finally settling into a career and adulthood.*

She got a job as a receptionist in the commissary control office at nearby Fort Meade, Maryland.

At a New Year's Eve party in 1981, Angie met Rick C. Rick was home from the Navy, working as a sheet-metal mechanic, installing commercial duct work. They started dating the day they met. *"Things were going great,"* wrote Angie. *"I was on top of the world and loving life again!"* In 1984, Angie and Rick got an apartment together.

"Then in October 1984, I started having that all-too-familiar pain in my left leg again. I couldn't believe it. 'It' was back again. I just knew *it!"* Angie went back to the doctors at NIH, who confirmed her own diagnosis. She had cancer again; this time, it was osteogenic sarcoma. The doctors told Angie that her left leg, pelvis, and hip would have to be amputated. The operation is called a "hemipelvectomy." After that, she would receive still more chemotherapy and radiation. *"I would finally lose the leg I struggled so hard to keep for so long. Sure I cried, but I knew in my heart, that this would be the end of all my pain and suffering."* The amputation was performed on November 20, 1984, five days after her twenty-fifth birthday.

After the operation, Angie and Rick moved in with Angie's parents, Nettie and Dan. Dan had adapted the Stoners' roomy Maryland ranch house to accommodate Nettie's wheelchair, and now it would accommodate Angie's as well. Mother and daughter developed another bond.

The Stoners say they talked to Rick to see if he wanted out. "Life in a wheelchair is no fun," says Dan. But Rick was committed to Angie and said he was going to stick around. The Stoners and Rick had never had a particularly close relationship. They felt he didn't give Angie enough support. "In fact, the day of her surgery, when they took her leg, he wasn't there. And the next day, it was Thanksgiving. Well, she kept asking for him all the time. And he was never there," says Nettie. Rick acknowledges a certain amount of friction with his mother-in-law. "Nettie didn't think we could handle it, Angie being sick and all. Like everything else, Nettie took over. One day Angie is in the hospital, and the next thing I know all my stuff is in her mom's house."

Nettie shouldered the burden of Angie's care, taking her to NIH for doctors' visits and caring for her at home. Rick moved out after about six months and went to live with his own mother. Angie remained at home with her parents during her yearlong recuperation from surgery and then for her forty-three-week course of chemotherapy. In addition to the usual side effects, Angie suffered serious complications. She was hospitalized for blood clots in her lung, and bacterial infections. She had constant problems with her chemotherapy IV. "Because they stick you so many times, she just looked like a pin cushion," says her dad. But as before, Angie fought her way through it. Rick and Nettie even started getting along better.

In February 1986, just as Angie's chemotherapy was ending, she and Rick moved into an apartment of their own again. "Angie wanted a normal life because actually she'd never really had one," says Nettie. "She didn't go through what all the teenage girls go through because of her disability. It was hard for her, but she didn't let on like it bothered her. I guess when she found Rick—I think she did love him. And maybe he loved her, too. I don't know—it was a strange relationship."

Angie started working again, as an Avon Lady for a while, then at the local senior citizens center directing arts and crafts programs, and eventually taking children in for baby-sitting. After being in and out of work, Rick had also gotten a job as a mechanic at Maloney Air. The couple got engaged. On November 17, 1986, Angie and Rick were married at Saint Louis Catholic Church in Clarksville, Maryland.

They settled in, staying home to watch TV most weeknights, going out with friends on Fridays and Saturdays. After the wedding, Nettie kept her concerns to herself and by all accounts Angie had never been happier. Angie had what she had wanted most: a home and husband.

> I made it, and I can tell you—if it hadn't been for the support of many loving and caring people (family and friends) and my fantastic outlook on life, (positive attitude) and faith in the wonderful God above, I wouldn't be here to tell you my incredible story today.

Angie prepared to take the next step in life—planning her own family. During the previous year, she and Rick had talked about having children, and they had decided to wait until after they were married. Now, as usual, she didn't waste any time. Six weeks after the wedding, Angie was pregnant. The couple was thrilled.

"She was great with kids and her nephews and nieces. She talked about what she was going to do for the baby and just couldn't wait until it was born," says Rick. Angie wanted a boy; he was hoping for a little girl.

When Nettie heard the news, she was just plain scared. "When she told me she was pregnant, I said, 'Oh, Angie, why?' And she said, 'You're just not happy for me anytime.' I said, 'I am, honey, but I'm so scared.' And then I just [said], 'If you're happy—and it's your life—do it.' " It wasn't easy for Nettie to adjust to the idea that Angie was on her own, old enough to be making her own decisions and managing her own health care. "When she got married, when she got pregnant, I thought, 'It's time.' Let her handle these things on her own. I felt like I was butting in all the time in her business. I thought, 'Maybe she doesn't want me to do that.' "

Angie's gynecologist referred her to the high-risk-pregnancy clinic at George Washington University Hospital, where she was accepted as a teaching case, free of charge. According to Dr. Lewis Hamner, who became Angie's doctor at G.W., the clinic staff had never seen anybody with Angie's outlook and attitude, or with the guts and determination to attempt a pregnancy without a leg or pelvis. "The nurses all knew her and looked forward to seeing her every week," he said. Hamner searched the literature for cases like Angie's and found little. There was one article in a Russian journal describing a similar case, and based on that and the ideas of G.W.'s own staff, they built an adjustable harness, or sling, to support Angie as her pregnancy progressed.

She came in to G.W. every two weeks beginning in March 1987. In April, Angie got bronchitis. Dr. Hamner took an X-ray, didn't notice anything new or problematic, and prescribed some antibiotics. He told her to quit smoking, which she did not do. Angie also developed gestational diabetes, requiring additional blood work on each visit, but through it all, Nettie recalls, "She was laughing and talking, joking. Those people in the clinic said they had never seen anybody so happy."

Less than two months later, on June 9, a Tuesday, Nettie took Angela in for a checkup. She had been complaining of shortness of breath and a new kind of back pain, higher up. "Angie was very upset. She was having the same pain as when she had her tumor in her leg, and was very worried," recalls Dr. Hamner. He examined her and found nothing abnormal. He ordered a chest X-ray, scheduled additional heart and lung studies, and sent her home. He suggested that a muscle relaxer might help, and told her to come back the next day for the results.

Angie was worried enough to call her doctor at NIH, Dr. Jeffrey Moscow. When Dr. Moscow called back that afternoon, Angie was taking a nap. But Nettie's description of the pain as being similar to her earlier leg pain was "very ominous to me," recalls Moscow. "That is a statement that I have only heard on a few occasions and every time it has been accurate."

The next day, Wednesday, June 10, Dr. Hamner got the results of the chest X ray. The film showed a white haziness covering Angie's right lung from the base almost to the top. Dr. Hamner called Angie and told her that it looked like fluid and that she needed to come in for further tests. The plan was to extract some fluid and test it for malignant cells. Angie said, "I was afraid of something like this." She asked if she could come in the following morning, as she couldn't get a ride into D.C. that afternoon. Dr. Hamner said that would be fine.

On June 11, Thursday, Angie's back was hurting but she was not terribly short of breath. Rick took her down to G.W., where she was admitted to the hospital for tests.

By the next morning, Friday, June 12, Angie was having trouble breathing and was in severe pain. The Stoners, increasingly worried, waited for the doctors to tell them what was wrong. Dr. Moscow, having heard nothing either, came down to G.W. Hospital as well.

When he arrived, Moscow found Angie sitting in a chair in the waiting room smoking a cigarette. He told her that was the worst thing she could be doing. She responded with a dirty look. He then went to look at the X rays. He saw a tumor the size of a football in Angie's right lung.

In the late afternoon, Dr. Moscow, Dr. Laurence Lessin (the head of the Division of Hematology and Oncology at G.W.), and Dr. Hamner discussed the options. The first step was to perform a CT scan and then a biopsy to confirm that the tumor was, in fact, a recurrence of osteogenic sarcoma. Assuming that it was, the doctors agreed that Angie could not be cured. The best outcome they could hope for was, in Moscow's words, "a healthy but motherless child." Moscow thought their best hope would be to prolong Angela's life through treatment long enough to allow her to give birth and spend some time with her baby. Moscow felt that "would be a fulfillment of her life, and something good that would come out of a horrible situation."

As of that Friday, June 12, Dr. Moscow figured that with treatment, Angie had "months," and if she did not respond to the treatment, possibly "weeks." Dr. Hamner agreed. A CT scan and biopsy were scheduled. Dr. Hamner recalls Angie's reaction: "She just wanted to get on with it. She had always been the type of person who thought, 'Just do whatever need[s] to be done.' " Dr. Lessin examined Angie and told her that her lung might have to be removed. She asked him, "Can I live with one lung?" He said, "Well, you won't be able to run a hundred-mile race, but yes, you can live without one lung." Angie replied, "Well, I can't run anyway. I only have one leg."

"But then," says Nettie, "after they told us that, nobody said another word. Here comes Saturday, here comes Sunday, nobody knew anything. I kept saying, "They were going to do a biopsy; they were going to remove her lung. What's going on?"

On Saturday, some of Angie's relatives went to see her. Dr. Alan Weingold, chairman of the Department of OB/GYN, was on duty. He examined Angie and found her to be "reasonably comfortable."

By Sunday, Angie was in a lot of pain. She was having trouble breathing, even with an oxygen mask. Nettie and Dan were at the hospital all day, and Rick arrived in the evening after work.

By Monday, June 15, Angie was worse. No tests or procedures had been performed over the weekend. The Stoners called Dr. Moscow, who came down from NIH. He got to Angie's room around noon. She was lying on her side and she had a fever. She was also sweating and breathing rapidly and she was so short of breath she was unable to speak. The nurse told Dr. Moscow that Angie had been that way all day, and he, in turn, instructed the nurse to find Dr. Hamner.

Dr. Lessin appeared and the three doctors reviewed the situation. They agreed that Angie's condition had deteriorated greatly. She was critically ill. Moscow thought she could die within hours if nothing was done.

They agreed to transfer Angie to intensive care, where they would begin treatment, but the options were limited. The tumor was too large to be removed surgically. A blast of radiation to shrink the tumor seemed the most promising alternative. Because of Angie's hemipelvectomy, she was carrying the fetus far over to the left. Hamner thought this would allow the fetus to be shielded from the radiation. Chemotherapy was trickier. Moscow felt that the existing literature supported chemotherapy treatment during the second and third trimesters of pregnancy. Lessin thought that view was overly optimistic and believed the treatment might, in fact, worsen Angie's condition as well as possibly harm her fetus, now at twenty-five weeks. In any event, the fetus's chances of survival were slim.

The doctors agreed that their goal would be to treat Angela in the hope of extending her life by several weeks to give the baby a better chance of surviving. The statistics showed a marked improvement in survival rates for premature infants after twenty-eight weeks of gestation. The doctors elected Moscow to explain the situation to Angie.

"I wanted to give her as much hope as possible, to present her situation to her in a way that would give her both a reason to live and a means of coming to grips with her impending death. I felt that this could best be done by focusing on the chance that the baby might be able to survive," he says. Angie's parents and sister Sherri were present when Dr. Moscow sat on Angie's bed and told her, "It's not like the other times. We can't cure you. We can't remove the tumor like we could all the other times when you had surgery. We can't just cut it out."

Dr. Moscow explained that they could radiate and follow up with chemotherapy in an attempt to gain several more weeks for the fetus. If Angie's cancer responded to the treatment, she might be able to give birth to a healthy baby and go home with it for a short while. He explained that the fetus was too small to be delivered at that time, but that a few weeks could make a big difference in its ability to survive. He also explained that at some point it might be necessary for Angie to be placed on a ventilator and that, though she might not want to do this, it would be best for the fetus.

At first, Angie wavered a little bit, then she nodded and mouthed the words, "Okay. Do whatever you guys have to do to make me better." It was around 4 p.m.

Hours went by. "She got worse and nobody did anything," Nettie says. "She just kept laying there. They told us they were going to take her up to critical care, she could hardly breathe and she couldn't get up. I took blankets and anything I could find to put under her. I just wanted her to be comfortable."

At approximately 7 p.m., Angie was transferred to the ICU. Around 8 p.m., the Stoners were heading home just as Rick arrived. They told him Angie was dying.

The next morning, Tuesday, June 16, the Stoners' phone rang at 6 a.m. Angie was not doing well. Dan and Nettie headed for the hospital, arriving around 7:30 a.m. Angie had tubes in her nose and throat, an IV, a catheter, and, as Nettie recalls, "all these machines buzzing and clicking." Angie was sedated and had been placed on a ventilator but still wasn't receiving enough oxygen. She had not had any radiation and was expected to die soon. The Stoners asked for a priest. Rick and his mother arrived. The priest gave Angie her last rites. Cousins arrived. Rick, Nettie, Dan, Sherri, and other family members visited Angie throughout the morning.

By the time Dr. Hamner arrived at around 8:30 a.m., the ICU staff believed that Angie had only another few hours to live. They were having enormous difficulty maintaining her oxygen, her blood was becoming increasingly acidic, and she had a fever. The staff was concerned that Angie's poor respiratory condition was also compromising the condition of her fetus. The night before, the fetus had turned twenty-six weeks old; technically, it was viable, capable of surviving outside the mother's womb (albeit with intensive neonatal care).

Viability is an important point medically, legally, and ethically. Medically, Dr. Hamner believed that viability created an independent obligation on the part of the hospital to attempt to save a fetus, in case the mother dies. Thus it would be a doctor's duty to perform a postmortem Cesarean section. Legally, in *Roe v. Wade*, the Supreme Court found viability to be the point at which the state's interest in potential life becomes compelling. In Angela's case, there was also a question of liability. If the hospital failed to act on behalf of the fetus could it later be held liable? Ethically, many other questions were raised. Now that the fetus was viable, were there two patients to be treated? Was the same treatment best for both? What if it was not? Did one patient take precedence over the other? Which one? Any way Dr. Hamner looked at it, the decision was a difficult and a heartbreaking one.

Dr. Hamner talked to the family. He mentioned the possibility that Angie could suffer a heart attack, and raised the question of performing a postmortem Cesarean section to deliver the fetus in the minutes after Angie's death. Nettie responded, "Let Angela die in peace. This was her baby. She wanted this baby. Let her take the baby to heaven with her. Please don't put her through any more suffering." Rick agreed, Hamner recalls. "I don't want to look at that baby without Angela," he said.

Dr. Hamner was somewhat surprised at the family's reaction. He had already mentioned the possibility of a postmortem Cesarean to Dr. Maureen Edwards, director of Nurseries, whose staff was beginning to prepare for such an event. He went downstairs to speak to Dr. Weingold, the head of the OB/GYN department. Dr. Hamner described Angela's condition and the family's wish for nonintervention. Hamner and Weingold agreed that the fetus's condition was "compromised" and that its chances of survival were less than those of an average twenty-six-week fetus. Dr. Weingold said he would respect the family's wishes and that no postmortem Cesarean would be performed. Weingold informed a hospital administrator of the likely developments in the unusual case. Dr. Hamner went back upstairs and informed Dr. Edwards and the family that Angela would die "intact."

Family members were in the waiting area near Angie's room, taking turns by her bed. At around twelve noon, a hospital social worker told the Stoners and Rick that a meeting was going to take place, and asked them to come downstairs. Unbeknownst to them, the hospital administrator whom Dr. Weingold had informed of Angela's condition had called the hospital's lawyer.

The lawyer was aware that the previous year, a nineteen-year-old Muslim woman had arrived at D.C. General Hospital pregnant with a full-term fetus. Her water had broken almost two days before, and she was nearly seven centimeters dilated. Because the baby was at risk of infection, the doctors recommended a Cesarean section. The woman refused, based on her religious beliefs and her confidence that the baby was not at risk. A hospital hearing was convened, and a judge ordered the hospital to deliver the baby by Cesarean.

Given this precedent, G.W.'s lawyer was concerned about the decision to let the fetus die with Angela, and called the D.C. Superior Court to request a hearing. Judge Emmet G. Sullivan rushed to the hospital with a police escort. Volunteer attorneys were also summoned. The Stoners were shown into a conference room and introduced to Robert Sylvester, who they were told would be Angie's lawyer.

Minutes before the Stoners arrived, Judge Sullivan had told the hastily assembled lawyers that they could choose whom they wanted to represent. Barbara Mishkin, herself the mother of four children, chose the fetus. Robert Sylvester, whose own wife had died at the age of twenty-nine, chose to represent Angela. Vincent Burke represented the hospital. There was also a lawyer, Richard Love, representing the state, which in this case was the city of Washington, D.C. Love had also argued for the city in the previous year's Cesarean case. For everyone involved, on a personal and professional level, the stakes could not have been higher.

The hearing was to be a mini-trial, with opening and closing arguments by the lawyers as well as direct questioning and cross-examination of witnesses. Formally, the hospital was seeking a declaratory judgment from the court, so as to determine its responsibility and course of action. But to the nonlawyers, it seemed that their fragile world was spinning out of control. They heard voices, but they couldn't understand them. They saw faces they had never seen before. No one had spoken to them in the past five days; now they were confronted with a roomful of people—social workers, administrators, doctors, lawyers, and a judge. All they really knew was that while all these people were talking, Angela lay dying upstairs.

"We were in shock," says Dan. "We really were."

"We had no idea what was going on," says Nettie. "Why didn't they come to us and say, 'This is what we have to do'? Why did they just throw it into the lion's den?"

The judge called the hearing to order. Vincent Burke, the hospital's attorney, summarized the situation. Burke asked the court to tell the hospital what it should do. The court then asked Mishkin and Sylvester if they wished to be heard. Barbara Mishkin spoke first. "My view of this is that we are confronted, very sadly, with a need to balance the interest of a probably viable fetus, presumptively viable fetus, with whatever life is left for the mother."

The Stoners didn't realize it at the time, but the topic of discussion had just changed from a postmortem Cesarean to an emergency one.

Sylvester spoke next. He argued that Angela did not want intervention. Her family and her doctors were confident of that. He put the state's interest on the side of abiding by the patient's wishes and her right to refuse treatment. The foundation of his argument was Angela's right of personal autonomy, her right to be let alone.

Dr. Hamner was called as the first witness. Angie's prognosis was terminal due to the tumor on her lung, he stated. She had been heavily sedated since the previous evening simply in order to maintain her status. She was unable to carry on a meaningful conversation and was expending enormous amounts of energy just to keep her heart going. He estimated that if nothing was done, Angie had about twenty-four hours to live.

Dr. Hamner gave his opinion that at twenty-six weeks a fetus would have a 50 to 60 percent chance of survival, but in this case the

chances would be smaller. The baby was probably chronically asphyx-
iated and was already receiving less oxygen than it had been the day
before. It had an elevated heart rate. It had been exposed to multiple
medications, its blood was becoming increasingly acidic, and it had an
abnormal electrolyte balance.

Dr. Hamner stated that the day before, Angie had agreed to treatment to prolong her own life, with the goal of delivering the baby at
twenty-eight weeks. But, he pointed out, she had never squarely faced
the question of delivering the baby earlier, or of choosing between her
own life and that of the fetus. On behalf of the hospital, Vincent Burke
asked Dr. Hamner, based on his knowledge of Angie, what he would
recommend.

Dr. Hamner answered, "My impression at this point is that Angela
realizes what she has been through throughout her life, and would not
want to bring a fetus into this world that would potentially have to go
through the same long course she has been through. . . . She has been
through multiple, multiple surgeries, multiple episodes of radiation
and chemotherapy, in and out of hospitals most of her life since the
age of thirteen. She understood the increased risk of cerebral palsy,
neurological defects, hearing loss, blindness that can go along with
premature delivery. My feeling from the ten or eleven weeks I have
known her, she would not want to bring a baby into this world that
potentially would have to undergo those type of problems."

Under questioning from Barbara Mishkin, Hamner acknowledged
that as far as the fetus was concerned, if a C-section was to be performed, the earlier the better. The longer it was delayed, the less oxygen the fetus would receive.

The next witness was Dr. Weingold. The judge questioned him.

Q: Your recommendation is similar to Dr. Hamner's that the appar-
   ent wishes of the mother and her family be honored?
A: That's correct.
Q: And that the mother and the fetus be allowed to die?
A: Correct.

Under cross-examination by Barbara Mishkin, Weingold expressed
his view that there was a paradox: The medications used to treat
Angela in the hope of extending her life, and thereby improving the fetus's chances of surviving could, at the same time, be detrimental to

the fetus. He repeated that Angela's prognosis was "imminent and grim. We are talking about hours of survival." When asked whether Angela could be questioned directly at that point, he stated that any attempt to raise the level of her consciousness in order to obtain her consent would shorten her life. Only heavy sedation would keep her from fighting the respirator.

In response to questions from Robert Sylvester, Dr. Weingold confirmed that the chances of Angela's baby surviving would be smaller than those of other twenty-six-week fetuses. "A message was sent to her that the earliest we would feel comfortable in intervening . . . would be twenty-eight weeks. Much prior to that, the prognosis was poor enough that we would be extremely uncomfortable intervening.

"We thought we had a patient who had survived three years of surgery and chemotherapy, that everything was focused on her having a baby to take care of at the end of the pregnancy," Dr. Weingold continued. "I don't think she had any mind-set at that point of leaving a child without a mother."

The court then called Dr. Maureen Edwards, the G.W. Director of Nurseries. She was a neonatologist, specializing in the care of premature and newborn infants. Were a Cesarean to be performed, Dr. Edwards would be responsible for the baby's care.

Vincent Burke's first question was, "Is the fetus viable?" Dr. Edwards answered, "Yes." Burke then asked for her recommendation. She answered that since she had not been involved with Angela or her family, she could not recommend a course of treatment for Angela. Regarding Angela's fetus, however, Dr. Edwards had an opinion: "The fetus is at a point in gestation where there is significantly measurable survivability, albeit with relatively protracted care in the nursery." She said that in her nursery, 80 percent of babies born at twenty-six weeks survived. Babies as young as twenty-three or twenty-four weeks had also survived. Taking Angela's condition into consideration, she estimated the chances of fetal survivability to be 50 to 60 percent.

She then outlined the possible handicaps that the baby could suffer, were it to survive. These included mental retardation, cerebral palsy, blindness, other sensory defects, and chronic lung disease. She estimated the chances of these handicaps at less than 20 percent. Acute complications such as jaundice, bowel problems, and cardiac problems were also possible. Dr. Edwards went on to state that although it is extremely difficult to predict prior to delivery what will happen to any particular baby, neonates are surprisingly resilient. However, she emphasized the risks to the fetus of further delay, given Angela's deteriorating condition.

It was Barbara Mishkin's turn to cross-examine Dr. Edwards. As she did so, a remarkable exchange took place.

Q: If this were your baby or your sister's, what do you think you would suggest?

A: Do I need to answer that?

Q: It would be very helpful if you could. . . .

A: This is an area that's really unclear to many of us who are caring for these children, what is right. We are heavily guided by what families are asking us. I personally would ask for intervention but I am not this family. I'm not this mother.

Dr. Lessin, director of the Division of Hematology and Oncology, was called as the next witness. He described Angela's tumor and condition. He told the court that the options were narrowing. The radiation therapist had now decided that there was "no role" for radiation. Chemotherapy had not been administered because of possible harm to the fetus.

The judge then questioned Dr. Lessin.

The Court: Doctor, at some point in time Ms. C. unequivocally stated she wanted to have the baby?

The Witness: She did. That was, I believe, Friday afternoon.

The Court: And yesterday . . . you had another conversation with her?

The Witness: Dr. Moscow was asking the questions.

The Court: Her response yesterday to the questions was?

The Witness: I don't know. I think so.

Barbara Mishkin jumped in.

Q: Have you heard anything from this patient that would make you think that she would refuse permission for a Cesarean section at this time in order to save the baby?

A: No.

Q: The answer is No?

A: I have not heard anything that would support that position.

Nettie Stoner was called next. Robert Sylvester began asking questions.

Q: What we are trying to determine is . . . what Angela C.'s state of mind would be relative to this fetus. If I may ask you, she indeed wanted a baby very badly, didn't she?

A: Yes.

Q: And she was looking forward to this baby's arrival?

A: Yes.

Q: Excitedly?

A: Yes.

Q: When she thought of the baby what did you think she was thinking of?

A: She thought everything was going to be all right. . . . She didn't know she was going to die until 4:00 p.m. yesterday . . . and at that time, she said, "I'll take the chemo and the radiation to keep my baby alive for a couple of weeks," only because she said to the doctors, "How long do I have?" and they said, "Months." They did not say "hours." They said "months." And when they took her out of her room yesterday to put her in ICU she said, "I only want to die. Just give me something to get me out of this pain."

"The only reason she would agree to any of this," Nettie continued, "was because she thought she was going to live to hold this baby, even though she knew she was terminal. She thought she would be here. She's a fighter. She's always been a fighter. She could not fight this. It was too much."

Barbara Mishkin now cross-examined Nettie, asking whether the family had health insurance to cover the care of the baby. Nettie answered no. "Nobody would insure a baby," she said. "Nobody would insure my daughter. Nobody."

Q: So there is no family insurance that would cover the baby's care.

A: That doesn't even enter into it. I don't care about the money. It's just that I know there will be something wrong with this baby. I can't handle it. I've handled her and myself.

Q: I understand.

A: Nobody else can love a child like that and I know what it would be.

Q: Would you even have resources to handle a healthy baby?

A: No.

Q: If the baby was not compromised?

A: Not really. Rick, her husband, they have only been married eight
    months. I mean, he hasn't even had her long enough. How is he
    going to cope with a baby? They don't have any family, it's just
    Rick and his mom. It's me and I'm in a wheelchair. I can't put
    the burden on us anymore. Angela is the only one who wanted
    that baby to love. She said she wanted something of her very
    own.

Q: Would you consider placing the baby for adoption?

A: Never, never.

Q: If the baby was born?

A: Never.

Q: What would you do if the baby survived?

A: Who wants it?

Q: I guess I'm asking you a terribly difficult question. . . .

A: I would take care of that baby. I would never put it up for adop-
    tion. I would do the best I could, but we don't want it. Angela
    wanted that baby. It was her baby. Let that baby die with her.

Rick, silent but visibly upset, interjected, "Please."

Nettie repeated, "It's hers."

No one had any further questions.

Dr. Hamner then asked the court for permission to speak. He read
a note from Dr. Weingold, who had stepped out of the room. The
note reiterated the reluctance of the Department of OB/GYN to participate in a Cesarean section. For the record, Weingold had written,
the department's position was, "We should abide by the wishes of the
family."

The court asked Rick if he would like to be heard. Rick answered,
"I don't think I could handle it, to tell you the truth."

The court took a short recess. When it returned, Dr. Minogue, the
hospital's medical director, stated that the hospital would assume the
costs of caring for the baby. Then it was time for closing arguments.

Barbara Mishkin went first. "We are not confronted with the problem of choosing between the life of the mother and the life of the fetus. Sadly, the life of the mother is lost to us at this point. On the
other hand, we have a potentially viable fetus. . . . The state has an obligation . . . to protect the life of a viable fetus, and unfortunately for

the family . . . the extent of potential disability of that fetus does not enter the equation so far as the law is concerned. . . . I would urge the Court to order performance of a Cesarean section and everything possible medically that can be done to try to save the life of the fetus," she said.

Robert Sylvester was next. He summarized Angie's commitment to her own health and to a twenty-eight-week-old fetus, and her recent wavering responses. "I would argue for the state to make a judgment to intervene at this point, they must have a very compelling reason and I just don't think there is a compelling enough reason to override . . . Angela C.'s view not to have this fetus delivered by Cesarean section. I do not believe this fetus delivered in that manner was the baby she expected or contemplated or would have wanted."

Mishkin interrupted. "We have no statement from the patient as to what she wants in this instance. . . . This is not a question of the woman's right to refuse treatment. This is the question of the state's obligation to protect this baby."

Sylvester objected that Angela's rights did not cease upon the twenty-sixth week of her pregnancy—the date of viability of the fetus. He said that Angie's wishes were critical to the court's decision, and argued that Angela's views *were*, in fact, known—to her family and her doctors. Her ambiguous responses of the previous day were less important than the wishes she'd expressed throughout her pregnancy: to have a healthy baby, delivered at a minimum gestational age of twenty-eight weeks.

The city's attorney, Richard Love, then addressed the state interest. He spoke of the need to balance the rights, including the right to privacy, of the mother against the "compelling state interest in protecting the potentiality of life." "The mother will die regardless of what we do," he concluded, "and under those circumstances the interest to protect the fetus becomes even more compelling . . . I think the court has no course but to order intervention."

Sylvester asked the court for permission to speak. "If we were to do a C-section on this woman in a very weakened medical state, we would in effect be terminating her life, and I can't—"

The judge interrupted him. "She's going to die, Mr. Sylvester."

Then Rick spoke. "Who is to say she is going to die?"

Sylvester continued. "But is our task to hasten this?" He said that under the Supreme Court's abortion decisions, a trade-off between a woman's health and fetal survival was not permitted. A woman's health must be the physician's primary consideration; she is, after all, the patient. He argued that Angela's constitutional rights to privacy and bodily integrity would be violated by a Cesarean. Her express refusal of treatment was not being honored.

The judge then turned to Mishkin and asked why he should risk hastening Angie's death by ordering a C-section. Mishkin conceded that the C-section could shorten Angela's life, but suggested that Angela might have wanted that, given Nettie's testimony. Mishkin also argued that the court was not being presented with a choice between two lives. Angela's life was already lost. Rather, the question was whether the state had "an obligation to rescue a potential life from a dying mother."

The court then asked Dr. Edwards and Dr. Weingold for their opinions. Both doctors agreed that if the goal was fetal survival, the sooner the Cesarean was performed, the better.

Then Dr. Weingold stunned everyone. He stated that, based on their evaluation of Angela's wishes, none of the doctors on the staff would perform a Cesarean.

The court took a five-minute recess.

When the hearing reconvened, the judge summarized the facts. "The uncontroverted medical testimony is that Angela will probably die within the next twenty-four to forty-eight hours. . . . A complicating factor is that Angela is pregnant with a twenty-six-and-a-half-week viable fetus who, based on uncontroverted medical testimony, has an approximately 50 to 60 percent chance to survive if a Cesarean section is performed as soon as possible."

He then stated, "The Court is of the view that it does not clearly know what Angela's present views are with respect to the issue of whether the child should live or die. She is presently unconscious. As late as Friday of last week, she wanted the baby to live. As late as yesterday, she did not know for sure."

He concluded: "It's not an easy decision to make, but given the choices, the Court is of the view that the fetus should be given an opportunity to live." He ordered the hospital to "promptly deliver by Cesarean section the fetus of Angela C."

Sylvester immediately asked for a stay. Vincent Burke asked when the hospital would be ready to operate if no stay was granted. Dr. Weingold answered that the hospital needed about an hour. The court told Sylvester he had an hour to appeal, but declined to issue a stay.

The hearing concluded. It was 4:15 p.m.

Before anyone could leave the room, word came that Dr. Hamner was on his way back down from the ICU. Hamner told the court that Angie was now lucid. He had explained to her that a Cesarean was to be performed to give the baby a chance to live. "I asked her, 'Would you agree to this procedure?' She did say yes. I said, 'Do you realize that you may not survive the surgical procedure?' She said yes. And I repeated the two questions to her again [and] asked her 'Did she understand.' She said yes." Dr. Hamner said that a nurse and two relatives had also been present. The judge asked whether Angie would be overwhelmed if he or the attorneys were to question her. Hamner replied, "I think she's pretty overwhelmed by the whole environment." After some discussion, they decided not to go.

The court took another short recess.

When the hearing resumed, Dr. Weingold testified that he had just come from the ICU, where he had been present at a second conversation between Angie and Dr. Hamner. "Dr. Hamner went into the room to attempt to verify his previous discussion with the patient, with the patient's husband at her right hand and her mother at her left hand. He, to my satisfaction, clearly communicated with Ms. C. She understood."

The Court:	You could hear what the parties were saying to one another?
Dr. Weingold:	She does not make a sound because of the tube in her windpipe. She nods and she mouths words. One can see what she is saying rather readily. She asked whether she would survive the operation. She asked Hamner if he would perform the operation. He told her he would only perform it if she authorized it, but it would be done in any case. She understood that. She then seemed to pause for a few moments and then very clearly mouthed the words several times: "I don't want it done. I don't want it done." Quite clear to me.

Weingold added, "This is an environment in which, from my perspective as a physician, this would not be informed consent one way or the other. She's under tremendous stress with the family on both sides, but I'm satisfied that I heard clearly what she said."

Sylvester asked the court to reconsider its decision based on Angela's recent conflicting responses. Angie's "Yes" had been at 4:40, her "No" at 5:00. Dr. Weingold clarified his earlier statement regarding Angela's capacity for informed consent. "I think she's in contact with reality, clearly understood who Dr. Hamner was. Because of her attachment to him, wanted him to perform the surgery. Understood he would not unless she consented and did not consent. That is, in my mind, very clear evidence that she is responding, understanding, and is capable of making such decisions." Dr. Weingold added, "When I said 'informed consent,' that in my mind has to take place in an environment other than an intensive care unit with a weeping husband and mother and all the paraphernalia."

The court concluded that Angela's intent was still not clear. The hospital's medical director said it would now take another hour before they could operate, as preparations had been halted when Angie began communicating again.

The court ordered the hospital to proceed.

"I had no idea what was going on," says Nettie.

"It was strange," adds Dan. "Here you are, pitting mother against her fetus. Isn't that something?"

"And us against the fetus," says Nettie, adding, "We wanted that baby as much as Angie did. But I wanted Angie more than the baby. . . . I guess it would have been different if we knew the baby. But we didn't know the baby. It wasn't a person. All I wanted was for Angela to be okay. I wanted them to do what they could for her. And make her life, or the rest of it, a little easier."

By 6:15 p.m., in an effort to overturn the judge's decision, Sylvester had gotten three judges from the D.C. Court of Appeals on the telephone. Angela had been moved from the ICU down to the operating room, and the doctors planned to operate in fifteen minutes—at around 6:30. The lawyers took turns on the speakerphone to the three-judge panel. At 6:40 p.m., the court denied Sylvester's request for a stay and hung up the phone.

In the meantime, Dr. Weingold had contacted five doctors who refused to perform the operation. Dr. Margaret Davis, his sixth prospect, reluctantly agreed, based on her belief in the rule of law. Dr. Weingold supervised. It was an uneventful operation. The baby was a girl. Rick named her Lindsay Marie. Dr. Weingold carried the baby across the hall where Dr. Edwards and her team were waiting. After a while, they brought the baby to the family to hold. "She was darling," says Nettie.

"That baby didn't have a chance," says Dan. Resuscitation attempts were unsuccessful, and about two hours later the baby was declared dead. The cause of death was listed as "extreme immaturity." That night, Rick told Angie they had a beautiful daughter with brown hair like her daddy. She gave him a hug and told him she loved him.

The next day, Wednesday, June 17, around noon, doctors asked the Stoners whether they would now agree to chemotherapy for Angie. On behalf of the family, Nettie declined. On Thursday, June 18, they were asked to consider turning down Angie's respirator, since the doctors felt there was nothing more they could do for her. "You just couldn't stand to watch her, her whole body was shaking. They said she had such a strong heart that she just wouldn't give up, even though the ventilator had blown a hole in her other lung," says her father. "They said she wouldn't feel any pain and she would just go to sleep. And that's what she did."

"But why did they ask our opinion on that?" asks Nettie.

Angela C. died that night around 8 p.m., June 18, 1987. She was buried with her daughter.

ANGELA'S long ordeal was over, but the legal controversy surrounding her fate was just beginning. On November 10, 1987, the same three-judge panel of the D.C. Court of Appeals that had taken part in the telephone conference on June 16, issued a formal opinion explaining its decision that night. By then, the case was known as *In re A.C.*, and Angela was identified only by her initials.

The court acknowledged that its decision may have shortened A.C.'s life by a few hours. It reviewed the legal literature and found that a case like A.C.'s had never been decided before. So the court compared A.C.'s case to the two types of cases it found most relevant. There were cases of adults asserting the right to refuse medical treatment—cases in which, for the most part, an adult's right to bodily integrity precludes the state from intervening. But there were also cases involving the right of parents to refuse medical treatment for their children. In those cases, the court found, the state may more easily override a parent's refusal to consent to medical treatment for their child. The court concluded that A.C.'s case required a balance between these two legal principles.

The court found that the judge at the emergency hearing was correct to balance the rights of the mother against the rights of the fetus. However, the court also emphasized that courts were not the proper places to resolve such emergency decisions and commended the judge and lawyers on "a difficult task well done despite the pressures created by time and tragic circumstances."

Robert Sylvester and an ACLU lawyer, Lynn Paltrow, appealed the decision to the full D.C. Court of Appeals. Of course, at this point the court's decision would have no effect on Angela or her family. But her dilemma raised important issues for the resolution of future cases. It was those issues and the procedures used to resolve them that were truly before the court.

On behalf of A.C., Lynn Paltrow argued that the judge had gone about resolving the case in the wrong way. She said that the legal system should not view pregnancy as a hostile relationship between the pregnant woman and the fetus. The judge should not have "balanced" the rights of one against the other. Instead, the woman's life and health should have been considered paramount. "Under common law, constitutional principles and common sense, [the decision belongs] to the woman on whom the surgery is proposed," she argued. Considered cumulatively, A.C.'s uncertainty the night before the hearing, the opinions of her family and treating physicians, and her words "I don't want it done" shortly before the Cesarean was performed were enough to constitute an informed refusal.

Paltrow criticized the trial court for failing to specifically determine whether A.C. was competent. If she had indeed been declared incompetent, then the judge should have used a "substituted judgment analysis," in which a family member's judgment is substituted for that of the patient. Had the judge done so, Paltrow said, the C-section would not have been ordered.

Attorneys for the American Medical Association and the American College of Obstetricians and Gynecologists also weighed in. They said that in cases like A.C.'s, hospital bioethics committees or hospital staff should be enlisted to participate. If the patient is not competent to make the decision, a family member's judgment should be substituted. Through this process, a consensus will almost always be reached, the attorneys claimed. Only in very rare instances should a patient or family member's decision be reviewed by a court. Furthermore, they argued, the specter of judicial involvement destroys the element of trust in the doctor-patient relationship and threatens to drive women out of the health care system. Finally, they urged the court to rule that hospitals should not face liability for following the wishes of a patient, and claimed that an effort to avoid liability was the real motivating force behind the rushed hearing to determine A.C.'s fate.

Vincent Burke, on behalf of the hospital, said that at the hearing the judge had, in fact, tried to determine what Angela would have wanted, but had been unable to do so. At the same time, Burke argued, the judge had correctly recognized the state's interest in potential life.

Burke argued that even under the AMA's proposed guidelines, A.C.'s case was one of the few that would require court involvement. The conflict between Dr. Edwards and the obstetricians, the sense that the family was perhaps arguing their own wishes rather than Angela's, and the question of whether the state had a compelling interest in potential life, as well as the earlier precedent of a court-ordered Cesarean section, required the hospital to call a judge. More important, Burke argued, the judge would have reached the same result under a substituted judgment analysis.

Like Burke, Barbara Mishkin argued that the judge had reached the correct result, even if it had been arrived at through the wrong legal method. She claimed that it was the result A.C. would have wanted. A.C. had agreed to a Cesarean at twenty-eight weeks, so, Mishkin argued, it was reasonable to assume that she would have agreed to a Cesarean at twenty-six weeks if it represented the best chance for the baby to live, regardless of the consequences to her own deteriorating condition.

While the D.C. Court of Appeals was pondering these arguments, the Stoners, still bitter and furious, filed a lawsuit against George Washington University Hospital and its doctors, nurses, and administrators. The Stoners claimed, among other things, wrongful death and malpractice arising out of Angela's treatment and the court-ordered Cesarean.

"I just knew they had done something that should not have been left up to the courts. It should have been left up to Angie, her husband, her parents, anybody that could speak for her if she wasn't able. I guess that's why we had such a terrible feeling when it all

happened," says Nettie, adding, "After all this started, there wasn't anything private anymore—her death, her last days. There was no dignity
left at all."

According to Dr. Weingold, the lawsuit was unjustified. "It was an
ugly case because instead of focusing on the basic issues of process and
consent, it focused on issues of malpractice. That was really unnecessary. There were a number of things in this case that were less than
optimal, but none of them were negligence or malpractice. I mean,
bad things happened, but they were not malicious and they would not
in any way have changed the outcome."

A further complication was that by the time of the lawsuit, Rick
had decided that if he had spoken at the hearing or had had time to
reflect while Angie was alive, he would have wanted the Cesarean, and
so would Angie.

ON APRIL 26, 1990, nearly three years after Angela's death, the full
D.C. Court of Appeals issued its opinion. The court found that there
were two issues to decide: first, who has the right to decide the course
of medical treatment for a patient who, although near death, is pregnant with a viable fetus; second, how should that decision be made if
the patient cannot make it herself?

The court held that "in virtually all cases the question of what is
to be done is to be decided by the patient—the pregnant woman—on
behalf of herself and the fetus." The court said its decision was based
on the principle of informed consent, the right of any person, if competent, to make an informed choice to accept or forgo medical treatment. This doctrine is rooted in common-law principles and based on
the right of bodily integrity. The court also found the right to be one
of constitutional magnitude.

Under the common law, there is no duty to rescue another or to
submit to a significant intrusion upon one's bodily integrity for the
benefit of another's health. (For example, a court had refused to order
donation of bone marrow by one cousin to save another cousin's life.)
Furthermore, the court noted, "the right of bodily integrity is not extinguished simply because someone is ill, or even at death's door." In
response to the argument that fetal cases are different because a
woman has an enhanced duty to the fetus, the court wrote, "Surely,
. . . a fetus cannot have rights . . . superior to those of a person who
has already been born."

The court relied on two additional arguments in support of its conclusion. It accepted the arguments of the medical profession that court intervention and court-ordered Cesareans erode the element of trust that is crucial to the doctor-patient relationship, and can drive women at risk of complications out of the health care system in an effort to avoid forced treatment. The court also found that the emergency nature of proceedings such as A.C.'s does not allow the parties adequate time to prepare and communicate, which undermines the authority of whatever decision the judge reaches. In A.C.'s case, the court noted that Angela's lawyer never met his client, her medical records were not brought before the court, and Dr. Moscow was not called to testify. In the rush to judgment, neither the court nor the attorneys ever mentioned the doctrine of substituted judgment, which the court of appeals now deemed critical to the outcome of the case.

The court held that when a patient is incompetent or a court is unable to determine competency, the procedure known as substituted judgment most clearly respects the right of the patient to bodily integrity and is the proper procedure to be followed.

In a case of substituted judgment, the court must put itself in the patient's position and attempt to ascertain what the patient would do. The greatest weight should be given to the patient's previously expressed wishes; next, the court should consider the patient's overall value system. Then the court should turn to the family (bearing in mind, however, that in certain instances family members may express their own opinions, rather than the patient's wishes). Consulting with physicians and reviewing prior medical decisions in similar cases may also be helpful. If the court is still uncertain, it should then consider what most persons in a similar situation would be likely to do. If the patient is pregnant, the viability, condition, and risks to the fetus could also be factors for the court to weigh, as they are factors that the mother would consider.

The court then turned to A.C.'s case. Because the trial judge had not followed the substituted judgment procedure, the court of appeals set aside his decision. It repeated that under the substituted judgment process, the patient's wishes are paramount, and that circumstances in which a conflicting state interest would override those wishes would be "extremely rare and truly exceptional." "This," the court wrote, "is not such a case."

But the court went no further. The court found that there was conflicting evidence as to what decision A.C. would have made. "We see no need to reach out and decide an issue that is not presented on the record before us; this case is difficult enough as it is. We think it sufficient for now to chart the course for future cases resembling this one, and to express the hope that we shall not be presented with a case in the foreseeable future that requires us to sail off the chart into the unknown."

A few months later, in November 1990, the Stoners and G.W. settled their lawsuit for an undisclosed sum. G.W. also agreed to revise its guidelines on "informed consent" and "substituted judgment" and to strengthen the role of its ethics committee. The hospital issued a statement declaring that it would "virtually never" be appropriate to seek judicial intervention to resolve ethical issues, and that the use of courts to resolve maternal-fetal conflicts is "almost never warranted."

However, in Dr. Weingold's opinion, agreeing to respect bodily integrity and the patient's right to make decisions will not put an end to such controversies. "I think it would be an error to assume that these cases will not occur again," he says, "because the tolerance of individual physicians for the patient to make the "wrong" decision is not uniform." To Weingold, Angela's case was not even a truly difficult one. He says, "This was the worst case to test the principle because it was lose/lose from the very beginning." Neither Angela nor her baby had a good chance of surviving.

According to Weingold, the toughest cases are those in which doctors are certain that a medical procedure will produce a healthy mother and baby, but without the procedure the baby may die, and the mother refuses to consent. "You have a normal baby being subjected, by virtue of maternal decision, to death or risk of significant damage," he says. "What do you do in that situation? Basically, you have to ride with the mother's decision, but it's not easy. It's just not easy."

Passing Judgments

IN A December 1988 car accident, a Long Island woman suffered serious brain damage and was hospitalized in a coma. By February 1989, she was still comatose. She was also seventeen weeks pregnant. In an effort to improve the woman's condition, her husband, with the approval of her parents, petitioned to be appointed her guardian in order to authorize an abortion.

Two men, affiliated with a pro-life group but strangers to the family, also petitioned to be appointed guardians, one for the woman and one for the fetus, in order to oppose the abortion. A judge denied their application.

The court held that a nonviable fetus was not a "person" for whom a guardian could be appointed, that the law prefers the appointment of relatives as guardians, and that the strangers failed to show that the interests of the husband and wife were adverse enough to preclude the husband's appointment. The court concluded its opinion with the observation "Ultimately, the record confirms that these absolute strangers to the family, whatever their motivation, have no place in the midst of this family tragedy."

In re Klein, New York 1989

PROSECUTION OF PREGNANT WOMEN

CAN A MOTHER who uses cocaine while she is in labor be prosecuted for "delivery of a controlled substance to a minor"? The state of Florida tried.

A woman, pregnant with her second child, smoked pot and crack cocaine throughout her pregnancy. On the morning of January 23, 1989, she went into labor. After smoking cocaine, she went to the hospital. Her delivery was normal with no complications.

The woman was convicted of "delivering" cocaine to her

newborn child in the minute and a half between the time the baby's head emerged from the birth canal until her umbilical cord was clamped. She was sentenced to fifteen years' probation.

On July 23, 1992, the Supreme Court of Florida threw out the conviction. In a unanimous opinion, the court ruled that the Florida legislature had not intended to use the word "delivery" to prosecute mothers for the presence of drugs in their bloodstream which pass through the umbilical cord into their children.

Johnson v. Florida, Florida 1992

————

THREE WEEKS later, the Supreme Court of Connecticut went even further. A twenty-three-year-old pregnant woman shot up with cocaine after her water had broken, just as she was about to go into labor. After the birth of the baby, child welfare authorities took the infant away and placed her in foster care. A trial judge terminated the woman's parental rights.

On August 18, 1992, the Supreme Court of Connecticut reversed the lower court ruling. In a unanimous opinion, the court wrote, "Certainly no one approves of the intravenous injection of cocaine by a pregnant woman, who had been warned of the risks to her fetus. . . ." However, the court concluded that because the baby was not legally a "child" until after it was born, the mother was not legally a "parent" at that point either. Therefore, her actions before birth could not be considered parental conduct.

Like the Florida Supreme Court, the Connecticut justices deplored the mother's conduct but questioned whether penalizing expectant mothers might lead to even more dire social consequences.

In re Valerie D., Connecticut, 1992

————

IN 1989, concerned about the crack epidemic and its tragic consequences for newborns, the Medical University of South Carolina Hospital began testing pregnant women for evidence of illegal drug use. Any woman who tested positive for illegal drugs was shown a videotape about the dangers of drug use during pregnancy and was asked to sign an agreement saying that she would complete a drug treatment program (although there were none in the area). The names of those who refused, failed to show up, or tested positive a second time were handed to the police, and the women were arrested.

Over the next four years, around forty women were arrested and sent to jail, where they were given another chance to sign up for treatment. Four were prosecuted. According to the local prosecutor, "It worked like a charm." The number of pregnant drug users dropped from twenty-four a month to around five or six. In 1990, members of the hospital staff published an article on the program in a medical journal.

In October 1993, a lawsuit was filed on behalf of the women who were tested. The lawsuit accused the hospital of violating the women's Fourth Amendment rights by testing them for drug use without their consent, violating their right to privacy and due process by releasing confidential medical information to the police without the women's knowledge, and conducting illegal human experimentation in violation of federal research guidelines. In February 1994, the federal government opened a civil rights investigation into the program and threatened to cut off research funding to the hospital.

In September 1994, the hospital and the federal Office of Civil Rights signed an agreement under which both the program and the investigation would be discontinued. The civil lawsuit for $3 million is still pending. The local prosecutor has been elected South Carolina's attorney general.

Ferguson v. City of Charleston, South Carolina 1994

FORCED CONTRACEPTION

A SANTA CRUZ, California, mother of two sons, aged two and four, practiced an extremely strict macrobiotic diet. In the fall of 1980, her doctor warned her that the diet was dangerous for her as a breast-feeding mother, as well as for her young children. The doctor diagnosed the children as severely malnourished, emaciated, and at risk of starvation.

On November 25, another doctor, finding one child semicomatose, called the police, who hospitalized the boy. Upon his discharge, the child was placed in a foster home. While visiting him, the mother abducted him and fled to Puerto Rico with both sons. In September 1981, an FBI agent found them and arrested the mother. (The agent testified that the living quarters were squalid and that the only foodstuffs he observed were bags of beans, some millet, and a few other grains and noodles.) The woman explained that she had abducted her son because he had been eating eggs and sugar in the foster home and "getting fat."

When the children returned to California, doctors determined that as a result of diet and maternal neglect, one boy was seriously underdeveloped and the other had suffered severe growth retardation and permanent neurological damage.

The mother was convicted of child endangerment and violation of a custody decree. She was sentenced to five years' probation on various conditions, including that she serve one year in jail, participate in a counseling program, and have no unsupervised visits with her younger son. The final condition of her probation was that she not become pregnant within the probationary period. Her attorneys challenged this last condition as an unconstitutional restriction of her rights to privacy and procreation.

A California court agreed. The court held that there were other, less drastic measures by which to protect the public and prevent injury to a future child. (These might include periodic pregnancy testing with required prenatal care, and the removal of any child into foster care if necessary.) Furthermore, the court pointed out that if the woman did become pregnant, the only way for her to avoid prison would be to have an abortion. The court concluded that this was an unconstitutional choice.

The woman went on to have three more children. In June 1991, she was again arrested for child endangerment. Police found her three daughters, aged two, four, and six, in a garbage-filled apartment. Two were screaming. One was hiding under piles of filthy clothes, terrified. None was able to communicate in anything beyond animal-like grunts.

In September 1991, the woman was committed to a mental hospital to determine her competency to stand trial. She told psychiatrists that rock star Rod Stewart had fathered her children, and that she was Elvis' wife. Despite these obvious fantasies, she was found mentally competent. After a trial and conviction, she received the maximum sentence: eight years in a mental hospital.

Her common-law husband and the father of her three daughters was convicted of child neglect. However, he was sentenced to only six months in jail and ordered to attend parenting classes. Two of the children were placed in foster care, and one with a relative.

People v. Pointer, California 1984

―――――

ANOTHER California woman with five young children was arrested for possession and being under the influence of heroin. It turned out that she had spent much of her adult life in custody, for petty theft as well as drug possession. On the new charges, the judge sentenced the woman to five years' probation on condition that she enter a drug treatment program and that she not become pregnant during the probationary period. The judge said, "I want to make clear that one of the reasons I am making this order is you've got five children. You're thirty years old. None of your children is in your custody or control. . . . And I'm afraid that if you get pregnant, we're going to get a cocaine- or heroin-addicted baby."

The judge then ordered her to return to court two months later to report on her progress. He added, "If you get pregnant, I'm going to send you to prison in large part because I want to protect the unborn child. But . . . second of all, because you have violated a term and condition of your probation." The woman's lawyers appealed the condition as unconstitutional.

The court of appeals agreed, finding the "no-pregnancy" condition to be "impermissively overbroad." The court determined that the crime of heroin possession was not related to children, born or unborn. Even if protecting the health of children yet to be conceived was a proper subject for probation conditions, the court said that there were other, less drastic means by which to accomplish that goal. The court noted that other states (Kansas, Florida, and Ohio) had also concluded that a ban on pregnancy during probation was unlawful. The judges explained that even if they considered certain maternal actions deplorable, they were nevertheless "constrained by our oath to refrain from imposing our personal views on people brought before the bench."

People v. Zaring, California 1992

QUILL v. KOPPELL

The Right-to-Die Cases

WINTER WAS coming when Diane found out that she had leukemia. Her doctor for the previous eight years, Timothy Quill, an internist and medical school faculty member in Rochester, New York, was the one to break the news. Without treatment, her death would come within a few months. Even with aggressive treatment—chemotherapy, radiation, and bone marrow transplants—her chances of surviving were only one in four.

For Diane, the odds were not good enough. She wanted to spend her remaining life at home with her husband, her college-age son, and her friends, she told Dr. Quill, not in and out of hospitals. She refused the proposed treatment. Quill knew Diane to be a strong and self-aware person. In the previous few years, after successfully battling alcohol and depression, it seemed to Quill that Diane had become happier, experiencing a renewed closeness with her family and satisfaction in her professional life as an artist.

Although earlier in his career Dr. Quill had spent eight years as the medical director of a hospice, and so had experience treating patients in the final stages of life, at first he was uncomfortable with Diane's decision. He was concerned that once the shock of the diagnosis wore off, Diane would change her mind, but by then it would be too late to treat the disease.

However, it would be Dr. Quill who eventually changed his mind. Today he describes himself as an outspoken advocate of active, informed patient choice and of a patient's right to die with as much control and dignity as possible. "There is nothing more personal than the whole process of dying," he says. "Many people who are dying—not everybody, but many people—become more themselves than they have ever been. They think about what their life is about, about what they have accomplished and what they haven't, what they're leaving behind. Who you are as a person can be expressed very fully at that time."

Quill believed it was his obligation to make sure that Diane had considered the consequences of refusing treatment and that she was prepared to confront the inevitability of her death. Over the next few weeks and months, Dr. Quill met frequently with Diane, treating her for medical complications, referring her to other doctors and a psychologist when necessary, and talking her through periods of despair. Their conversations convinced Quill that Diane's refusal of treatment was not the result of depression or hopelessness but of her desire to live her life with dignity, and to make the most of the time she had left.

Then Diane presented Dr. Quill with another challenge. She explained her great fear of a lingering and painful death and asked him to help her die. "Knowing of her desire for independence and her decision to stay in control, I thought this request made perfect sense. . . . I also thought that it was out of the realm of currently accepted medical practice and that it was more than I could offer or promise," Dr. Quill later wrote.

Dr. Quill explained to Diane that when she began to feel pain, he could administer pain medication. If she suffered great pain, Dr. Quill could even administer a dose of pain medication that might be high enough to kill her, so long as his intention was to relieve her pain, not to cause or hasten her death. (In medical parlance, this is known as the "double effect death.")

But Diane was not reassured. She became preoccupied with avoiding a drawn-out death, and began to contemplate a violent suicide. After a series of conversations with Diane and her family, Dr. Quill became convinced that only the security of knowing she had enough sleeping pills to commit suicide would allow Diane to concentrate on living. He prescribed the barbiturates and made sure that Diane knew how many she would need to help her sleep or to end her life.

"I wrote the prescription with an uneasy feeling about the boundaries I was exploring—spiritual, legal, professional, and personal. Yet I also felt strongly that I was setting her free to get the most out of the time she had left, and to maintain dignity and control on her own terms until her death," Quill recalled.

Over the next several months, Quill believes, Diane did make the most of life. Her husband and son stayed home to be with her, and she spent time with her friends. After a series of good-byes, one spring morning Diane asked to be left alone. An hour later, her husband and son found her on the couch. She seemed to be at peace.

Dr. Quill listed the cause of death as acute leukemia. "Although [it] was the truth, it was not the whole story," he recalled. Quill believed that any mention of suicide would give rise to a police investigation. He knew that he might be criminally prosecuted, and was worried that Diane's husband or son could also face charges for their part in her death.

In March 1991, with the consent of Diane's family, Dr. Quill published an article on her death and his role in it. It concluded, "Diane taught me about the range of help I can provide if I know people well and if I allow them to say what they really want. She taught me about life, death, and honesty and about taking charge and facing tragedy squarely when it strikes. She taught me that I can take small risks for people who I really know and care about. Although I did not assist in her suicide directly, I helped indirectly to make it possible, successful, and relatively painless."

Quill wondered aloud how many other doctors secretly help suffering patients to die, and how many ill and dying people take their own lives. Perhaps his greatest regret, wrote Quill, was that, in order for their families to escape criminal charges, Diane and others like her are forced to die alone.

Dr. Quill admits that he was "naïvely unprepared" for the public reaction to his article. He had expected it to spark debate in academic circles or to arouse strong negative reaction in the pro-life community, but he had not anticipated the intensity of mass-media and public interest. He was certainly not prepared to be charged with second-degree manslaughter.

Quill says he had sought legal advice before publishing the article. But it was "academic legal advice, not criminal legal advice, and it turns out they're fairly different," he says, in an understatement. The answer he got—that he could not be successfully prosecuted—turned out to be correct, but, he explains, "what I didn't understand was what you can go through on the way to not being successfully prosecuted."

In July 1991, the local prosecutor, Charles Simpson, presented the case to a grand jury for three days. Quill himself testified for three hours. Quill says he basically retold Diane's story and explained the reasons behind his decisions. When he finished, he recalls, one grand juror said, "Why are you here?"

The grand jury refused to indict Dr. Timothy Quill on charges of second-degree manslaughter. "It was a perfect solution for the prosecutor," says Quill, "He didn't want to prosecute particularly, but didn't want to have the decision not to prosecute be on his shoulders."

The New York State Health Department conducted its own inquiry to determine whether Quill was guilty of professional misconduct. In August 1991, the three-member panel unanimously cleared his name. In support of their conclusion, they cited Quill's long-standing relationship with Diane, as well as the fact that he had not directly participated in the taking of life.

By 1992, physician-assisted suicide was front-page news. In Michigan, Dr. Jack Kevorkian had already helped five terminally ill people to kill themselves. *Final Exit*, a book containing a recipe for suicide, was on the best-seller list. A referendum on physician-assisted suicide had been narrowly defeated in the state of Washington the year before, and the issue was on the November ballot in California. (That initiative was written by an attorney whose wife had died in his arms after a long and agonizing battle with ovarian cancer.) Efforts to put the issue before voters in Oregon were also under way. Dr. Quill, with two colleagues, wrote an article proposing clinical criteria by which to evaluate dying patients' requests for help. Public opinion surveys indicated support for the idea of physician-assisted suicide, but also confusion and anxiety over its implementation.

There was also strong, vocal, and well-organized opposition to the legislative efforts. Religious groups and other critics charged that physician-assisted suicide violated the sanctity of life as well as the state's legal duty to preserve and protect life. They said that the proposed laws also violated medical ethics by placing physicians in the role of killers rather than healers. Furthermore, the issues were far too complex to be resolved by means of a simple ballot question.

Opponents said that the proposals also contained an intolerable risk of pressuring vulnerable patients into choosing death: the elderly or infirm who might ask to die rather than impose financial and emotional burdens on their families; the handicapped, the poor, and minorities, who are already victims of social indifference and exploitation; people suffering from depression or pain who might choose to live if these conditions were treated; or those who simply wished to change their mind but could find no one to listen.

The California ballot measure went down to defeat. But the efforts on behalf of physician-assisted suicide continued. In 1993, Dr. Kevorkian filed suit challenging a Michigan law prohibiting assisted suicide as unconstitutional, and a trial court ruled in his favor. In May 1994, a jury acquitted him of criminal charges. A measure was placed on the ballot in Oregon in 1994, with stricter safeguards than those in California's proposed legislation. Other state laws were challenged in court, and efforts to change them in the state legislatures began to pick up momentum.

In July 1994, Dr. Quill coauthored another article proposing the legalization of physician-assisted suicide and setting forth a number of crucial safeguards. According to the article, physician-assisted death should be considered as a "non-standard medical practice reserved for extraordinary circumstances, when requested voluntarily by a patient whose suffering has become intolerable and who has no other satisfactory option." The option of physician-assisted death would be available only to competent adults capable of making decisions and requesting help themselves. The request must be an "enduring" one, repeated over time. Informed consent must be in writing, or witnessed by others. An independent second opinion would be required from a physician experienced in the care of the severely ill and dying. That opinion could be reviewed by a regional committee which would also be responsible for educating doctors and the public. Layers of professional review are required, in Quill's opinion, to protect vulnerable patients from abuse. Given the legislature's ability to design adequate safeguards, oversight, and review, legislation was the preferred vehicle of reform.

To Dr. Quill, the two most important elements of his proposed system are the long-term commitment of physicians to care for their dying patients, and the truly independent and thorough nature of the second opinion. These are also the elements that, he believes, set his approach apart from that of Dr. Kevorkian.

"The physician who is involved should be the physician who is going to care for the patient, no matter what—who will not abandon them," says Quill. "People need to be able to change their minds. They need to be able to talk about this without acting on it. My belief is that most people want to have this [the drugs] as a possibility that they will never use. . . . But most of the time, if they get good palliative care [pain relief], they won't need it.

"So you need a clinician who is skilled and knows how to work with people who are dying, who are committing to work through this process with them, who, reluctantly, on rare occasions may allow somebody to be helped actively, when all else fails. That's the kind of system we ought to have set up."

In contrast, Quill says that Dr. Kevorkian is not the long-standing personal physician who will provide continuity of care to the terminally ill patients he assists in dying, if they change their minds. Instead, says Dr. Quill, "He comes in and connects with them around this very specific issue [suicide] and that's very dangerous."

The second crucial element in Quill's plan is the verification of the patient's decision by an independent and skilled clinician. Quill makes clear that this is not a second opinion from a "buddy in practice." Rather, a hospice doctor, or someone experienced in the care of the sick and dying, must revisit and reverify every aspect of the decision. If there is any uncertainty about the patient's mental state or competency, a psychologist should be brought in. If there is a question of pain, a palliative care expert should become involved. "The clinical assessments here are very, very difficult," says Quill. "You can be very fooled about depression. You can be fooled about other things. You want really skilled people making these decisions."

Under Quill's proposal, the patient must have an "incurable" illness. The term "incurable" is broader than "terminal." This, however, is an area of intense debate. Quill explains that people suffering from incurable diseases like Lou Gehrig's disease (ALS) will often suffer intolerably for long periods of time, and he believes they should be eligible for assistance in dying. Most legislative proposals, however, confine eligibility to patients who are terminal—that is, those not expected to live more than six months.

Dr. Quill also believes that in some extraordinary cases doctors should even be allowed to administer the lethal dose to their patients directly. This is called "voluntary active euthanasia." "The moral differences between physician-assisted suicide and voluntary active euthanasia are not significant," says Quill. "With physician-assisted suicide, the patient has to ultimately take, or not take, the medication, so there is a little more assurance of voluntariness. The downside is that people have to have a certain level of strength, or their body has to be intact in certain ways, in order for them to do it, so it discriminates against some people whose state is the most horrible."

Quill believes that "if your other safeguards are in place, then you [the doctor] should do what is best for that particular patient. If you're going to do such an extreme intervention, you should do it in the way that is most effective and humane."

Quill says he recognizes that politically, voluntary active euthanasia is not a realistic possibility. Therefore, he is trying to begin reform by legalizing physician-assisted suicide. On July 20, 1994, Quill, two other doctors, and three terminally ill patients filed a lawsuit in federal district court claiming that New York's ban on assisted suicide violated their constitutional rights to privacy and equal protection.

The patients claimed they had a constitutional right to refuse unwanted medical treatment, even if that refusal would result in their death. They argued that the right was also broad enough to allow them to seek a doctor's help in hastening that death. They based their arguments primarily on two sources: the Supreme Court's 1990 decision in *Cruzan v. Director, Missouri Department of Heath*, and the line of abortion decisions culminating in *Planned Parenthood v. Casey* in 1992.

In *Cruzan*, the Supreme Court had addressed the "right-to-die" issue for the first time. A 1983 car accident had left Nancy Cruzan, a young Missouri woman, in a persistent vegetative state. When it became obvious that her condition would not improve, Nancy's parents requested the withdrawal of the feeding tube that was keeping her alive. The hospital refused to comply. Missouri law required "clear and convincing evidence" of the patient's wishes before treatment could be withdrawn.

Nancy's parents testified in court about Nancy's beliefs and outlook on life. She would not want to be kept alive in her present condition, they said. Nancy's roommate recounted conversations in which Nancy had said she would rather die than live as a "vegetable." The Missouri Supreme Court concluded that such testimony did not establish "clearly and convincingly" that Nancy Cruzan would choose to die under these circumstances. The feeding tube could not be removed.

In a 5-to-4 decision, the United States Supreme Court upheld the rigorous Missouri standard. Chief Justice William Rehnquist wrote that for the purposes of Nancy Cruzan's case, the Court would assume that a *competent* person had a constitutionally protected right to refuse life-saving medical treatment. But that did not mean that if a patient was *incompetent*, then family members could simply step in and make the decision to end his or her life. Nothing in the Constitution prohibited a state from requiring that certain precautions be taken in such life-

and-death matters. Given the state's interest in preserving life and guarding against abuse, as well as the finality of the decision at stake, the "clear and convincing" standard was not too high, the Court said.

Although *Cruzan* was viewed as a setback for the so-called right-to-die movement in the context of *incompetent* patients, Dr. Quill and others saw an opening for *competent* terminally ill individuals. Dr. Quill and his colleagues seized on the Court's "assumption" that a competent person had a constitutionally protected right to refuse medical treatment. If the terminally ill have a right to end their lives by refusing treatment, Quill and his patients argued, then they must have a right to enlist a physician's aid in ending their lives as well.

Thus, the plaintiffs argued that the law banning physician-assisted suicide violated the constitutional guarantee of Equal Protection. There was no constitutional difference between refusing life-sustaining treatment when that refusal would lead to certain death, and administering drugs to oneself to hasten death.

Dr. Quill explains, "What's odd about this is how you are falling apart and what your medical condition is determines whether doctors are able to help you." For example, he says, if someone wants to be unhooked from a respirator or a feeding tube, or wants to stop dialysis, they can openly discuss with their doctor the withdrawal of treatment which will lead to their death. If they are in pain, they can ask for more pain medication, until the pain is relieved or until they die.

But patients whose suffering may be excruciating in other ways (those who may be so weak they cannot move, swallow, or administer drugs to themselves, for example) cannot be helped. "If you are one of those people," says Dr. Quill, "and you talk about dying, you might be accused of being crazy. If I talk about helping you, I might be accused of being a murderer. That's pretty crazy. That's pretty discriminatory."

Dr. Quill and his patients also drew on the Supreme Court's abortion decisions, which had recognized a sphere of liberty broad enough to include personal decisions of profound significance. They quoted directly from the Court's opinion in *Casey*, the case that upheld a woman's right to choose abortion before viability: "At the heart of liberty is the right to define one's own concept of existence, of meaning, of the universe, and of the mystery of human life. Beliefs about these matters could not define the attributes of personhood were they formed under the compulsion of the State."

Dr. Quill and his patients argued that surely the right of a competent person to control his or her death is a decision of the utmost magnitude, equal to that of terminating a pregnancy. Therefore, it should be included among our fundamental rights. Following the reasoning in *Casey*, they asserted that the law banning assisted suicide constituted an "undue burden" on this fundamental right. They argued that the competing state interest was weaker in the case of the terminally ill than in the abortion context since there was no other potential life at stake. Only the life of the person trying to commit suicide is involved, and that person is competent and able to communicate his or her wishes.

One federal district court, in Seattle, Washington, had accepted these arguments. In May 1994, it held that Washington's ban on assisted suicide violated the constitutional right to privacy.

However, in December 1994 two other courts issued decisions rejecting the right to assisted suicide. The Michigan Supreme Court upheld that state's law banning assisted suicide against a challenge by Dr. Kevorkian. Then a federal district court issued a preliminary injunction that prevented Oregon's new law allowing physician-assisted suicide from being put into effect.

In Dr. Quill's case, the three patient plaintiffs had died by the time the court issued its opinion. On December 15, 1994, the court held that New York's law banning assisted suicide did not violate the Constitution.

The court rejected the analogy to the abortion decisions, particularly *Casey*. The abortion issue was unique and the legal reasoning in these decisions could not be applied to other situations, the court said. Rather, the inquiry should follow the analysis set forth in *Bowers v. Hardwick*, in which the Court held that there was no right to homosexual sodomy, even between consenting adults. In *Hardwick*, the Supreme Court refused to recognize a right as "fundamental" unless it could be demonstrated to be "deeply rooted in this nation's history" and "implicit in the concept of ordered liberty." Just as the Supreme Court in *Hardwick* had reviewed the history of laws prohibiting sodomy, so the *Quill* court reviewed the history of the crime of suicide.

In England, suicide had been a crime according to common law as far back as the thirteenth century. Originally, the American colonies adopted this rule, although they gradually abandoned it. While no state now criminalizes suicide or attempted suicide, the same cannot be said for assisted suicide, which remains illegal in almost all fifty states. Therefore, the court found that even the limited form of physician-assisted suicide suggested by Quill and his colleagues was not a "fundamental right" under the Constitution.

Likewise, the court rejected the Equal Protection claims. It found that the state could recognize a difference between refusing treatment and allowing nature to take its course, on the one hand, and intentionally "using an artificial death-producing device" on the other. The determination that a physician cannot assist a patient in committing suicide was a valid exercise of the state's interest in the preservation of life. The court concluded with the observation that resolution of the issue should be left to the democratic process. Dr. Quill and the other doctors have appealed.

IN MARCH 1995, a three-judge panel of the Ninth Circuit Court of Appeals in California overturned the decision by the Washington district court judge who had found physician-assisted suicide to be protected by the Constitution. "The decision of the district court lacks foundation in our recent precedent. It also lacks foundation in the traditions of our nation," the appellate court declared.

In a blistering opinion, the court rejected a comparison to *Casey* or *Cruzan*. "In the two hundred and five years of our existence, no constitutional right to aid in killing oneself has ever been asserted and upheld by a court of final jurisdiction. Unless the federal judiciary is to be a floating constitutional convention, a federal court should not invent a constitutional right unknown to the past and antithetical to the defense of human life that has been a chief responsibility of our constitutional government." The plaintiffs have appealed (to the full Ninth Circuit), and many predict that the case will wind up in the United States Supreme Court.

Whether or not the Supreme Court addresses the issue soon, Dr. Quill believes it will not go away. "The goal is to allow someone to die intact as a person, not to disintegrate before dying. Disintegrating before death is a true medical emergency. You can't let people stay in that state. You have to help them find a way out of it, even if that means helping them to die."*

*For an update to *Quill v. Koppell*, please turn to page 339.

Passing Judgments

IN AUGUST 1989, an elderly Massachusetts woman suffered irreversible neurological damage and became comatose. The woman's daughter said that her mother had always wanted everything medically possible to be done for her if she became incompetent. The woman's doctors believed such care would be futile, and issued a "Do Not Resuscitate" order over the daughter's objections. The woman died.

In April 1995, a jury found the hospital and two doctors not guilty of neglect or of imposing emotional distress on the daughter.

Gilgunn v. Massachusetts General Hospital,
Massachusetts 1995

IN 1986, after a blood vessel burst in her brain, an elderly comatose New York woman was transferred from the hospital where she had first been taken to a Long Island nursing home, where she remained in a persistent vegetative state. Over the next three years, her husband begged nursing home officials to remove the feeding tube that was keeping the woman alive, saying that his wife had repeatedly stated she would not want to be kept alive by artificial means. Officials at the nursing home refused. Under New York law, they said, they were prohibited from terminating life support without "clear and convincing evidence" of the patient's wishes. In 1987, the husband stopped paying the nursing home's bills. The nursing home sued him. He countersued, and asked the courts to order the removal of the tube.

In 1989, an intermediate court ruled in his favor. The woman was transferred to a hospice. The feeding tube was removed and she died a week later. But the lawsuit continued. In 1993, New York's highest court ruled that the man was liable for the $100,000 in nursing home bills for the unwanted treatment, plus interest and legal fees.

Grace Plaza of Great Neck, Inc. v. Elbaum, New York 1993

———

A 1972 MOTORCYCLE ACCIDENT, and another incident in 1976, left a young Pennsylvania man in a persistent vegetative state with no hope of recovery. After overseeing his care and visiting him several times a day for twenty years, his mother asked that his feeding tube be withdrawn. His doctors agreed. At a court hearing, she testified that her son had never expressed his views on the termination of life-sustaining treatment, but that when active, her son loved life and would not have wanted to be kept alive in this way. The nursing home and state attorney general opposed her request.

In January 1995, by which time the man was forty-three, a Pennsylvania appeals court ruled that the consent of a close family member along with the approval of two qualified physicians is sufficient to warrant terminating life-sustaining treatment for a person in a persistent vegetative state. In Pennsylvania, clear and convincing evidence is not required.

In re Fiori, Pennsylvania 1995

———

A 1987 CAR ACCIDENT left a Missouri high school student in a persistent vegetative state. The girl's father did not know whether his daughter had ever discussed her views of life and death, but he knew that a Missouri law (upheld in *Cruzan*) required "clear and convincing evidence" of a patient's wishes before life-sustaining treatment could be withdrawn. In other words, he would be unable to persuade the hospital to remove his daughter's feeding tube. In 1991, the man won court approval to move his daughter to Minnesota, where families are allowed greater discretion in such decisions. Missouri officials battled him to the state's highest court, and called state troopers to prevent him from moving his daughter from the hospital.

Then, in January 1993, as his first official act, Missouri's new attorney general asked the court to dismiss the case on the ground that the state should not intrude into private family matters. On January 26, 1993, the court did so without issuing an opinion.

In re Busalacchi, Missouri, 1993

———

IN 1988, a California mathematician and computer software scientist was diagnosed with an inoperable malignant brain tumor. Doctors said that continued growth of the tumor would cause the man to enter a persistent vegetative state, and to die within five years. The man sought assistance to be cryogenically suspended (frozen) before he entered a vegetative state, until a future time when a cure had been found and his body could be reanimated for treatment. But under the law, he would be dead if he were cryogenically suspended. He asked the court to rule in advance that he had a constitutional right to assisted suicide.

In 1992, a California appellate court found no such right.

Donaldson v. Lungren, California 1992

DOE v. CITY OF NEW YORK

The Other Constitutional Right to Privacy

IN FEBRUARY 1992, John Doe, a former Pan Am employee, filed a complaint with New York City's Human Rights Commission against Delta Airlines. He claimed that during a pre-employment interview, he was first asked unlawful questions regarding his living arrangements, marital status, and relationship with his male roommates, then denied employment because of his sexual orientation and perceived disability (his HIV-positive status). Approximately three hundred similar complaints were filed with New York City's Human Rights Commission alleging discriminatory employment practices by Delta Airlines.

Doe's case was the first to be settled. Under the settlement worked out by the city, Delta hired Doe as a customer services agent. He was awarded back pay, seniority privileges, and a monetary settlement—a total of $13,958. The settlement agreement contained a confidentiality clause under which the parties agreed not to identify Doe by name. He started work in August.

A couple of days later, without checking with Doe or Delta, New York City officials issued a press release reporting on the settlement. Although Doe was not identified by name, he claimed that the press release contained enough information to cause him to be identified by coworkers and others, thereby revealing his HIV status to his colleagues.

Doe filed another lawsuit, this time against the city. He claimed that the city had violated his constitutional right to privacy in his medical information. He based his claim on a 1977 Supreme Court decision, *Whalen v. Roe*.

The controversy in *Whalen* centered on a New York statute which required that the name, address, and age of every patient obtaining certain "dangerous yet legitimate" prescription drugs be recorded in a centralized computer data bank. The drugs included opium and other narcotics, cocaine, methadone, and amphetamines. The law required the use of a new triplicate form: The doctor kept one copy, the pharmacy kept the second, and the third was forwarded to the New York State Department of Health in Albany. The patients argued that disclosing their names would violate their privacy and deter them from seeking needed medical treatment.

The Supreme Court unanimously declared that the Constitution protects two types of privacy. One aspect of privacy covers the right to make fundamental decisions (familiar from the abortion context). The other, lesser-known and relatively uncontroversial aspect of the constitutional right to privacy covers the interest in avoiding disclosure of personal matters.

The Court recognized that disclosing the prescription drug information to the state implicated this constitutionally protected privacy interest. Nonetheless, the Court held that the New York law was constitutional. The Court found that the disclosure required by the statute was not "meaningfully distinguishable from a host of other unpleasant invasions of privacy that are associated with many facets of health care." The Court also noted that New York had recognized the sensitive nature of the information and had instituted safeguards to prevent its disclosure. For example, the processing room at the Department of Health was protected by an alarm and surrounded by a locked wire fence. The paper forms were kept in a vault and destroyed after five years, and the tapes were stored in a locked cabinet. When the tapes were in use, the computer was off-line.

After recognizing the routine nature of disclosures to doctors, hospitals, and insurance companies, the Court also pointed out that states already required reporting on other personal matters that could reflect unfavorably on an individual, including venereal disease, child abuse, injuries caused by deadly weapons, and certifications of fetal death. Finally, the Court said the state has broad powers to regulate the use of drugs and to take other measures to protect the public health.

Although the New York law was upheld, *Whalen* was considered a milestone in the fight for privacy. The recognition of a constitutionally protected interest in certain personal information was important, as was the recognition of the vulnerability of information in the electronic era. "We are not unaware of the threat to privacy implicit in the accumulation of vast amounts of personal information in computerized data bases or other massive government files," the Court wrote.

The *Whalen* decision also reflected the real-world role of the right to privacy. Although the justices recognized the privacy interest as important, and even constitutionally protected, they determined it was outweighed by the state's competing interest in controlling the widespread illegitimate use of drugs. The state is responsible for protecting public health, and that, of necessity, requires the collection of certain medical information.

The Supreme Court has not addressed the issue again, but following *Whalen*, a number of lower federal courts recognized a privacy interest in confidential medical information, including medical records. They also began to fashion a framework by which to balance an individual's privacy rights against the government's need for access to and disclosure of some personal information.

In January 1994, the U.S. Court of Appeals for the Second Circuit joined those courts. In Doe's case (regarding the New York City press release), the court extended the protection previously granted to medical records to include a person's HIV status. The court rejected the city's claim that Doe had given up his right to privacy when he filed a complaint with the city's Human Rights Commission, and his HIV status had thereby become a matter of public record. (By law, there is no privacy in information in the public record.)

Instead, the court found that under *Whalen*, Doe had a constitutional right to privacy in his HIV status. "Extension of the right to confidentiality to personal medical information recognizes there are few matters that are quite so personal as the status of one's health, and few matters the dissemination of which one would prefer to maintain greater control over," the court declared. "Clearly, an individual's choice to inform others that she has contracted what is at this point invariably and sadly a fatal, incurable disease is one that she should normally be allowed to make for herself. This would be true for any serious medical condition, but is especially true with regard to those infected with HIV or living with AIDS, considering the unfortunately unfeeling attitude among many in this society toward those coping with the disease. An individual revealing that he or she is HIV-seropositive potentially exposes himself or herself not to understanding or compassion, but to discrimination and intolerance, further necessitating the extension of the right to confidentiality over such information."

Even though the court recognized Doe's right to privacy, it also recognized the city's need to disseminate information about the settlements it reached in the public interest. The Second Circuit sent the case back to the trial court to balance Doe's privacy interest against the public's right to know. Doe died before the case was completed. His estate settled with the city for an undisclosed sum.

While we do have a constitutional right to privacy in certain medical information, it is important to note that it is a limited right. Anyone wishing to bring a constitutional privacy claim must remember that the Constitution only protects us against violations by the government. Doe could not have made the same claim had Delta Airlines issued the press release instead of New York City. Furthermore, in the area of public health, state interests are often compelling enough to override an individual's right to privacy.

Still, there are other sources of legal protection in addition to the Constitution. Although there is no general federal medical privacy law, almost every state has a statute protecting the confidentiality of medical records and of doctor-patient relationships. But in the area of HIV testing, the laws vary widely. For example, New York and California prohibit the disclosure of HIV test results without the consent of the patient, while Colorado requires reporting by name of all people testing positive for HIV. State workers then track down and notify the sex partners of infected individuals.

In the area of HIV and AIDS, plaintiffs have had more success in asserting a claim of discrimination rather than invasion of privacy. Now there is a new and potentially powerful weapon: the Americans with Disabilities Act. The ADA specifically prohibits discrimination on the basis of a disability (such as HIV or AIDS). Although it does not protect privacy directly, it does provide a remedy for the forms of discrimination which often result from a breach of confidentiality.

Passing Judgments

In March 1987, Jane Doe, her husband, and a friend were driving through the borough of Barrington, New Jersey, when they were stopped and questioned by a police officer. Mr. Doe was arrested. He told the police officers that he had tested positive for HIV and that they should be careful in searching him. All three were taken to the police station where Mr. Doe was detained. Jane Doe and the friend were released and drove to the Does' house. They left the car running and it somehow slipped into gear and rolled down the driveway into a neighbor's fence. The neighbor worked in the local school district.

Police officers who responded to a call about the incident told the neighbor that because Mr. Doe had AIDS, she should wash her hands with disinfectant to protect herself. The woman then contacted other parents with children in the school that her daughter and the four Doe children attended. She also notified the media. A panic ensued. Eleven parents removed nineteen children from the school. The story was covered by local TV and newspapers. The Does' name was mentioned.

The Does sued on behalf of themselves and their children. They claimed that as a result of the disclosure by employees of the government, they had suffered discrimination, harassment, and humiliation. Mr. Doe died before the case was decided.

In January 1990, a federal district court found that Mrs. Doe and her children had a constitutional right to privacy in Mr. Doe's HIV status. The court recognized that a disclosure that one family member had AIDS had caused the entire household to be ostracized. It found no societal or governmental interest in disclosure that outweighed the Does' privacy rights.

Doe v. Borough of Barrington, New Jersey 1990

WHEN A New York woman who had tested positive for HIV was incarcerated in the Erie County Holding Center, she was segregated from the rest of the female inmates and placed in an area reserved for mentally disturbed and suicidal inmates. She was refused permission to attend religious services or to use the prison's law library. A red sticker was placed on all of her documents and belongings (including her clothing bag, court papers, belt, wallet, change, and keys) to indicate that she had a contagious disease.

The woman sued, alleging violation of her constitutional right to privacy and New York's public health law requiring medical confidentiality. The prison claimed that the red-sticker policy did not specifically disclose her HIV status and that segregation was necessary to protect her as well as other inmates and staff from illness or violence.

In October 1991, a federal district court held that the red-sticker policy was unconstitutional. It found that the policy had been developed in response to the fear of AIDS and that it was not "reasonably related to legitimate penological interests." A system of universal precautions did not violate privacy rights and provided more effective protection against transmission of the virus. The court also held that the red-sticker policy violated New York's public health law.

Regarding the woman's segregation, the court noted that segregation of HIV-positive prisoners had been upheld by an Alabama court. However, the court found the segregation to be an "exaggerated response" and a violation of the woman's constitutional right to privacy. Segregation also violated the woman's privacy rights under New York law because it disclosed confidential medical information to nonmedical staff.

Nolley v. County of Erie, New York 1992

———

DR. JOHN DOE was an obstetrics and gynecology resident at Pennsylvania's Hershey Medical Center and the Harrisburg Hospital. In May 1991, during an invasive procedure, Dr. Doe was accidentally cut through his glove by the attending physician. No one could be certain that the patient had been exposed to the doctor's blood. Dr. Doe voluntarily submitted to a blood test, which confirmed that he was HIV-positive. He voluntarily withdrew from further surgery and took a leave of absence.

Internal investigations showed that 447 patients had been in contact with Dr. Doe during his residency. The hospitals argued that they had a "compelling need" to inform these patients of their possible exposure to HIV. Dr. Doe's name would not be disclosed to the patients, but the hospital wished to inform other departmental physicians of Dr. Doe's identity. The doctors would be prohibited from revealing his identity to anyone else. Dr. Doe objected that the disclosures would violate his right to privacy. He also argued that if people at risk for HIV infection could not be certain that their test results and HIV status would remain confidential, they would refrain from being tested, and thereby hinder efforts to combat the disease.

In July 1991, a Pennsylvania appellate court upheld the disclosures. It found that although Pennsylvania law protected the confidentiality of AIDS test results, there was an exception for a "compelling need." The court decided: "The public's right to be informed in this sort of potential health catastrophe is compelling and far outweighs a practicing surgeon's right to keep information regarding his disease confidential."

In re Milton S. Hershey Medical Center, Pennsylvania 1991

IN 1982, a Florida man sitting on a park bench was hit by a car. He was hospitalized and received a transfusion of fifty-one units of blood. In 1983, the man was diagnosed with AIDS. In an effort to prove that he had contracted the disease from the transfusions, he sought to discover the identity of the blood donors.

In 1987, the Florida Supreme Court denied his request. The identities of the blood donors were protected against disclosure by both federal and state constitutional privacy interests. The court found that "AIDS is the modern-day equivalent of leprosy. AIDS, or a suspicion of AIDS can lead to discrimination in employment, education, housing and even medical treatment." . . . The court concluded that "Disclosure of donor identities in any context involving AIDS could be extremely disruptive and even devastating to the individual donor." In addition, the court said that society had a vital interest in maintaining a strong blood supply which would be jeopardized if donor identities were disclosed. These concerns outweighed the man's interest in discovery.

Rasmussen v. South Florida Blood Services, Inc., Florida 1987

Privacy v. The Press

A woman is kidnapped, taken to an apartment, stripped, and terrorized. The police—and the media—surround the apartment. The police eventually overcome the kidnapper and rush the woman, who clutches a dish towel in a futile attempt to conceal her nudity, to safety. A photograph of her escape is published in the next day's newspaper.

In a split second, a man in a crowd deflects a gun aimed at President Gerald Ford. The media celebrates the man as a hero. A reporter discovers that the man is homosexual, a fact of which even his family is not aware. But everyone finds out when the reluctant hero's sexuality becomes part of the national story.

A man, Ricardo, becomes a woman, Rikki. She scrupulously changes all of her life records from birth certificate through high school transcripts and begins a successful life as a woman. She enrolls in a community college and is elected its first female student body president. A reporter finds out about Rikki's past and publishes the story.

A Pittsburgh Steelers fan is photographed in the stands at a football game with his fly unzipped. The picture is published in a popular sports magazine.

IN THESE stories, and others like them, lies the clash between privacy and the press. Media coverage once focused on a small group of very famous people, while average Americans watched from the sidelines. But in recent years the "information age" has burst into the information *explosion.* To the traditional daily newspapers, add record numbers

of books, newsletters, magazines, and other periodicals. Radio and
television have become ubiquitous, often running twenty-four hours a
day. And we stopped counting cable television channels when they hit
triple digits.

All of these outlets need to be filled with information. As a consequence, people who in another time would have lived their lives in
quiet obscurity now find themselves in the spotlight. Some offer themselves up willingly, dishing out intimate information by the shovelful
on national television. More poignant, and problematic, are the private
people who unwittingly or unwillingly become "news": the woman
who is kidnapped or the man who saves the President. More and
more, ordinary Americans have come to know the hunted feeling previously the province only of celebrities.

These lesser-known people are shaping the law in the area of privacy and the press. Perhaps surprisingly, although clashes between
public figures and the media are the most visible, actual celebrity lawsuits for invasion of privacy are scarce. As illustrated in this chapter,
when faced with the First Amendment rights of the media, even private individuals have a difficult time winning a privacy case. Public figures, whose lives are much more open to public scrutiny, have even
less of a chance of prevailing, and therefore rarely file suit. It is left to
the people in these stories—the California widow or the North Carolina mother—to attempt to vindicate their right to privacy when personal matters appear in the press.

While new mass communication is making the privacy/press clash
more immediate and personal to ordinary Americans, there is also
something fundamental and very old about the conflict. The idea of
man in control of his own private sphere has always been a basic or-
ganizing principle of American society. At America's birth, we adopted
from our English ancestors the belief that a man's home is his castle
and that man is king of that domain and, by extension, the whole of
his private life. The Bill of Rights was drafted to limit government interference in people's lives. Later, the rugged, solitary individual was
celebrated on the American frontier, in business, and in literature
and popular entertainment, and became an integral part of American
mythology.

But this mythology is antithetical to another American ideal: an
open and outspoken press. Americans have always been proud of a
strong First Amendment. Every schoolchild knows that the Founding
Fathers considered a free press to be the bulwark of liberty, and

that some "bad" speech must be tolerated so that "good" speech—and truth—can flourish. Indeed, in America freedom of the press is more than just a principle.

At times the press has even seemed to be something alive and feral. We call it the "watchdog" on our government, and First Amendment scholar Zechariah Chafee wrote: "The press is a sort of wild animal in our midst—restless, gigantic, always seeking new ways to use its strength."

When the media uses its strength to uncover government corruption or lay bare a public lie, it is the country's watchdog. But when the animal roams into our cherished private sphere, it seems to turn dangerous and predatory. Then we Americans turn on the press. We want a free press, we say, but not *that* free. In a country where individuals treasure their personal sovereignty as much as free expression, the current legal conflict between privacy and the press was inevitable. In fact, it was outrage at the press that "created" the legal right to privacy in the first place.

THE RIGHT TO BE LET ALONE

The Press is overstepping in every direction the obvious bounds of propriety and decency. Gossip is no longer the resource of the idle and of the vicious, but has become a trade which is pursued with industry as well as effrontery. To satisfy a prurient taste the details of sexual relations are spread in the columns of the daily papers.

I T IS a common criticism of the media today, voiced by celebrities and private individuals alike. However, this particular view of the press was expressed by two distinguished legal scholars in a *Harvard Law Review* article more than a century ago. The article, entitled "The Right to Privacy" and published in 1890, was authored by Samuel D. Warren and Louis D. Brandeis (later a Supreme Court justice). It was reportedly prompted by Warren's outrage at coverage of a family wedding in the gossip columns. From these somewhat petty beginnings, a major new legal right was founded. The Warren and Brandeis article is credited with creating the "right to privacy" and, consequently, the right to sue for "invasion of privacy."

In their article, Warren and Brandeis famously described the right to privacy as the "right to be let alone." As society became more complex and technology became more intrusive, they asserted, protection of privacy became more urgent. They recognized that an invasion of privacy would usually cause spiritual or emotional harm, rather than physical injury, but argued that the damage was just as serious and should be compensated through legal action. "Only a part of the pain, pleasure, and profit of life lies in physical things," they wrote.

"Thoughts, emotions, and sensation demand legal recognition." Courts began to accept Warren and Brandeis' argument, and the legal right to privacy was born.

It is important to note that this right is distinct from a constitutional right to privacy. The Constitution protects individuals against *government* action only. Warren and Brandeis were arguing for a right against private individuals—friends, neighbors, employers, and especially members of the press. This right of privacy is called a "tort."

A tort is a legal cause of action that is specifically set out in a statute (as opposed to the Constitution), or is part of what is known as the general "common law"—i.e., law that courts recognize based on legal history and other cases. For example, some well-known torts are "negligence," "trespass," and "defamation."

Tort law, unlike federal constitutional law, can vary from state to state. There is only one federal Constitution, and when the United States Supreme Court interprets the Constitution, its ruling becomes the law of the land for the entire country. In contrast, in tort law each state legislature is free to draft statutes recognizing certain torts while rejecting others. Likewise, each state court system interprets its own statutes and case law according to precedent in that particular state. As a result, the same case may provide a valid cause of action for invasion of privacy in one state but be thrown out of court in the state next door.

If the privacy tort was born in 1890, then it came of age in 1960, again because of a legal article. After "The Right to Privacy" was published, courts recognized suits for invasion of privacy, but only intermittently and in a hodgepodge fashion. A Peeping Tom, a shopkeeper who publicized a customer's debt, a newspaper that published a photograph of a nursing mother, and a reporter who sneaked into a hospital room—all were brought to court for invasion of privacy. Then, in 1960, a legal scholar, Dean William Prosser, compiled the varied privacy cases and wrote an influential article arguing that the tort known as "invasion of privacy" was really four distinct but related torts. He called these four torts: intrusion, public disclosure of private facts, false light, and appropriation. They are generally defined as follows:

> *Intrusion:* Intruding (physically or otherwise) upon the solitude of another in a highly offensive manner. For example, a woman sick in the hospital with a rare disease refuses a reporter's request for a photograph and interview. The reporter photographs her anyway, over her objection.

Private facts: Publicizing highly offensive private information about someone which is not of legitimate concern to the public. For example, photographs of an undistinguished and wholly private hardware merchant carrying on an adulterous affair in a hotel room are published in a magazine.

False light: Publicizing a highly offensive and false impression of another. For example, a taxi driver's photograph is used to illustrate a newspaper article on cabdrivers who cheat the public when the driver in the photo is not, in fact, a cheat.

Appropriation: Using another's name or likeness for some advantage without the other's consent. For example, a photograph of a famous actress is used without her consent to advertise a product.

After Prosser's article clarifying and defining the tort, invasion of privacy lawsuits became more common. Indeed, Prosser's four torts were generally accepted by the courts as the only causes of action for invasion of privacy. Even so, each state went its separate way. Some state legislatures recognized the torts and wrote them into statutes. Some states left it to the courts to decide which of the four torts would be recognized and under what circumstances. Others are still picking and choosing as cases come up. And like the constitutional right to privacy, the privacy torts have been under attack for as long as they have been recognized.

These attacks come from several fronts. Some complain that the law in this area is just plain confusing. The Supreme Court has discreetly described it as "somewhat uncharted," while exasperated commentators liken it to a haystack in a hurricane. One basic problem is that all of the four torts—intrusion, private facts, false light, and appropriation—are grouped under the same heading of "privacy," even though they seem at first glance to have little in common. In fact, some argue that two of the torts have little to do with ordinary notions of privacy at all. (False light seems to have more in common with defamation, and appropriation is similar to a property right.)

In addition, the standards to be applied under each tort have been criticized for ambiguity. In each tort except appropriation, the key is to prove that information has been used in a manner that is "highly offensive to a reasonable person." Clearly, the phrase leaves room for interpretation. (How high is high? How reasonable is reasonable?) But the "reasonable person" standard haunts most areas of the law. Because of the flexibility of the English language and the various ways of interpreting it, such standards can take on meaning only over time, case by case. Still, critics of the privacy torts argue that when the First Amendment freedom of the press is at stake, as it most often is in these privacy cases, then such ambiguity is unacceptable. Editors are left guessing what any given judge or jury may deem to be "highly offensive."

This state of affairs, the argument continues, is particularly unacceptable when there are other ways for people to seek relief. The four privacy torts often overlap with other torts. For example, there is a cause of action known as "intentional infliction of emotional distress," which, with its emphasis on emotional harm, clearly overlaps with the privacy torts. Intrusion is similar in many ways to "trespass" and false light is akin to "defamation." Thus, some argue that the privacy torts are unnecessarily muddying the law, clogging the courts and posing an additional threat to the First Amendment. However, even the critics admit that the overlap is not complete. There are still some harms, intangible but grievous emotional damages, that are only covered by the right to privacy.

The fundamental question becomes whether we should provide a legal remedy for this kind of harm at all. Some assert that the injury caused by invasions of privacy, especially by the press, is "often as exquisite pain as mortals know." Others refer to the harm as mere "hurt feelings" and claim that such injury is the price we must pay for living in a free society.

The debate over the right to privacy in tort law has not been as publicly wrenching as in the constitutional area. But for those who are involved—the coed whose lover secretly videotaped their lovemaking and distributed the tape on campus, or the family whose father's dying moments were broadcast on the nightly news—the effect on their lives is profound. The question of whether and under what circumstances we should continue to recognize these privacy torts raises the much larger issues of what kind of society we want to be and how we prioritize our freedoms versus our restrictions. These questions are most stark and controversial when privacy torts go up against the First Amendment, for although the torts can be used against anyone, they are most often used against the media. Then it is a clash between the right to be let alone and the right to know, a clash between privacy and the press.

HALL v. POST

The Case of an Adoption Revealed

I T WAS in September. It was at the time when the fair was in Salisbury," Mary Hall says, recalling the autumn of 1967.

It was a time when she was struggling to rear three children in rural Rowan County, North Carolina. Mary had a grade school education and worked at the local mill. Her husband, Earle, drove a long-haul tractor-trailer. The Halls had three children: an older daughter from Mary's first marriage and two young boys, one six months and the other two years old. Child care was an unending problem.

"I couldn't get no one I could depend on to look after my children," Mary says. So she left the mill and opened a day care service in her home, advertising for other children in the local paper. It happened that the carnival had come to town, and with it came a young carnival barker and his wife. The couple needed someone to look after their baby girl while they were at the fairgrounds. They called Mary Hall.

"I told them if she was a good baby and didn't cry, that I would keep her," Mary remembers. Later that day, the carnival couple showed up with the little girl. "They had her in this little car bed," Mary says. "She looked up and all you could see was her eyes. I knew right then. I said, 'Yeah, I'll keep her.' "

Each day, the couple would drop the baby off in the afternoon, go to work at the carnival, and pick up their daughter around midnight. The "carnival baby" seemed no different from the others Mary had taken on at her new day care. Then, after two weeks, the fair folded its tents in Salisbury and moved on, taking the carnival barker and his family with it.

But Mary heard from the carnival barker again. "He called me long-distance," she says. The fair had moved to Charlotte and the man wanted Mary to continue to look after the baby for a while. Mary said that would be fine.

When the father brought the child up from Charlotte, for the first time Mary asked the little girl's name. She explained that her two-year-old son had been calling the baby "Susie." Mary had previously cared for a baby girl with that name, so to her son all girls of a certain age were "Susie." Mary worried that the name had begun to stick and asked the child's given name. The man smiled and said "Susie."

A few days later, the mother called to check on her baby. Mary told the woman that the girl was happy and healthy, even cutting a tooth. The mother asked if the Halls needed a payment from them and Mary replied that she would wait until they returned to pick up their daughter.

It was several weeks before Mary realized that the carnival couple was not coming back. "Well, I got to thinking after probably about a month," Mary says. "And then I worried more and more and more."

When Mary and Earle finally accepted that the baby girl had been abandoned, they asked the local social services agency to help locate Susie's family. However, Mary could not even tell the agency the names of the little girl's mother and father. The only clue the Halls had to the baby's identity was a tiny suitcase with a faded sticker from Jamaica, Florida. The authorities could find no trace of the parents in Florida, or anywhere else. The couple seemed to have vanished.

The Halls responded to a carnival barker abandoning a baby in their living room by keeping her, loving her, and raising her as their own. "Well, I feel this way," Mary says. "She was brought to my house. She was left there and never called for. I felt in my heart that God gave her to me and I was gonna raise her."

After about a year, Mary and Earle decided to make the adoption official and hired a lawyer to draw up the papers. They gave the little girl the name "Susie," which was what they had been calling her all along. A birth date, however, was harder to come by. Mary and Earle never learned the date of Susie's birth. But the little girl had always seemed to be at roughly the same stage of development as the Halls' younger boy, Herbert. So Mary and Earle chose a birthday close to that of their little boy: Herbert's birthday was March 23; Susie's became March 19. The adoption was finalized and, in accordance with North Carolina law, the records were sealed. So, with a name from one brother and a birthday from another, the little abandoned girl became Susie Jean Hall and, as the Halls are fond of saying, "That was that."

When Susie was six years old and entering first grade, Mary Hall told her daughter about her past. "I don't know if I really knew what she was talking about or not," Susie says now. "Because once she told me that I was adopted, I just looked at her and hugged her and said, 'You're my mama.'"

Susie and her siblings knew the circumstances of Susie's abandonment and adoption but nothing more, because no one had anything more to tell. For her part, Susie says she never had any interest in learning anything else. Even as she grew older, Susie did not want to find her biological parents, nor even know their names. "Mama and Daddy were my parents," Susie says of Mary and Earle Hall, "and that was it." After the conversation in which the Halls told Susie about her past, the family simply never discussed the subject again.

Susie flourished in the Hall family, which in a few years grew to include a new baby girl. Despite the four days' difference, Susie and Herbert celebrated their birthdays together in March. People began to assume that the two were twins, an idea the Halls encouraged. The family moved from Salisbury to Charlotte, and then moved again, finally settling in Mooresville, North Carolina, a modest resort community on Lake Norman.

Then, in the summer of 1984, as Susie was looking forward to her senior year in high school, her world came apart. Mary and Earle received word that someone claiming to be Susie's biological mother was in town looking for her. Mary cried so much that the children thought someone had died. Susie kept asking her parents what had happened and Earle finally told her about the call. "I just said NO," Susie recalls. "I just kept saying NO, NO, NO. Then I got my clothes packed up."

Susie fled to an uncle's house, fearful that somehow these strangers would find her. For a few days, the entire family was in a panic. Then, when they did not hear anything more, the Halls assumed that the people had given up and Susie came home. Soon after she returned, Susie, Mary, and Earle were visiting a grandparent who lived nearby when someone showed them a copy of the previous day's *Salisbury Post*.

The *Salisbury Post* is a daily newspaper serving approximately twenty-six thousand people in Rowan County, North Carolina. It reports the big national stories but is dedicated to extensive coverage of matters of local interest. For most of its readers, the *Post* is the only newspaper they receive.

On Wednesday, July 18, 1984, the lead headline reaching across the front page read: EX-CARNY SEEKS BABY ABANDONED 17 YEARS AGO. The story, written by veteran *Post* reporter Rose Post (no relation to the paper), detailed a meeting Rose had had in a local motel with a couple named Ann and Bob Gordon. The article began with a description of Ann and Bob's emotional state.

> Tears she struggles to control turn her clear blue eyes green in the
> dim lamplight of Room 173 of the Econo Motel. . . . Bob sits on the
> floor and stares into the unknown. . . .

According to the article, Ann had only recently married Bob, but she had been married before. When she was twenty-three, she met a carnival barker, Chuck Martin, who was traveling through her small Wisconsin farm town. She ran off with Chuck to escape an unhappy home life and literally to join the circus. On the road, the couple had a little baby girl. In 1967, they left the girl with a baby-sitter in Salisbury, North Carolina, thinking they would come back for her when the carnival season was over. But when the fair moved farther away and money became scarce, Chuck told Ann that he had signed papers giving the child up for adoption. Ann told Rose Post that she had believed her husband and thought there was nothing she could do. She stayed with Chuck, and with the carnival, and had three more children, whom she kept with her.

Ann said that she eventually left Chuck and life on the road and returned with the three children to her hometown. She never told her parents or anyone else about her first child. Nearly two decades later, when she married Bob Gordon, she finally told him her secret. Now they were in Salisbury trying to pick up the trail of the abandoned little girl.

"If she could just know [the child] is all right. . . . If she could see her, even from a distance . . . ," Rose Post wrote. The article described the Gordons' fruitless search for word of the little girl. Following department policy and state law, the Rowan County Social Services Department would not provide any information. The Gordons also failed to learn anything from talking with people at the local Holiday Inn where Ann remembered she had stayed with the carnival that year. Likewise, a search through the archives of the local press and the town's high school yearbooks turned up nothing about the child. To Ann and Bob, the little girl seemed to have vanished.

Looking at the *Salisbury Post*, Susie Hall was stunned. She was reading her personal history—a story she had never wanted to know. Suddenly, her birth mother had a name, a face (in a photograph accompanying the article), and a family history. Through the *Post* article, Susie learned for the first time that her original name had been "Becky." Through the article, Susie learned that her real birthday was June 1 and that she had been born when the carnival played in Philadelphia.

And through the article, Bob and Ann Gordon found Susie.

The *Post* story had ended with a plea:

> If anyone, they say, knows anything about a little blonde baby left here when the county fair closed and the carnies moved on in September 1967, Bob and Ann Gordon can be reached in Room 173 at the Econo Motel.

Apparently, enough people called the Gordons so that they were able to discover Susie's identity. Some even called offering the Halls' new telephone number, address, and directions to Mooresville.

At about the same time the Halls discovered the *Post* article, the Gordons showed up at their home. A relative answered the door and told the couple that Susie and her parents were at their grandmother's house canning beans. Soon after, the telephone rang at Susie's grandmother's home. Mary answered the phone, and when she heard who it was, she started crying and handed the receiver to Earle.

The man on the phone identified himself as Bob Gordon, and he apologized for the shock and distress he knew the Halls must be suffering. Bob said that he and Ann just wanted to talk with the girl who they believed was now called "Susie." Susie refused to take the phone, saying she wanted nothing to do with them. Bob left a telephone number where they could be reached in case Susie changed her mind.

If the Halls were surprised by the *Post* article, they were shell-shocked by the newspaper's follow-up story. On Friday, July 20, two days after the original story about the Gordons' search, the *Salisbury Post* ran a second article by Rose Post. It was still on page one, this time below the fold in the lower right-hand corner. The headline read: DAUGHTER FOUND; MOM HOPES FOR REUNION.

"They found her!"

They laugh, they cry, they believe, they don't believe, and they look at each other and tears and laughter mix and they must believe the unbelievable.

"They found her!"

The article recounted the Gordons' search for the abandoned child. The newspaper specifically identified Susie and Mary Hall of Mooresville as the lost girl and the mother who took her in. The article also related the Gordons' feelings about Susie, their failed attempt at a reunion, and their concern about the disruption their appearance had caused. Rose Post wrote:

> Maybe Mary Hall and her daughter, Susie, who used to be Ann's daughter, Becky, will come to terms with the shock of discovering through a *Post* article that Ann was looking for her daughter and will understand that Ann and Bob don't want to steal her, don't mean her any harm, just want to love her.

When Susie failed to return the Gordons' call or contact them, Ann and Bob returned to Wisconsin. That was the end of the story for the *Salisbury Post* and its readers.

But the Gordons continued to call the Halls and send Susie cards and letters. Ann's children also wrote to their "new sister." Susie threw away all of the correspondence and never replied. Like Mary, Susie had begun crying uncontrollably and both were having trouble sleeping. Susie even began sleepwalking, sometimes down two flights of stairs and into the yard which abutted the lake. She feared that the Gordons were trying to find her and became somewhat paranoid, hiding or running whenever she saw a car driving slowly in her neighborhood. Both Mary and Susie went for counseling. Then, in part because of Susie's sleepwalking by the lake, and in part to make themselves harder to find, the Halls finally moved.

Susie knows that some people in her situation would have reacted differently. Some adopted children, as well as some parents who give a child up for adoption, spend their lives in an anguished search for the biological parent or child. Others live in quiet fear that someday a

stranger will appear and turn their lives inside out. Susie did not want
to be tracked down. Ann felt that by looking for Susie, she could heal
what for her had been a seventeen-year heartache. It was a wrenching
dilemma.

But what was a newspaper doing in the middle of it?

"It was a hell of a story," says Steve Bouser, editor of the *Salisbury
Post*. "That's why I decided to stretch it across the top of the front
page." You did not have to be a journalist to recognize the human interest value in the saga of the abandoned carnival baby. But, Steve
Bouser is quick to point out, no one at the paper had any idea that the
story would have such real-life consequences. "To the degree that we
even thought about it, we assumed that Social Services would have followed the practice that they follow now, which is if they're going to
adopt a baby out, they adopt it somewhere far away," he explains.

Rose Post agrees. "It never, ever occurred to me in writing [the ar-
ticle] that the plea would have any impact whatsoever," she says.

But then there is the matter of the second article, detailing the
Gordons' attempt at a reunion and, most damaging, specifically identifying Mary and Susie Hall and their hometown. Steve Bouser was
out of town when the follow-up story ran, and says, "I'll be candid and
say that when I came back and saw the second story . . . I saw some
potential ramifications. . . . I did not think that we had invaded these
people's privacy, but I saw that there could be an argument there that
we had."

Rose Post, however, did not see it that way. After talking with the
Gordons, she asked around herself. According to Rose, several people
at the mill where Mary used to work and at the local bar knew all
about the Halls' "carnival baby." Clearly, at least some people knew
enough to call the Econo Motel with information after the first story
ran. Rose Post says that she even got a call from someone identifying
the Halls. It seemed to her that the second article had merely published facts that were common knowledge anyway. "I didn't view this
as a privacy issue ever," she says. "Because it was so much in the public domain."

"I hate them," Susie says of the *Salisbury Post*. Both Susie and Mary
Hall are convinced that the Gordons would not have found them without the far-reaching voice of the *Post*. They also feel they should have
had a say in whether the story was published. "They didn't come to
us or try to find us to find out if we wanted it printed or not," Susie

says. "They just up and put it all in the paper assuming they were doing a good deed, which they weren't. They just hurt us."

Yet even the Halls concede that everything the *Post* published was *true*. There may be questions of editorial judgment surrounding the decision to print either or both of the stories. But in the United States, under the First Amendment, is publishing an accurate account of an abandoned child *against the law*?

As it turned out, in North Carolina, the answer was up for grabs. Through a relative, the Halls hired a local attorney, Joe Millsaps, and sued the *Salisbury Post* for invasion of privacy. Their claim fell under the tort of public disclosure of private facts. Under this tort, the Halls had to prove that the *Post* had published highly offensive private information about them which was of no legitimate concern to the public. However, there was no privacy statute on the books in North Carolina and no court in that state had ever ruled on a private facts case. Thus, there was no precedent by which either the Halls or the *Post* could judge how likely they were to win or lose.

This lack of precedent is not as unusual as it may seem. Privacy law in general is unsettled in many states and the private facts tort in particular has proved troublesome. It is in the private facts tort that the right to privacy most directly challenges, and clashes with, the right to a free press, because it is here that a person can sue the press for publishing the truth.

THE UNITED STATES Supreme Court has considered private facts more often than the other privacy torts. However, the High Court has specifically refused to decide whether truthful publications must *always* be protected by the First Amendment. Rather, the Court has decided each case on its specific facts. And each case that has come before the Court has involved the quite narrow area of information that is already part of the public record.

For instance, in 1975 the Supreme Court held that a television station could not be sued for broadcasting the name of a rape-murder victim, which the station had obtained from public court documents. In 1977 and 1979, the Court held that newspapers could not be sued for printing the names of juvenile offenders when the papers had obtained the names from public officials or from attending public proceedings. And in 1989, the Court upheld a newspaper's right to publish a rape victim's identity, which the paper had learned from a document in the police press room, even though the victim's name had been included in the document by mistake. Although the press prevailed in each of these cases, the Supreme Court took care to confine its ruling to the specific facts presented. The Court stated: "We do not hold that truthful publication is automatically constitutionally protected."

Without a clear order from the High Court, fundamental questions remain unresolved. Some argue that the private facts tort is simply unconstitutional. The First Amendment is based on the concept that all speech should be allowed to compete in the marketplace of ideas. This theory has long protected all kinds of speech which many find repugnant, from Ku Klux Klan television programs to flag burning. Furthermore, in the much more developed area of defamation law, truth is an absolute defense. In defamation law, no matter how damaging information published about someone may be, if it is true, the press cannot be held liable. Hateful, even harmful, speech is simply the price we pay to live in a free society with an unfettered press. Thus, opponents of the private facts tort argue that any anguish caused by publication of private, but truthful, information is just part of the price of freedom.

On the other hand, a majority of states *have* recognized the private facts tort in some form. Many courts and commentators have accepted the argument that truth, in and of itself, is not always enough to protect the press and that some information, although truthful, does not really contribute to the "marketplace of ideas." Most important, they point out, the First Amendment has never been held to be absolute. Therefore, when a free press comes up against another important right—the right to privacy—a balance must be struck.

Under the private facts tort, the balance between privacy and the press is struck by the "newsworthiness" test. This is the highest hurdle that a plaintiff must clear. To win a private facts case, the plaintiff must prove that the offensive and private information published about him is "not of legitimate concern to the public"—i.e., is "not newsworthy."

Defining "news" has proved no easier for the legal community than for anyone else. One thing, however, is clear: Courts take a very broad view. "News" is not confined to matters of government or national import, but includes just about anything that occurs in a public place, material meant merely to entertain or amuse, and the vast arena known as "human interest." For example, an early case in the 1940s involved a former child prodigy, W. J. Sidis, a famous mathematics whiz at age eleven who subsequently had a breakdown, dropped out of sight, and lived his adult life in squalor, determinedly fleeing the spotlight. Decades after his fame, *The New Yorker* magazine ran an article on Sidis' fate. A court later described the piece as "merciless in its dissection of intimate details of its subject's personal life" and "a ruthless exposure of a once public character, who has since sought and has now been deprived of the seclusion of private life." Nonetheless, the court found that the question of whether the former prodigy had fulfilled his early promise "possessed considerable popular news interest," and rejected Sidis' claim for invasion of privacy.

The "newsworthiness" issue has also thrown courts into some odd areas of consideration. For some reason, there are an unusual number of cases involving lapses in clothing covering genitalia. A 1964 case held that a photograph of a woman with her skirt blown up by a fun-house air jet was not "news." More recently, courts have gone the other way, holding that a Pittsburgh Steelers fan photographed at a game with his fly unzipped and a high school soccer player photographed running for a ball with his private parts exposed were both participating in newsworthy events and could not claim invasion of privacy. In a case once removed, for the same reasons a court dismissed the case of a man who tried to sue for invasion of privacy because he was photographed leaving a portable toilet at a public rally.

Even if the "not newsworthy" element is satisfied, there are two more tests under the private facts tort. A plaintiff must also prove that the information published about him was indeed "private." To the courts, asserting that something is a "private fact" does not necessarily make it so, as two California cases have made clear.

In a split second, in 1975, O. W. Sipple deflected a gun aimed at President Gerald Ford. The incident, of course, received intense nationwide news coverage. When the *San Francisco Chronicle* uncovered the fact that Sipple was homosexual, that information, too, became a part of the national story. Sipple, whose parents, brothers, and sisters were all unaware of his sexual orientation, sued for invasion of privacy. In rejecting Sipple's claim, the court noted that Sipple was actually prominent in the gay community, openly frequented gay bars, and had been featured in several gay publications. Thus, the court held that Sipple's homosexuality was not a "private" fact.

In contrast, there is the case of Rikki, a transsexual. Rikki was born Ricardo, a male, but at age thirty-three underwent surgery and assumed a new life as a female. She enrolled in college and was eventually elected the school's first female student-body president. An *Oakland Tribune* reporter discovered Rikki's secret, published it, and suggested that classmates "may wish to make other showering arrangements." The court held that Rikki's prior sexual identity was a private matter. In doing so, the court relied heavily on the extraordinary steps she had taken to conceal her past—lawfully changing her name, as well as changing her driver's license, Social Security files, and even her high school records. The court concluded that, unlike Mr. Sipple, Rikki had proved her sexual identity was indeed a "private fact."

Finally, under the private facts tort, the plaintiff's case must meet the same elusive standard that haunts the other privacy torts: The publication of the information must be "highly offensive to a reasonable person." As in the other privacy torts, that standard remains ambiguous, but apparently quite high. In one leading case, *Sports Illustrated* published an article on the sport of bodysurfing. The article featured the acknowledged daredevil of the sport, and described some of his leisure-time activities, including putting cigarettes out in his mouth, hurtling down stairs to impress women, and eating insects. A California court agreed that while the facts were "generally unflattering and perhaps embarrassing," they simply did not rise to the level of offensiveness required for a private facts claim.

EACH OF the private facts elements—offensiveness, newsworthiness, and the question of what is private—was at issue in the *Hall* case.

The *Salisbury Post* argued first and foremost that the circumstances of Susie Hall's adoption were not even private. The newspaper provided affidavits from four people who stated they had long known of Susie's past. Ann and Bob Gordon supplied an affidavit stating they had received between twenty and thirty calls at the Econo Motel from people who identified Susie Hall as the abandoned child. Certainly, enough people had called the motel to enable the Gordons to find the Halls. Thus, the *Post* argued, Susie's adoption was simply not a "private fact." The *Post* also asserted that the facts about the abandonment and adoption were not "highly offensive." Indeed, the paper claimed that, if anything, Mary Hall had been portrayed as a devoted mother and something of a hero. Finally, the *Post* argued that under the very broad definition of "newsworthiness," a story with such obvious human interest on an important social issue like adoption easily passed the test.

The Halls countered by saying they found it embarrassing and offensive that people now knew not only that Susie had been adopted but that she had been abandoned in such a bizarre manner. They also disputed the number of people who called the Econo Motel with knowledge of their story. In any event, they argued, a few people knowing or having some pieces of the story was a far cry from the whole community reading it on the front page of the local paper. As for "newsworthiness," the Halls simply did not consider their life story "news." They relied on North Carolina's law protecting the confidentiality of adoption records to demonstrate that the facts surrounding an adoption are not considered to be of legitimate concern to the public. Even if their story was newsworthy, they continued, their names and hometown were not.

The North Carolina trial court judge agreed with the *Post*. The court did not issue an opinion, but dismissed the case without a trial. Joe Millsaps promptly appealed to the intermediate-level court in North Carolina.

This time, a three-judge panel ruled that the case *should* go to trial. The Court of Appeals held first that there was a genuine question as to whether the *Post* stories were newsworthy. The court relied on the North Carolina statute protecting adoption records and the fact that the articles not only told the story but also specifically identified Susie and Mary Hall. With respect to the private nature of the information published, the court wrote: "The fact that a plaintiff may have spoken freely to a small, select number of people about a private matter" does not necessarily make the matter public. Finally, the court simply stated that a reasonable person may well find that the information published about the Halls was highly offensive. Hence, the Halls should be allowed to go to trial and have a jury decide their case.

For the *Post*, the decision was a disaster. The Court of Appeals seemed to accept a relatively narrow definition of "newsworthiness," but a broad definition of "offensiveness." What was worse, the opinion left all of these issues for a jury (as opposed to a judge) to decide. The specter of juries second-guessing editorial judgments about "news" was alarming, especially with potentially huge jury verdicts at stake. The *Post* immediately appealed to the North Carolina Supreme Court, expecting to reverse the judgment or at least narrow the language in the Court of Appeals opinion.

For their part, Joe Millsaps and the Halls were overjoyed. The intermediate court opinion was very favorable to them. Moreover, the court seemed to respond not only to their legal arguments but also to the emotional dimension of the case. The Halls thought they had a very good chance of persuading the state's highest court as well.

On October 6, 1988, the North Carolina Supreme Court issued its opinion. Both sides knew they were exploring an unsettled area of the law, but no one expected the court to do what it did. The court held not only that the Halls could not bring their case to trial but that no one could bring a private facts case against the media. The decision outlawed the private facts tort in North Carolina.

The court noted that the United States Supreme Court had declined to rule that truthful expression is *always* protected by the First Amendment. But in considering the competing arguments, the North Carolina Supreme Court concluded that the private facts tort is, "at the very best, constitutionally suspect." The court also found that North Carolina already recognized the tort of "intentional infliction of emotional distress," which could often be used to recover for the same type of injury. Thus, according to the court, any possible benefits to people like the Halls did not justify adopting another tort that punishes the media "for the typically American act of broadly proclaiming the truth."

It was the worst possible outcome for the Halls and Joe Millsaps. They knew they might not win, but they did not expect to lose the larger privacy point for all of North Carolina. Millsaps says, "The case makes bad law and you hate to be a part of that." The Halls could have sued again under the "emotional distress" tort, but they declined. Mary and Susie felt they could not afford another lawsuit, either financially or emotionally.

Steve Bouser, the editor of the *Salisbury Post*, felt that the court had ruled the only way it could in order to allow journalists to do their jobs. He was greatly relieved that neither he nor other members of the media in North Carolina would have to worry about juries second-guessing their editorial judgment as to what is "news." But he concedes that the case had an impact on him. "The court ruled the right way in *Hall v. Post*, but there was always a certain uneasiness," Bouser says now. "It did open our eyes in a sobering kind of way to the impact you can have on people's lives in what seems like an innocent story."

Passing Judgments

AN INVESTIGATIVE REPORT on a county home published in the *Des Moines Register* described forced sterilizations of women, specifically identifying one of the women by name. The woman (who had not been contacted about the article) had since left the home and for years had been living a new life with new friends who knew nothing of her prior residence, or the sterilization. The woman conceded that the subject of the article was newsworthy, but argued that her specific identity was not. She sued for invasion of privacy. She lost.

An Iowa court held: "The identity of victims of involuntary sterilizations is a matter of legitimate public concern." The newspaper had a right to "name names" because it made the story more real to readers, "fostering perception and understanding."

Howard v. Des Moines Register, Iowa 1979

A WOMAN is kidnapped, taken to an apartment, stripped, and terrorized. The police—and the media—surround the apartment. The police eventually overcome the kidnapper and rush the woman, who clutches a dish towel in a futile attempt to conceal her nudity, to safety. A photograph of her escape is published in the next day's newspaper. She sued for invasion of privacy. A jury awarded her $1,000 in actual damages and $9,000 in punitive damages. On appeal, she lost.

A Florida court held that the event was newsworthy, "a typical exciting emotion-packed drama to which newspeople, and others, are attracted."

Cape Publications, Inc. v. Bridges, Florida 1982

A NEW JERSEY businessman and his wife were very happy to
purchase a new home. They were a lot less happy when, without their knowledge, their real estate agent gave the local
newspaper a press release. The *Asbury Park Press* published a
photograph of the house and an article on the sale under the
headline OCEAN TOWNSHIP ESTATE SOLD FOR ABOUT $250,000. The
article identified the purchaser, mentioned his job at a bank,
and described the interior of the home in detail. The couple
sued for invasion of privacy. They lost.

A New Jersey court held that the facts about the house
and sale were not really private and the publication was not
highly offensive.

   Bisbee v. Conover, New Jersey 1982

A SOUTH CAROLINA newspaper published a story on teenage
pregnancies. A sidebar article identified one boy as the father
of an "illegitimate" child. The reporter had reached the boy by
telephone, identified herself, and asked several questions, but
did not specifically request permission to name him in print.
The teenage father sued for invasion of privacy. A jury
awarded him $1,500 in actual damages and $25,000 in punitive
damages.

A South Carolina appeals court upheld the jury verdict and
the jury's finding that the item was not newsworthy.

   Hawkins v. Multimedia, Inc., South Carolina 1986

THE BODY of a murdered fourteen-year-old girl, partially de-
composed and wrapped in chains, was found in a Georgia
river. A newspaper photographer took pictures of the body,
which were later described by a court as "at close range, showing the gruesome effects of an atrocious crime, and displaying
the dead body . . . as an object of public curiosity." A Georgia
newspaper, *The Daily News Tribune*, not only published the photographs but also advertised that copies of the photos were for

sale. The paper invited the public to its offices to view the photographs firsthand and purchase them. The dead girl's parents sued for invasion of privacy. They lost.

A Georgia court held that, as reprehensible as the newspaper's actions might be, the recovery of a dead body was "newsworthy" and therefore there could be no cause of action for publication of private facts.

Waters v. Fleetwood, Georgia 1956

———

A SIX-YEAR-OLD girl was abducted in Orlando, Florida, in 1985. Nearly three years later, the family was notified that the police had found the little girl's sundress, along with a child's skull. The remains were identified as that of the missing girl. The family held memorial services for their daughter. On the day of the services, a reporter from Channel 2 News went to the police and asked to see the child's skull. For the benefit of the cameraman, the reporter staged having the police chief remove the skull from a box and tilt it for a close-up. The reporter then called her news producer and told her she had footage of the child's skull. The producer and news anchorman vehemently objected to using the videotape, saying it would be offensive to the community, as well as to the family. They were overruled by the news director, who declared, "Fuck it! We are going to run it."

The reporter submitted her segment from the field, and it ran without review by anyone at Channel 2. The piece began with an emotional story on the memorial services and smiling pictures of the little girl when she was alive. The camera then zoomed in for a shot of the skull—a frontal close-up aimed directly at the camera—as the voice-over declared it to be that of the murdered girl. The child's unsuspecting family saw the broadcast and the girl's twelve-year-old sister ran from the room screaming, "That cannot be my sister!" Channel 2 staffers were so upset by the broadcast that one of them called the family to apologize, and even the news director admitted the piece was a mistake and did not run it again.

The family sued for invasion of privacy and "outrage,"

Florida's version of "infliction of emotional distress." A Florida court ruled that they could not proceed with their privacy claim because the discovery of the little girl's remains was "newsworthy." However, the court held that the family could go to trial on the claim of "outrage," declaring the television station's actions to be "beyond all possible bounds of decency."

Armstrong v. H&C Communications, Florida 1991

A TEENAGE GIRL was abducted from New York City and brought, unconscious, to an apartment in Yonkers, New York. When she awoke, she was repeatedly raped and sodomized by two males over several hours. The girl was aware that the assailants were videotaping the violent assault. Two men were later arrested for the crime and the videotape was seized at their home.

The trial of the men was held in open court and all parties, spectators, and members of the media knew when the tape would be shown. However, the courtroom was small and, with the videotape machine positioned for the jury's benefit, only a few of the spectators would get a clear view of the tape. Several members of the media objected and demanded that the video be shown so that the entire courtroom could see. One media representative went immediately to a higher court on another floor, hoping to get someone to intervene. The trial judge declared that "court business gets priority" and that the tape would be shown to the jury in open court without any special setup for the benefit of others. The tape was shown twice in this manner. In addition, an enhanced version of the audio portion of the tape was played in open court and plainly heard by everyone in the room.

Gannett Suburban Newspapers and NBC both filed papers requesting that the videotape be made available to them for viewing so that they might further educate the public about the case. CBS filed papers requesting the right to copy the audio portion of the tape for "possible broadcast," offering to mask the victim's voice.

A New York court denied all of the requests. The court

said the media wanted access to "a grisly pornographic portrayal of thirteen forcible sexual acts perpetrated upon . . . an unwilling victim of tender age . . . shown in color with audio." The court noted the girl's courage in agreeing to go forward with the prosecution knowing that she would not only have to testify in "lurid detail" but also endure having the tape shown in open court. Given these facts, the court held that even in the face of the First Amendment, "viewing by only one additional unnecessary person would be an unconscionable further intrusion upon the victim's privacy rights."

People v. Colon and Cardona, New York 1992

MILLER v. NBC

The Case of the Televised Death

L ATE ON October 30, Dave and Brownie Miller were winding up a day in their Los Angeles apartment. In their fifties, the Millers were happily settling into a new phase of their lives. Their two children were now grown and off on their own. Dave and Brownie had sold the family house and bought a more practical two-bedroom duplex apartment. They had plenty of friendly neighbors and their children were nearby. Their son, Norm, lived north of Los Angeles, in San Rafael. Their daughter, Marlene, lived south, in Laguna Beach. She was married to Tom Belloni, an artist, and had two children of her own: an eighteen-month-old daughter and a son just shy of his fifth birthday.

The Millers relished their role as grandparents. Dave called his grandson every day to chat. In fact, Marlene and Tom and the kids had recently been for a visit.

Now Dave and Brownie were preparing for bed. Suddenly, Dave Miller collapsed to the floor. Brownie ran to her husband's side, screaming for help. A neighbor, hearing the screams, vaulted up the stairs of the Millers' duplex apartment and, seeing Brownie cradling her unconscious husband, dialed 911. It seemed the police arrived instantly. More neighbors ran to help. Then, just minutes later, two paramedics were rushing up the stairs and into the Millers' bedroom.

Right behind the paramedics, with camera and sound rolling, came a crew from the local NBC-TV station. The television crew, led by producer Ruben Norte, had been riding with the paramedics for an upcoming series on emergency medical services in Los Angeles. The KNBC crew was with the paramedics when the call came in about an apparent heart attack.

In the Miller bedroom, the paramedics immediately swung into action, placing an oxygen mask over Dave Miller's face and performing cardiopulmonary resuscitation (CPR). The police stepped aside. A frantic Brownie Miller and her neighbors were ushered out of the room. The only people in the bedroom with Dave Miller were the paramedics trying to save his life—and the television crew.

The year was 1979, before Big Brother took the form of a camcorder and ostensibly private moments began playing to a nationwide audience. Brownie Miller, one hand clutching her waist, the other covering her mouth in horror, peered around the bedroom door at her stricken husband. She did not even realize that the television people were there.

Then, as suddenly as it all began, Dave Miller was placed on a stretcher and whisked down the stairs, a paramedic running alongside pounding on Miller's heart. The stretcher was put in the ambulance. One paramedic and the KNBC cameraman and soundman jumped in. The ambulance rushed off to the hospital, siren screaming. Brownie Miller, dazed and frightened, stumbled to a car to follow her husband.

"I'll never forget the call I got at that time," says Marlene Belloni. "It was about 11:35 at night. Johnny Carson had just come on. We got the call and it was from one of my parents' neighbors who said my dad was very sick and I should come."

Marlene and Tom put their two sleeping children in the car and drove the one and a half hours from Laguna Beach to Los Angeles. They arrived at the Millers' apartment shortly after 1 a.m. Marlene's uncle answered the door.

"He looked at me and just started to cry," Marlene recalls. "And I knew my dad was dead." Dave Miller had died of a heart attack at the age of fifty-nine.

Someone called Marlene's brother, Norm. Throughout the night and the next day, other family members and friends were notified. "I was real close to my dad," says Marlene. "Tom was real close to my dad. So it was really . . . it was so hard." It was hardest of all on Brownie Miller. She had been married to Dave Miller for thirty-four years and now, at the age of fifty-five, she was suddenly alone.

The Bellonis stayed with Brownie for a few days and then returned to Laguna Beach to begin what Marlene calls "a difficult grieving process." She telephoned the doctor she trusted most. "He was our family doctor for years and years and years," Marlene explains. She talked with him about her father's death and the doctor assured Marlene that Dave Miller had probably died swiftly. "He said, 'Don't worry,' " Marlene recalls. "It was just quick and fine." That made both Marlene and Tom feel better. They celebrated their son's fifth birthday, and within a few weeks the Bellonis' lives slowly began to slip back into the usual routine. Tom went back to work on his art. Marlene returned to keeping the books for Tom's work and looking after their son and daughter.

Then, on November 19, about three weeks after Dave Miller's death, Tom was giving the children a bath while Marlene was in the bedroom watching the local six o'clock news on television. Marlene was only half paying attention to the broadcast when she heard the reporter talking about paramedics trying to save a fifty-nine-year-old man. "And I'm thinking, 'That's weird,' " Marlene recalls. She looked up at the television. "Then all of a sudden they kind of panned up a staircase, like going upstairs, and 'Oh!'

"I saw something on the wall, it was . . . my parents have this Hebrew saying on the wall in Scripture, and then it was like somebody just hit me. And then they walked in and you could see how they—oh, it gives me a chill—how they panned over the room and you could see my mom real quick. And then when they got into the bedroom, you saw them working."

Marlene had immediately recognized her parents' home and her mother. Then she saw her father dying as the paramedics pumped his bare chest. Marlene screamed for Tom and fled the room. Tom ran into the bedroom and over to the television set as several paramedics discussed the flaws in the Los Angeles emergency medical services system. Marlene was shaking, pacing back and forth in the hallway. When she thought enough time had passed and the segment was over, she went back into the bedroom. On television, the paramedics were wheeling a gurney out to the ambulance, and Marlene recognized two distinctive tattoos on her father's arms.

"Then I went hysterical again," she says. "Tom was holding me and he finished watching over my shoulder." As the experts debated how to improve L.A.'s emergency medical services, a picture of Dave Miller in the ambulance, a paramedic pumping on his chest, filled the screen. Miller was wheeled into the hospital, down a corridor, and into the emergency room. The reporter stated that the paramedics had worked on the stricken man for "nearly two hours" but could not save his life.

When the segment ended, Tom and Marlene were stunned. How on earth had Dave Miller's death ended up on television? Clearly, a television camera had been in the bedroom with the paramedics. But how did it get there? Why didn't anyone call them to ask permission to show the footage on television? Marlene called KNBC and said she wanted to talk to the person in charge of the segment on Los Angeles paramedics.

Ruben Norte was in the newsroom after the six o'clock broadcast when he received a telephone call. He recalls: "There was one call from a woman who said that she thought that one of the people in the paramedic story was her father. There was no hysteria . . . and I told her I didn't know who the person was . . . and that was it. It was a very short phone call among many phone calls, which is kind of a common thing. People call to say, 'I think that's my Uncle Joe that was interviewed today.' It was that kind of call."

"I was hysterical," Marlene says. "I was upset. He *knew* I was upset. I was crying and I just let him have it. 'How could you do that? How insensitive.' I just went on and on." Marlene recalls that she told Norte it was cruel to have filmed and then broadcast her father's death. "I said that it was very hurtful and that if any of my family members were to see it, it would be very hurtful, that it was just awful." She says that she asked Norte not to show the segment again. Marlene recalls that he replied that he would "look into it."

In the meantime, Marlene called her mother. "I know how she reacts to things," Marlene says, "and she would have been absolutely devastated [to see the KNBC piece]. I started out to explain to her and keep her calm, and said that there was something that I had to tell her, that I didn't want her to watch the news, that Daddy was on the news."

Brownie Miller was confused. How could the newspeople have pictures of her late husband? Why would they want to show them? Marlene explained all that she knew and just warned her mother not to watch the news.

That night, Marlene and Brownie stayed away from the television and Tom watched the eleven o'clock news on KNBC. He saw the same segment from the earlier broadcast, including the portions shot in the Miller home. The Bellonis' phone began to ring with calls from family members and friends who had seen the broadcast and recognized Dave Miller as the heart attack victim.

Marlene says that she called Ruben Norte again, complaining that they were still showing the footage of her father. "He didn't even apologize, really," Tom says. "We got this feeling from him that we were bothering him."

According to Ruben Norte, he reviewed the film footage and concluded that the heart attack victim was not identifiable. Ruben also says that he did not receive a second call from the Bellonis. "There was *one* phone call."

Brownie Miller did not want to risk seeing the segment featuring her husband. She did not watch the news all week. But one morning, around 10:30, she was flipping through the television channels looking for a soap opera when a promotional spot came on for an upcoming special on CPR. The station was KNBC. There, briefly, was her home, her bedroom, and her husband, dying. Brownie screamed and turned off the set.

By this point, Brownie and Marlene were absolutely certain that their privacy had been invaded. Through a friend, they hired a lawyer and sued KNBC and Ruben Norte for invasion of privacy. They could not believe that the members of the media thought they could get away with acting the way they had.

In a clear illustration of the gulf that sometimes exists between the press and the public it serves, over at KNBC the producers could not believe they were being sued. Tom Capra, news director of KNBC at the time, says, "We were doing a public service and all of a sudden this lady rises up and files a suit against us. . . . This one was like taking pictures of a swimming pool and an alligator comes up and bites your leg."

At the time, there was controversy surrounding emergency medical care in the Los Angeles area. Indeed, some asserted that an inadequate system was costing lives. KNBC had decided to devote a weeklong series to this important issue. According to the KNBC piece in which Dave Miller appeared, more than thirty paramedic services were operating in the Los Angeles area without any oversight. Even routine performance statistics were not compiled. The piece also included paramedics and members of their families discussing the terrible emotional and physical toll of a job that did not offer the same benefits as that of a police officer or firefighter.

In preparation for the series, Ruben Norte had researched the Los

Angeles emergency medical services for weeks, including arranging to ride along with the paramedics. In 1979, unlike today, "ride-alongs" were rare. Ruben says that he accompanied the camera and sound technicians in part to oversee the unusual operation, and especially to make sure the crew did not interfere with the paramedics' lifesaving work.

Before the call to the Miller home, Ruben and his crew had been riding with the emergency team for two days. They had entered more than ten private residences with the paramedics. Ruben says that about half the time people would ask what they were doing, that he would tell them, and that no one seemed to mind.

Always, he says, the focus was on the paramedics. "The victims were incidental to the story. So there was no reason to identify the victims or even really worry about who they were because we were much more interested in the work that these guys were doing." In the Miller bedroom, the crew tried to shoot the paramedics working on Dave Miller without showing Miller's face. And Ruben made sure that the final edited version did not reveal the heart attack victim's face.

Most important of all to Ruben, while they were in the Miller home, *no one asked them to leave.* Ruben says that "of course" he would have left if anyone had asked him to; indeed, he is offended by the question. But three men with video equipment were in the bedroom with the paramedics the entire time and nobody objected to their presence.

At the time of the lawsuit, Ruben recalled: "There was a woman in the hallway, which was outside of the bedroom where the heart attack victim was. I do remember seeing a woman there. I didn't speak to her." But neither the woman nor anyone else in the apartment told the television crew that they should not be there.

"Common-sense decency should tell them they shouldn't be there," says Tom Belloni. The Bellonis were amazed that the people from KNBC thought otherwise. Why *would* the television crew be welcome there? Who would want strangers in their bedroom observing a loved one's death, let alone strangers with cameras?

As for the argument that no one told them to leave, the Bellonis call it "ridiculous." Marlene says that her mother is a frail and emotional woman who obediently left the room where her husband lay because the professionals had told her to. The Bellonis thought it was unreasonable to expect even a strong person to deal with her husband's dying moments and at the same time sort the film crew from the emergency medical crew, ask them why they were there, and demand that they leave. Marlene and Tom thought KNBC had it backwards. The issue was not that no one told them to leave, but that no one invited them in.

But, Tom Capra says, it is difficult to see how the television crew's presence had harmed the Miller family. "I'm just amazed because we did no damage, we caused no problems for her, she didn't even know we were there. And she still brought a lawsuit. . . . *The woman never knew the crew was in her apartment.* How did her rights get violated?"

Marlene says that their privacy was invaded simply because the crew entered the Miller home without permission, even though, under the stress of the moment, no one realized they were there. She says it is "eerie" to think that someone has been in your bedroom without your knowing it. Furthermore, the broadcast of the footage of her father's death was extremely disturbing to both her and her mother. Out of the blue, Marlene was confronted with her father's last moments on television, and the image was not the one she had set in her mind.

"You think they die nicely," Marlene says. Her call to the family doctor had seemed to confirm that. "And then they're going through this whole dramatic thing of how they're pumping on him and working on him." When the newscaster talked of how long the paramedics tried to save the heart attack victim, Marlene thought, "My God, was he awake? Did he know what was happening?"

"It was probably really awful for her," Tom Capra says. "I understand that. She probably had a terrible experience and I'm sorry she did. But I think the series did a lot more good than it's ever been given credit for." According to Capra and Norte, the paramedic series exposed a lot of shortcomings in the way emergency medical services in Los Angeles were handled and led to some improvements in a system responsible for saving lives. They say that in the Millers' case, as in many cases involving the First Amendment, the harm suffered by some individuals is outweighed by the public benefit that results from a free and vigilant press.

"Compared to my harm, my mom's harm, the family's harm," Marlene says, "there was no public good." The Bellonis say they are not naïve. They understand that actual, dramatic, life-or-death footage is very desirable in television. But they feel that KNBC could have presented the information about emergency medical care just as successfully without going into the Miller home. Talking to the paramedics and showing them at work on practice dummies would not be as dramatic, the Bellonis say, but it would still get the point across without risking harm to others.

Tom Capra and Ruben Norte disagree. "Yeah, it could have been done different ways," Ruben says. "But you're never gonna see [the paramedics'] lives unless you see them in action, under stress, doing fairly heroic stuff. You can hear them talk about it until hell freezes over and you'll never, ever get the feeling of being in that room with them," Ruben says. "That's what television does best."

"Fine," says Tom Belloni. "Then get *permission.*"

And so Brownie Miller and Marlene Belloni took KNBC and Ruben Norte to court. Both parties entered the fray certain that they were right, confident that they would win, and simply amazed at the other side's position.

Ruben Norte and KNBC had the First Amendment on their side. Indeed, a report on the operation of a city's emergency medical services is the kind of information at the core of First Amendment protection. The media is in its "watchdog" role, reporting on public employees doing their jobs.

On the other side, Brownie Miller and Marlene Belloni had their claim for invasion of privacy. It was only a tort in the face of KNBC's constitutional right, and usually, when a tort and a constitutional right conflict, the tort must give way. But the private place that Brownie Miller claimed had been invaded was her home—the sanctum sanctorum in American law.

In addition, what the crew had filmed in the Miller home was a man's death. Surely, Brownie Miller and the Bellonis thought, a man's dying moments are among the most private of all.

On this last point, the Millers and Bellonis were in for a surprise. At first glance, it would seem that Brownie and Marlene had a private facts claim based on the broadcast of the paramedic series and the promotional spots. It seemed that a private incident—Dave Miller's death in his home—had been publicized without consent. But the right to privacy is considered a *personal* right. The only person who can sue for an invasion of that right is the person whose privacy has actually been invaded. If the alleged invasion of privacy is an article or photograph published in a newspaper, then in most instances, the only person who can sue is the subject of the article or photo. Of course, if it happens to be a photograph of a dead body, the only person who can sue for invasion of privacy is not around to file a claim.

By the time of the *Miller* case, there had been many instances in which relatives sued after the publication or distribution of photographs regarding a loved one's death. Some of the situations were gruesome, all were distressing, but none could give rise to a cause of action for invasion of privacy. In New York, a three-year-old boy and his two-year-old sister suffocated when they trapped themselves in the family refrigerator. In the commotion that followed, a freelance photographer entered the home, photographed the children's bodies, and sold the pictures to the newspapers. In New Mexico, grieving parents discovered that the local police had "improperly circulated" photographs of their murdered daughter's nude body. And in Florida, police videotaped the autopsy of a teenage boy without permission, then brought the tape home to show to friends at a "party." In none of these cases could surviving family members sue for invasion of privacy.

As each court pointed out, there are serious practical and policy reasons to limit such claims. First, this issue highlights one of the most vulnerable aspects of privacy claims: The damage alleged is almost always intangible emotional harm. In such cases, courts are wary of spurious claims.

Most important, if claims based on the invasion of another's privacy were allowed, it would be nearly impossible for courts to limit who would be allowed to sue. Where would the right end? With immediate family members? What about dear friends who may, in fact, be closer to the subject of unwanted publicity? In the *Miller* case, would Marlene be allowed to sue as well as Brownie? What about Marlene's husband, Tom? The aunt and uncle who came the night of Dave Miller's death? The specter of a nearly unlimited right to sue for emotional damages has been deemed by most courts to be too great a threat to the First Amendment. Thus, courts limit the right to sue for unwanted publicity to the actual subject of the publication, even if that person is dead.

Hence, Brownie and Marlene were told that they could try to assert a claim for invasion of privacy based on the *broadcast* of the paramedics working on Dave Miller. But in the opinion of most courts, the broadcast alone could not be considered an invasion of either Brownie's or Marlene's privacy. As in the other such cases, the only one who possibly had a right to sue for invasion of privacy based upon the broadcast was dead. (However, also as in the other cases, the relatives sometimes could recover under another legal theory, usually "infliction of emotional distress." So Brownie and Marlene asserted that claim in addition to their privacy claims.)

There remained the issue of the film crew's physical presence in the Miller home. This could be grounds for a traditional invasion-of-privacy claim. But again, only the one whose private space is invaded—the owner of the home—is allowed to sue. Brownie, not Marlene, might have a cause of action.

Brownie Miller's claim for invasion of privacy fell under the intrusion branch of the four privacy torts. The tort of intrusion is usually defined as "intentionally intruding, physically or otherwise, upon the solitude or seclusion of another or his private affairs . . . in a manner that is highly offensive to a reasonable person." As the definition indicates, intrusion does not necessarily require a physical invasion of another's private space. For example, wiretapping, eavesdropping, and persistent harassing telephone calls could all be grounds for an intrusion claim. When, as in Brownie's case, the alleged invasion is indeed physical, then intrusion resembles what we commonly think of as "trespass." However, to win a claim for intrusion, a plaintiff must still prove that bugaboo from the other privacy torts—that the intrusion was "highly offensive to a reasonable person."

Could an intrusion into a home be "highly offensive" when the owner of the home did not even know the intruder was there?

On April 24, 1985, after nearly five years of legal wrangling, a California trial court threw out all of Brownie Miller and her daughter's claims. The court noted the rule that one cannot recover for publicity about another, and dismissed all of the claims based on the broadcast of the paramedic series and promotional spots. Then the court dismissed Brownie's claims for intrusion, trespass, and infliction of emotional distress based on the physical entry into her home. The court decided that the widow had suffered no "actual harm" purely as a result of the unauthorized entry.

"Right!" said Tom Capra. The court had ruled exactly as KNBC had expected.

Brownie and the Bellonis were staggered. Strangers had come into a *home*, filmed a private man's death, and broadcast it—all without permission. Now a court had said the man's family could not even go to trial. Brownie and Marlene hired a new attorney, Mitch Ezer, to appeal the trial court's opinion.

With respect to the KNBC crew's presence in the Miller home, Ezer argued that Brownie's claim for intrusion should proceed to trial. Ezer argued that reasonable people may well believe that the unauthorized entry into her home was "highly offensive," even if she did not know the crew was there at the time. Brownie should at least be allowed to let a jury decide on the offensiveness of the actions.

Ezer also tried to find a way for both Brownie and Marlene to re-cover for the broadcast itself. He argued that the broadcast was a "nonphysical" intrusion, like eavesdropping or harassing phone calls. Ezer acknowledged the reluctance of courts to allow claims by rela-tives based on publications about a deceased loved one. However, he suggested a way in which the court could limit such claims and still al-low Brownie and Marlene to recover. Only immediate relatives should be allowed to recover, he said, and only if the footage was gathered in an unlawful manner in the first place. For example, Ezer argued, foot-age of Dave Miller had been obtained by an unlawful entry into the Miller home.

KNBC strongly objected to the plaintiffs' argument that the broad-cast of Dave Miller's image could be considered an invasion of Brownie and Marlene's privacy. "Recovery for even the most grisly and tasteless depictions of relatives has been consistently denied," KNBC pointed out. The Millers could not, by some new theory of intrusion, indirectly do something they could not accomplish directly. They could not recover for the broadcast of the paramedic series in which neither of them appeared. Any other decision, KNBC argued, would have a di-sastrous effect on the First Amendment protection of the press.

On December 18, 1986, the intermediate-level court in California, the Court of Appeals, made its decision. First, the court chose not to adopt the plaintiffs' new theory to allow recovery based on the broad-cast. The court followed the general rule and held that neither Brownie nor Marlene could sue for invasion of privacy based on the broadcast of Dave Miller's image.

Then it was Tom Capra and Ruben Norte's turn to be surprised. Regarding the television crew's presence in the Miller bedroom, the court lashed out at the media defendants. The court noted that there were few cases to guide them in evaluating whether KNBC's actions were indeed an "intrusion" under the law. "Probably," the court wrote, "because even today most individuals . . . do not go into private homes without the consent of those living there; not only do widely held notions of decency preclude it, but most individuals understand that to do so is either a tort, a crime, or both."

The court said that Ruben Norte's crew had clearly intruded phys-ically into Brownie Miller's private space. Noting that Ruben had tes-tified that he had seen "a woman in the hallway," the court wrote:

"Not only was the 'woman in the hallway' Dave Miller's wife, the hallway was a part of her home, a place where NBC had no right to be without her consent." The only real question, according to the court, was whether the unauthorized entry was "highly offensive to a reasonable person." If it was, then Brownie had made out a case for invasion of privacy under the intrusion branch of the four torts.

The court said it was mindful of Ruben Norte's testimony that he and his crew had entered numerous homes without objection. But the court did not think that proved the crew's conduct was inoffensive. Instead, the court wrote, "It illustrates, perhaps, a widespread loss of certainty about where public concerns end and private life begins [when] individuals are confronted by aggressive media representatives."

The court concluded that "reasonable people could construe the lack of restraint and sensitivity NBC producer Norte and his crew displayed as a cavalier disregard for ordinary citizens' rights of privacy . . . and as highly offensive conduct." Thus, Brownie Miller could proceed to trial and have a jury decide whether her privacy had been invaded. (The court also said that Brownie could proceed on her trespass and infliction of emotional distress claims.)

Both sides had mixed feelings about the opinion. Brownie and the Bellonis were happy with the court's decision to allow Brownie to proceed to trial for the physical intrusion into her home. But Marlene had again been told that she had no claim for invasion of privacy. "I thought my harm was much more devastating [than the court recognized]," Marlene says. They appealed the part of the opinion which ruled that Brownie and Marlene had no claim for the broadcast alone.

KNBC and Ruben Norte were satisfied with that part of the opinion. But they thought that the court's language regarding the entry into the Miller home had "devastating Constitutional implications." They thought the court had failed to consider the practical difficulties of covering fast-breaking, emergency news. They feared that all sorts of news coverage of emergencies might now be called into question. For example, would news footage of attempts to rescue earthquake or fire victims from their damaged homes now be prohibited? KNBC, too, appealed to the Supreme Court of California.

But the case was starting to get expensive. Although the parties had been at it for six years, they were only at the beginning stages— deciding whether the plaintiffs could go to trial. There was still the prospect of a long trial, and appeals from that, before it would be over. The two sides sat down to settlement discussions.

Under the agreement they reached, neither side may reveal the amount for which the parties eventually settled. Mitch Ezer says, "I can tell you that it was a significant sum. I can also tell you that it was less than I thought the case was worth, significantly less, for a very good but rather bizarre reason." During settlement discussions, Brownie Miller had told her attorney that she simply could not appear at a trial. Several years after her husband's death, Brownie was still too distraught by the events to testify in public. Without Brownie, Mitch Ezer did not have much of a case. "But NBC and the defense attorneys did not know that she was not going to appear," Ezer says. "In effect, it was a game of bluff poker at that settlement conference."

To KNBC, an amount that was "significantly less" than the Millers might otherwise get was beginning to look pretty good. It is always hazardous for media defendants to go to trial before juries, which sometimes hand out gargantuan damage awards to plaintiffs. Even if the jury award is eventually overturned on appeal, the process is costly. Settling seemed to be in KNBC's interest, too.

Thus, one of the very first cases involving a media "ride-along" ended with an intermediate court opinion in California. According to that court at least, "Others besides the media have rights, and those rights prevail when they are considered in the context of the events at the Miller home on October 30, 1979."

However, "ride-alongs" have become far more common now than they were at the time of the *Miller* case. According to Tom Capra, "Now all you have to do is stick your thumb out and hold your camera up." Indeed, entire television programs are based on "ride-alongs" like those in the *Miller* case. But one of the media's strongest arguments under the First Amendment is that lawsuits, especially successful ones, have a chilling effect on their work. Supposedly, a strongly worded opinion like that handed down in the *Miller* case would be chilling. So what happened?

"I really don't think this case has affected the way we do business," Tom Capra says. "Everybody in the newsroom is aware of the Brownie Miller case. Everybody knows about it. But I think most people believe that we were well within our own rights."

Passing Judgments

WHILE A Florida woman was away visiting a friend, a fire broke out in her home, killing her seventeen-year-old daughter. Fire and police officials at the scene invited news reporters and photographers into the burned-out home. The woman learned of her daughter's death from the newspapers, which ran an article on the fire and a photograph of the girl's "silhouette" left on the floor after her body was removed. The woman sued for trespass and invasion of privacy. She lost.

The Florida Supreme Court concluded that it was customary for the media to be invited, even into private property, where newsworthy events took place. Thus, because such activity was customary, there was no trespass or invasion of privacy.

Florida Publishing Company v. Fletcher, Florida 1976

———

AN INVESTIGATOR for the Humane Society of Rochester, New York, had a search warrant to enter a woman's home and seize any animals found in an unhealthy condition. The investigator called all three local television stations and invited them to come along. The investigator and several reporters and cameramen entered the woman's house and the newspeople filmed the search of the home—all over the woman's repeated objections. She sued for trespass and won.

A New York court expressly rejected the Florida court's reasoning that such actions could be justified as "customary." The New York court wrote: "What must be remembered is that news people do not stand in any favored position" and must respect private property like everyone else.

Anderson v. WROC-TV, New York 1981.

A LOCAL television news crew in Oregon accompanied police executing a search warrant for narcotics and stolen vehicles. The police, and the television crew, entered the home. The crew filmed the search, the couple that lived there as well as their four young children, and broadcast the footage on the evening news. The couple sued on behalf of themselves and their four children, claiming invasion of privacy. They lost.

A jury found that the intrusion into the family's home was not "highly offensive to a reasonable person" and an Oregon court upheld the verdict.

Magenis v. Fisher Broadcasting, Inc., Oregon 1990

———

THE UNITED STATES Secret Service entered a New York apartment with a search warrant looking for evidence of credit card fraud. The Secret Service agent in charge wore a microphone for the benefit of a CBS crew which he had invited along to film the raid. The suspect was not home, but the camera crew filmed while the agent in charge interrogated the man's wife. She repeatedly objected to the camera and attempted to cover her face and that of her young son, who was hiding behind his mother and crying. The crew also recorded the contents of the family's drawers and shelves while the agent narrated the details of the crime of credit card fraud. No evidence of any crime was found in the apartment. The only material seized was a family photograph, which CBS also filmed. The man was later indicted. He sued CBS to obtain the tape of the search to use in his defense and a federal court ordered the network to turn over the tape. The man's wife then sued on behalf of herself and her son for violation of their privacy rights. A federal court judge held that they could proceed to trial. He declared that the only reason CBS was present at the search was to "titillate and entertain others," and that "CBS had no greater right than that of a thief to be in the home."

Ayeni v. CBS, Inc. et al., New York 1994

BRAUN v. FLYNT

The Case of the Swimming Pig
(False Light)

RALPH STOOD at the center of the diving board. On cue, he trotted to the end of the board, leaped, and, with legs outstretched, ears pricked up, and tail curled, executed a perfect swan dive deep into the pool. Ralph was a diving pig. He surfaced and swam eagerly to feed from a baby bottle held by his trainer, Jeannie Braun. Ralph and Jeannie were the headline act at Aquarena Springs amusement park in San Marcos, Texas.

San Marcos is a small community about forty-five minutes' drive south of Austin. Aquarena Springs is the town's biggest, and only, entertainment center. In the 1970s, the park was open every day of the year except Christmas, and during the summer it attracted two thousand to three thousand visitors daily. Among other programs, Aquarena Springs featured an underwater show. Set against a background of a colorful volcano, the act included an underwater ballet, ducks that dove for food, a "witch doctor," and Ralph. Visitors could watch from seats alongside the large pool or from a submerged submarine.

Jeannie Braun grew up in Lockhart, Texas, seventeen miles south of San Marcos. She started working at Aquarena in the late 1960s at age nineteen, as a swimmer. She was one of several women who, using air hoses or holding their breath, would execute ballet sequences, eat, drink, and perform other stunts underwater, sometimes eleven times a day. Jeannie worked her way up to become show director, responsible for training the swimmers, both human and porcine. The

191

underwater show was the biggest draw at Aquarena Springs and Ralph its most celebrated performer.

Actually, there were five Ralphs at any given time. Jeannie would begin training piglets when they were just three days old. "I'd raise 'em," she says. "They'd be in my office when I was doing schedules. They would just follow me all over. That's how we got 'em to go in the water. Then to teach 'em to swim, you put your hand under their stomachs, hold 'em up, and they'd start paddling their little feet, going after the bottle."

Ralph's career really took off when his original trainer, Barbara Backus, appeared on the television programs "To Tell the Truth" and "What's My Line." Ralph himself later appeared in a segment on Charles Kuralt's television show. Aquarena Springs distributed publicity brochures, glossy photographs, and postcards featuring Ralph. One of the most popular postcards showed Ralph in midair, in good form, diving toward Jeannie Braun in the pool with a baby bottle.

For nearly ten years, Jeannie could not have been happier with her job. "Oh, I loved it!" she says. "I went a lot of places with Ralph. We promoted tourism. And we were in the River Parade in San Antonio on a float with Ruby Begonia, the famous turkey."

Then, one day in 1977, Jeannie was driving from work to her home in Lockhart when she stopped for gas. "I had never, ever, ever in my life gotten gas at this particular place," she says. "It was in a little town called Maxwell." Jeannie filled her gas tank, then walked into the convenience store to pay.

A man she had never met walked up to Jeannie and said, "Hey, I know you, your picture's in *Chic* magazine." Jeannie replied that she had never heard of the magazine. But the man persisted. "You know, you know," he said. "Your picture is in *Chic*. Do you train swimming pigs for a living?" When Jeannie said she did, the man responded, "I knew it was you. I recognized your face. C'mere, I'll show it to you." The stranger went to the back of the store and pulled out a copy of *Chic* magazine (properly pronounced "sheek," but with the possible double pronunciation intentional).

"[This man] went and got the magazine," Jeannie recalls. "And I stood there because I was really terrified. I thought something is going to happen, my picture is not in that magazine. My legs were like jelly, I couldn't untrack. I was petrified. And he was thumbing through these pictures. I was raised in private Catholic school and I had never seen anything like this. And I was terrified, I didn't know what he had in mind. I thought something horrible was going to happen to me. He flipped through that book and my picture was in that book. I didn't believe it. I stood there like a dummy."

The postcard featuring Ralph and Jeannie was printed in a regular *Chic* feature entitled "Chic Thrills." The section collected approximately twenty blurbs and photographs, mostly sexual in nature, and tried to put a humorous spin on them. The "Chic Thrills" section in which Jeannie and Ralph appeared included a piece called "Mammaries Are Made of This" about men sprouting breasts, a photograph of a naked woman advertising "Bellybuttons" (a $4.98 plastic disc that "glues to your lady's navel" and carries suggestive messages), and a report on an International Chicken Flying Meet described as "flipping the bird."

The Aquarena Springs postcard of Jeannie and Ralph was reproduced—without alteration—at the top of the third page of the "Chic Thrills" feature. The caption read:

Swine Dive: A pig that swims? Why not? This plucky porker performs every day at Aquarena Springs Amusement Park in bustling San Marcos, Texas. Aquarena staff members say the pig was incredibly easy to train. They told him to learn quick, or grow up to be a juicy ham sandwich.

Chic would later be described by a court as a "glossy, oversized, hard-core men's magazine." The magazine is published by Larry Flynt, who also publishes *Hustler*.

Apparently, the appearance of Jeannie and Ralph's picture in *Chic* was something of a fluke. In May of 1977, Henry Nuwer, editor of the "Chic Thrills" column, had been unable to get a hotel room in Austin. He ended up in San Marcos and happened upon Ralph and Jeannie's act. "Then I saw these postcards which struck my sense of humor," he said. "Then the whole idea of a swimming swine and the idea of a swine dive just struck me as a funny thing." Nuwer called Aquarena and requested negatives of Ralph. Jeannie had signed a release authorizing Aquarena to use pictures of her for publicity as long as the use was in "good taste." Not being familiar with *Chic*, Aquarena's publicity director asked about the nature of the magazine.

Here the stories diverge. Nuwer says he told Aquarena that *Chic* was a men's magazine specializing in men's fashion, travel, and humor. As for the idea of nudity, Nuwer says the issue "never came up." The Aquarena publicity director says Nuwer told her *Chic* was a fashion and travel magazine with the same readership as *Redbook* or *McCall's*. In response to Nuwer's request, Aquarena sent *Chic* several negatives of publicity photos and some additional information on Ralph.

Jeannie just looked at her photograph in *Chic* and, without saying a word, walked out of the store, got into her car, and drove straight home. She recalls, "My first feeling was, I couldn't believe it." Then she started getting angry. "I was getting madder and madder," she says. "I have never in my life been as mad as I was when I drove up my driveway." She found her husband, Ed, and said right out, "My picture is in a pornographic magazine." Ed could not quite believe it either, so the next day Jeannie found a copy of *Chic* and proved it.

"It was *real strange* the way people reacted," Jeannie says. No one in her family would talk about it with her. "My husband discussed it with my father," she says. "That's how *my* family is." She found out later that her stepson, who was in high school at the time, actually knew of the photograph in *Chic* before she did, but had been too embarrassed to bring it up. A cousin later told Jeannie that they, too, had found out, but were afraid to ask her about the photo in case she had actually consented to *Chic's* using it. Even at work, Jeannie says, people did not know how to react. "At Aquarena Springs, I almost felt like people were avoiding me. I don't know if it was my own self-consciousness about it, but I got a feeling people were making circles to avoid me."

Her relationships at Aquarena became more strained when Jeannie decided to take legal action. She wanted Aquarena to join her in a lawsuit against *Chic*, but the park's president tried to dissuade her. He pointed out that a lawsuit would only bring more publicity to the magazine, and said he did not want to spend the time and money on something they might well lose.

Jeannie's husband, Ed, was also against the idea. He was a man who simply "had no use for lawsuits." Jeannie did not care. "I said, 'This didn't happen to any of you, it happened to me, and I'm not going to take it.' " She hired a lawyer and sued *Chic* magazine and Larry Flynt for defamation and invasion of privacy.

At first, *Chic* tried to get the case dismissed, arguing that it was not even about defamation or privacy. Larry Flynt's attorneys asserted that the magazine had permission to publish the photographs. If anything, Aquarena might be able to sue *Chic* for misrepresenting the nature of the publication. Jeannie Braun, in turn, might be able to sue

Aquarena for carelessly allowing her photograph to be used in violation of the release. But, *Chic* argued, the magazine was answerable
only to Aquarena, not to Braun.

The court rejected *Chic's* argument, and because Aquarena chose
not to get involved, the issue of fraud and misrepresentation fell away.
The central issue became: Was the publication of Braun's photograph
in *Chic* defamatory and an invasion of privacy?

Jeannie's claim of invasion of privacy was based on the false light
privacy tort. False light is generally described as "giving publicity to a
matter concerning another that places that person in a false light that
is highly offensive to a reasonable person"—in short, creating a highly
offensive false impression of someone.

Of the four privacy torts, false light is probably the one least related to what one commonly thinks of as "privacy." The complaint is
not that something secret has been invaded or publicized, but that a
false impression has been created. Thus, the "privacy" that is protected
under false light is not confidential information or a private place, but
a person's very personality—"his image of himself."

False light actions are not necessarily limited to the media. For example, a shopkeeper who posts a sign falsely accusing a customer of
owing the store a large debt might be sued under a false light theory.
But because one of the elements of this branch of privacy is "publicity," the press is the most likely to be sued for false light.

Like the other privacy torts, false light has come under attack. One
major criticism is that it overlaps with other torts—most significantly,
the thorny laws of defamation. A person can sue for defamation if
false information is published about him and he can prove that the
falsehood harmed his reputation. Thus, both defamation and false light
require publication of false material. But defamation requires damage
to a reputation, whereas in false light the false publication need only
be "highly offensive" and cause great distress. Some critics are concerned that false light will be used when a case does not rise to the
level of defamation. This fear has led at least one state court to reject
the tort of false light altogether, and other states to question its
validity.

Nonetheless, a majority of states do recognize false light. Some
courts reconcile the overlap with defamation by treating false light as
just another way of saying defamation and requiring that all of the
same elements be proved. Others make the "highly offensive" standard

even higher than it usually is. And while most courts allow plaintiffs to bring both actions, false light and defamation, they allow only one recovery of money damages.

There is actually one quirky kind of false light case that is distinct from defamation. This is the rare instance in which the published falsehood is not disparaging; indeed, it may even be flattering. For example, the former baseball star Warren Spahn successfully sued over an unauthorized biography which, among other things, incorrectly stated that he had won a Bronze Star in World War II and wildly overromanticized his relationship with his wife and teammates. Although the description was flattering, it was not true. Spahn won his claim for invasion of privacy.

Some have suggested that because these flattering false light cases do not overlap with defamation, they should be the only kind of false light action recognized by the courts. Others argue that the flattering false light case is actually least justifiable. They question whether there is any true harm to the individual and worry that because the material is not derogatory, it raises no red flag which would warn the editor that extra care must be taken with the story.

However, those who support a false light theory of invasion of privacy point out that both kinds of cases—flattering and disparaging—provide an important protection for the press that the three other privacy torts do not. All false light cases, by definition, require that the plaintiff prove a false impression of him has been created. As in defamation, truth is an absolute defense. No matter how derogatory (or flattering) the published information may be, if it is true, false light provides no cause of action. (This resolves the biggest criticism of the private facts tort.)

Indeed, even some falsehoods published by the press are protected. The First Amendment has been interpreted to allow the media some room for errors so that it may realistically do its job without threat of a lawsuit. Therefore, inconsequential errors, like stating someone's age to be a year more than it actually is, would not be grounds for a lawsuit.

Even in the case of significant errors, there are still protections for the press. In the older, more developed area of defamation, there are two standards to be applied, depending on whether the subject of the press coverage is a public figure or a private person. A public figure is someone who is well known, such as a movie star or elected official, or someone who has been involved (even involuntarily) in a public event, such as a crime. The public figure suing for defamation has a higher standard to meet. He has to prove that the press either *knew* the disparaging information was false or was *recklessly indifferent* as to whether it was false or not. The private person has to prove only that the press was negligent, or careless, in publishing false information about him. The public figure has a higher standard because he has either sought the spotlight or been thrust there by some event important to the public. It is also thought that the public figure has better access to the media and can more easily rebut negative press coverage.

It is clear that this higher standard also applies to public figures claiming they have been placed in a "false light." However, it has not yet been determined by the Supreme Court what standard applies to *private* persons suing for false light. That makes a difference.

An Oklahoma man was shocked to see his photograph in a local newspaper illustrating a story about a mentally ill former schoolteacher who had committed a gruesome murder. The man's photograph had been submitted years earlier upon his high school graduation, and the newspaper inadvertently put it in the file for a psychotic murderer. The newspaper had clearly been careless in mixing up the pictures. But an Oklahoma court held that even though the man was a private person, the higher standard applied. The man could not prove that the newspaper either knew of the error or was reckless (which is worse than merely being careless) in publishing his photograph. So he lost his false light case. In other states, however, it may have been enough for the man to show that the newspaper was merely careless. Thus, editors and potential plaintiffs are often left guessing as to what standard will be applied to any given story.

The problem of uncertainty in false light is most apparent in the cornerstone of the tort: The false impression must be "highly offensive to a reasonable person." As always, there are an infinite number of ways in which the press can purportedly offend someone, creating a hodgepodge of examples that do not necessarily relate to one another. For example, a Georgia court held that it was not highly offensive to mistakenly publish an obituary, complete with date and time of funeral services, for a young woman who was still very much alive. And a Michigan court held that a newspaper's description of a hairdresser's style as the "blowtorch technique" was not highly offensive (and that the woman's proper remedy was to cancel her subscription, not to bother the courts).

In a case similar to Jeannie Braun's, a doctor and his wife were standing in an airport next to an enormous pile of boxes which did not belong to them when their photograph was taken without their knowledge. The picture was published in *Forbes* magazine with the caption: "Some Latins buy so much in Miami they've been known to rent an extra hotel room just to store the purchases." A Pennsylvania court held that the photo itself was not offensive and the use in *Forbes* did not make it otherwise.

However, in other cases similar to Braun's, certain uses of photographs have been held to be highly offensive. In fact, Larry Flynt, by virtue of the number of lawsuits against him, is almost single-handedly shaping the law in this area. The "Beaver Hunt" feature of *Hustler* is the standout. It has generated so many lawsuits that there is apparently now a consensus that publishing a nude photograph of someone without their consent is "highly offensive to a reasonable person."

Thus, Jeannie Braun's case raised a novel question: Does publishing an accurate and otherwise inoffensive photograph of a public performance *become* highly offensive because it is placed in a hard-core men's magazine?

Chic argued that there was simply nothing "false" or "highly offensive" about the material it published concerning Jeannie Braun. *Chic* had accurately reproduced a widely distributed postcard and written a lighthearted caption. All parties agreed that there was nothing offensive about the photograph, or even the caption, standing alone.

However, Jeannie Braun argued that the photograph had to be taken in the context of the "Chic Thrills" column and *Chic* magazine. According to Braun, the ordinary reader would receive a false and highly offensive impression of her character because her photograph had appeared in *Chic*. Braun claimed that the reader would believe she was "unchaste or promiscuous," or at least that she had consented to the publication, implying that she approved of the magazine and its depiction of women.

Chic countered that Braun's photograph in the magazine did not imply anything about her personality and that the average reader does not draw conclusions about a performer's character based on the periodical in which a publicity photo appears. This is clear, Flynt's attorneys argued, if you look to other publications. "Does somebody whose picture appears in *Time* magazine thereby imply that he or she has given permission for that picture to appear in the magazine . . . or that he or she agrees with the editorial policy of the magazine? I think the answer is clearly no."

Chic argued that, under the First Amendment, people taking part in public events could not sue simply because they did not like the magazine in which their photograph appeared. *Chic* stressed that Jeannie and Ralph performed in front of hundreds of people daily and had been featured in many articles, parades, and television programs. Indeed, the very postcard reproduced in *Chic* was sold at Aquarena Springs and distributed all over the world. *Chic* said Jeannie Braun was a public figure who could not expect to keep her public performance private.

Flynt's attorneys compared *Braun* to a similar case that clearly held there was no claim for invasion of privacy. The performer Ann-Margret had sued when a partially nude still photograph from her recent motion picture appeared in *Celebrity Skin* magazine without her consent. In that case, a New York court held that "when an individual consents to be viewed in a certain manner during the course of a public performance . . . it cannot then be argued that a subsequent faithful reproduction of that appearance constitutes an invasion of privacy."

Chic argued that the precedent set in Ann-Margret's case must prevail. To hold otherwise for Jeannie Braun would present a grave threat to the First Amendment. If performers could sue simply because they did not want to appear in *Chic*, then they could sue because they did not want to appear in *Rolling Stone*, or *The New York Times*, or any other publication. The First Amendment had to protect all publications equally.

Jeannie Braun responded by arguing that anyone trying to sue under false light would still have to prove that use of a photo in a particular publication created a highly offensive false impression. In her case, Braun emphasized her distress and humiliation and how she "felt like crawling in a hole and never coming out." She described how the publication strained her relations at work, eventually prompting her to leave her job. She said that although she took part in a public performance, she was a private figure for the purposes of the First Amendment and entitled to greater protection than public figures.

Braun also voiced a common complaint of plaintiffs in lawsuits against the media. She spoke of a feeling of helplessness in the face of a publishing conglomerate with resources she could never match.

But Larry Flynt says that at least in *his* case, this "David and Goliath" dynamic gets turned inside out. His pornographic magazines may be very successful, but they have few admitted readers in a jury box. As Flynt says, "Most attorneys, if they have anything on the ball at all, know that they're the favorite when they go in the courtroom against me." In fact, Larry Flynt, perhaps more than most publishers, literally depends on the First Amendment for his livelihood. As one commentator put it: "Popular or inoffensive speech, by definition, needs no protection. Easy cases are foreign to the First Amendment. People do not sue Mr. Rogers. They sue Larry Flynt."

For his part, Flynt could not believe the fuss being made about the "Chic Thrills" column. He knew that much of the contents of his publications had enraged many people, but to him the "plucky porker" piece was not the stuff of controversy. He shrugs, saying "It was just kind of cute for our satirical section." Flynt's in-house counsel at the time told him not to worry . . . the case was a "slam-dunk."

DID *Chic*'s use of the photograph defame Jeannie Braun or invade her privacy? That question was put to a six-person jury in a Texas federal district court in February of 1982. Given the general confusion and competing interests in this area of the law, the jurors had an understandable response. They could not make up their minds. (A local paper reported that the jurors were "hog-tied.") The judge had no choice but to declare a mistrial.

But the case did not end there. Jeannie Braun became even more determined to vindicate herself, and Larry Flynt was just as committed to vigorously defending his position under the First Amendment. By April, there was a second trial. This time, the jurors did reach a verdict.

The second jury found that *Chic* had both defamed Jeannie Braun and invaded her privacy under false light. For defamation, the jury awarded Braun $5,000 for actual harm and $25,000 in punitive damages; for invasion of privacy, the jury awarded her $15,000 for actual harm and $50,000 in punitive damages—a total of $95,000 in damages.

Jeannie Braun was elated. "It really kind of renewed my faith in people," she says. "I had begun to think maybe I was too prudish, maybe I'm just not rollin' with the flow." Now, Jeannie felt the verdict confirmed that using her photograph in *Chic* did indeed place her in a "false light."

But Larry Flynt and his attorneys saw something else in the verdict. For a defamation/invasion of privacy suit against a major publisher, the damage award was quite low. In such cases, it was not unusual for a jury to hand out hundreds of thousands, if not millions, of dollars. Flynt's team suspected that a familiar dynamic was at work. The verdict was not in favor of Jeannie Braun. It was against Larry Flynt. Had the jury truly believed the case met the standards of false light and harmed Braun, they reasoned, the damages would have been much higher. They felt Braun's lawsuit would go the way of many others. On appeal, when put before less emotional judges strictly applying the law, the verdict would be reversed.

They were wrong. On March 9, 1984, the Fifth Circuit Court of Appeals upheld the verdict against *Chic*. First, the court concluded that Jeannie Braun was a private person and therefore entitled to greater privacy protection than public figures. Then the court held that "the publication of Mrs. Braun's picture in the 'Chic Thrills' section of the magazine was fully capable of conveying a false impression of Mrs. Braun." The court said that "common sense" dictated that the photograph not be considered alone, but be viewed in the context of the entire magazine. And the court made clear its opinion of the magazine, calling it a "glossy, oversized, hard-core men's magazine . . . devoted to the publication of lewd pictures of women and to sexual exploitation . . . containing vulgar cartoons and jokes." As for the allegation that the *Chic* editor told Aquarena that his magazine had the same clientele as *Redbook* and *McCall's*, the court wrote: "The same clientele indeed; in the sense that both sets of readers were featherless bipeds." To the Fifth Circuit, the fact that the photograph of a "respectable" woman appeared in a magazine like *Chic* was enough to win a false light case.

Still, the court held that because false light was so similar to defamation, Braun could not recover damages for both. The court noted that the damages she suffered—"personal humiliation and embarrassment"—fit more clearly under false light. Therefore, the court concluded that Jeannie Braun could either simply accept the damages already awarded by the jury for invasion of privacy ($65,000 total) or have a new trial to address just the issue of damages.

Jeannie, thrilled that the court agreed with her in principle and exhausted by the legal process, happily accepted the damages already awarded and ended the case. (This time, a local paper declared the Brauns were "bringing home the bacon.") Larry Flynt paid the relatively modest damage award. The money did not concern him nearly as much as the precedent that had been set. Flynt's current attorney calls the case "extremely dangerous." However, he points out, "It hasn't turned out to be as harmful as it could have been. I don't think it has been followed." Indeed, in a later, similar case in which the plaintiff complained of the use of a photograph in *Hustler*, a California court rejected *Braun* and ruled in favor of Flynt's First Amendment right.

In the ongoing match between the First Amendment and the right to be let alone, Jeannie Braun (and Ralph) fought one of the rare cases in which privacy trumps the press. However, in late 1994 the Texas Supreme Court decided that the state would not recognize the tort of false light. The court noted that many other courts interpreting Texas law, including the Fifth Circuit in *Braun, had* recognized the tort. But the Texas Supreme Court had never before ruled on the issue. When it did, the state's highest court decided that false light did little more than duplicate the claim of defamation and, as such, posed an unnecessary threat to the First Amendment. Today, not only would Jeannie Braun not win her false light case—she could not even bring suit at all.

Passing Judgments

Article in the *New York Post*:

HEY, THERE'S A BODY ON THE PATIO, DUMMY!
by Leo Standora

Cops are trying to find out who owns the nude and life-size female doll that scared the pants off a Roslyn, Long Island, man this weekend.

The mystery began late Friday when a strange sound in the backyard of Mr. and Mrs. Jerry Grossman prompted them to turn down the TV and perk up their ears.

. . . Bravely Jerry strode out into the night.

Seconds later, Jerry bellowed in fright and came running back into the house.

"There's a body on the patio," he gasped to his wife. . . .

IT TURNED out that the "body" was really a female dummy used in CPR courses, left on the Grossman patio by persons unknown. Mr. Grossman sued for invasion of privacy. He lost.

A New York court held that although the facts were embellished ("scared the pants off"), they were true. Thus, the Grossmans were not presented in a false light.

Grossman v. News Group Publications, New York, 1983

———

A MODEL posed for a Viceroy cigarette ad making the famous "V for Victory" sign. *Hustler* published the photograph in its own version . . . airbrushing out one of the model's fingers so that he appeared to be making an obscene gesture. The caption read: *"Up Your Ad. You might remember having seen this gentleman with two fingers—instead of one. But the reader who sent us this couldn't resist the temptation to change the picture. We can't blame him. This is probably what the cigarette companies are saying to Americans."* The model sued for defamation and false light. A jury awarded him a total of $10,000 in damages. On appeal, he lost.

A Florida court held that no false impression had been created because the caption made it clear that the magazine had altered the photo on its own.

Byrd v. Hustler Magazine, Inc., Florida 1983

A NEW JERSEY high school yearbook contained a section entitled "The Funny Pages." The section consisted of photographs of students and faculty members accompanied by purportedly humorous captions. One picture showed a female teacher, Ms. S., seated next to a male teacher with his hand to his head. The caption read: "Not tonight, Ms. S. I have a headache." The female teacher failed to see the humor and sued the school, the principal (who happened to be Ms. S.'s sister), and the yearbook supervisor (who happened to be Ms. S.'s niece). She claimed defamation and false light.

A New Jersey court dismissed her claim, stating that both defamation and false light required proof of falsity. When, as here, the material is so obviously parody or satire, there can be no false impression created.

Salek v. Passaic Collegiate School, New Jersey 1992

A FRONT-PAGE headline in the tabloid weekly the *Sun* read: PREGNANCY FORCES GRANNY TO QUIT WORK AT AGE 101. The accompanying story told of an Australian woman, Audrey Wiles, who had to quit her paper route at the age of 101 because an extramarital fling with a millionaire on her route had left her pregnant. The story was illustrated with the photograph of an elderly woman with a stack of newspapers under her arm smiling for the camera. It turned out that the photo was really of a woman who lived in Mountain Home, Arkansas, not Australia. She did indeed have a paper route, but she was 97, not 101, and she was definitely not pregnant, by a millionaire or anyone else. The woman sued for defamation and false light.

At the trial, the author of the "granny" article, Manny Silver, explained the paper's editorial process: The editors piled random photographs and headlines on a table. Writers picked a headline and/or photo from the pile and then made up stories to go with them. They would also choose a pseudonym for the byline. The woman's attorney asked how Silver researched the "granny" story after he had chosen the headline.

Q: What information did you use to write [the story]?
A: It's total fiction. I made it all up.
Q: Just off the top of your head?
A: That's right. I'd say about 90 percent of my stories are off the top of my head.
Q: Just created out of whole cloth?
A: That's right.

The woman lost the defamation claim. But a jury found in her favor on the false light claim and awarded her $850,000 in punitive damages and $650,000 in compensatory damages.

On appeal, the *Sun*'s principal defense was that the story was so obviously ridiculous that no reasonable reader would think it true and thereby receive a false impression of the woman. However, the appellate court decided that even if much of the contents of the newspaper was "total fiction," the *Sun* did not hold itself out as such to its readers. Rather, the newspaper claims that it brings its readers the "news," and includes factual articles along with the fiction, as well as some articles that have a little of both. The court upheld the punitive damages award, but reduced the amount for compensatory damages. The woman ended up with $1 million.

Peoples Bank & Trust Co. v. Globe International Publishing, Inc., Arkansas 1992

The "Hard Times" section of Penthouse *magazine has spawned almost as many lawsuits as some of the Hustler features. "Hard Times" is described in the magazine as "a compendium of bizarre, idiotic, lurid, and oftentimes witless driblets of information culled from the nation's press." Among others, it featured the following two stories.*

IN 1986, a forty-six-year-old woman unexpectedly gave birth to a second son weighing almost six pounds. It was unexpected because less than two days earlier, doctors had assured the woman that her stomach pains were caused by a urinary tract infection and a case of hemorrhoids. Apparently, neither the woman nor her doctors was aware that she was pregnant. The surprised mom gave an interview and posed for a photo, both of which were picked up by the wire services.

"Hard Times" featured the story under the headline BIRTH OF A HEMORRHOID.

———

IN ANOTHER case, four elementary-school girls in Rhode Island were photographed giving the "thumbs-down" sign to show disapproval of their principal's decision. Conflicts between boys and girls had led the principal to segregate them on the playground. One eleven-year-old boy was quoted as saying, "They beat us up all the time. I've been kicked where it counts." The photo and story were picked up by the wire services.

"Hard Times" ran the story and photograph under the headline LITTLE AMAZONS ATTACK BOYS.

———

IN BOTH CASES, the subjects of the articles sued under false light. (They did not mind their photographs appearing in the mainstream press, but objected to their use in *Penthouse.*) In both cases, the courts dismissed the complaint. There was no false impression created, the courts said, because the stories were clearly taken from the wire services.

Grimsley v. Guccione, Alabama 1988

Fudge v. Penthouse, Rhode Island 1988

―――――――

One tricky area in false light involves statements of opinion. To win a false light case, one must prove that published material is indeed false. An opinion, by definition, cannot be true or false. (Someone is a "jerk" or has a "bad" haircut.) Thus, courts have long held that there is no false light claim regarding opinions, as opposed to statements of fact, which are capable of being proven true or false. However, in some instances, determining just what is an opinion is, well, a matter of opinion. . . .

A COLLEGE sociology textbook was the target of a false light claim. A chapter entitled "Selecting the Criminal" included a photograph of a white male police officer in Port Authority prodding a black man with his nightstick in order to prevent the man from falling asleep. The caption read: "The social status of the offender seems to be the most significant determinant of whether a person will be arrested. . . . Would the officer [in the picture] be likely to do the same if the 'offender' were a well-dressed, middle-aged white person?" The police officer sued, claiming defamation and false light. He lost.

A New Jersey court held that the picture caption was a statement of opinion and therefore could not be "false."

Cibenko v. Worth Publishers, Inc., New Jersey 1981

―――――――

AN OREGON WOMAN founded an anti-pornography group. *Hustler* then published an article featuring her as "Asshole of the Month," accompanied by a picture of her superimposed over the rear end of a bent-over naked man. The article depicted the woman as a "tightassed housewife" and "deluded

busybody" who presided over a "wacko group" and was in
need of "professional help." She sued, claiming defamation and
false light. She lost.

A federal court held that although the woman had "clearly
suffered a grievous assault to her human dignity, the law does
not offer protection from such disgusting and distasteful
abuse." The *Hustler* article's statements were merely opinions
and could not be grounds for a privacy or defamation lawsuit.

Ault v. Hustler Magazine, Inc., Oregon 1988

———

A HARTFORD, Connecticut, radio program included a segment called "Berate the Bride." Listeners were invited to call in
and vote for the "dog of the week," selected from photographs
of recent brides on the "Weddings" page of the local newspaper. On July 7, 1988, one woman was selected whom the disc
jockey declared "too ugly to even rate." She was awarded the
"dog of the week" prize—a case of Ken-L Ration and a dog
collar. The woman sued for defamation and false light. The
disc jockeys and radio station's defense was that their characterization of the bride was a matter of opinion.

In a surprise, a Connecticut court held that the woman
should be allowed to go to trial. Characterizing the bride as a
"dog" was *not* a matter of opinion, the court held. Furthermore, the court said, the woman had a good chance of
proving the statement was *false* because it is "common knowledge that a woman generally reaches the zenith of her attrac-
tiveness and desirability at or about the time of her marriage,
and that wedding photographs capture her beauty."

Murray v. Schlosser, Connecticut 1990

ARRINGTON v.

THE NEW YORK TIMES COMPANY

The Case of the Cover Photo

I N THE FALL of 1978, the staff of *The New York Times Magazine* was preparing its year-end issue. The *Magazine* is part of the Sunday edition of *The New York Times*, which has a nationwide circulation of more than one and a half million. Edward Klein had been hired the year before as editor in chief, and his mandate was to make the *Magazine* more up-to-date and vital by dealing with relevant, even controversial issues. Klein recalls, "I tried early on to grapple with issues that were not yet paid enough attention to and that would grab people's attention because they were important."

He found such an issue in a story submitted by William Brashler detailing something the author identified as a new social trend: the rise of the "black middle class." Blacks who had rushed through the doors opened by the civil rights movement in the 1960s had, throughout the 1970s, created a new, upwardly mobile middle class. The existence of this new class directly contradicted findings in a celebrated 1968 study which had concluded that a black middle class could not offer an "escape hatch" from the ghetto. Brashler interviewed a number of African Americans for the article, focusing on two women in particular.

Klein recalls that the article "forced itself upon us as an important enough story to warrant running it on the cover." That raised the question of what would appear on the cover of the *Magazine* to illustrate the story. The individuals included in the article had been photographed going about their daily lives. But a cover photo had to be special. It must, as Edward Klein puts it, "drag people inside the magazine and make them want to read this article."

The New York Times art department contacted a freelance photographer, Gianfranco Gorgoni, and assigned him to "photograph well-dressed blacks on the street." Gorgoni spent several days in New York and Chicago on the assignment, then submitted over a hundred color transparencies to the Times. Out of the take, it was decided that the cover of The New York Times Magazine would be one of the photographs depicting a black man, clad in a three-piece suit, striding purposefully across a street in New York City.

"In no instance did I request permission to take a subject's photograph," Gorgoni would later say. Nor, apparently, did anyone at The New York Times request the subject's permission to use the photograph on the cover of a magazine.

ON SUNDAY, December 3, 1978, Clarence Arrington was at his home in Mount Vernon, a suburb of New York City, getting ready to go to work. Arrington had received an M.B.A. from Columbia University and was working as a senior financial analyst at General Motors. As such, he was responsible for reviewing compensation and benefit plans, as well as preparing summaries of capital budget plans, profit plans, and other financial documents for the GM board of directors. Year-end was a busy time for Arrington and it was not unusual for him to work seven days a week. He was just about to leave when the telephone rang. It was a coworker, already at the office.

Arrington recalls: "My colleague essentially said, 'I didn't know you were doubling as a model.' And I said, 'Well, actually I'm not. What are you talking about?' And he said that there was a full-length color picture of me on the front cover of The New York Times Magazine. And I said, 'No, that's not me. You're mistaking me for somebody else.'"

Just as Arrington was hanging up the phone, his brother, Lloyd, who lived in the neighborhood, was knocking at the door. Lloyd had gone to the local newsstand to pick up the Sunday Times. Now he was standing at Clarence's door with a huge stack of the papers under his arm and a grin on his face. Lloyd handed his brother The New York Times Magazine. The headline read: THE BLACK MIDDLE CLASS: MAKING

IT. And filling the front cover was a photograph of Clarence Arrington, hand thrust in his pants pocket, crossing Fifth Avenue.

"It was rather strange to see it there," Arrington says in an understatement. He had had no idea that his photograph had been taken, much less that it would wind up on the cover of a magazine. Arrington guessed that the picture had been taken one day when he was returning from lunch. He says that the photo was actually quite flattering and at first he got a kick out of the unexpected public exposure. "It was, more or less, kind of a welcome experience," Arrington says. "But," he continues, "that was, of course, before I read the article."

The cover story reported on the rise of the "black middle class," stating that this new phenomenon meant that many of the assumptions about race from the 1960s would have to be rethought. The author documented the new social trend with statistics on education, employment, and salaries, but most of all with a detailed depiction of a new class obsessed with making money and acquiring fancy homes, clothes, and cars. The article often reads like a hip insider's guide to a group of former outsiders now consumed by the need to secure the trappings of the white middle class. One exchange between two members of this new class, a receptionist and a visitor to the office, was reported:

In midmorning, Rachel looks up and greets a visitor she knows.

"Hey, Alvin," she says. "How are ya?"

"Hey, Rachel. What you up to?" Alvin says. He is here on business, looking business-like in a three-piece suit, close-cut natural, an attaché case held with one finger pointing to the ground.

"Gettin' around," Rachel says, just as creamy as ever. "Livin' up on the North Side."

"Oh, yeah? I been up there for some time now. Eugenie Square," Alvin says.

"Still got the Mercedes?" Rachel asks.

"Got it. Four-fifty *es-el*," Alvin says. He winks.

"Then you must know Floyd. Lives in Eugenie. Drives a Mercedes."

"You sure? You really sure?" Alvin says, and looks concerned. "Don't remember the man and I know ev-ree-body in the Square who drives a Benz. . . ."

Alvin's appointment shows him in, and he walks by Rachel, a

most puzzled, troubled look on his face. He *thought* he knew every-body in his building who drove a Benz. It will bother him for the rest of the day.

As for Rachel, the article states, "She would like to ride in Alvin's Mercedes."

The article also reported that some of the "haves" in the new black middle class are "keeping up the fight," dedicating themselves to find-ing jobs for black youths and ridding black neighborhoods of drugs. "But it is a struggle," the article continues, "to counteract the preva-lent middle-class black backlash against the black underclass." This new class of blacks was "drifting more and more distant from its less fortunate brothers," even from black culture. "Who needs that jive when he drinks Tanqueray and drives a BMW?" the author wrote.

The cover story focused on two central characters: an industrial re-lations manager in her twenties who had worked her way out of a tough neighborhood in Detroit but who had a brother in jail on drug charges ("a street dude who took a fall when he decided to hold up a drug pad"), and a Chicago receptionist who had successfully left be-hind a life of prostitution but had a sister who was still a prostitute and two brothers in jail. Others mentioned in the article were primarily from Detroit or Chicago.

Clarence Arrington was appalled. He objected to almost every-thing about the article. First of all, Arrington says, "I didn't feel that there needed to be a singling out of a black middle class [as distinct from] the middle class of America." To the extent that a black middle class could be defined, Arrington did not feel that its members were as materialistic and frivolous as the article portrayed them to be. And he did not even think that the people profiled in the article could ac-curately be called middle class. "In my opinion, they were upper-lower class, or less," Arrington says. He certainly did not identify with the backgrounds or values of those highlighted in the story. And, as he points out, they were not even from the same city as he. Finally, Arrington says it did not help that the article, which he found to be inaccurate and patronizing, was written by a white author. "I was deeply offended by the whole thing," Arrington says.

He was not the only one. There was, as Edward Klein recalls, "a minor storm of controversy." Letters to the editor criticized the article for conveying "stereotypes" and "caricatures" of successful blacks. Re-buttals were published in black periodicals. And the *New York Amster-*

dam News, a newspaper with a predominantly black readership, stated that the cover story "managed to bring to new heights the *Times Magazine* tradition of insulting, disparaging and distorting black life. . . . The article is patronizing in the extreme."

Most important to Arrington, he began to hear from almost everyone he knew. "Neighbors, friends, cousins, coworkers—they all called," he says. They wanted to know why Arrington would have agreed to pose for a photograph illustrating such an article. Everyone just assumed that a magazine could not put a private person's photograph on the cover without his consent. Therefore, Arrington must have agreed to be featured with the article. Arrington explained over and over that he had quite enough to do at work without "moonlighting" as a model and that he knew nothing about the photograph or the article prior to its publication. "Well, how can the press just use your photograph like that?" his friends and family wanted to know. Arrington didn't think they could and decided to sue *The New York Times* (as well as the photographer and his agent, who sold the photo).

A friend who was an attorney at a prominent New York law firm agreed to take the case for free. Otherwise, Arrington says, he never would have been able to afford a lawsuit against *The New York Times*, let alone one which was destined to go all the way to the highest court in New York State. For, contrary to the general public perception, under New York law it was not at all clear that *The New York Times* had done anything wrong.

NEW YORK has a statute protecting the right to privacy, but it covers only what is generally viewed as the appropriation branch of the four privacy torts. The statute prohibits the use of a person's "name, portrait, or picture . . . for advertising or trade purposes" without the person's consent. For example, the model Christie Brinkley successfully sued under this law to halt the sale of unauthorized pinup posters with her photograph. The New York statute is one of the earliest laws specifically protecting the right to privacy, and, in fact, grew out of a case similar to Brinkley's that had occurred nearly a century earlier.

In 1902, a company used a young girl's photograph, without her consent, on a poster distributed throughout the country advertising the company's brand of flour. The girl's family sued for invasion of privacy. New York's highest court noted that the state legislature had not passed a law protecting the right to privacy. Then, in a crucial part of the ruling, the court refused to find a right to privacy in the "common law" of New York—that is, deriving from legal history or other cases in the state. The court said it could not just declare that a right to privacy existed based on legal tradition. If such a right was to be protected in New York, the court held, then the legislature would have to pass a law. The girl's family lost the case, causing a public outcry. Within a year, the New York legislature enacted the right to privacy statute prohibiting the unauthorized use of one's name, portrait, or picture for advertising or trade purposes—i.e., appropriation.

Of the four privacy torts, appropriation is often characterized as the most justifiable. After all, it seems only fair that another should not profit from your name or likeness without your consent. Most important, appropriation, with its emphasis on the *commercial* use of one's identity, appears to pose less of a threat to the core values of the First Amendment than do intrusion, private facts, and false light.

The New York statute became a model for other states as the right to privacy grew. However, many other states also wrote laws protecting the other three branches of the right to privacy, or their state courts recognized such causes of action as part of the common law. But in New York, for nearly a century, there remained only the 1903 statute.

Under the statute, Clarence Arrington could not argue that his picture had been used for "trade or advertising purposes" simply because *The New York Times* was in the business of selling newspapers. Early on, New York courts decided that if such an argument were to prevail, publishers could not operate. They would have to obtain prior consent for every photograph in every publication, whether it was the President of the United States making a speech, a defendant walking into the courthouse for trial, or an athlete celebrating a victory on the field. New York courts ruled that as long as an article is on a subject of "legitimate public interest" and the photograph used to illustrate the article is "reasonably related" to the subject matter, then the photo has not been used for advertising or trade purposes under the statute.

Thus, Arrington first argued that his photograph was not reasonably related to the *Times* story. He did not agree with the views in the article, did not know any of those featured, and did not even feel he was in the same "class" as those portrayed.

The *Times* argued that it was enough that Clarence Arrington was indeed a member of the "black middle class," the subject of the article. The press simply had to be free to illustrate such articles with photographs taken in public. If the law were otherwise, the *Times* argued, "Pictures of Sunday strollers down Fifth Avenue, people sitting on a stoop on a hot summer evening, or the faces of people reacting to news of an assassination, would all be banished from the press."

Clarence Arrington countered that he was not trying to prevent the press from using crowd shots or covering public events, only that he should not be singled out and featured as the illustration for a story he knew nothing about.

The *Times* knew that Arrington had a case that would arouse public sympathy. The newspaper's attorneys said that when they discussed free press issues and mentioned Arrington's situation, even ardent First Amendment supporters said, "Well now, wait a minute. . . ." Nonetheless, the *Times* maintained that it was their First Amendment right to use Arrington's picture as they did, and that there was no way, consistent with a free press, to make a rule to cover Arrington's case. If his complaint was that he had been singled out from a crowd and made to look as if he had consented to appear in the cover photo, then presumably the answer would be to use a crowd shot. But then could the entire crowd sue?

"Some might say that if we had not had just Clarence Arrington, but, say, *three* African Americans crossing the street, all looking prosperous and middle class, that wouldn't have been as 'bad,' " Edward Klein says. "But suddenly the line gets smudged more and more, because why is it okay to have three black people crossing the street? Most people would say, 'Three people, well, that's okay. Two? Well . . . One? Wait a second.' " As always, the question becomes: Where do you draw the line?

The media's position is that such lines are necessarily arbitrary and last only until the next set of facts comes along to challenge them. Therefore, no lines should be drawn at all. The press cannot operate freely, the argument goes, if it is under constant threat of a lawsuit, especially from inevitably ill-defined and changing rules.

The *Times* asserted that New York courts had long recognized this basic First Amendment principle. The newspaper pointed to several cases indicating that their use of Clarence Arrington's photo was perfectly acceptable under New York law.

The cover of *New York* magazine had recently featured a photograph of a man watching the St. Patrick's Day parade under a headline for the cover story: THE LAST OF THE IRISH IMMIGRANTS. It turned out that although the man was dressed in Irish garb, he was not even Irish and had not consented to the use of his picture. In another case, an article on Hindu mystics who used hypnosis to convince audiences that they were watching "Indian rope tricks" was illustrated by a photo of a Hindu man. However, the man was a musician and had nothing to do with hypnosis or rope tricks and, again, had not known his photo would be used. In still another case, a picture of a man at a construction site eyeing a woman passerby was used to illustrate an article on "psychological rape." Not surprisingly, the man had not consented to his photograph being used in this way.

Each of the men sued under the New York statute. And each of them *lost*. The photographs were deemed to be "reasonably related to an article of legitimate public interest."

But, as often happens in the area of privacy law, Clarence Arrington could point to other cases that seemed to support *his* claim. A photograph of three boys used to illustrate an article on a neighborhood beating was held to be a violation of the statute when it was discovered that the boys had nothing to do with the assault. Also, a college student won under the statute when her photo was used without her consent on the cover of a book about applying to colleges. Thus, Arrington argued, he should prevail under the New York statute as well.

Furthermore, Arrington said these cases were part of a trend. Arrington's attorneys asserted that for several years New York courts had been stretching older rulings under the appropriation statute to allow recovery against the press. Some of these courts had even opined that New York's highest court, the Court of Appeals, was ready to overrule the earlier cases and declare the other privacy torts to be part of the common law of the state. (Most important for Arrington would be the recognition of false light. Arguing that the *Times* had created a highly offensive false impression of him made for a stronger case than alleging that the paper used his likeness for advertising or trade.)

By now, most other states recognized at least some of the other privacy torts and allowed greater room for recovery for invasion of privacy than did New York. Arrington's case, his attorneys argued, presented the perfect opportunity for bringing New York in line with these other jurisdictions. It was time, they said, for New York to recognize a general right to privacy under the common law.

On April 7, 1982, the New York Court of Appeals declined to do so. Like many people, the members of the court were sympathetic to Arrington's complaint. They agreed that because his picture had been used to illustrate the cover story, "others quite reasonably took the article's ideas to be ones Arrington shared." They also recognized his "perfectly understandable preference that his photograph not have been employed in this manner." Nonetheless, the court held that under New York law, Arrington had no cause of action and his case should be dismissed. The Court of Appeals found that it was indeed enough that Arrington was simply black and middle class for his photograph to be "reasonably related to an article of legitimate public interest."

Most important, the court refused to overrule the earlier cases and find a right to privacy in the common law of New York. The court noted that for nearly a century it had consistently refused to do so, stating that it was up to the legislature to protect privacy by statute. The legislature had just as consistently declined to heed the call, content to let cases like Arrington's be dismissed.

Then, in a statement that went to the heart of Arrington's case, indeed to the heart of the entire conflict between privacy and the press, the New York Court of Appeals wrote: "An inability to vindicate a personal predilection for greater privacy may be part of the price every person must be prepared to pay for a society in which information and opinion flow freely."

However, in a surprise, the court went on to hold that the *photographer* and his *agent* might be liable under the statute. The court said that the sale of the photograph to *The New York Times* was arguably for "trade purposes." Therefore, Arrington could proceed to trial against the photographer and agent, but not the *Times*.

Arrington, of course, thought the court had it backwards. He was harmed, he said, not so much by the taking or sale of the photograph, as by its publication on the cover of a magazine. He tried to pursue the case against the photographer and agent, but after several years of depositions and court papers, he gave up. "Frankly, by that time I had lost interest," he says.

Arrington's case ended up having an impact on New York law after all. The New York legislature *did* heed the call and change the privacy statute as a result of the court's opinion in *Arrington v. The New York Times*, but not in the way Arrington expected. The legislature thought that the court was wrong to allow the case to proceed against the photographer and agent—thus, the New York privacy statute was amended to protect photographers and agents from such lawsuits as well.

Passing Judgments

CHILDREN'S BOOK author Jill Krementz photographed a toddler hammering pegs into a toy workbench at his nursery school. Krementz did not have the child's parents' consent to use the photo (indeed, the parents claimed they had specifically refused to allow their son's picture to be used). Krementz published the photograph anyway in her book entitled *Katherine Goes to Nursery School*. The caption correctly identified the toddler by his first name, but with no last name. The parents sued for invasion of privacy. They lost.

A New York court frowned on the author's use of the photo. Nonetheless, the court felt constrained to hold that a book dealing with a child's initiation into the education system is clearly a matter of public interest and the photograph was reasonably related to the subject.

McWhir v. Krementz, New York 1980

A COUPLE sued when a photograph of them on a nude beach appeared in a book entitled *World Guide to Nude Beaches and Recreation*. The author said he was documenting a worldwide movement encouraging a more natural perception of the human body, in addition to listing nude beaches around the globe. A New York trial court held that the subject of the book was not of legitimate public concern and therefore the couple could go to trial. The judge noted that most of the photographs (200 out of 208 pages) were not of resorts but of nudes in close-up. Therefore, the court concluded, the primary purpose of the book was not to disseminate information, but "to print 200 pictures of naked people." On appeal, the couple lost.

The appellate court in New York held that "a guide to beaches where nude bathing is permitted is a matter of some public interest" and the couple's picture was reasonably related to the subject.

Creel v. Crown Publishers, New York 1985

A *New York Post* photographer snuck onto the grounds of a private psychiatric facility and, using a telephoto lens, surreptitiously photographed Hedda Nussbaum. Nussbaum had been at the center of a highly publicized murder case against her abusive live-in companion, Joel Steinberg. When the photographer was discovered, he was ordered to leave and the medical director phoned the *Post* asking that no photos of patients be published. The next day, the *Post* published on the front page a full-length picture of Nussbaum walking with another female patient. The other woman in the photo sued for invasion of privacy, saying that her family, friends, and business associates had not known she was at the psychiatric facility until she appeared on the front page of the newspaper. The woman recognized that Nussbaum's recovery was of legitimate public interest, but she argued that she should have been cropped from the photo. She lost.

New York's highest court unanimously held that the photograph in its entirety was reasonably related to the public interest story. Indeed, the photograph illustrated the story of Nussbaum's recovery by showing her with a "smiling companion."

Howell v. New York Post Co., New York 1993

A COUPLE was shocked to find a picture of their family in *Omni* magazine illustrating an article on research involving caffeine-aided fertilization. The article was entitled "Caffeine and Fast Sperm." Accompanying the story was a photo of the couple and their six children with the caption "Want a big family? Maybe your sperm needs a cup of Java in the morning. Tests reveal that caffeine-spritzed sperm swim faster, which may increase the chances for *in vitro* fertilization." The family was not identified, but neither was their permission asked to use the photograph. The couple sued for invasion of privacy. They conceded that the subject of the article was newsworthy, but argued that their picture was not reasonably related to the subject. None of their children had been conceived by in vitro fertilization, or any other artificial means, and they had nothing to do with the research, indeed they knew nothing about it. They lost.

The New York Court of Appeals held that the theme of the article was "fertility." Therefore, there was a reasonable relationship between the subject of the article and a picture of "six healthy and attractive children with their parents to whom each child bears a striking resemblance."

Finger v. Omni Publishing, New York 1990

———

TWO CONSTRUCTION WORKERS, a male and female in hard hats, were strolling hand in hand down Madison Avenue in New York City when they noticed that they were being filmed by a television crew. The crew was doing a story on romance in the city. The male construction worker told the television reporter that he was married and his companion was engaged, and demanded that the film of them walking together be destroyed. Instead, the pictures ran twice on a CBS-TV broadcast entitled "Couples in Love in New York." The construction worker sued. He lost. A New York court held that the subject matter—romance—was of public interest.

DeGregorio v. CBS, Inc., New York 1984

The Right of Publicity

If people who have never been in the spotlight, such as Clarence Arrington or Mary and Susie Hall, do not win privacy cases, then it is easy to see why celebrities rarely prevail. By definition, information about much of a celebrity's life is deemed to be "newsworthy" and therefore protected by the First Amendment. Thus, public figures often do not even attempt to file a privacy claim. However, some states provide additional protection for at least a celebrity's commercial interest in his identity by recognizing a relative of the appropriation tort—the "right of publicity."

A MICHIGAN manufacturer decided to call his new line of portable toilets "Here's Johnny" and advertise them as "The World's Foremost Commodian." Johnny Carson, the popular talk show host, sued for use of his signature introduction. The court held that even though Carson's name and likeness were not used, his "identity" had been appropriated and he had a claim for violation of his "right of publicity."

Carson v. Here's Johnny Portable Toilets, Michigan 1983

———

THE Ford Motor Company used a "sound-alike" in a commercial for Lincoln Mercury cars. Bette Midler had declined to sing "Do You Wanna Dance" (a song she popularized in the 1970s) for the commercial. So Ford hired one of Midler's former backup singers to sing the song and sound as much like Midler as possible. Bette Midler sued. A California court held that because it was not Midler's actual voice in the commercial, she could not sue for appropriation of her voice. However, the court said she did have a claim under the "right of publicity" for appropriation of her "identity."

Midler v. Ford Motor Company, California 1988

———

SAMSUNG ELECTRONICS ran a series of ads set in the twenty-first century, each depicting an item of popular culture with a Samsung product. The point was that Samsung products would still be in use far into the future. One ad featured a robot dressed and made up to look like Vanna White standing on a futuristic "Wheel of Fortune" set. White sued. Again, a court found that because her actual likeness had not been used, White did not have a claim for appropriation. But she could sue because her "identity" had been used without her consent.

White v. Samsung Electronics America, Inc., California 1992

Privacy v. The Voyeur

LONG BEFORE a man named Tom peeped at Lady Godiva riding naked through Coventry, voyeurs were threatening privacy. Indeed, voyeurism is probably the oldest, not to mention the most basic, form of invasion of privacy. It is also the sort of privacy invasion which makes us feel most vulnerable.

By definition, the Peeping Tom spies on our most intimate activities. In a cruel twist, his violation may also be a betrayal of the most intimate trust, as in the lover who secretly records a couple's lovemaking. And the invasion usually occurs in a place we consider secure—a hotel or dressing room—or a place we consider private—a bedroom or bathroom—even of our own home. We are all inescapably vulnerable to voyeurism in one form or another.

Indeed, one of the biggest and most unpleasant surprises during our research was just how many "peeping" cases there are. Reading one after another is unnerving. It may not make you paranoid, but you will likely think twice the next time you enter a public rest room or try on clothes in a dressing room, and you may even start checking your own mirrors.

Making matters worse, as usual, is new technology. Of course, voyeurs can and do still simply push aside a blind to spy on others. But now, as one young couple found out, "peepers" can be aided by two-way mirrors, as well as telephoto lenses and high-powered listening devices. In addition, video cameras can secretly record the most private of activities, ensuring that the violation can be repeated over and over again for new viewers.

The good news is that claims against voyeurs are the most successful of all claims for invasion of privacy. The legal cause of action is usually the tort of intrusion. Unlike many privacy claims against the government, press, or employers, where there are important competing interests at stake, there is no societal interest on the side of the voyeur. And when the case involves the invasion of an intimate space or the act of spying on an intimate moment, the hurdle of proving that the intrusion was "highly offensive to a reasonable person" does not seem so high. As inured as we may have become to certain invasions of privacy by bosses, bureaucrats, or computers, invasions by voyeurs still have the power to outrage. We may be most vulnerable in this area, but we are also most likely to achieve vindication.

COOPER v. ANDERSON

The Sex Tape Case

THERE WAS nothing remarkable about the way Debbie Anderson and Jeff Cooper met. Jeff, seventeen, sandy-haired and baby-faced, was a senior at a public high school in Houston, Texas. "I guess I considered myself as hanging with one of the 'in' crowds," he says. "We were interested in having fun. Although I did keep up with my grades and do well . . . we mostly just hung out with our friends." Debbie, nineteen, tall and lean with long brown hair, was a senior at a local Catholic girls' school. An average student, she excelled at extracurricular activities. Elected to the school's homecoming court, she was also a cheerleader and All-State volleyball player. It was May of 1985, nearing graduation and summer, a time of celebration, parties, and the prom. At one of the graduation parties in Houston, Debbie was introduced to Jeff by a mutual friend.

Nor was there anything remarkable about the relationship that developed between Debbie and Jeff. Debbie had dated often throughout high school but had not yet had a sexual relationship. She says that as soon as she met Jeff she thought he was "wonderful" and "gentlemanly," and a few days later invited him to her senior prom. Jeff had also dated throughout high school, having had "a few" sexual relationships and one long-term girlfriend. He says that if Debbie hadn't called about the prom, he probably would not have given her another thought, but once she called, he was happy to go. He picked her up at her house, met her mother, and escorted Debbie to the prom. Jeff and Debbie slept together that night, and the next day Debbie confided to her best friend that she had lost her virginity to Jeff Cooper.

Debbie and Jeff talked on the phone and saw each other about eight or ten times over the next couple of months. Sometimes, if a friend's parents were out of town, they would go to that house to make love. Debbie says that Jeff was always "polite, a gentleman." She thought she was falling in love. Jeff, on the other hand, says, "I felt the relationship was strictly casual sex and, in my opinion, there were no ties."

"When I look back," Debbie says now, "he was acting like he was interested, but wasn't *real* interested. When you look back, you can see." But she could not see it then. And Jeff was content with the way things were going. Nothing unusual, he says: "It was a typical relationship that a lot of my other friends had."

The remarkable thing about Debbie and Jeff's relationship occurred on the night of August 10, 1985, one day shy of Jeff's eighteenth birthday. Debbie had invited Jeff to attend a wedding with her. He declined, but the two made plans to meet later that night. Jeff was hanging out at a friend's house with a group of ten or twelve other boys, drinking beer and shooting pool. "When one kid's parents go out of town, all the kids end up at that house for the weekend," Jeff explains. "So I knew Kevin Baker's parents were out of town, and quite honestly, I saw that as an opportunity." The group was going out anyway, so Jeff asked if he and Debbie could use the house. Kevin said okay.

Then Kevin said he would like to set up a video camera.

Jeff recalls: "Kevin said, 'Sure, but I'd like to tape it,' or 'I want to video it' or something like that, and I said, 'Sure, whatever.' " And with that, the boys decided to videotape Debbie and Jeff making love—without Debbie's knowledge.

Jeff went to pick Debbie up at the reception. Kevin got out the family camcorder. He and two of the other boys at the house then proceeded to tape an "introduction" to the video they were about to make. Laughing, joking, and hollering, they described in crude and graphic terms what they expected to capture on tape. Acting as "emcees" to an entertainment event, they described what Debbie, as an unwitting participant, was going to do and what would be done to her. "There were [lots of] people at that house that night who knew what was going on," Jeff says. "They're all peers of mine and not one of them thought, bing, 'Wait! We're making a mistake. Somebody stop.' " Instead, Kevin hid the video recorder in the closet of his bedroom with the camera on, the lens facing the bed.

Jeff met Debbie at the wedding reception. She says she thought they were going to a get-together at Jeff's friend's house, but when they got to the house, no one was there. So instead, the two had a beer and chatted awhile. Then Jeff led Debbie to Kevin's room, where they had sex under the blankets on the bed. Debbie had no idea that a video camera was recording them.

Jeff later drove Debbie home and returned to the Baker house. The others had already come back. When Jeff walked in, there were ten or twelve high school boys partying, having a good time watching the tape. Jeff watched with them, then took the tape when he left.

Within a week or two, both Debbie and Jeff were off to college. Jeff went to the University of Texas at Austin, Debbie to Southwest Texas State University in San Marcos, about thirty miles from Austin. Her two best friends, Judy Paulo and Stacey Romano, went there as well. Debbie brought pictures of Jeff to college with her, still considering him a "boyfriend" and hoping to pursue the relationship. She called him a few times from her dormitory and even ran into him when she visited UT on weekends, but Jeff acted cold toward her. Debbie soon realized that he "wasn't interested."

Debbie did not know of the videotape's existence, much less that word of the episode had already begun to spread. Jeff's high school friends had, of course, seen the tape right away. In addition, Jeff had pledged a fraternity at UT and told some of the fraternity brothers what he had done. He showed the tape at three different friends' apartments, each time to a different group of male friends and fraternity brothers. And there were many more people who wanted to see it. "There were a lot of others who would have loved to have been there, but they weren't," Jeff says. "Guys were calling that I know. [Guys] in another fraternity heard about it and wanted me to bring it over and show it. . . . I said, 'Look, leave it alone. You can't see anything.' "

By all accounts, the tape was of very poor quality—dark, shadowy, and fuzzy. In the section in the bedroom, at least, it was difficult to discern much detail. "It was very hard to see," Jeff says. "I maybe helped to focus in on the picture and what it was [when I was showing it]. There were a couple of funny things involved with it. But you couldn't see anything."

Still, everyone knew who was on the tape. The word was out. Although Jeff's college in Austin, Debbie's college in San Marcos, and their hometown of Houston were all separated by many miles, this kind of news transcended geographic boundaries. One of Debbie's friends says simply, "Everybody knew. Everybody." Well, at that point, everybody but Debbie and her closest friends.

Then, on December 6, Debbie, Judy, and Stacey traveled to UT to attend the big fraternity and sorority rush parties on campus. There, another of Debbie's high school friends, Gail Gammon, came up to her and told her to stay away from Jeff. Debbie wanted to know why. "She didn't want to tell me," Debbie recalls. "She just kept saying, 'Don't talk to him again. Don't see him again. Don't anything.' I kept asking why and she wouldn't tell me. And this went on for five minutes." Debbie kept insisting on an explanation and Gail finally told Debbie about the videotape.

"I didn't believe her at first," Debbie says. But Gail told her how many people had either seen or heard about it. Debbie froze. For a few minutes, she just stood there, unable to say or do anything. "I was furious and upset and hurt and in shock," Debbie says. She finally decided she had to confront Jeff, so she, Judy, and Stacey went to his fraternity.

"I wasn't in very good shape at that point," Jeff recalls. "It was a rush party and I was pretty drunk. . . . I just didn't want to deal with it." He told Debbie he was sorry and had not meant to hurt her. He also told her it was no big deal and to go away. Debbie's friends tried to talk with him but did not get much further than Debbie had, so the girls eventually just drove back to school in San Marcos.

But Debbie did not stay there long. She was reeling. Her first sexual relationship had ended not only in betrayal but also in public humiliation. She imagined all of the young men she knew seeing her naked in the act of love, and she was unbearably embarrassed. She was also beginning to feel an anger—rage, really—that she had never felt before. That night, Debbie says that she could not sleep and could not stop crying. She could not reach Jeff by telephone either. She finally decided that she had to go back to UT and get the tape.

Debbie, Judy, and Stacey again made their way to Austin. When they arrived at Jeff's apartment, he was at the library. In a telephone conversation with a friend, he found out that Debbie was looking for him, so he stayed away most of the night. "I just didn't want to deal with it," he says. "I stayed at [a friend's house] until two or three in the morning . . . and then decided they have got to be gone by now." When Jeff approached his apartment, there was no sign of Debbie or her friends. Jeff pulled into a parking space, and Debbie pulled in right behind him. The girls had been waiting around the corner.

When Debbie confronted Jeff about the tape, he apologized to her again and said he would destroy it. Debbie said that was not enough; she wanted the tape. Jeff kept promising to destroy it, but Debbie wanted to make absolutely certain that it was out of circulation. "I also wanted to see what everyone else was seeing," she says. Jeff finally reached into a compartment in his car and brought out the tape, apologizing again. Then he gave it to Debbie. For the second time, he did not realize the enormity of his action or its consequences. After the confrontation with Debbie, Jeff merely assumed that the whole in- cident was over and he basically forgot about it.

Debbie says she, too, tried to forget, but could not. It was the end of the semester and finals were coming up. "I don't remember any- thing except sitting in my room and crying and rocking back and forth," she says. "I don't remember taking one final." She would find out later that she failed every one of her tests.

Debbie went home for the Christmas holidays and her parents immediately became concerned about her appearance and behavior. Debbie's parents had been divorced since she was eight. She and her two sisters lived primarily with their mother but saw their father and stepmother, who lived nearby, quite often. In fact, Debbie was sup- posed to do some data processing work at her father's manufacturing plant over the holidays. Both Debbie's mother and father noticed that their daughter was uncharacteristically sullen and withdrawn. When they asked her what was wrong, she just told them not to worry.

For most people, there comes a time when they realize that they are looking at the world in a different way, with a little less trust and a little more cynicism, than they had when they were younger. Usually, it is a gradual process, one that is hardly noticed until eventually they look back and realize they had once been much more innocent, more naïve. Debbie says she can point to the very moment in her life when she lost that sense of innocence. She says finding out about the tape changed her forever.

At the time, however, she merely tried to get through each day, and did not do a very good job of it. Although she had viewed the tape and now knew it was not as revealing as she had feared, she was still angry and still felt a deep sense of betrayal and shame. Her feel- ings of rage and humiliation were beginning to overwhelm her.

First, she had a terrible fight with her mother. "[It] was over something as insignificant as being late for a wedding," Faye Anderson, her mother, says. "She was just undeniably out of control." Debbie didn't attend the wedding, and when Faye returned from the celebration, she found a note from Debbie saying she had left home. "That had never, ever happened before," Faye says.

Debbie lived first at Judy's house, then at another friend's, Lucy Brown. She tried to go back to work for her father, but she was distracted and would cry during the day; and she drank and had trouble sleeping at night. Judy, Stacey, and Lucy were calling all the time to check on her. Debbie's father, Walt, says, "I decided I needed to have a serious confrontation with her." Walt Anderson called his daughter into his office and closed the door. "I told her, 'You're not going to leave here until you tell me what's bothering you.' " He asked Debbie if she had flunked out of school, if she was on drugs, or if she had been raped or physically assaulted in any way. Debbie just started crying again, told her father to leave her alone, and fled.

Walt Anderson was still in his office trying to decide what to do when the telephone rang. It was Judy Paulo. She told Walt that Debbie was at her mother's house and that he should come right away. Apparently, Judy had decided that her friend needed help and if Debbie could not tell her parents herself, Judy would do it for her.

Walt went in the front door of the house, he recalls, to find "Debbie sitting on the couch with her knees up, rocking back and forth and sobbing quietly. Judy Paulo was there, and she was crying. Sally, my younger daughter, was there, and she was crying." At first, no one seemed able to talk. Then, Walt says, Judy "just kind of blurted out that a film had been made of Debbie making love to a boy."

"I went over to Debbie and got her to stand up and we just held each other. I tried to calm her down a little . . . then I got my younger daughter and we all three huddled together. There was very little discussion, actually."

Debbie's mother and her older sister soon returned to the house. Walt took each of them aside and explained to them what had happened; Debbie was unable to do so herself. Faye recalls, "We couldn't talk that night because everybody was so upset, just mass hysteria and hurt."

"We think daughters are fragile and need to be protected," Debbie's father says. "I felt a great sense of wanting to take the hurt. I felt like I had somehow not protected her as I should have. . . . Within a week, I had gone out and purchased a gun."

That Christmas holiday, the Anderson family was in turmoil. "[There wasn't one minute when] somebody wasn't crying or somebody wasn't totally outraged or somebody wasn't hurt and somebody was always trying to stay next to Debbie because we didn't know what was going to happen," Faye says. "We had never experienced anything like this before. She was a whole person at one time, and she was not a whole person again. . . . We didn't know what the magnitude of what had happened was and we didn't know where to go to find out about it. She wasn't 'a rape victim.' Where do you go? What do you do?"

Debbie's stepmother finally got the name of a psychotherapist and Debbie went for counseling. Her parents and sister also went to a session with her. Walt says he decided to put the gun away. And by the time winter break ended in late January, Debbie felt ready to go back to school. "I elected to try and forget about it and just move on with my life," she says.

However, Debbie soon found out that was not so easy to do. "Everyone would look at me. Everyone would ask me questions," she explains. Some of the people who approached Debbie were her friends, some were acquaintances, and others complete strangers. Some knew the truth and some had assumed that Debbie had volunteered to be taped. It got to the point where, Debbie says, "I didn't want to tell anyone my name when I met them." She says that there was no getting away from it. Debbie was no longer known as a cheerleader, volleyball player, or homecoming queen. She was the girl in the videotape.

Even her good friend Lucy Brown says, "When you think of Debbie Anderson, you think of the videotape. I know I do. I try not to . . . but it's all you can think of."

And when Debbie and Jeff's peers thought of the taping, what they felt was not outrage at Jeff Cooper but revulsion toward Debbie Anderson. Of his own acquaintances, Jeff says, "I can tell you none of them thought it was bad. I guess they all thought it was kind of a novelty. . . . I have always said I never lost a friend because of this." Instead, Debbie was "branded."

"All of my girlfriends went the other way, except my three closest friends," says Debbie Anderson. "People would confront me or confront my friends. Stacey Romano was informed by six girls we knew in high school that she shouldn't be seen with me because I now had a reputation of a porno queen."

"People didn't want to have anything to do with her anymore," says Lucy. "She was like an outcast."

Finally, Debbie came to the conclusion that she "couldn't sweep it under the rug." She now wanted to take action. She wanted to let people know she had not willingly participated in the taping. She also wanted to prevent it from happening to someone else. "I have a little sister who could not, I don't think, handle something like this," she explains. "And the whole thing just wasn't right. Everyone was laughing at me and he looks like a big hero. It made me mad."

The next time Debbie went home from school, she looked for a lawyer. Her father contacted his business attorney, who said he did not think there was any legal action that Debbie could take. Debbie and her mother went to see several lawyers who specialized in the criminal area, including the local district attorney, but they all said the same thing: What had happened to Debbie was not a crime. Finally, Debbie's godfather came up with the name of an old fraternity brother who practiced law, including the law of torts. Debbie went to see her godfather's friend, Ken Burch.

"Debbie was the most devastated, despondent client I have ever had," reports Ken Burch. "She almost couldn't tell her story to me." Ken advised Debbie that she might well have a case for invasion of privacy and infliction of emotional distress. But he also advised her that if she was going to file a lawsuit and testify at a trial, she would have to forgo whatever privacy she had left. Debbie thought about it and concluded that she had to take action. She reasoned that she had already been humiliated. She returned to Ken Burch and told him she wanted to file a lawsuit.

Ken enlisted the help of a friend, Dick Morrison, and later, Morrison's law partner, Ronnie Krist. Morrison and Krist are attorneys in the Texas cowboy mold, outfitted in studded boots and ready with a colorful phrase. But they are no "simple country lawyers." Both are seasoned tort attorneys. They generally take personal injury cases on a contingency basis—that is, rather than charge clients an hourly fee, they receive a percentage of the damages paid to their clients as a result of the lawsuit. Their clients do not pay the lawyers unless damages are awarded. Contingency-fee attorneys absorb the cost of the trial and assume the risk that no money will be paid. If money is paid, however, the attorneys get a sizable chunk—often 30 to 40 percent. Thus, attorneys like Dick Morrison and Ronnie Krist do not usually take on a case unless they think there is a good chance of winning substantial damages for their client.

On behalf of Debbie Anderson, they filed a lawsuit alleging invasion of privacy and negligent infliction of emotional distress. They named Jeff Cooper, along with Kevin Baker, Win Wilcox, and J. R. Talbot, who appeared in the "introduction" to the tape. They also named Kevin's older brother, Ken, who was in the house at the time and is mentioned on the tape, although he does not appear in it. None of the other boys who were in the Baker house that night was named in the complaint. "There are a lot of people that don't realize how lucky they are," Jeff says now, looking back at the trial.

At first, taking legal action only made things worse for Debbie. Once word of the lawsuit got around, people stopped talking to her altogether. Gail Gammon suddenly could no longer recall that she had been the first one to tell Debbie about the tape. And Lucy Brown had a confrontation with Jeff and J. R. Talbot in a restaurant. Lucy said it ended with the boys taunting her for being Debbie's friend and throwing a drink on her. According to J.R., "I kind of spilled my drink on her." In any event, it was clear that the boys did not yet understand the seriousness of what was about to happen.

Debbie's attorneys, however, knew a major tort suit when they saw one. "I always felt that we would get money," recalls Dick Morrison. "We always had confidence there," adds Ronnie Krist. "Always."

At first glance, Debbie's case may not have seemed particularly promising. She had been emotionally distressed, not physically injured, and the people she was suing were all just out of high school. "[Usually] jurors don't want to give a lot of money against teenagers," says Krist. "They're not what we call target defendants. This wasn't Exxon; it wasn't some big company—it was a bunch of kids. So that would hold damages down."

But, Krist reasoned, what would keep the amount of the damages high was the quality of the plaintiff. When Krist and Morrison first interviewed Debbie, they could not believe their luck. "She was a Sally Field look-alike. She was an All-State volleyball player. She was a cheerleader at a Catholic girls' school," Krist exulted. "We literally had the All-American Girl!"

Just as important, they also had the videotape. "If that tape had been destroyed, the case would have been worthless," Krist says candidly. As it was, though, "We couldn't argue this case as well as the defendants did it for us [on the tape]."

Unaccountably, even once the lawsuit was under way, some of the boys still did not "get it." The defendants, along with their fathers and attorneys, all showed up at Ken Burch's office to view the videotape. As the tape played, showing the three boys describing in graphic terms what was going to happen to Debbie Anderson, Kevin Baker, seated next to his father, was laughing. When Debbie's attorneys asked Kevin why he had laughed at the tape, he said, "It amused me." When Kevin's brother Ken was asked in his deposition if he had any remorse, he replied, "The only remorse I have is because I've been sued."

Debbie's attorneys could barely contain their glee. The case just kept betting better. They sued the five defendants for $3 million in actual damages and $9 million in punitive damages—a total of $12 million. Each.

The trial began in May of 1989, nearly four years after the videotaping. The participants, who at the time had been boys and girls graduating from high school, were now young men and women graduating from college. Local media coverage was intense. The judge moved the trial to the largest courtroom available, but still could not accommodate everyone. The parties themselves took up a lot of space. Debbie Anderson was at the plaintiff's table with her three attorneys. The five defendants,—Jeff Cooper, Win Wilcox, J. R. Talbot, and Kevin and Ken Baker—were each there with their own attorneys. All the parties' families and friends were packed in the front rows. A jury of seven women and five men was impaneled.

Ronnie Krist opened the trial in the most powerful way he could. He played the tape. Actually, he did not play the entire tape, only the "introduction," arguably the most damaging segment. All parties agreed that in the interest of both Debbie's and Jeff's privacy, the second half of the tape would not be played in open court. The jury would be given the tape and a VCR for use in the jury room during deliberations.

The tape having spoken for itself, Debbie's attorneys spent most of the trial trying to show that, as a result of the taping, Debbie's reputation had been terribly damaged and she had suffered awful emotional distress. Several of Debbie's friends testified about her "good" and "chaste" reputation before the incident. They repeated that, in contrast, Debbie was now "branded," an "outcast," a "porno queen."

"Sister Jane even came!" Dick Morrison recalls. Sister Jane Meyer was the principal at Debbie's Catholic high school. She testified at length about Debbie's outstanding achievements at school and her reputation for "chastity." Brushing aside questions from the defense attorneys about the Catholic Church's view of premarital sex, Sister Jane declared that "in a sacred moment which Debbie entered into as an act of love, she was violated and exploited" by a "despicable" act. The defense attorneys then left Sister Jane's testimony alone.

The defense offered depositions from other students who indicated that Debbie's reputation had not really been harmed—because it was not so sterling to begin with. The most damning testimony came from Gail Gammon, the friend who now could not recall that she was the one who originally alerted Debbie to the existence of the tape. Parts of Gail's deposition were too graphic to be read into the record, but she concluded that Debbie's reputation was not "any worse" as a result of the videotape.

More people, including Debbie's mother and father and Debbie herself, testified to the dramatic change in her personality since she had found out about the videotape. Before December of 1985, they said, Debbie was "outgoing," "self-confident," a "leader," a girl with "goals" and a "sparkle in her eye." Her many athletic awards were ticked off. She not only was an All-State volleyball player but had been elected captain by her teammates. When she had to choose between volleyball and cheerleading for the nearby boys' school, she chose volleyball, then promptly joined the Spirit Club so she could continue to root for the brother school's teams. The boys at that school responded by electing Debbie to the homecoming court. In short, Debbie says she was "on top of the world."

Then each witness described the change in Debbie after she found out about the videotape. They said she became "withdrawn," "depressed," and "mistrustful." They testified that she did not socialize nearly as much as she had before and seemed unable to make new friends. Debbie said that she had had trouble sleeping and experienced stomachaches and dizziness. She said her grades had suffered as a result, eventually prompting her to transfer to a different college. Debbie stated that the betrayal and humiliation of the taping had simply changed her forever. Even now, she said, she worried about the future and how she would explain the incident to a husband and child.

On cross-examination, the defense attorneys tried to show that there were alternative explanations for some of Debbie's problems. Debbie's parents admitted on cross that Debbie had "always had trouble with school" and barely maintained a C average. The defense brought out that Debbie had had lifelong problems with her hip and sinuses, and on at least one occasion serious problems with her stomach when she was twelve. She had also missed an unusual number of days of high school. The defense asked about the trauma Debbie suffered because of her parents' divorce at age eight and, more recently, because of a car accident. With every question, the defense attorneys suggested that not all of Debbie's woes could be blamed on the videotape.

Indeed, the defense argued that Debbie's distress over the tape was not even that severe. Witnesses testified that within months of finding out about the tape, Debbie entered into a long-term sexually active relationship and that she later had two other such relationships. The defense also argued that Debbie's grades at her new school were among the best she had ever received. Finally, there were dueling expert witnesses in the field of psychology who debated whether Debbie was suffering from "post-traumatic stress syndrome" or was merely a little depressed.

The most dramatic testimony came from each of the defendants, now young men in their twenties, who also took the stand. At long last, they each understood the gravity of the lawsuit; their pretrial cockiness was gone. Or, as Dick Morrison describes it, "Once we got 'em down [at the courthouse] and put a blowtorch on their ass, then it was a different story." Each of the defendants said they were truly sorry for their role in the taping and for any harm they had caused Debbie. J. R. Talbot even apologized directly to Debbie from the stand.

But Ronnie Krist kept after J.R., asking him about the time he'd thrown a drink on Debbie's friend, hammering away about Kevin Baker laughing at the tape and Ken Brown saying that his only regret was that he had been sued. Over and over, Krist recounted the defendants' actions in the years after the taping. Pointedly and effectively, he asked each of the young men: "Now, when exactly did this flood of remorse wash over you?"

"It was really a lot of fun," Krist says. "It really was. It was just *fun*."

This is not to say that none of the defendants regretted his participation in the taping. "I would be as insensitive as they were," Ronnie Krist says, "if I told you with a straight face that Jeff Cooper didn't suffer from this. One [of the accused] was such an idiotic little ignorant son-of-a-bitch that he didn't have enough sense to know what he had been proven to be. But this Jeff Cooper was the best of the bunch."

Debbie agrees that "Jeff was the best of all of them."

"When he was barbecued in that courtroom for a week," Ronnie Krist says, "the guy suffered. He was downright regretful of what he did."

Indeed, by the time of the trial Jeff Cooper was fully aware of the trouble he had caused Debbie, himself, and his family. He took the stand, apologized for his actions, and said he could see that he had harmed Debbie. He admitted to everything he had done, from making the tape to showing it to friends. He only hesitated when asked whether he had "sexually exploited" Debbie Anderson. So Ronnie Krist got out a dictionary definition of "exploited" and marched through every possible definition.

Q: Was the tape utilized by you?

A: Yes, sir . . .

Q: You used it?

A: Yes, sir, I used it.

Q: And you misused it?

A: Yes, sir, I misused it.

Q: And you walked all over Ms. Anderson by using it without her consent?

A: That is correct.

Q: And you deceived her?

A: Yes, sir, I did.

Q: And you beguiled her?

A: Yes, sir.

Q: And you deluded her?

A: Yes, sir.

Q: And you hoodwinked her?

A: Yes, sir.

Q: And you duped her? Pulled something over on her?

A: Yes, sir.

Q: Fooled her?

A: Yes, sir. She didn't have any knowledge of it. . . .

Q: [A]fter having gone over each aspect of the definition of "exploitation," do you agree that this is a case involving sexual exploitation?

A: After going over that, I agree it is.

By the end of his testimony, Jeff Cooper was weeping on the stand. "And it wasn't a fake deal," says Krist.

JUST BEFORE the case was submitted to the jury, two things happened. First, Ken Baker was dismissed from the suit because, though he had been present in the house that night, he had not actively participated in making the videotape. Second, and much more important, Debbie's attorneys dropped the invasion of privacy claim, leaving only the claim for negligent infliction of emotional distress. It was a move that would ultimately have stunning consequences, but at the time, the change in claims did not mean much to anyone other than the lawyers.

The question to the jury was: Did the defendants negligently inflict emotional distress upon Debbie Anderson? In less than a day, the jury answered yes, by a vote of 10 to 2. (Of the seven-woman and five-man jury, all of the women and three of the men voted in Debbie's favor.)

The jury awarded $500,000 in actual damages and $500,000 in punitive damages. Of the total $1 million in damages, the jury assessed $650,000 against Jeff Cooper, $200,000 against Kevin Baker, and $75,000 each against Win Wilcox and J. R. Talbot.

Jeff says he was flabbergasted by the amount of the jury award. "Debbie Anderson was hurt," he says. "She deserves some type of damages—there's no question in my mind. But a million dollars? I don't think that's a fair judgment." Furthermore, the judgment was not, as some people believed, merely symbolic. Jeff, right out of college and looking for a job, did not have $650,000 to give to Debbie Anderson. But the insurance company behind the Cooper family's homeowner's policy did.

That's right, the insurance company.

It was because of the insurance company that Debbie's attorneys dropped the invasion of privacy claim, leaving only a claim for negligent infliction of emotional distress. Invasion of privacy is generally recognized as an *intentional* act, not something done negligently or carelessly. In Texas (as in most places), homeowners' policies generally cover only accidents, or what is known as negligent conduct, and specifically exclude intentional acts. So an *intentional* invasion of privacy is not covered by insurance, but *negligent* infliction of emotional distress is. Debbie's attorneys were going after Jeff Cooper's family insurance policy, knowing that was the only way they could secure a large payment of damages.

This strategy is not uncommon. In South Carolina, a photographer advertised for swimsuit models, then secretly videotaped the women as they changed clothes for the photo session. When the women found out and sued for invasion of privacy, the photographer turned around and sued his insurance company for not covering the cost. (He lost because the invasion was intentional.) In New York, a man who had been sued for molesting a child in his home appealed all the way to the state's highest court, insisting that his insurance company should pay the damages. (He lost, but by a very slim margin.) And in Maine, a male college student was convicted of raping a coed at his fraternity. After the criminal trial, the woman sued the rapist in civil court for damages. Both the woman and her attacker argued that the assault had been negligent—he thought he had consent—and that the insurance company should pay.

In Jeff and Debbie's case, none of Jeff's codefendants followed through on an appeal of the judgments against them. The insurance companies holding the policies for each of the boys' families simply paid. Jeff Cooper alone waged an aggressive appeal. First of all, the $650,000 judgment against him exceeded his family's policy limits, so even the insurance company could not satisfy the judgment.

More important, the insurance company, USAA, felt there was a crucial issue of law at stake. Cases like Jeff's—disputes over personal matters between two individuals—were becoming more common, often resulting in huge jury verdicts, with insurance companies footing the bill. The company feared that the tort of negligent infliction of emotional distress opened them up to potentially unlimited liability, in a way that invasion of privacy did not. This was clearly bad for the insurance industry, but USAA thought there were strong policy arguments why lawsuits like Debbie's were also harmful to society.

Most individuals who are sued do not have the resources to compensate the people they have harmed. The law often further insulates some defendants by allowing them to declare bankruptcy but keep certain valuable assets (such as a home or land, even lavish estates) safe from legal judgments. Therefore, in many cases insurance coverage provides the only means of recovery for many plaintiffs who suffer real and grievous injury.

Insurance coverage also indirectly provides something else to a plaintiff: a lawyer to fight the case. Most plaintiffs could not afford the expense of a lawsuit if they had to pay their attorney by the hour as the case went along. Enter the contingency fee attorney, who takes the case for free in exchange for a large percentage of any damages that are awarded. If there is no real prospect of financial recovery—in other words, if it is not possible to attack the deep pockets of an insurance company—then an attorney will be much less likely to take the case. Attorneys like Ronnie Krist and Dick Morrison argue that this system provides legal representation to individuals who otherwise could not afford it, as well as real compensation for the harm they suffered.

The catch, of course, is that the cost to the insurance company is ultimately passed on to the consumer in the form of higher insurance premiums. At first, this is more of a problem for the consumer than for the insurance company. But at some point, the argument goes, premiums could be raised so high that insurance coverage will not be affordable for any but the wealthiest companies and individuals. If that happens, the system threatens to go into a deadly spiral. Small companies could go out of business and municipalities might have to close down public facilities because they wouldn't be able to afford the insurance coverage they require. Individuals, too, would go uninsured, risking everything they owned. Ultimately, even insurance companies, with a dwindling number of customers, could fold.

Fear of such a spiral is at least one of the reasons there have been cries for tort reform. Dozens of proposals have been put forth, from limiting the amount of damages that a jury can award, to eliminating causes of action that result in giant verdicts, to doing away with contingency fee attorneys. Some insurance companies have reacted the way that Jeff Cooper's did—fighting case by case, state by state, to limit their liability under current laws.

Jeff's insurance company provided him with a new attorney, Barry Chasnoff, to handle the appeal. Chasnoff's job was to convince the Texas Supreme Court that Texas should not recognize negligent infliction of emotional distress as a valid cause of action. There was a problem, however. Just a few years earlier, the Texas Supreme Court had affirmed that very cause of action in another case, involving a hospital. When Debbie's attorneys dropped the invasion of privacy claim in favor of the one for negligent infliction of emotional distress, they felt they were on sure ground because they were relying on that recent case.

Chasnoff tried to make a distinction between the two cases, arguing that the hospital case applied only to those peculiar facts. Mostly, he argued policy: He said it was not in the interest of the people of Texas to recognize the tort of negligent infliction of emotional distress. Some of the arguments were the same as those used against its close kin, invasion of privacy. Chasnoff asserted that the cause of action was too ambiguous and subject to abuse, creating unlimited occasions for liability. The problem, he said, was that the tort required proof of only emotional distress, an injury notoriously hard to prove and quantify—one of the common criticisms of invasion of privacy. But unlike invasion of privacy, this tort required only a showing of negligence, a standard quite a bit easier to prove than intentional. For example, Chasnoff argued, if Jeff Cooper had not videotaped Debbie Anderson but broken up with her in a distressing manner, she could sue for negligent infliction of emotional distress. Chasnoff argued that recognizing such a tort would create a burgeoning liability, which neither the courts nor society could handle.

This was particularly unnecessary, Chasnoff asserted, when there were other causes of action which would give people like Debbie Anderson some relief. Debbie may well have a case for invasion of privacy, or even for *intentional* infliction of emotional distress. Because these are intentional torts, they would not be covered by insurance, but Debbie would get a jury verdict and whatever small amount of damages she could recover from the defendant who caused the harm. Chasnoff reminded the court that Debbie's attorneys had deliberately dropped the privacy claim so that they could trigger insurance coverage with a negligent tort.

"There is nothing evil about that," answers Ronnie Krist. "The lawyer is charged with the responsibility of enhancing the probability of recovery for his client. . . . [They say] we're looking for the deep pocket as if we had done something terrible. Well I say, 'Yes, that's right. And my malpractice carrier is glad I did it.' They would think I was a moron if I tried a case and said I could present it in one fashion and have an insurance company stand behind it, as well as the family; but I chose to present it in another fashion and have only the family."

As for the policy arguments against negligent infliction of emotional distress, Krist says they are as old as the law itself. There are many torts that could conceivably create open-ended liability, but none of them has been abandoned. Krist argued that judges and juries should simply be allowed to do their jobs: They should weed out the frivolous lawsuits without penalizing people with legitimate claims.

"The judge just says, 'Your case is silly. You're out of here.' " In any event, Debbie's attorneys said, all of these policy arguments were beside the point. The Texas Supreme Court had already recognized negligent infliction of emotional distress as a legitimate cause of action in Texas.

The appeal clearly came to be about something much greater than the dispute between Debbie and Jeff—it was now a case that would either reaffirm or condemn the system itself. The process dragged on for three more years. During that time, Debbie and Jeff's case took yet another twisting turn in its journey. The central incident, which had gone from the campus, to the courtroom, to a national legal controversy, now moved on to its next, and probably inevitable, stage—it became a media event.

Debbie, Ronnie Krist, and Jeff Cooper's trial attorney showed up on "Larry King Live." Sister Jane even called in to the program to stand up for her former pupil. Then Debbie and her attorney appeared on "Inside Edition," "Donahue," and a local Houston program. Krist says they turned down the many other television offers that were streaming in because they were "sleazy."

Jeff Cooper, on the other hand, refused all requests for interviews. He was now experiencing, on a national scale, the kind of treatment Debbie had received right after the taping. The public did not react in the same supportive way that his peers had. Just the opposite. Now Jeff was the one who was "branded." Although his friends and family stood by him, Jeff says, "I couldn't get on with my life. I mean, I had problems at work. It came up and I almost lost my job. That's when you feel like a pawn. . . . It never ended. It kept coming back up." Ironically, Jeff now felt exactly the same way Debbie had in trying to get on with her life after the tape became common knowledge. "Every time I met somebody," Jeff says, "I thought . . . 'Do they know?' "

On December 2, 1992, more than seven years after the original taping incident, the Supreme Court of Texas issued its opinion. But even that did not end the saga. In its opinion, the Texas Supreme Court did two unusual things. The court overruled its recent decision and now concluded that Texas should *not* recognize the tort of negligent infliction of emotional distress. Thus, the verdict against Jeff Cooper was set aside. However, in the "interest of justice," the court *also* said that Debbie Anderson could have a new trial based on another theory, presumably invasion of privacy.

The court said that continuing to allow claims for negligent infliction of emotional distress would "not only strain judicial resources, but would dignify most disputes far beyond their social importance." The court stated: "Tort law cannot and should not attempt to provide redress for every instance of rude, insensitive, or distasteful behavior, even though it may result in hurt feelings, embarrassment, or even humiliation." The court said that plaintiffs could still recover damages for the emotional distress they had suffered, but only if they could prove that the defendant had committed some other independent wrong and had not merely caused them distress in a careless manner. For example, if Debbie could prove that her privacy had been invaded, then she could recover damages for any emotional distress she had suffered as a result of the invasion.

The majority of justices went on to say that they considered what Jeff Cooper had done "egregious conduct" for which the law provides a remedy under other legal theories. It was under one of these other theories that Debbie could have a new trial.

Three justices filed an extremely angry dissent. They accused the majority of characterizing what happened to Debbie as a "mere trifle." Noting that the majority had left intact the right to recover for negligent infliction of emotional distress in certain previously recognized cases (such as the mishandling of corpses), the dissent stated: "Greater protection is thus extended to negligent mishandling of the dead than outrageous treatment of the living." The dissenting justices also said that the majority was failing to keep up with the times and counseled that "the law is not irretrievably locked in the days before television and videocameras." Finally, the dissent argued that if unlimited liability was the concern, then the solution was to take steps to limit the tort, not throw it out altogether. "The message of the majority is clear," the dissent wrote. "Don't bother this court to separate the injustice from the inconsequential, better to bar both."

Neither Debbie nor Jeff was happy with the decision. Although the court all but said that Debbie would win on a different legal theory, she did not want to endure another trial. Her attorneys immediately asked for a rehearing so that the justices might reconsider their decision.

Jeff Cooper was left in the most troubling position of all. The decision was a small victory for him in the short term—the jury verdict against him was overturned. But in the long run, it could be a disaster. Jeff did not want to go through a new trial any more than Debbie did. In addition, a new jury would almost certainly find that he had invaded Debbie's privacy. This time, though, a million-dollar verdict would not be covered by insurance, and paying the damages would leave Jeff bankrupt. In fact, Jeff had gone along with the appeal expecting that either the Texas Supreme Court would throw out the jury verdict and he would be off the hook entirely or the verdict would be upheld and the insurance company would cover it. Jeff's attorneys also asked the court to reconsider its decision to allow a new trial.

On May 5, 1993, the Texas Supreme Court declared that it would not rehear the case, but it then issued a new opinion to "clarify" the original decision. This time, the rhetoric was even more inflamed. The court left the legal conclusions intact but defended itself against attacks that it had been insensitive. The majority specifically accused the dissenting justices of "mischaracterizing" its opinion. The justices in the majority said that when they had written that the law could not redress all "rude" behavior, they were speaking generally, not about Jeff Cooper. They emphasized that Jeff's actions were "egregious" and that he should be punished, only under another legal theory that was not so open-ended.

One of the justices also wrote a concurring opinion attacking the dissenting justices: "As a result of the posturing by the dissenting justices, what has been lost in the shuffle is the pivotal role that insurance played in this case. . . . It does not take a rocket scientist to determine why Ms. Anderson's lawyers elected to proceed solely on the tort of negligent infliction of emotional distress. . . . This case has a lot to do with a search for a deep pocket who can pay. If the purpose of awarding damages is to punish the wrongdoer and deter such conduct in the future, then the individuals responsible for these reprehensible actions are the ones who should suffer, not the people of Texas in the form of higher insurance premiums."

The dissent was angriest of all. "What has occurred here with the issuance of a revised opinion," three justices wrote, "is roughly comparable to Jeff Cooper having erased those portions of the videotape featuring his friends making crude remarks, then replaying the remainder of the tape so damaging to Debbie Anderson. Excising a few insensitive phrases in no way alters the insensitivity of the majority's opinion." The dissent agreed that insurance had played the pivotal role in the case, but "in the sense that excessive concern for the effect of every opinion on insurance companies seems to have become the predominant and overriding issue here, even to the exclusion of a woman's most basic rights. Debbie Anderson loses today because of the majority's misdirected concern about the potential liability of insurers for some hypothetical rude behavior that might some day give rise to a lawsuit." The dissent concluded: "It defies logic to have a system of justice that will compensate the victim of a car wreck but will refuse to compensate the recipients of the most devastating of emotional injuries."

Most of the rhetoric was lost on both Debbie and Jeff. At this point, seven years and nine months after the original incident, they wanted most of all to put it behind them. Barry Chasnoff urged Jeff's insurance company to pay, even though the court had thrown out the negligent cause of action. The company had won the larger legal point; and Jeff had agreed to appeal, expecting that either the insurance company would pay the judgment or the case would be over. Jeff's insurance company offered the policy limit, $500,000, to settle the case and Debbie accepted it. There would not be another trial.

Debbie and Jeff's case lives on, however, in the Texas legal system. Barry Chasnoff says, "I think [the case] has eliminated a big area of potential exposure. I really do believe that it has taken a lot of cases out of the courtroom."

Debbie's attorneys think the Texas Supreme Court decision may have even farther-reaching consequences. Judges are elected, not appointed, in Texas, and the supreme court opinion overturning Debbie's jury verdict was unpopular with a lot of Texans. Ronnie Krist hopes that will translate into votes at the polls, changing the face of the state's highest court. "Heads are going to roll," he predicts.

In its way, the case also lives on with both Debbie and Jeff. Even though her verdict was overturned on appeal on somewhat technical legal grounds, Debbie still feels that she won. "The most important part was the jury verdict," she says. "What the boys did to me wasn't right and they needed to know that it was [at least] against society's view or opinion."

Since the trial, Debbie has married and had a baby girl. She has chosen to live on a ranch hundreds of miles from Houston and visits her hometown only rarely. Although her life has moved on, Debbie is certain that the secret videotape changed her forever. The incident eroded her trust in people and flattened her spirit in such a way that it will never be completely mended. "[Those guys] said it was just one night they were goofing off," she says. "Well, them just goofing off one night affected my whole life."

Jeff, too, is still affected. Like Debbie, he has married, but has chosen to stay in the Houston area. He works in commercial real estate and still sees the same friends who stood by him, including some of his codefendants. After eight years, he can now shake someone's hand without wondering, "Do they know?" Even so, Jeff says, "I don't think it will ever completely go away. . . . It's always out there."

McCALL v. THE SHERWOOD INN

The Peephole Cases

Q: *You've told us that you made love in the Jacuzzi and twice on the bed,
a total of three times during the course of the hours you were there at
the penthouse suite. You've told us about that; have you not?*

A: *I have told you about it, yes.*

Q: *You've told eight strangers about it as well?*

A: *[The witness indicates yes.]*

Q: *And anyone that's in this courtroom. Has that been easy for you to
come in and discuss this in front of strangers?*

A: *No.*

Q: *Why have you brought this lawsuit then which would force you to do
this or require you to do this, Terry?*

A: *Because I feel that it's very wrong and I want to make sure that it
never happens to anybody else.*

TERRY NELSON was in an Iowa courtroom describing her engagement night to Peter McCall. She and Pete had both grown
up in Iowa City. They met in 1980 in junior high school, but it
was not until 1986 that they began "going steady." She had just graduated from high school and was beginning classes toward a nursing
degree while working as a nurse's assistant. Peter had been to community college for a year and a half and, upon leaving college, worked at
a pizza parlor, then at a pawnshop, both in Iowa City. In 1987, Peter
moved to Dubuque to manage another pawnshop owned by his employer. All the while, he continued to see Terry.

The couple had discussed marriage several times, and by the summer of 1988, when Pete was twenty-two and Terry twenty, Pete decided it was time to propose. However, he did not want his engagement to be a casual affair. Pete says, "I wanted the night to be really special and I wanted to really impress Terry." Indeed, he planned an entire weekend to celebrate their engagement in a way they would always remember. Pete chose the Sherwood Inn, just outside Iowa City, as the place to spend the special weekend. The Sherwood Inn had approximately 130 rooms and was designed around a Knights of the Round Table motif. Two of Pete's siblings worked in the inn's restaurant, the House of Lords.

Pete knew that the Sherwood Inn had one special room, a penthouse suite located on the third floor. In addition to a wet bar and refrigerator, the suite had one Jacuzzi in the room and another outside on an enclosed deck. The cost for one night's stay was $116.95. Pete could not afford two nights in the penthouse, so he reserved the suite for Friday night, July 1, 1988, the night he planned to propose, and booked a standard room for the next night.

On July 1, Pete checked into the suite early to make sure everything would be just right. "I took candles and placed them around the outdoor hot tub," he recalls. "I figured when it was later at night I could go outside [and light them] and it would be kind of more romantic, being outside." Pete also arranged for his sister to bring cheese and crackers and champagne up from the restaurant. Then he double-checked that the diamond engagement ring was in his pocket and went to meet Terry and her parents for a drink in the House of Lords restaurant.

After cocktails with the Nelsons, Pete and Terry went up to the suite. Terry put away their clothes and Pete filled up the indoor Jacuzzi. They made love in the hot tub and drank champagne. Then Peter took out the diamond ring, placed it on Terry's finger, and asked her to marry him. She said yes and began to cry. Pete lit the candles around the hot tub on the deck and led Terry outside. They ran into a bit of a snag when the water in the Jacuzzi did not heat up, making it too cold to use. But Pete simply brought the candles inside and placed them around the room. He and Terry played the radio, ate cheese and crackers, drank champagne, and twice more made love on the bed. It was everything they could have wanted on their engagement night.

Only one thing seemed slightly awry. Throughout the evening and into the night, Pete and Terry heard noises behind the wall of the suite. At first, they didn't think much of it. Pete says, "I figured it could be somebody in the hallways or whatever, and I was just more concerned with the night and what was going on." Each time they heard the sounds, Pete and Terry just assumed that people were going to and from their rooms or the swimming pool. But when the noises continued well into the early morning hours, Pete decided that "something just did not add up right."

"But then again, I didn't know what it was," he says. "It sounded like a creaking sound, something I'd associate with somebody walking on something, and then like a shuffling of some type.

"Later on," Pete continues, "Terry was getting something out of the small refrigerator and I was lying on the bed, and I was just sitting there kind of looking over to her, and all of a sudden something just clicked inside of me.

"I was looking at the mirror and I don't know what made me go over there. The noises just led me to the wall. And then all of a sudden I [went] over there and I literally pushed Terry out of the way and I said, Something is wrong here."

Pete examined the mirror near the wet bar but did not see anything that could explain the sounds. Then he did something unexpected. He placed his hand up against the mirror, checking to see if there appeared to be a space between his fingers and the glass. It was a procedure he had seen on television. "I don't recall what show it was on or what I watched," he says, "but I heard somewhere if you put your finger up against a mirror and there's not a space, that's an indication that it could be a two-way mirror." Pete had no idea what reminded him of this trick just then. But when he checked the mirror in the penthouse suite, he did not see a space between his fingers and the glass.

Alarmed, he tried to take the mirror off the wall, but it was bolted on. Moving to the side of the mirror, he was able to pull it back from the wall a few inches. And behind the mirror, Peter saw a square hole cut into the drywall. The hole was approximately eight inches wide by eight inches high, giving someone on the other side a view into the penthouse suite.

Pete and Terry were horrified. "I took a towel and threw it over the mirror to conceal it," he says. "Then Terry and I quickly got dressed."

At first, they were simply dumbfounded at discovering, of all things, a peephole and a two-way mirror. Then they looked at each other. At the same time, they each realized that the noises they had heard may have come from someone behind the wall looking through the hole and the two-way mirror into the suite. They began to get a creeping sensation that someone, maybe several people, had been watching them. Slowly, they realized that someone may have seen all or part of their special engagement night, including Peter and Terry, naked, making love in various parts of the room.

Terry began to cry. Pete went around the room checking all of the other mirrors over and over, but found nothing. Neither Pete nor Terry could be sure exactly what time they discovered the peephole, except that it was in the early morning hours, and they did not sleep for the rest of the night. They say they just spent the time "consoling" each other. At daybreak, Pete went down to the front desk to report what he had found.

It turned out that the front desk clerk, Ray Fowler, had gone to high school with Pete and at first thought his former classmate must be joking. Pete told Ray to follow him to the suite. There, Pete and Ray together pulled the mirror out farther than Pete alone had been able to. Now, with daylight beginning to stream in, they could clearly see the hole cut out of the wall behind the mirror. They also got the glass out far enough to look through it from the other side. It was indeed a two-way mirror.

Terry already had their things packed to go. She was so upset she wanted to leave the Sherwood Inn altogether. "I didn't want to stay because I was so embarrassed and humiliated," Terry says. "But Pete said he wanted to make it up to me." Pete was trying to salvage what he could of his special engagement plans and suggested that they move to the second, standard room he had booked. They had been up all night and were exhausted anyway, he said, so they might as well stay.

Terry relented and they checked into the standard room. "The first thing I did," Pete says, "is I went around and I checked the locks and I checked the mirrors." Everything seemed to be secure. But neither Pete nor Terry could relax, let alone have a good time. Of that day and night at the inn, Pete says, "It wasn't too enjoyable." They went home the next morning.

A few days later, Pete and Terry were surprised that they had heard nothing more from the Sherwood Inn. Their discovery was so startling and their experience so disturbing, they were expecting some kind of explanation from the management. When none came by July 6, five days after the incident, Pete called the inn and asked for the manager, Ned Taylor. Peter McCall and Ned Taylor remember their first conversation differently.

According to Pete, Ned got "defensive" and said, "I've heard that rumor for years and I've checked it out and there's not a two-way mirror in that room." Pete said that Ned agreed to look into it only after he reported that the front desk clerk had seen the two-way mirror as well.

Ned Taylor says that he never told Pete McCall that he had "heard that rumor for years." He states that he could not have said that because he had never heard such rumors; indeed, Pete's call was the first he'd heard of a two-way mirror in the penthouse suite. Ned says that Ray Fowler never reported the incident to him. In fact, Ned recalls, at first he was so surprised by Pete McCall's assertions that he assumed it was a crank call. It was Pete's insistence and "calm manner," Ned says, that convinced him he should take the allegation seriously.

It is undisputed that when Ned took a maintenance man with him to the penthouse suite, they did find the two-way mirror concealing a peephole in the wall. Ned says he immediately told the maintenance man to seal the hole and replace the mirror with proper glass.

Ned then called Pete McCall. Both men agree that Ned admitted he had found the mirror and peephole and apologized on behalf of the inn. Then Ned said he had not known the mirror and hole were there, nor had he ever heard a rumor concerning them. He said he had no idea how long the peeping setup had been in the suite, nor how it came to be there. Then he offered Pete a gift certificate for a free weekend at the Sherwood Inn. Pete accepted.

Terry, however, wanted no part of another night at the Sherwood Inn, even if it was free. But Pete said he wanted to give it a try. He thought he might be able to make up for the fiasco of their engagement night. "I was living up in Dubuque at the time and I wanted to try to salvage what I could of our engagement celebration," he says. Terry argued with him for a while but finally agreed to go back "because Pete wanted me to." She says she was uneasy the entire weekend and Pete later admitted it had been a mistake to return.

Although Pete and Terry availed themselves of free room and board at the Sherwood Inn, they say it did not make up for the violation they felt they had suffered. Indeed, it only seemed to make things worse. "It brought back more of what had happened," Pete says.

In fact, as time went by, the fallout from the incident intensified for Terry and Pete. They say they began to get more than a little paranoid. "[If] I go into a public rest room, I have to check the mirrors myself and make sure that they are not two-way mirrors and nobody is behind them," Pete says. "I have on occasion gone as far as to take a mirror off a wall in a public rest room. . . . I have tried not to think about it, but it's something that I just can't get rid of."

Even walking about town made Pete and Terry uncomfortable. They had lived in and around Iowa City all of their lives and were familiar with many of the people in the community. They began to wonder who could have been behind the peephole spying on them. Was it someone they knew? "It's pretty humiliating to have to face people, wondering . . . ," Terry says. In addition, in a community the size of Iowa City, an event like the discovery of a peephole and two-way mirror at the local inn was no small matter. Pete and Terry say that people in town began to stare at them and point them out as the couple who had apparently made love in front of a Peeping Tom. Some acquaintances began to make jokes about eight-by-ten glossy photographs and videotapes, and Pete and Terry realized with horror that there could be a photographic record of what someone had seen in the suite that night. They had no proof that anyone had actually seen them, let alone taken videos or pictures, but the prospect was enough to cause them terrible anxiety.

"It's just something I never expected to happen to me, especially on an engagement night, which is supposed to be one of the biggest nights of my life," Pete says. "All I think of now is how the night should have been so special. . . . I mean, this is going to be with me for the rest of my life. . . . It's not like I just stayed there. It was a night I stayed there for my *engagement*."

Terry especially could not shake her sense of violation and resentment at the Sherwood Inn for allowing such a thing to happen. At the time, she said, "In the morning when I'm listening to the radio, anything with the name Sherwood in it makes me very mad. And one time they had this commercial on—it was for Valentine's Day—and you could win an evening for two . . . an unforgettable evening." The irony was not lost on Terry. And seeing Terry so upset riled Pete even more. For both, their initial shock and embarrassment was giving way to anger and a determination to do something about it.

Pete and Terry went to a local attorney who agreed to take on their case for invasion of privacy against the Sherwood Inn. But weeks and then months went by with nothing happening. As their case languished, Pete and Terry began to worry that the statute of limitations would run out and they would miss having their day in court. When the attorney stopped returning their phone calls, Pete and Terry decided that it was time to find new representation.

They went to Tom Riley, a lawyer who specialized in personal injury cases. Like many personal injury attorneys, he worked on a contingency basis; he would take a percentage of whatever damages he recovered for his client either in court or in a settlement. Tom Riley had never tried a privacy case before, and was aware that much of the law in this area was untested, but he felt sure that Pete and Terry had a strong case.

What worried Riley most about their chances actually had nothing to do with the unsettled nature of privacy law, or even anything of a legal nature. Iowa City is a university town, which, it is generally thought, makes for a more liberal jury pool. But according to Riley, people affiliated with the university usually do not show up on juries, leaving the older, more conservative members of the community to serve. Riley was worried about something that had never occurred to Pete and Terry: the jury's reaction to a couple sleeping together before marriage. "My sainted mother tells me she would have voted for the other side for that reason," Riley says.

Nonetheless, Pete and Terry said they had done nothing to be ashamed of and wanted to push ahead. Riley filed a lawsuit against the Sherwood Inn claiming invasion of privacy, as well as seven other counts including negligence, negligent misrepresentation, intentional infliction of emotional distress, and breach of contract. The privacy claim was based on an intrusion theory—that Pete and Terry's solitude had been intruded upon in a manner that was highly offensive to a reasonable person. Although Pete and Terry could not prove who had actually spied on them (or indeed that anyone had), they felt that the peeping setup and shuffling noises were solid evidence that someone had been behind the two-way mirror looking in—and they were holding the management of the hotel responsible for the intrusion. The gist of their claim was that the management was negligent because it either knew or should have known about the peeping setup and should have put a stop to it.

The Sherwood Inn was covered by a standard business insurance policy. The insurance company, Maryland Casualty Company, made an in-house decision that the lawsuit fell within the insurance coverage; if the hotel was found liable, it would be covered to the extent of the policy limit—$1 million. Maryland Casualty hired a local attorney, Keith Stapleton, to defend the suit. The inn's defense was that although the peephole and mirror existed, there was no proof that anyone had actually used them to spy on Peter and Terry that night. Furthermore, Stapleton would argue, no one in management knew of the peephole and mirror, and therefore the inn could not be held responsible.

Before the trial began, the attorneys for both sides discussed settling the case. Tom Riley recalls, "They offered, or suggested that they might be able to come up with, something like $13,000. Well, of course, the clients had now spent almost four years waiting to get to trial and they had some expenses. This was a contingency fee case . . . and they didn't have any legal fees, but they had deposition costs and things of this kind. So it was easy to reject that offer."

In addition, through discovery (preparation for trial), Terry and Peter were finding out that as shocking as they thought their case was, it was not unique. One southern attorney alone was representing twenty-one people who claimed they had found peepholes in their rooms at Holiday Inns across South Carolina, Tennessee, and Florida. Those cases did not involve two-way mirrors, but had to do with an even simpler method of snooping. The guest rooms of the hotels backed up along a service corridor. From that corridor, holes were drilled at points in the wall where a mirror hung on the other side. The silver coating on the back of the mirror was then removed, allowing a clear view into the guest rooms. In some instances, piles of cigarette butts were found in the corridor beneath the peepholes. Holiday Inn said the hotels involved in the lawsuits were franchises operated by local businessmen, not the company. Nonetheless, the hotelier promised to check all seventeen hundred hotels in its chain for peepholes.

Even in their own case, Peter and Terry learned, the peeping setup at the Sherwood Inn came as no surprise to at least some people. Tom Riley found several former employees who were willing to testify that the existence of the peephole and two-way mirror was "common knowledge" among many of the workers. In fact, some had themselves looked through the setup and into the penthouse, although all said they had done so when no one was using the suite.

All of this new information just "fueled the fire," according to Pete and Terry. "One of the things we wanted out of the lawsuit was public awareness," they say. "This is going on and it's our responsibility to let other people know."

The trial began on June 22, 1992, in the Johnson County Courthouse in Iowa City. Pete McCall took the stand first. He walked the jury through his plans for an engagement celebration, his activities in the suite with Terry, and his discovery of the mirror. He said that there was no doubt in his mind that the noises they had heard meant that someone was behind the two-way mirror spying on them. He recounted his first telephone call with Ned Taylor in which, Pete says, Ned responded that he had "heard that rumor for years." Then he told the jury of the gossip and joking he and Terry had endured, of his own humiliation, anger, and growing paranoia, and especially of the effect the whole incident had had on his fiancée. "My anger really stems from seeing how it's affected Terry," he testified. "Things come up, she gets upset and actually will cry. . . . And it just hurts me to see that, you know, what has happened to her."

On cross-examination, Keith Stapleton emphasized the fact that Pete had two siblings working at the inn's House of Lords restaurant at the time of the incident, and that another sibling had worked there previously. Stapleton also emphasized that Pete had waited until morning to notify the front desk, had not asked to have his money refunded, and indeed had stayed the next night at the inn. In addition, Stapleton had Pete confirm that he and Terry had used the gift certificate offered by Ned Taylor and spent another weekend at the inn, free of charge, several weeks after the incident. Finally, he asked Pete if he had seen any pictures or videos that could substantiate the alleged peeping, and Pete said no.

Tom Riley then called several former employees at the inn who established the existence of the snooping setup and how it could be used. They testified that there was a closet on the second floor, down the hall from where the penthouse was located on the third floor. A crawl space above the second floor, abutting the penthouse, could be accessed through an opening in the ceiling of the closet. The opening, approximately eight feet from the ground, could be reached by standing on a ladder, or even on one of the laundry carts that were stored in the closet. Once up in the crawl space, a person could walk or crawl along the rafters to reach the wall of the penthouse suite. There, behind the insulation, was an eight-by-eight-inch hole looking into the suite through a two-way mirror. The closet door had a lock, the former employees testified, but the workers had keys and, anyway, the lock was often broken.

Rita Gershon, the former head of housekeeping at the inn, reported that she had never actually seen the two-way mirror but had overheard two women in her department talking about it. "Basically, the conversation was just that there was a two-way mirror," Rita testified. "And, of course, there was no doubt when they mentioned it, it was the penthouse . . . they were laughing about it and carrying on. And then I walked in and the conversation ceased." Rita said that she told Ned Taylor about the conversation she had overheard and that Ned said he would "follow up on this." On cross-examination Rita said she could not remember exactly when she had talked to Ned about the mirror and that, whenever it was, Ned had reprimanded her for not coming to him sooner. That ended the testimony on the first day of trial.

On the second day, Tom Riley and Keith Stapleton again discussed settling the case. Riley says he asked for $100,000. "That was more than I would have taken, by the way, but I didn't want to start any lower than that." According to Riley, Stapleton replied that he might be able to get $20,000 and Riley turned him down. "But if they had offered $75,000," Riley acknowledges, "they would have gotten a settlement just like that."

Instead, the trial continued with another witness, Cal Johnson, who had worked in the maintenance department at the Inn from 1980 to 1987. He testified that he had heard about the two-way mirror pretty much from the start of the job. In fact, he had seen it for himself when he went into the crawl space to replace some insulation. He said he put new insulation over the peephole but did not cover it up. Under questioning from Keith Stapleton, Cal said that he had talked freely to many coworkers about the peephole and mirror, often in the House of Lords restaurant after his shift. Cal testified that he might well have talked to the McCall siblings about it, but he could not be sure.

Stapleton was trying to raise another defense for the inn. If the existence of the peephole and mirror was such common knowledge among employees, as the plaintiffs themselves claimed, didn't it stand to reason that Pete McCall's siblings, who worked in the restaurant at the inn, would have known about them as well? Then might not Pete McCall himself have known, and planned the whole incident as a setup for the Sherwood Inn? That was a possibility Keith Stapleton wanted to raise in the minds of the jurors.

The next witness was another former housekeeper, Kirt Fulton, who said that he, too, had seen the peephole from the crawl space. He had begun work at the inn in 1986 and had heard rumors about the mirror from several coworkers. So, Kirt said, one day he decided to see for himself. He stood on one of the laundry carts in the linen closet to reach the opening in the ceiling, pulled himself up, and crawled along the rafters. He said he peeled the insulation back with little effort and could see clearly into the penthouse suite, although no one was there at the time. On cross, Kirt Fulton testified that he never told anyone in management about what he had seen. "It really wasn't any of my business, I didn't think. I was there to clean rooms and collect my paycheck," he said.

The next witness was Kirt's sister, Janet Fulton, who had worked in the housekeeping department in 1987 and 1988. She, too, had heard gossip about the two-way mirror. "It was discussed quite liberally in the break room," she said. And like her brother, she did not tell anyone in charge at the hotel. "[That] was management," she explained when Keith Stapleton asked why not. "We were the workers. We never really mixed." She specifically did not tell Ned Taylor, she said, because, "I never really mixed with Ned."

Then, just when it seemed that Janet Fulton was simply repeating the testimony of other witnesses, she dropped a bombshell. Keith Stapleton asked her about another former coworker, Dave Fitzpatrick. Janet said that Dave had told her he had gone up into the crawl space and seen the peephole and mirror.

Stapleton continued to question her:

Q: Did he tell you that he told anybody about the mirror?
A: Upon one occasion after I stopped working at the Sherwood, he himself was no longer working at the Sherwood, he mentioned to me that he had told some people he knows about the existence of the mirror.
Q: And who [were] the people that he told?
A: He named Pete McCall by name but not Terry.
Q: So he told you that he told Pete McCall about the mirror before Pete McCall ever rents the room?
A: Yes, he told me that.

Tom Riley was stunned. Janet Fulton was his own witness, supposedly testifying for the plaintiffs, and this was the first he had heard of this damning account. He looked at Pete, but his client said he was just as surprised and had no idea what Janet was talking about. When

Riley got his chance to question her again (on redirect), he brought out the fact that Janet had never mentioned this conversation with Fitzpatrick either in her pretrial deposition or in other interviews with the plaintiffs. Riley also had her confirm that she was angry about having been called as a witness in the first place. But when he asked her to confirm that she had told someone in his office that if she was called she would "dump on Mr. McCall," Janet replied, "I believe my exact words were, 'I am not going to help Pete McCall cheat the Sherwood.' I told them I had information that would help out Mr. Taylor and that I didn't appreciate being bothered."

Finally, Keith Stapleton rose and asked Janet if it was true she had been fired from the Sherwood Inn, implying that she had no reason to help the hotel. She said she had indeed been fired.

The court took a midmorning recess at 10:25 a.m. and Tom Riley immediately put a call in to his office. He wanted someone to locate one Dave Fitzpatrick, formerly employed at the Sherwood Inn. Riley believed that Pete had never met the man and wanted Fitzpatrick to say so. But of course someone had to find him first. In fact, they had to find him by the end of the day, because the trial would be over by then.

After the break, Tom Riley called Terry Nelson to the stand as he had planned. Riley's strategy had been to open and close his case with Pete and Terry, to remind the jury of the human beings involved and the distress they had suffered. But now he first had to ask Terry about Dave Fitzpatrick. She testified that she had never met Fitzpatrick and that, to her knowledge, Pete had never met him either. She said that before her engagement night, she had never heard anything about a two-way mirror in the penthouse and there was "no way" she would have stayed in the suite if she had.

Then Terry told of their engagement night and of finding the mirror. She also testified about her anguish, telling the jury that she was still angry and embarrassed. "When people joke about it, or if I drive by the Sherwood, I start getting real upset, wondering if anything is ever going to be done about it, and if I am going to run into the person that was behind there." Like Pete, she said she had developed a paranoia about mirrors in public places and was uncomfortable everywhere from public rest rooms to dressing rooms in stores.

In a strange coincidence, it turned out that two-way mirrors had actually been a part of Terry's job. At the hospital where Terry worked, some patients were observed behind a two-way mirror while they were eating. "I was assigned to this patient, to feed her," Terry testified. "We have to feed them, and then the therapist on the other side will observe for feeding problems. And I felt so uncomfortable, I knew that when I came back the next day I wouldn't be able to go in and feed her again." Terry had to be reassigned.

Then Terry, under questioning by Tom Riley, explained why she was in court, concluding, "Because I feel that it's very wrong and I want to make sure that it never happens to anybody else."

Riley then recalled Pete to the stand to refute Janet Fulton's testimony. Pete testified that he had never met Dave Fitzpatrick and had certainly never heard anything about a two-way mirror in the penthouse suite prior to spending his engagement night there. As far as he knew, Pete said, the testimony about Fitzpatrick was a "complete fabrication." At that point, with Fitzpatrick nowhere in sight, Tom Riley rested the plaintiffs' case.

Keith Stapleton then opened the defense by calling his primary witness, Ned Taylor. Ned testified that he had been associated with the Sherwood Inn since 1972, becoming the on-property manager in 1982. He testified that in all of the time he worked at the inn, he had never heard a rumor about a two-way mirror until Peter McCall called him on July 6, 1988. He said that neither the front desk clerk, Ray Fowler, nor any of the other employees had said anything about it to him. As for Rita Gershon's testimony, Ned said that she had indeed told him that she had overheard a conversation between two employees about the mirror, but that was *after* the lawsuit had been filed. He confirmed that he had been furious with her for not telling him sooner. Finally, he testified that he had no idea how the peephole and mirror had gotten there.

On cross-examination, Ned confirmed that he had a large stake in the continued success of the Sherwood Inn. Not only had he been employed there for more than twenty years, he was a part-owner of the inn as well.

After Ned Taylor's testimony, Tom Riley rose to ask the court's permission to reopen the plaintiffs' case. Riley's office had found Dave Fitzpatrick. He was currently employed by a local construction company and happened to be working at a job site just a few miles away. Riley could not tell the court exactly what Fitzpatrick would say, except that his testimony would refute the surprise testimony of Janet Fulton. Riley's associate had subpoenaed Fitzpatrick right off the job site and he was waiting outside the door to the courtroom.

Keith Stapleton objected but it was overruled.

So Dave Fitzpatrick, who less than an hour before had been going about his business at work, took the stand. Yes, he said, he had worked at the Sherwood Inn and knew about the crawl space and two-way mirror; in fact, he had been up there and seen it for himself. Yes, he said, he also knew Janet Fulton. However, Fitzpatrick testified, he did not know Peter McCall and had never even laid eyes upon him until this moment. So, Fitzpatrick continued, he certainly never told Pete McCall about the two-way mirror, nor had he ever told Janet Fulton that he had done so.

Then, under further questioning from Riley, Dave Fitzpatrick dropped a bombshell of his own.

Q: You told the person that served the subpoena what you've told the jury. Is there anybody else within the last week that you've had a conversation with about this same subject?

A: Just Ned.

Q: And who is Ned?

A: Ned Taylor.

Q: That's the gentleman sitting over there next to Mr. Stapleton, the lawyer?

A: Yes.

Q: And did he come out and see you or call you, or just what?

A: He stopped out to the job site and talked to me a little bit about it. He just wanted to know the same questions, I guess. I gave him the same answers.

Q: So he knew what your testimony would be?

A: Yes.

Q: And you have not been asked to come in and testify to this jury by Mr. Taylor; have you?

A: No.

In his closing argument, Tom Riley said that not only had Peter McCall and Terry Nelson's privacy been invaded in the basest way, but now the hotel was trying to pin the incident on them. Riley said the defense sprang Janet Fulton's surprise testimony, knowing all the while that Dave Fitzpatrick was out there to refute it. He said the inn was trying to deceive the court and jury into believing Pete McCall had masterminded a fraud, rather than owning up to its responsibility for a gross invasion of privacy.

Keith Stapleton countered that Janet Fulton's testimony was entirely credible. After all, she had been fired from the inn so she had no reason to go out of her way to help the defense. In addition, Stapleton said, it was believable that although several employees knew of the two-way mirror, management did not. And if the employees did know, then wouldn't Pete McCall's siblings—the ones who helped arrange for the room—have known as well? Finally, while Peter and Terry had testified about their distress, they offered no actual documentation of their damages. They had submitted no doctor's reports, no medical bills, nor any evidence of lost wages. They had not offered "a dime's worth" of actual damages, Stapleton said. Thus, a jury award, if any, would have to be quite modest.

Before the case was submitted to the jury, Tom Riley dropped all of the causes of action except "invasion of privacy." He felt that the privacy claim was the strongest and would hit the jurors on the most personal, visceral level.

The jury received the case late in the afternoon of June 24, 1992. By 1:30 p.m. the next day, the jurors had reached a verdict.

The forewoman read it aloud:

"We, the Jury, find in favor of the Plaintiff Peter McCall and fix the amount of his recovery against Defendant Sherwood Inn, Ltd., at $100,000 on his claim for invasion of privacy (intrusion upon seclusion)."

"And We, the Jury, find in favor of the Plaintiff Terry Nelson and fix the amount of her recovery against Defendant Sherwood Inn, Ltd., at $200,000 on her claim of invasion of privacy (intrusion upon seclusion)."

Whatever the jurors thought of Pete and Terry sleeping together before marriage, they thought less of the actions of the Sherwood Inn. And that was not all. The $300,000 total covered only compensatory damages—that is, the amount of money awarded to Pete and Terry to compensate them for the specific harm they had suffered. After that, the court moved on to inquire about *punitive* damages.

"What amount of punitive damages, if any, do you award to Plaintiff Peter McCall?"

Answer: $2 million.

"And what amount of punitive damages, if any, do you award to Plaintiff Terry Nelson?"

Answer: $2 million.

A case that one lawyer had ignored, and another was willing to settle for less than $100,000, had just produced a $4.3 million jury verdict. Everyone in the courtroom was stunned, including the plaintiffs and their attorney. Tom Riley says, "In my wildest imagination I didn't expect a verdict that would approach a million dollars, let alone exceed a million dollars."

Keith Stapleton planned an immediate appeal. Insurance would cover only $1 million of the verdict and the $3.3 million balance would ruin the Sherwood Inn. But before the appeal process even got under way, Tom Riley called to say he would recommend that his clients settle for the $1 million in insurance proceeds. "It wasn't any charity on my part, or sympathy for the hotel," Riley explains.

The state of Iowa has a special rule regarding punitive damages. In many states, if an appellate judge decides that a jury's punitive damage award is excessive, the judge has the power to simply reduce the award. (For example, in one of the Holiday Inn peephole cases, a $10.1 million jury award to five plaintiffs was later reduced to $500,000.) But in Iowa, the judge does not have such power. He must either let the damage award stand or throw it out altogether and order a new trial. Thus, Tom Riley felt that Pete and Terry faced the very real possibility of having to start all over again.

They agreed to accept the $1 million in settlement. But Pete and Terry did not retain that amount for themselves. Tom Riley was entitled to his legal fee. And Iowa had another special law regarding certain kinds of punitive damages. In response to cries for tort reform, especially with respect to enormous jury verdicts, Iowa had created a rule declaring that when punitive damages are awarded in a case that is really on behalf of the public good, a portion of the money goes to the state. For example, the peephole at the inn was a danger to the entire community; Peter and Terry just happened to be the ones who uncovered it. Thus, a part of their punitive damages would go to the government.

So after their lawyer and the state of Iowa each took its share, Pete and Terry received a total of $375,000. It was still far more than they ever expected. "They were happy," Riley says.

Peter and Terry felt that the original jury verdict was extremely important as well. "We wanted to send a message, and they sent a message," Pete says. "The coverage that it got opened a lot of doors. Most everybody has heard about this, at least we hope they have, and they will think and check their mirrors." Pete says he still does. "For me, it's like, I wash my hands, I check the mirror. I'll probably do that for the rest of my life. Whether that's good, I don't know." Good or bad, for Pete and Terry it is necessary. "The government is there for certain reasons," Pete says, "but when it comes down to it, you've got to watch out for yourself. You've got to protect yourself."

Passing Judgments

A CALIFORNIA MAN engaged in sexual activity with several women on different occasions in the bedroom of his home. The women had no idea that a video camera hidden in a closet was recording everything they did. They found out only when police officers came to their door to inform them that the secret videotapes had been recovered from the man's home. Like most states, California did not have a law specifically declaring surreptitious videotaping of sexual activity to be a crime. However, it did have a criminal "eavesdropping" statute prohibiting the secret recording of confidential communications. So the man was prosecuted and convicted of violating that law. In his defense, he argued that sexual activity was not the kind of "communication" contemplated by the statute, so it was not fair to convict him under it.

A California court upheld the man's criminal conviction, declaring, "[W]e are convinced the defendant received fair warning. There can be little doubt he knew that in recording the sexual activity without the woman's consent, he was violating her right of privacy." One judge, however, dissented, saying that he disagreed with the majority's "strained construction" of the eavesdropping statute.

People v. Gibbons, California 1990

———

A KANSAS PHOTOGRAPHER invited females as young as fifteen to his attic studio to photograph them modeling clothes. When the women changed outfits, the photographer would leave the studio and close the door. What the women did not know was that the man had installed a two-way mirror in the studio and drilled a hole in the wall behind the mirror. He had a camera set up on a tripod behind the peephole and secretly took photographs of the women in varying stages of undress.

Police later found the pictures in the photographer's house. Like the man in California, the photographer was criminally prosecuted under an existing "eavesdropping" statute. He, too, defended himself by saying the statute was not meant to cover his conduct. A Kansas court disagreed, stating, "We believe what defendant did is not only immoral but is a violation of [the eavesdropping statute] and criminal in the State of Kansas."

Kansas v. Martin, Kansas 1983

———

FOUR YOUNG WOMEN wanted to join the Louisiana National Guard. They contacted the local recruiting officer for the guard. He came to the home of one of the women, where he interviewed each of the four. He also deceived them into thinking that he had the authority to conduct a physical examination and "proceeded to examine each female's breasts, rectal area, and vagina." When the women found out that the officer had no authority to perform physicals, they sued for invasion of privacy and battery. A trial court awarded the women $8,500 apiece.

The verdict was upheld on appeal. However, the appellate court found that the amount of damages was "clearly" too high. The court said that the women had testified only about their embarrassment and mortification but had offered no proof of "serious" psychological harm as a result of the "unnecessary" exam. Furthermore, the court noted, "All were adults, one was married, and two of the four had children . . . and the physical was not conducted in a manner to sexually arouse any of [them]." The appellate court reduced the damages award to $4,000 each.

Turner v. Louisiana and Sudduth, Louisiana 1986

———

ONE DAY, a twenty-five-year-old woman discovered two circular scratch marks on the bathroom mirror in her Maryland apartment. When the woman could not clean the marks off, she reported them to the management but heard nothing further. A few weeks later, an upstairs neighbor informed the woman that he had been in the vacant apartment adjacent to hers to look at the renovations taking place. He said that it was possible to see most of the interior of the woman's bathroom through two holes that had been scratched in the back of her bathroom mirror. The holes were approximately four and a half feet from the floor and had been scratched to accommodate a pair of human eyes. It turned out that the management of the building knew of similar incidents that had taken place in other apartments undergoing renovations. But the manager had not warned tenants, nor even told construction workers to stop the activity, for fear of "exacerbating the problem." The woman moved out of her apartment and sued the management for invasion of privacy and negligence. A jury awarded the woman $20,000 in compensatory damages and $150,000 in punitive damages.

On appeal, a court reversed the verdict on invasion of privacy because the woman could not prove who had spied on her. The court let the negligence verdict stand, but threw out the punitive damages award because the management's conduct "did not constitute anything more than negligent inattention" and was not "extraordinary or outrageous."

New Summit Associates v. Nistle, Maryland 1987

A COUPLE rented a house in New Hampshire from the landlord, who lived in an adjacent home. After a year, the husband discovered a microphone hidden in the bedroom he shared with his wife. Wires ran from the microphone to the landlord's house next door. The couple sued for invasion of privacy. The landlord argued, in part, that there was no proof that anyone had actually listened in on the bedroom activities. A New Hampshire court held that such proof was not necessary and it was "obvious" that "an intrusion of this type" would be highly offensive to any reasonable person.

Hamberger v. Eastman, New Hampshire 1964

There are some forms of "peeping" that are sanctioned by the courts. Indeed, most of us have probably been "peeped at" at one time or another in a public place. If you've ever been in a store dressing room with a notice that you "may be under surveillance," chances are that you were.

AN OFF-DUTY security guard was trying on clothes in the dressing room of a men's store. An employee climbed a ladder in back of the dressing room and peered in through a vent based on a suspicion that the man was shoplifting. The store clerk saw the guard's gun and promptly had him arrested. The guard sued for invasion of privacy. He lost. A Michigan court held that the guard did not have any real expectation of privacy in the dressing room—the door did not lock and signs warned of "surveillance." In light of the serious problem of shoplifting, the court held, such surveillance was reasonable. However, the court did go on to say that the employees doing the "surveillance" must be of the same sex as the person being observed.

Lewis v. Dayton Hudson Corp., Michigan 1983

HOWEVER, another Michigan court said that installing see-through panels in a women's rest room to control vandalism was going too far. The manager of a roller-skating rink had installed the panels in the ceiling of the ladies' room, permitting him a clear view of the area from above, including the partitioned stalls. When a mother and daughter using the rest room discovered the panels, they sued for invasion of privacy. The manager argued that the women could not prove that anyone had actually peeped at them. The Michigan court said that was not necessary and that "installation of the hidden viewing devices alone constitutes an interference with privacy which a reasonable person would find highly offensive."

Harkey v. Abate, Michigan 1983

ON THE other hand, when a customer of an Atlantic Zayre
store in Georgia complained that homosexual activity was occurring in the store's rest room, Zayre's loss prevention manager investigated the complaint. In the rest room he observed
what a Georgia court later called "an exhibition of highly suspicious behavior": Three or four men seemed to be waiting for
the second and third stalls, both of which were occupied, even
though the first stall was empty and in working order. So two
security employees went to a storage area above the rest room
and peered in through a crack in the ceiling. Based on their
observations, a man was arrested and charged with sodomy (a
crime in Georgia). The man sued for invasion of privacy. He
lost. A Georgia court held that "[the man's] interest in privacy
was subordinate to the store's interest in providing crime-free
rest rooms for its customers."

 Elmore v. Atlantic Zayre, Inc., Georgia 1986

*Even full-scale surveillance of public rest rooms by the police is not out of
the question. However, in such cases the subjects have the additional protection of the Fourth Amendment, as well as state constitutions, because the
"peeping" is being done by government officers. Whether such surveillance
is legal can depend on anything from specific constitutional language to the
layout of a particular bathroom stall.*

A RANGER at Mills Park in Carson City, Nevada, received numerous complaints from park visitors that the men's rest
rooms were being used for homosexual activity. Members of
the Carson City Sheriff's Department observed the rest room
and saw what they considered to be suspicious behavior (messages on the wall indicating the desire to meet certain men;
several men who visited the rest room multiple times in an
hour). The detectives then obtained a court order allowing
them to conduct surreptitious surveillance of the rest room.

The officers drilled a peephole in the ceiling over the stalls and installed a miniature video camera. They set up a monitor and videocassette recorder in a maintenance room next to the rest room. The officers monitored all activity in the rest room constantly, but videotaped only when they observed "criminal conduct." Twenty-one men were arrested for engaging in acts of masturbation and/or oral copulation in the Mills Park rest room. The men claimed that the secret videotaping violated their Fourth Amendment rights and could not be used against them.

The Supreme Court of Nevada noted that courts had come to different conclusions regarding the legality of such surveillance, citing more than a dozen cases of secret police surveillance in public rest rooms across the country. Some courts held that such clandestine observation always violates the Fourth Amendment, expressing concern that it "permits spying on the 'innocent and guilty alike.' " Other courts focused on the design of the rest room, especially on whether the stalls had doors, and if so, if they locked. If not, these courts held, there was no "reasonable expectation of privacy" regarding what went on in the stalls. The Supreme Court of Nevada adopted the latter approach and, noting that the Mills Park stalls did not have doors, held that the secret surveillance did not violate the Fourth Amendment.

Young v. Nevada, Nevada 1993

————

SEVERAL such surveillance operations were set up, without a warrant, in public rest rooms along Oregon highways after complaints of homosexual activity. In one instance, a hidden video camera was directed at two doorless stalls separated by a partition. The officer operating the camera from a hiding place knew when people entered the rest room by radio communication from another officer stationed outside in a van. The operator activated the camera "whenever he thought illegal activity might occur." Several men who were arrested for masturbating in the public rest room challenged the surveillance.

An Oregon court held that the surveillance may not be considered a violation of the Fourth Amendment, because the stalls did not have doors and thus the activity could be seen by anyone entering the rest room. However, the court held that the surveillance *was* a violation of the stricter standards of the Oregon state constitution. "A person in a public rest room anticipates that another person might enter and see what is going on," the court wrote. "What a person does not anticipate is that his activity will be seen by concealed officers or recorded by concealed cameras."

One judge dissented, stating, "Had defendant performed his acts on the 50-yard line of a Seahawks game during half-time, he could not successfully contend he had a right not to be videotaped. I see little difference between that and performing sexual acts in front of another, knowing that a member of the public could walk in at any moment."

Oregon v. Owczarzak, and *Oregon v. Casconi,* Oregon 1988

Privacy in the Workplace

MANY PEOPLE spend eight hours a day, five days a week at work where, whether we know it or like it, intrusions into our privacy can take place on a regular basis. The application process now routinely includes urine testing, while workers on the job are subject to video surveillance or telephone and computer monitoring. Sophisticated technology now permits management to monitor not just the work but the workers themselves; not only job performance, but off-duty behavior—including what employees have been eating, drinking, and smoking. However, many people are willing to sacrifice a certain amount of privacy in recognition of the employer's obligation to provide a safe and productive work environment, not to mention the right to make a profit. But how much intrusion is too much?

On the privacy side of the equation is the deeply held belief that people should be judged solely on the quality of their work. Most of us assume that while our boss has a right to know what we do on the job, what we do on our own time is our own business. In fact, federal and state laws prohibiting discrimination on the basis of race, sex, age, religion, national origin, or disability were passed to codify the principle that we should not be judged on our lifestyle, off-duty behavior, looks, or religious beliefs.

Employers, on the other hand, argue that in today's increasingly competitive economy, they have a right to choose the workers who best fit the job, and in order to make informed choices, they need information; information that can only be acquired through such procedures as background checks, credit checks, and drug tests. Once workers have been hired, the argument goes, monitoring is then essential to maintain and often improve productivity.

Driving much of the expanded need for information are the expanded responsibilities of the employer in two important and costly areas: health insurance and liability. Health insurance costs have been eating into corporate profits at an exponential rate. Insuring high-risk workers, like smokers or skydivers, further drives up the cost of insuring everyone else. But to know which workers are high-risk requires still more information, whether from medical tests or personal questions and surveillance. A second justification for workplace monitoring is that employers face liability for the actions of their employees. Also, under the fast-growing tort of "negligent hiring" an employer can be sued for its failure to adequately check the past histories of its workers. Indeed, in some workplaces, such as day care centers, employers are required to check the background of their job applicants (pursuant to the "Oprah" law).

There is nothing new about corporate control over people's lives. Articles on the subject invariably refer to the stories of Henry Ford's investigative team, which went door to door checking on the hygiene and morals of the first assembly-line workers. Nineteenth-century company housing evolved into the twentieth-century company town where, directly or indirectly, the boss knew about every aspect—personal and professional—of the workers' lives.

Today, a host of new privacy issues are coming over the horizon. We have tried to highlight some of them in the stories that follow. Does an employer's need to ensure a safe workplace justify asking intrusive questions? Can an employee's personal life or sexual orientation be grounds for dismissal? And what happens when privacy can be invaded by new technology and no law exists to cover a perceived injury?

A robust economy is obviously in everyone's interest. Improving efficiency and performance contributes to that end. Careful selection and monitoring of workers are important management tools that entail some intrusion into personal lives. But might we reach a point at which the workplace has become so dehumanized that any increase in profit is not worth the sacrifice of privacy?

SOROKA v. DAYTON HUDSON CORP.

Psychological Testing

SIBI SOROKA, an aspiring San Francisco actor in his twenties, doesn't doubt that one day he'll hit the big time, but in April 1989 his plans to open a pet supply store had fallen through and he found himself cruising the aisles at his local Target store. He ran into an old boss of his who was working at Target as an "asset protection manager" (the current term for a supervisor in the store's security department). When Soroka mentioned that he needed a job, his ex-boss encouraged him to apply at Target. During college, Soroka had worked as a security guard at similar stores, so he thought his chances of getting hired were good. He decided to apply for a full-time job, save up some money, eventually switch to part-time, and continue developing his own business plans.

Target Stores is a rapidly expanding high-end discount retailer selling housewares, toys, and clothing. It is owned by the Dayton Hudson Corporation, which also owns and operates Dayton's, Hudson's, and Marshall Field's department stores. As of 1994, Target operated 661 stores in thirty-two states, employed approximately one hundred thousand people, and in 1993 earned $11.74 billion in sales. Target is headquartered in Minneapolis, with regional operations and distribution centers around the country. California has 115 Target stores—more than any other state.

Target's entire asset protection division has about two thousand employees, most of whom work in the stores. Each Target store has an asset protection manager and several asset protection specialists, who rotate among a few different stores. They are responsible for securing store safety, preventing shoplifting, and detecting employee theft.

In Soroka's experience, store security work was a fairly low-key way to pick up some extra money. "[Asset protection specialists] are not security guards *per se*. They are undercover observation people. They are usually young people dressed in jeans and a sweatshirt. They might have radios in their bag, and they radio to other store personnel that people are putting stuff in their pockets, or taking five garments in the dressing room and walking out with two. It's no big Miami Vice–type operation at all."

Once a shoplifter is spotted, the rules are strict. According to Target guidelines, says Soroka, "I have to actually see [the customer] remove the item from the shelf. I have to maintain constant observation all the way through the store." Target also instructs its security force to give the customer every possible opportunity to pay for the merchandise. Consequently, confrontations usually occur outside the store. Says Soroka: "Generally they're busted and they know it. They go back in the store and your partner has called the police."

Soroka showed up for his interview at Target's Walnut Creek store in Northern California early in April 1989. He filled out some standard forms, was interviewed by the area asset protection manager, and took a preliminary test called the Target Screening Inventory, consisting of about one hundred twenty true/false questions. He was told to come back to take a second longer test, the Psychscreen, given only to those applying to the asset protection division. He scheduled his appointment for the following week.

"I arrived with five sharpened pencils and erasers to take the test, you know, like when you go to a [final] exam at school," he says. Before Soroka was allowed to open the test booklet, an administrator read aloud from the "Participant Agreement":

> The hiring process at Target consists of several steps, one of which you are about to complete. This step is a psychological inventory and its purpose is simply to give us some ideas about you that relate to the world of work.

The administrator then explained that the answer sheet would be forwarded to Martin-McAllister, a psychological consulting firm in Minneapolis, who would then "share their ideas . . . with the appropriate management personnel" at Target.

Soroka signed the form where required and turned to begin the test. For the most part, he found the first few questions easy to answer.

5. Our thinking would be a lot better off if we would just forget about words like "probably," "approximately," and "perhaps."
9. I usually go to the movies more than once a week.

There were also relatively harmless questions dealing with such subjects as what sections he turned to when he read the newspaper and if he enjoyed parties and being with groups of people. But some of the questions struck him as odd.

3. I looked up to my father as an ideal man.
23. When a person "pads" his income tax report so as to get out of some of his taxes, it is just as bad as stealing money from the government.

As he went further into the test, Soroka began to wonder about the relevance of some of the questions. He was asked to choose the better of two of the country's early presidents, to judge whether women should be able to drink in public taverns, and to give a positive or negative response to a classic children's book.

Odder still were questions about religion, sex, and politics. The test probed for his feelings about racism and whether he should get involved in solving that societal problem. It had questions about his views on dealing with income taxes. The test probed into the environment of the home he grew up in and there were fairly intimate questions about his romantic relationships and sex life.

Soroka needed the job, so even with his growing distrust of the test, he continued. The questions became more outrageous and, he felt, even less relevant to the job he was applying for. They probed deeper into his sexual feelings, clearly searching for any kind of abnormal tendencies and reactions toward the opposite sex. They even asked about aches and pains in different parts of his body.

Then he came to a stretch of questions that pushed him to the edge of disbelief. They asked about the regularity of his bowel movements, about any homosexual urges he might harbor, about perverted sex acts he might practice or want to practice. The test also asked questions about his religious beliefs: whether he believed in the afterlife, his feelings about sins and sinners, and if he believed in the resurrection of Jesus Christ.

After answering over five hundred questions, "I had to put the pencil down," Soroka says. "I pushed my chair back away from the table and then finally I said, 'Okay, let me just write some of these questions down, because I've got to ask somebody about this.' I did not major in history but I had enough knowledge to know that questions that asked me 'Children should be taught all the main facts of sex,' or 'I am worried about sex matters,' or 'I believe in heaven and hell and an afterlife,' I mean, questions like this just don't get asked of people when they're applying for a job!"

Soroka began copying down the questions but stopped when he hit question 606: "I believe there is a God." He says, "I mean, it was ridiculous! I couldn't copy all these questions down. I didn't bring enough paper and I didn't have enough time."

Soroka felt like quitting, but because he needed the job, he completed the test. By the time he finished, the administrator had gone to lunch and Soroka felt uncomfortable handing his test in to anyone else. So he sat down to wait. "I was kind of sleepwalking through the steps at this point because I was numbed by this whole event. And yet underneath that numbness, there was anger percolating inside, and there was just complete, utter disbelief. It seemed so ridiculous, it seemed like *anybody* who ever looked at this test would say, 'This is ridiculous. We cannot possibly ask this of potential employees. We would be laughed out of the [ballpark].' "

While he was waiting, it occurred to Soroka that although he did not have time to write down the hundreds of questions on the Psychscreen, he might have time to photocopy it. He called a friend to come get him, and they went to a nearby shop and photocopied the test. When Soroka returned to Target, the personnel administrator was still not back, so he handed the test in to a secretary and left.

Soroka says he was shaking and felt sick to his stomach. He and his friend got a glass of milk at Foster's Freeze. Then Sibi went home to bed. "I don't know if you've ever been robbed," he says. "Or someone has broken into your apartment or your house, or someone has said something about you that got out in public. It's like you've been violated and you can't get it back."

When he got up later that afternoon, Soroka says he looked at the test, shook his head, opened up the yellow pages, and started calling attorneys. He called the ACLU and other organizations listed under "employment law" in the phone book.

Soroka chose Brad Seligman to be his attorney because, says Soroka, "he interviewed the best." For his part, Seligman admits that he wasn't sure about the call at first. "I got this phone call from this guy who starts describing this test. Frankly, I thought he was hallucinating. The questions are ridiculous, about religion and urine, and all the rest of it. I was about to brush this guy off and then he said, 'I have a copy of the test.' I almost fell out of my chair."

Over the next couple of weeks, Soroka waited to find out whether he had gotten the job. He was told that a decision couldn't be made until the test results came back. Soroka was afraid that his answer sheet had gotten lost in the mail, or worse. "They probably passed it around the store. You know, everybody's going to read it and laugh before they get around to mailing it. . . . Here I've been asked to reveal my entire emotional and personal life—political, sexual, religious beliefs. If I get the job, I'll be thinking, 'Well, gosh, what do they know about me?' " A few days later, Soroka was offered a job with Target, and started working soon after. It didn't last long, about two weeks.

In the meantime, Soroka was planning his lawsuit. He decided he did not want to bring a personal injury claim against Target in which, if successful, he would be compensated for any damages he had suffered from having to take the Psychscreen. Rather, he and Brad Seligman wanted to stop Target from using the Psychscreen altogether. On September 7, 1989, they filed a class action lawsuit, claiming that the Psychscreen had invaded the privacy of Soroka and all those who had taken the test.

When officials at Target heard about the lawsuit, they were shocked. They had viewed the screening process, including the Psychscreen, as a necessary step benefiting both customers and employees. The process had been developed in response to financial problems and safety issues that had plagued Target Stores for some time. Target executives did not view a security position in their stores as the low-key job it seemed to Sibi Soroka.

First of all, asset protection specialists are charged with the task of battling the biggest money losers for Target: shoplifting and employee theft. In 1993, the last year for which figures are available, Target lost $168 million to a combination of shoplifting, employee theft, and

systems inventory discrepancies. The Bureau of National Affairs esti-
mates that nationwide, employee theft is the leading cause of retail
loss, costing U.S. businesses $15 to $25 billion annually.

Asset protection specialists also possess unique power over fellow
employees. Sheilah Stewart, Target's director of employee relations,
says simply, "They have the power to cost somebody their job." If a
discharged employee is falsely accused, it is Target that gets sued, not
the asset protection specialist.

Asset protection specialists also have power over Target customers.
An ugly confrontation or a careless accusation of shoplifting by a
store's security officer does nothing for Target's image with the public.
And if a customer feels that he has been unjustly detained and falsely
accused, again, it is Target who will be sued.

In addition, Target, like all employers, faces potential liability
under the tort of negligent hiring. In lawsuits for negligent hiring, employers are held liable for the actions of an employee whose past they
have failed to investigate, or about which they knew and did nothing.
For example, the parents of a child who was sexually assaulted on the
premises of a New Mexico hotel sued the hotel for negligent hiring
and negligent retention of an employee whose history of alcoholism
and violent behavior was known to management. Similarly, the Supreme Court of Minnesota imposed liability on the owner of an
apartment complex for hiring a manager who raped a tenant, because the owner failed to investigate the employee's prior criminal
record.

Although Target Stores does not have a higher incidence of violent
crime than other retailers, it has not been immune to the general epidemic of crime across the country. Asset protection specialists are responsible for overall store safety. Though their usual job is to handle
belligerent customers, on occasion, according to Target's management,
guns have been fired in the stores and cashiers have been shot.

Target's vice president and general counsel, Bob Sykes, adds,
"[Store security officers] are threatened verbally, and there is an attempt in many cases to physically intimidate. Weapons may be drawn
. . . and that is part of the everyday fare. The very severe examples occur on perhaps a weekly basis. But day to day, all sorts of things happen. And it's the unpredictability, the uncertainty, which creates great
stress and anxiety."

It was this level of stress, coupled with the power and potential for danger, as well as liability, that led Target to review its security personnel and procedures in 1987. Target concluded that its security staff was inadequate and took steps to improve the performance of those already on the job. For example, asset protection specialists were trained to encourage shoplifters to discard merchandise (by making eye contact with the suspect and pulling out their radios), rather than risk a violent confrontation. Target was also concerned about new security personnel coming on board. The company feared that people who had been rejected for police work, possibly because of emotional instability, were applying for store security jobs. Management decided to institute a screening procedure to stop the potentially problematic or even dangerous employee before he or she got in the door. As King Rogers, Target's Vice President, Loss Prevention, puts it, "We wanted to make darn sure that the people we were selecting were people who were going to treat our customers in a respectful manner, and that they were not nuts who were going to be unleashed at our stores."

King Rogers, Sheilah Stewart, and Karen Grabow, Vice President, Human Resources Development, were aware of various techniques used to screen applicants for high-stress, safety-sensitive jobs. For example, emotional stability is considered essential for police officers, firefighters, and nuclear power plant engineers—jobs in which a lapse could have life-or-death consequences for fellow workers or members of the community. So Target turned to Martin-McAllister, a psychological consulting firm which had screened police candidates for the city of Minneapolis. Over the years, Martin-McAllister had also evaluated applicants for Target's high-level executive positions.

At Martin-McAllister's suggestion, Target decided to adopt some of the same screening procedures used for police work. According to Bill Kirkpatrick, one of Martin-McAllister's senior psychologists, an evaluation for a law enforcement applicant consists of a background investigation, a personal interview lasting about an hour and a half conducted by a licensed psychologist, and a battery of psychological screening tests. Since Target's asset protection division has to hire over a thousand people a year, the company decided that the entire police evaluation process would be prohibitively expensive. Martin-McAllister then suggested that a condensed version of the psychological screening tests be administered to Target applicants.

The test, known as the Psychscreen, is designed to focus on the applicants' emotional stability. It is a combination of two psychological screening tests originally developed for use in clinical settings: the Minnesota Multiphasic Personality Inventory (MMPI) and the California Personality Inventory (CPI). The MMPI was designed in the 1940s to detect psychopathology, or extreme deviant personality types; the CPI was first introduced in the 1950s to evaluate aspects of the normal personality, such as interpersonal behavior or emotional responsibility. Each of these tests takes the better part of a day to complete and many questions overlap. The Psychscreen eliminates the overlap, consists of 704 true/false questions, and can be completed in three to four hours.

To score the test, Martin-McAllister psychologists broke the answers down into six scaled categories: Response Set, Emotional Stability, Interpersonal Style, Addiction Potential, Dependability/Reliability, and Socialization. The psychologists were also prepared for those who tried to look too good. If a person tries to predict the "right" answer, psychologists mark the test "Invalid."

According to Target and Martin-McAllister, the goal of the scoring system was not to discover the sexual orientation, fantasies, or religious beliefs of any particular person. Rather, the process of comparing the overall pattern of a person's answers to the overall patterns of answers accumulated over many years of use will reveal extreme or deviant personalities. In practice, most people score somewhere in the middle range. Those who score at one extreme or another are the ones that Target was seeking to screen out. As Karen Grabow puts it, "I would not expect to see the caliber of our whole workforce improve as a result of this test. What I would expect was that we might identify lunatics and keep them out of our workforce."

Finally, Target emphasizes that the psychological testing procedures were designed with a concern for employee privacy in mind. No one at the company ever saw an applicant's actual answer sheet. Martin-McAllister sent back only a numerical rating in each of the categories, and a general recommendation as to whether the applicant posed a security risk. Target had enthusiastically begun using the Psychscreen as a hiring tool in January 1988.

Target was not alone in experimenting with workplace testing. The 1980s saw an explosion of both old and new forms of screening, including polygraph testing, drug testing, honesty testing, medical exams, and AIDS testing. As in Soroka's case, most of this testing was administered to people applying for work. In the pre-employment area, most of the testing has been upheld by the courts. The trend most likely will continue, with more futuristic possibilities—like hair testing for drugs, and genetic testing, just over the horizon.

Although each type of workplace testing raises somewhat different privacy issues, they have common elements, and a ruling in one area can have important consequences in others. Because Soroka's case was believed to be the first serious challenge to a private employer's use of psychological testing, and because California courts have led the way in many new areas of the law, the case was closely watched by corporations across the country. The arguments centered on the California state constitution's right to privacy. When California voters amended their state constitution in 1972 to add privacy to the list of protected "inalienable rights," they created possibly the strongest privacy protection in the country.

The ballot arguments approved by the voters made clear that the privacy provision of the California constitution was aimed not only at the more familiar types of privacy, such as freedom from unreasonable search and seizure, and reproductive privacy, but also at the newer threat from the widespread dissemination of personal information, so-called informational privacy. California voters affirmed that, "Computerization of records makes it possible to create cradle-to-grave profiles of every American. [The right to privacy] prevents government and business interests from collecting and stockpiling unnecessary information about us and from misusing information gathered for one purpose in order to serve other purposes or to embarrass us."

Soroka argued, and Target conceded, that the Psychscreen revealed personal information. However, even under California's constitution, an individual's right to privacy is not absolute—that is, it can be overridden by a stronger right, or a more compelling societal interest. Thus, the core of the case became: Did Target's interest in ensuring an emotionally stable security force justify the invasion of privacy caused by taking the Psychscreen? The California courts were split on an important issue central to that question: Do job *applicants* enjoy the same privacy rights and protections as those already on the job?

Some courts had found that applicants are entitled to less protection, reasoning that the applicant can choose not to submit to an overly intrusive pre-employment evaluation. Employees, the argument goes, deserve greater protection because they are less free to go elsewhere, and furthermore, the employer can observe their job performance directly, thereby eliminating the need for intrusive testing. Target argued that, particularly in the case of applicants, it had only to demonstrate that its use of the Psychscreen was *reasonable*.

Soroka argued that the state constitution was intended to protect individuals, regardless of whether they happen to be applicants or employees at any given time. Furthermore, he asserted, applicants deserve the same level of protection as employees. Soroka points out that often applicants may be more vulnerable, as they are required to disclose personal information to many different companies before they get a job. He argued, therefore, that in order to overcome a constitutional right, Target should have to demonstrate that it had a *compelling* interest in the private lives of its workforce.

Soroka also argued that the nature of the job and the relevance of the test were the truly important considerations. A key principle in the area of workplace privacy—one that links public and private sector, applicant and employee, and the various forms of testing—is whether and how closely the intrusion is related to the job. In legal parlance, it is known as "the nexus requirement." The principle is somewhat flexible, and a sort of sliding scale is often applied. For example, if a job is truly high-risk, like that of a police officer, nuclear power engineer, or train operator, greater intrusion into the employee's privacy will be permitted than in the case of a clerical or administrative employee. Not surprisingly, the parties in the *Soroka* case differed over whether the job was, in fact, high-risk and, assuming that it was, whether the Psychscreen was relevant to job performance.

Soroka's lawyer, Brad Seligman, claimed that the job was not high-risk, describing the asset protection specialists as "the folks at your discount department store standing around the door to see if you're wearing three pairs of pants." Furthermore, he argued, there was no evidence that the Psychscreen, as used by Target (without the clinical interviews central to the police screening process), was reliable or accurate. No in-depth validation studies had been conducted, and Target admitted that it had tested only fifteen to twenty APSs before introducing the Psychscreen as part of its application process.

Finally, he said that the questions regarding Soroka's religious beliefs and sexual orientation or activities were unrelated to his ability to perform the job. According to an ACLU brief filed on Soroka's behalf, "An inquiry into the contents of the mind is an inquiry into the human soul. That inquiry may be the province of our God, our priest, or perhaps our spouse. It is not properly the province of our government, or our employer."

Target strenuously countered that the position of asset protection specialist was, in fact, a high-risk job for which psychological testing was necessary. Target executives recited the incidents involving violent confrontations in the stores and elaborated on the unique power of the asset protection specialists over the public as well as over employees. Target also asserted that the Psychscreen did, in fact, meet the nexus requirement. From Target's vantage point, an emotionally stable security force was absolutely critical, and the Psychscreen was a professionally recommended and administered tool designed to achieve that goal.

On October 25, 1991, a California court of appeals ruled in favor of allowing Soroka to go to trial. It found that the California state constitution applied to private employers and made no distinction between applicants and employees. The court also found that any violation of the right to privacy must be justified by a *compelling* interest and must serve a job-related purpose.

Turning to Soroka's case, the court found that Target had failed to demonstrate a compelling interest or a job-related purpose connected with the Psychscreen's questions on religious and sexual matters. It found that Soroka was likely to prevail at a trial. In the meantime, the court held that Target could not use the test while awaiting trial, declaring that the harm to applicants from continued administration of the Psychscreen outweighed the harm to Target, which could use other means to determine emotional fitness for the job.

Target appealed, and in January 1992 the California Supreme Court agreed to take the case, leaving the intermediate court's conclusions in doubt. The state supreme court joined *Soroka* with another important privacy case also working its way up the system, *Hill v. NCAA*.

Hill involved a challenge by student athletes at Stanford University to the NCAA's drug testing program. The trial court and intermediate court had both ruled in favor of the athletes, finding that the privacy provision of the state constitution applied to the NCAA, and that the NCAA had not demonstrated a compelling interest in testing student athletes for drugs.

By joining *Soroka* with *Hill*, the California Supreme Court indicated its willingness to issue a major ruling interpreting the privacy provision of the California constitution. Workplace privacy has been among the fastest-growing areas of tort litigation, and California has been a recognized leader in the area. A supreme court decision in that state not only would clear up the confusion among the different divisions of the appellate courts but would have important ramifications for testing programs around the country.

While both sides were waiting, the most important workplace legislation in twenty years—the Americans with Disabilities Act of 1990—took effect. The ADA prohibits job discrimination against a qualified individual because of a disability. It provides that a pre-employment medical exam can be required only after a conditional offer of employment has been made. The ADA also requires that any pre-employment physical or medical exams be job-related. The ADA was so new, it was anyone's guess as to how broadly such provisions would be interpreted. Would the ADA apply to a test like the Psychscreen?

Soroka was convinced that the ADA would bolster his arguments. He believed that the Psychscreen would be perceived as a medical exam, and if so, it could be found to violate the ADA.

In addition to the uncertainty posed by the ADA, Target was also increasingly concerned about the impact of Soroka's testimony upon a jury. Target executives believed that Soroka had distorted the use and purpose of the test throughout the lawsuit by quoting questions out of context and glossing over the fact that no one at Target saw the applicants' responses. Still, Target's attorneys recognized the emotional impact of Soroka's strategy. In the summer of 1993, Target decided to settle.

Under the settlement agreement, Target did not admit liability but put $1,300,000 in a fund to be divided pro rata among people who had taken the Psychscreen, with each claimant receiving at least $500 per test. The three named plaintiffs were to split $60,000. Soroka received the largest share: $22,000.

Target also agreed not to require future California applicants for positions in the loss prevention department to take the Psychscreen or any other test based on the MMPI or CPI. It agreed to collect all Psychscreen rating forms from people who had already taken the test in California and keep them in a secure, confidential location. Target was prohibited from using those ratings except to defend itself in a lawsuit for negligent hiring or if ordered to do so by a court. Target agreed to destroy the documents relating to people it did not hire after one and a half years, and after five years for employees. The company remained free to refer individual employees to a psychologist for evaluation.

Soroka is pleased with the settlement, but says he won't be happy until all the records are destroyed. "I would still like to be evaluated on my past record of performance," he says, "not on what I do on Sunday, not on what I do in the bedroom, not on what happened to me as a child." He remains convinced that "whether you are a little guy or a CEO, job performance should be the key."

Today, Target has replaced the Psychscreen with a more structured interview process in which three people pose specific questions. The company also conducts background and criminal records checks of applicants to its loss prevention department, and recruits on college campuses.

But Bob Sykes and King Rogers remain adamant that none of these other measures is an adequate substitute for psychological testing. Says Sykes: "There is a rhetorical question that is at the core of this entire issue: Assuming that emotional stability is relevant to these positions, and we've answered that it is, how does one go about measuring emotional stability? Is it something you can ask in a question in an interview? I think the professional community of psychologists and psychiatrists would say there are but a few, if not one or two, assessment tools that effectively and accurately make that evaluation. And those were the ones that we used. We don't know how else to do it, quite frankly."

THE CALIFORNIA Supreme Court issued its decision in the *Hill* case on January 28, 1994. It found that the NCAA's drug testing program did *not* violate the athletes' state constitutional right to privacy. The court held that the NCAA's interest in health and safety outweighed the diminished privacy expectations of the athletes.

Perhaps most important, however, the court laid out a test for future invasions of privacy under California's state constitution. A plaintiff must prove a legally recognized privacy interest, a reasonable expectation of privacy in the circumstances, and a serious invasion of privacy by the defendant.

The court ruled that when the case involves an "obvious invasion" of a "fundamental" privacy interest, such as freedom from involuntary sterilization or freedom to pursue "consensual familial relationships," a "compelling interest" must be present. However, it found the compelling interest test to be too rigid in other circumstances. When the invasion affects informational privacy, a balancing test should be employed to determine if the invasion is reasonable.

Passing Judgments

DRUG TESTING

The hottest workplace privacy issue of the 1980s was drug testing. As a central weapon in the Reagan administration's "war on drugs," government agencies led the way in instituting drug testing programs for their workforces. These were challenged as a violation of the Fourth Amendment's prohibition against unreasonable search and seizure. In 1989, the Supreme Court upheld post-accident drug testing of railroad workers, and testing of Customs Service personnel involved in drug interdiction efforts. Since then, drug testing programs affecting government workers in public safety jobs, like pilots, train engineers, or police officers, have generally been upheld, whereas blanket testing of administrative or clerical workers has not.

In the private sector, where workers are not protected by the Fourth Amendment, drug testing has become widely accepted, particularly in the pre-employment context. According to the American Management Association, an estimated 91 percent of large companies now test their workers for drugs.

IN 1990, a woman who worked for the Ford Meter Box Company in Wabash, Indiana, was fired for flunking a drug test. But what she tested positive for was nicotine. Ford Meter Box forbade its employees to smoke, even on their own time at home. Although the woman did not get her job back, her case led the Indiana legislature to pass a law prohibiting companies from firing employees for smoking. The legislation does, however, permit employers to charge additional health insurance premiums for employees who smoke.

Bone v. Ford Meter Box, Indiana 1991

IN APRIL 1989, a benefits clerk at the Conagra Poultry Company in Denver, was notified that her employer planned to institute a drug testing program. In addition, Conagra required employees to disclose all prescription medications they were taking. The clerk refused to sign the disclosure form and was fired. She sued for invasion of privacy, among other claims. The court dismissed her case.

Mares v. Conagra Poultry Co. Inc., Colorado 1991

POLYGRAPH TESTING

Lie detector testing also enjoyed a surge in popularity in the 1980s. By 1987, an estimated 1.8 million polygraph tests were being conducted annually, with 75 percent of those being administered to job applicants. For years, however, polygraph tests had been criticized as intrusive, inaccurate, and unreliable.

IN 1982, the city employees of Long Beach, California, challenged the use of polygraph tests as a violation of the California state constitutional right to privacy. In 1986, the California Supreme Court wrote: "A polygraph examination is specifically designed to overcome . . . privacy by compelling communication of thoughts, sentiments, and emotions which the examinee may have chosen not to communicate." The court found that there was no compelling state interest to justify the use of the tests. It cited a polygraph examiner's manual in which the following questions were suggested:

Have you had any major operations in the past ten years?

Have you ever suffered a nervous breakdown?

Have you ever filed or collected workmen's compensation insurance from an on-the-job injury?

Have you ever had an automobile accident while you were driving?

Are you now or have you ever been a Communist sympathizer?

Have you written any bad or insufficient checks in the past three years?

Long Beach City Employees Ass'n. v. City of Long Beach, California 1986

IN 1982, an employee of a New Hampshire Papa Gino's for nearly ten years was confronted by a superior with rumors that he had been seen using drugs outside work. The employee took a polygraph test and answered questions relating to his alleged drug use. When the examiner reported his belief that the man was lying about using drugs, the man was fired. He later claimed that he had been forced to take the test under the threat of losing his job and had been asked numerous non-job-related questions about private matters. A jury found Papa Gino's investigative techniques "highly offensive to a reasonable person" and awarded the employee $398,200. In 1986, the U.S. Court of Appeals for the First Circuit upheld the verdict.

O'Brien v. Papa Gino's of America, Inc. New Hampshire 1986

IN 1988, Congress passed the Employee Polygraph Protection Act (EPPA) of 1988, which essentially bans the use of polygraphs, voice stress analyzers, and other physiological tests as job-screening devices by private employers. Exceptions were made for the pharmaceutical industry, security-guard companies, and government. Testing of employees suspected of specific incidents of theft is still permitted under the EPPA.

SHAHAR v. BOWERS

Lifestyle Monitoring

AFTER GRADUATING magna cum laude from Tufts University in Boston in 1986, Robin Brown wanted to live in a city with warmer weather and good jobs for women. She chose Atlanta, Georgia. Robin was hired to be the program director for the B'nai B'rith Youth Organization, and later took a job as a paralegal, but her long-range goal was to work in the public sector.

In December 1986, Robin attended a winter solstice party, which is, as she puts it, "the politically correct version of a Christmas party." There, she was introduced to Francine Greenfield, known as Fran, who had moved to Atlanta from New York to get her Ph.D. in clinical psychology. Robin and Fran fell in love. As their relationship developed, they bought a house together, got a couple of dogs, and settled down to pursue their respective careers.

Robin considered applying to a graduate school in social work, but in September 1988 wound up instead at Emory Law School as the winner of a Woodruff Fellowship, a prestigious full academic scholarship. Robin did well at Emory. She made the dean's list every semester, received two American Jurisprudence Awards (given to the student in each course who received the highest grade), and was selected as an editor of the *Law Review.* Robin also passed the Georgia Bar Exam while she was still in her third year of law school, and graduated sixth in her class of over two hundred students.

While in law school, Robin decided she would like to do criminal work after graduation. She was also concerned about having a secure, steady job and earning enough money to help support Fran while she completed graduate school. During her second year at Emory, Robin applied and was accepted for a summer job in the office of the attorney general for the state of Georgia, Michael Bowers.

Robin enjoyed the work that summer, especially the criminal appeals and death penalty cases. Deciding how to integrate her personal life with Fran into everyday office socializing, however, required thought and a plan of action. It was a process Robin says many gay people in the workforce must go through.

For her part, she did not want to avoid talk of her personal life altogether—that seemed unnatural. She could, as some people she knew did, discuss her private life but constantly edit her descriptions. For example, she could refer to Fran as a "friend" or to the two of them as "we" and avoid references to "she" or "her." But that, too, seemed unnatural, not to mention exhausting.

Robin decided that for her, the best approach was to steer a middle course. "Wherever I would work, I would want to be honest about who I am. But that doesn't mean I want to come in the first day and put a big sign on my door," she says. "So what I usually do is try to get to know people—sort of get a feeling for when they're liking me and thinking okay things about me. Then, once I've got that established, if I come out to them, hopefully they won't rule me out as a person."

Robin eventually came out to her fellow summer law clerks and three or four permanent employees in the office, including her supervisor. As far as Robin could tell, her sexual orientation did not cause much of a stir among those who knew. And by the end of the summer, Robin had received an offer from the attorney general to become a full-time prosecutor in his office. She happily accepted.

Nineteen ninety-one was to be a big year for Robin for another reason as well. For some time, Robin and Fran had been meeting with a rabbi to discuss sanctifying their relationship through a religious marriage ceremony. They finally chose a date—July 28—after Robin's graduation but before the start of her job. The weekend celebration was to take place on a campground at Table Rock State Park in the South Carolina mountains. Robin and Fran had made all the arrangements. They expected about a hundred people, including their parents, grandparents, and friends. Fran had invited the entire psychology department from the federal penitentiary where she was working, and Robin had invited a couple of people from the attorney general's office.

As part of the ceremony, Robin and Fran had also decided to

change their names. "We weren't satisfied with any of the combina-
tions of Brown and Green we came up with, so we decided to take a
name that had a different kind of meaning for us than variations of
our fathers' names would have," says Fran. They chose Shahar, which
in biblical Hebrew means "an act of seeking God" and in modern Hebrew translates as "dawn."

In mid-June 1991, Robin called Bob Coleman, the deputy attorney
general in charge of administration, to confirm her starting date (September 23) and her division assignment (division 3, criminal appeals
and death penalty work) and to inform him of her upcoming name
change. "I had this big thing about changing my name," says Robin.
"I thought I just couldn't go in and have a new name. I decided to say,
'I'm getting married and I'm changing my name.' Just like that. I
didn't know him well enough to get into it with him, and I assumed
he would say, 'Congratulations. Okay, what's your new name going to
be?' And he would change my paperwork and that would be the end
of it."

"But," she says, "what happened was, he got very excited when I
told him I was getting married. Then I found out through the grape-
vine a few weeks later that he had been running around the office telling everyone that I was getting married. The assumption behind it was
that I was marrying a man. Certainly, when I said to him, 'I'm getting
married and I'm changing my name,' I didn't think he would think I
was marrying a woman. But it was very difficult because I didn't know
him well enough to say, 'Bob, I'm having a ceremony with my female
partner.' I didn't feel comfortable telling him that."

"I was horrified because it meant that when I got to the job, they
would all be saying, 'Oh, I heard you got married,' and I would be in
this awkward position over and over again—'Do I tell them that I married a woman, or do I let it go?' If he had just said 'Congratulations,'
then I would have come to work and I would have been able to come
out at my own pace. . . . I just didn't really think it through."

But as it turned out, she didn't have to. A couple of weeks later,
on July 9, Bob Coleman's secretary called to ask Robin to come down
to the office for a brief meeting. When Robin got to Coleman's office
the next day, he was there with Stephanie Manis, another deputy attorney general. Coleman handed Robin an envelope and said her job offer
was being withdrawn. Robin asked if she could speak with Michael
Bowers personally and was told his schedule was full. That was it. She
was fired before she had started work.

"I really think I was in a state of shock," says Robin, haltingly. "I mean, I just remember feeling so hot, and my body just kind of shaking—it's sort of mind-blowing. I had done very well in law school. I could have had a lot of choices of where to work. I *wanted* to work for them. And my work was good. There was never any question of [whether] I did a good job for them. It was like a bomb going off in my face.

"I left. I opened the letter. I saw what it said," Robin continues. The letter read:

> I regret to inform you that I must withdraw the State Law Department's offer of employment. . . . This action has become necessary in light of information which has only recently come to my attention relating to a purported marriage between you and another woman. As the chief legal officer of this state, inaction on my part would constitute tacit approval of this purported marriage and jeopardize the proper functioning of this office.

"I went to a pay phone and called Fran. Then I called my parents. I called the director of career services at Emory. I went to an appointment which I cut short. Then I came home and Fran had left work and come home."

Fran says she, too, was shocked. "Just absolutely shocked. The timing made it worse, coming about two weeks before the ceremony. We were already in a state of total confusion. Unlike traditional families, we were doing it ourselves, all of it. So there was a lot of stress. Plus, Robin's job was our income. We had these tickets to go to Greece for a month, and I know what I earn working part-time just doesn't cut it. We were spending all our money on this wedding. The idea was that Robin was going to have a decent-paying job. And then it was, no job."

In deciding how to respond to Michael Bowers, Robin faced a dilemma. On the one hand, she says, "I felt like he was baiting me, like, 'Come on, sue me. I'm putting it in writing for you.' " But she was aware of the personal difficulties she would face as an open lesbian bringing a lawsuit against a popular politician in a conservative community. Robin says she was concerned she would be used as a "pawn to advance his political career." On the other hand, she felt that if she did not take official action, she would always "be left with this feeling of being a victim."

THE RIGHT TO PRIVACY

THE RIGHT TO PRIVACY

The heart of the case lay in Shahar's claim that her sexual orientation bore no relationship to the quality of her work, and that her job offer could not be withdrawn solely because of activities conducted outside the office. At first, it seemed to be a quintessential privacy claim: Her private life had nothing to do with her job. Instead, Robin's case became a prime example of the *limitations* of the right to privacy. And in what some would call a twist of fate, and others a setup, Michael Bowers was the reason why.

Michael Bowers is a somewhat infamous figure in the struggle for gay rights. His rise to prominence began in 1982, when Georgia police entered the home of a man named Michael Hardwick and found Hardwick in bed with another man. Hardwick was arrested and charged with violating the state's sodomy law. At that time, Georgia's sodomy law, like those of many states, defined sodomy as "any sexual act involving the sex organs of one person and the mouth or anus of another." It applied to heterosexuals as well as homosexuals and carried a prison sentence of up to twenty years. Hardwick challenged the law as unconstitutional. He argued that private sexual behavior between consenting adults was within the zone of privacy that the Supreme Court had created in other decisions involving contraception and abortion. Michael Bowers, as Georgia's attorney general, fought to keep the sodomy law on the books. Bowers argued that homosexual sodomy was not within the zone of privacy that protected heterosexual reproductive decisions.

The Supreme Court agreed with Bowers. In a 5-to-4 decision, the Court refused to recognize a "fundamental right to engage in homosexual sodomy." The dissenters, led by Justice Harry Blackmun, rejected that characterization of the case. Blackmun wrote: "What the Court really has refused to recognize is the fundamental interest all individuals have in controlling the nature of their intimate associations with others. . . . [This] poses a far greater threat to the values most deeply rooted in our Nation's history than tolerance of nonconformity could ever do."

After their defeat in *Hardwick*, gay rights advocates retreated from the right to privacy as the legal rationale for their cause. For example, current battles over gays in the military are usually litigated under the Equal Protection Clause as cases of discrimination, not as violations of the right to privacy. Paradoxically, too, the loss in the courts reflected the growing strength of the gay rights movement and a new social reality. Maybe as a practical as well as a legal matter, "privacy" was not the answer. In the 1990s, according to Ruth Harlow, Shahar's lawyer and the associate director of the ACLU's Lesbian and Gay Rights Project, "Privacy is not really what we are looking for."

Instead, Harlow describes the central issue in Shahar's case as "allowing us to live in the public realm, just like everyone else does, and not having to keep private decisions about who we have relationships with, or what we do in the context of our religion." In other words, Robin should be able to steer a middle course and talk freely with people at work once she gets to know them, rather than constantly having to hide her personal life.

Harlow says, "Robin Shahar was doing the same thing that heterosexual people do all the time. She had mentioned entering into a relationship with her partner, and that they were going to take a trip together. These are the kinds of things that people talk about every day, but if it happens to be in the context of a lesbian or gay relationship, it becomes a different issue. . . . So the right to privacy just [doesn't] mesh with our whole theory of what the case is about."

Instead, Robin claimed that the withdrawal of her job offer violated her freedom of religion and association (under the First Amendment) and unlawfully discriminated against her on the basis of her sexual orientation. First, Shahar argued that the ceremony was purely religious in nature; it was performed by a rabbi; it was private; it was conducted far from the office in a remote location; and it was not a legally recognized marriage, only a religious ceremony. Secondly, Robin argued that her relationship with Fran and their private gathering were both protected by the constitutional right of intimate association. That right has been developed in a number of court cases involving the traditional family unit, but Robin broke new legal ground by arguing that her relationship with Fran should also be protected. Finally, she argued that she had a straightforward case of discrimination: Michael Bowers withdrew the job offer simply because she was a lesbian. The case became a rallying point not only for gay rights advocates but also for workplace privacy advocates concerned about employers' control over the off-duty behavior of their employees, whether it be sexual practices, religious affiliations, or recreational activities.

For his part, Bowers rejected Shahar's claims of freedom of religion and association. He argued that it was the homosexual nature of the marriage, not Robin's religious beliefs or practices, that had led to

the withdrawal of her job offer. He pointed out that he had not prevented the ceremony, and that Robin remained free to associate with
Fran or whomever she wished. Finally, he said that withdrawing
Shahar's job offer was not an act of discrimination but, under the
circumstances, the only reasonable response from the state's chief
legal officer. Bowers pointed out that he had broad discretion over
the hiring, firing, and administration of the Law Department. The
attorneys who work for him are the legal counselors for the state.
They must defend and enforce the laws of Georgia, including the sodomy law.

Bowers relied heavily on his role in the *Hardwick* decision and his
visibility as a defender of public morality. He claimed that if the department had to prosecute a sodomy case in the future, or litigate a
civil case involving benefits for homosexual partners, Robin's presence
in the department would undermine public confidence in the department's ability to enforce the laws in general, because presumably she
herself would be in violation of a law. He stated in his deposition:
"The natural consequence of a marriage is some sort of sexual conduct, I would think, to most people, and if it's homosexual, it would
have to be sodomy."

Bowers contended that Robin's ceremony was a public political
statement of the type prohibited by departmental regulations, not a
private religious ceremony. As Dorothy Kirkley, the lawyer representing Michael Bowers, put it, "In every job there are some constraints on
what you do given the legal responsibility of the office, its duties, the
fishbowl nature, the culture, the work ethic, whatever. Your conduct
has to be calibrated to be appropriate to the office where you work
. . . particularly in a place like the attorney general's office, which is
very public, very visible in the state of Georgia."

Bowers had been forced, he claimed, to choose between compromising his position by approving Shahar's public conduct, or withdrawing her job offer. In fact, some people in the Law Department saw
Robin as a political activist who had applied to work for Bowers precisely because of his visibility—in other words, she had set him up.

Not surprisingly, Shahar objected to Bowers' interpretation of the
facts. She portrays herself not as a crusader, but as naïve. Her primary
objection, however, was to the assumption that she was a lawbreaker
simply because she was a lesbian. She pointed out that she had not
been accused of sodomy, and there was no evidence that she had engaged in such behavior. She claimed it was discriminatory to assume

that she, as a lesbian, had engaged in sodomy, while not assuming the same of heterosexual attorneys.

Furthermore, argued Robin, whether or not she was a homosexual had no bearing on whether she could perform the job of staff attorney, even in a case involving sodomy. "I can think of very few lawyers who would have the luxury of being in a job where they would believe in every case they were handling, where they would always think that they were on the right side of a case," she says. "Part of what I have to deal with as a lawyer is that I'm going to get certain cases that I'm just not going to agree with. But nonetheless, I have to advocate on behalf of my client to the best of my ability. And it's offensive to think that, because I'm a lesbian, I'm not going to be able to put my personal beliefs aside to advocate on behalf of my client."

One of the most hotly debated issues in the case was which legal standard should be used to measure Michael Bowers' action. Shahar argued that because her fundamental rights (freedom of religion and freedom of association) had been infringed, the most demanding standard should be applied. In order to justify his withdrawal of her job offer, Shahar argued, the state had to show that it had a *compelling* interest in refusing to employ her, and that Bowers had taken the most limited step necessary to achieve that goal.

Bowers contended that a different analysis should be applied. When government is acting as an employer (as opposed to when it is acting on behalf of all citizens), its actions should be measured by balancing the employee's interest—here, Robin's interest in her same-sex marriage—against the government's interest in the efficient delivery of public services.

On October 7, 1993, the federal district court in Atlanta issued its opinion. In potentially significant language, it found that Robin and Fran's relationship is protected by the Constitution's right of intimate association. The court also agreed with Shahar that she had "pursued her desired association only at the price of her employment."

The question then boiled down to whether Bowers justifiably imposed that price. On this issue, the court agreed with Bowers and applied the balancing test. The court found that the ceremony was public, not private, and that continued employment of Shahar could undermine "the efficient and credible operation of the Department which requires attorneys to refrain from any conduct which appears improper or inconsistent with Department efforts in enforcing Georgia law."

The court concluded that "the unique circumstances of this case show that [Bowers'] interests in the efficient operation of the Department outweigh [Shahar's] interest in her intimate association with her female partner." Robin was out of a job.

Robin Shahar went to work for the city of Atlanta's Law Department and is appealing her case.

Update on Shahar v. Bowers

ON *December 20, 1995,* the Eleventh Circuit Court of Appeals reversed the lower court's opinion in Robin Shahar's case. On the first crucial point, the appellate court, relying heavily on the religious aspects of Robin and Fran's marriage, agreed that their relationship was protected by the First Amendment right to "intimate assocation." But the Eleventh Circuit said that the lower court had used the wrong Constitutional standard to judge Michael Bowers' actions. The lower court should not have merely balanced Bowers' interest in the effective operation of his office against Shahar's interest in pursuing her personal relationship with Fran. Instead, the circuit court said, where the important right to "intimate association" is at stake in the manner that it was here, Michael Bowers should be held to a higher standard. The burden should be on Bowers to demonstrate that the state had a *compelling* interest in the situation, and that withdrawing Shahar's job offer was the most appropriate way Bowers could serve that interest.

The circuit court wrote, "Though the religious-based marriage in which Shahar participated was not marriage in a civil, legal sense it was intimate and highly personal in the sense of affection, commitment, and permanency and ... it was inextricably entwined with Shahar's exercise of her religious beliefs. Strong deference must be given to her interests and less to the employer's interest."

Although the question of which standard to apply appears to be a technical point, it could mean the difference between victory and defeat. Under the simple balancing test, Bowers' interests were deemed to outweigh Shahar's. But with the burden on Bowers to prove a compelling state interest, the case could go the other way. The Eleventh Circuit sent the case back to the lower court to be decided under the higher "compelling interest" standard.

But in still another twist, in the fall of 1996, the full panel of judges for the Eleventh Circuit agreed to rehear Shahar's case, leaving the state of the law and Robin's fate on hold.

Passing Judgments

LIFESTYLE AND OFF-DUTY BEHAVIOR:
PRIVATE SECTOR

IN OCTOBER 1990, Sue Everett, manager of corporate training and development at Rohr Industries (a California aerospace manufacturer), was fired after nine years of "above-standard" performance. Rohr had conducted a clandestine investigation into her personal life to confirm rumors that she was dating Ken Bingham, the unmarried director of human resources, to whom she did not report. He was also fired. The couple sued Rohr for invasion of privacy, among other claims. In November 1992, after a seven-week trial, a jury awarded Ken Bingham $3,265,568 and Sue Everett $1,035,693.

Rohr appealed the verdict. Meanwhile, Bingham has not been able to find another job. Though Everett was employed at an eyeglass-lens company at the time of trial (which accounted for the lesser amount of her damages), she has since been laid off. The couple is still together. Neither has received any money.

Bingham and Everett v. Rohr Industries, Inc., California 1992

LAURAL ALLEN and Samuel Johnson met while working as sales associates at the Wal-Mart store in Johnstown, New York. Allen was separated and Johnson was single at the time they began seeing each other. When Allen's estranged husband served divorce papers on her at work, both Allen and Johnson were fired. It turned out that their relationship was in violation of company policy on fraternization set out in an employee handbook: "Wal-Mart strongly believes in and supports the 'family unit.' A dating relationship between a married associate and another associate . . . is prohibited."

In July 1993, the attorney general of New York filed suit against Wal-Mart for violating a brand-new state law prohibiting employers from firing workers who engage in lawful recreational activities off-duty and off-premises. In January 1995, a New York court held that "dating" was not a "recreational activity" protected by the statute, and issued a decision in favor of Wal-Mart.

The company has, however, altered the fraternization policy. The new version requires evidence of improper conduct at work (including "open displays of affection" and "making the work environment uncomfortable") before an employee can be fired.

State v. Wal-Mart Stores, New York 1995

IN FEBRUARY 1993, Katz Media, a company that sells radio and television advertising time, fired the man who was its vice president and New York sales manager. Two days later his girlfriend, who had worked at Katz for eleven years as an administrative assistant, was demoted to an entry-level position. She resigned in June 1993 and sued the company, claiming she was discriminated against because she lived with the vice president.

Katz argued that under *Wal-Mart*, the case should be dismissed. However, in August 1995, a federal judge refused, ruling that cohabitation is in fact a "recreational activity" protected by New York law, and is not usually grounds for firing.

Pasch v. Katz Media Corp., New York 1995

IN INDIANA, it would be wise to adopt a healthy lifestyle if one wants to keep a job. A man went to work for the Best Lock Company in 1984. Best Lock had a TAD rule, which prohibited the use of tobacco, alcohol, or drugs at any time—

whether on or off the job. In 1989, the man admitted he had been drinking off-duty in a bar on a few occasions between December 1985 and February 1986. He was fired. He sued for unemployment compensation, claiming that the TAD rule was unreasonable. He won.

Best Lock v. Review Board, Indiana 1991

LIFESTYLE AND OFF-DUTY BEHAVIOR: PUBLIC SECTOR

Government workers are protected by the federal and state constitutions and certain statutes which often enable them to be more successful than their private-sector counterparts when suing their employer.

MICA ENGLAND, a thirty-year-old chef from Oologah, Oklahoma, had wanted to be a police officer since she was in high school. When the Dallas Police Department sent recruiters to Tulsa in 1987, she applied. She passed the written test and the physical agility exam, but when she took the polygraph, she lied, claiming she was not gay. She flunked.

In 1989, the police recruiters came back, and so did England. She filled out the necessary forms, revealed her homosexuality, and made an appointment to go to Dallas for testing. When she arrived in Dallas, a recruiter took England aside to tell her that the department had a policy of not hiring lesbians or gay men. Mica was shocked and angry. She waited for an hour hoping to talk to somebody. As she describes it, "Everybody knew. I went downstairs; I'm bawling; I have a dress on; I'm walking out of the building. I see this Equal Opportunity poster on the bulletin board. So I went into Office 101 and I say, 'Do you have one of those posters I can have?' I'm upset, and this woman is looking at me like I'm crazy. She goes, 'No.' I said, 'Okay, I'll just take that one out there.' Then I ripped it off the wall and I left."

Her dramatic exit was followed by an appearance the next morning at a meeting of the city council, where she denounced the discriminatory hiring practices of the police de-

partment. She also filed a lawsuit challenging both the police
department's ban on hiring gay and lesbian officers and the
state sodomy law upon which the policy was based.

Mica won the first part of her action when the Texas
Court of Appeals held that the city of Dallas had violated her
right to privacy under the Texas state constitution. Following
that decision, another trial had to be held to determine
whether money damages should be paid. In September 1994,
the case settled for $73,000, of which Mica received $42,000. After being rejected by the police department a second time on
other grounds, Mica has decided to remain a chef and an activist for the time being.

　　Dallas v. England, Texas 1993

————

In 1980, the city of El Segundo, California, had eighty-three
police officers, only two of whom were women. When the city
announced a promotion exam, a woman who had worked in
the police department as a clerk-typist since 1973 decided to apply. The exam was open only to permanent city employees
and consisted of written and oral components, psychological
and polygraph testing, a background check, and a physical agility exam. The woman passed them all. However, she later
testified that when she submitted to the polygraph exam, she
was asked a large number of questions about her sexual activities, including when she first had sex, with whom, etc. The
polygraph examiner had also been told to look into a "female
problem." The woman had reported a pregnancy and miscar-
riage on her questionnaire, and was questioned about the
identity of the father. She was reluctant to reveal the information but admitted that the father had been a former police
officer. Upon further questioning, she revealed that the
father was actually a married police officer still with the department, and asked the examiner to keep the information
confidential.

Two months later, she was informed that her name had
been removed from the eligibility list. Three reasons were

given: her record of frequent tardiness and sick time, her poor performance on the physical exam (which was attributed to her being "a very feminine type person who is apparently very weak in the upper body"), and her "only recent interest" in becoming a police officer. The woman sued, claiming an invasion of her constitutional rights to privacy and free association, and sex discrimination.

The U.S. Court of Appeals for the Ninth Circuit decided in her favor. On her privacy claim, the court wrote: "The Constitution protects two kinds of privacy interests. One is the individual interest in avoiding disclosure of personal matters, and another is the interest in independence in making certain kinds of important decisions. Both are implicated in this case. [She] presented evidence that defendants invaded her right to privacy by forcing her to disclose information regarding personal sexual matters. She also showed that they refused to hire her as a police officer based in part on her prior sexual activities, thus interfering with her privacy interest and her freedom of association."

Thorne v. El Segundo, California 1983

IN 1978, a prostitute in Phoenix, Arizona, revealed that sexual relationships existed between herself, another prostitute, and two police officers. A police department investigation revealed that the relationships had "involved intimate contact while on duty, that the prostitute involved with [one officer] was accepting city money from him as a paid informant, and that both relationships were carried on openly and publicly, and were well known among prostitutes and in the County Attorney's office." The city discharged the officers.

The officers claimed that the city had violated their constitutional right to privacy by punishing them for their private sexual activities. The case went to the U.S. Court of Appeals for the Ninth Circuit, the same court that decided *Thorne*. The court took a dim view of the officers' claim. It refused to extend *Thorne* to cover "sexual behavior that is not purely private, that compromises a police officer's performance, and that threatens to undermine a police department's internal morale and community reputation."

> *Fugate v. Phoenix Civil Service Bd.*, Arizona 1986

IN 1977, a man who began working as a part-time police officer in North Muskegon, Michigan, in 1969, separated from his wife and moved in with another woman. He informed the police chief of his new living arrangements and was promptly suspended, then terminated. He sued the police department for intruding upon his constitutionally protected rights of privacy and association, claiming that his off-duty living arrangements bore no relationship to his job performance.

The district court agreed. The court found evidence that the man was a good officer doing a satisfactory job. "This Court rejects the notion that an infringement of an important constitutionally protected right is justified simply because of general community disapproval of the protected conduct. The very purpose of constitutional protection of individual liberties is to prevent such majoritarian coercion." The U.S. Court of Appeals for the Sixth Circuit affirmed the case.

> *Briggs v. North Muskegon Police Dept.*, Michigan 1983

ALSO in 1977, a patrolwoman for the Amarillo Police Department began dating a sergeant, who was an eleven-year veteran. The sergeant informed his immediate superior that the couple would probably be spending the night together. The supervising officer told him "that would probably be fine, [but] that I didn't want the two of them setting up housekeeping." The couple spent a lot of time together but, as instructed, maintained separate residences. In the fall of 1977, the chief of police heard rumors that the couple were living together. The chief neither confronted them nor contacted their supervisors. Instead, he ordered officers in the detective division to conduct surveillance of their off-duty behavior. The detectives rented an apartment across the street from the sergeant's to monitor the woman's comings and goings. They also observed the couple from a car parked across the street. As a result, the patrolwoman was suspended for twelve days and then was assigned to solitary, isolated field patrols. She resigned in March 1978. The man was also suspended, then demoted and transferred to the records division, where he stamped file reports, wrote up telephone reports, and was isolated from the officers he had previously supervised. He resigned in February 1978. The couple later married.

The U.S. Court of Appeals for the Fifth Circuit found no privacy or due process violation.

Shawgo v. Spradlin, Texas 1983

SHOARS v. EPSON AMERICA, INC.

High-Tech Monitoring

A LANA SHOARS IS one of those lucky workers who seem to have all the training they will need to succeed in the rapidly changing, technology-driven workplace of the future. Alana breezily offers to demonstrate the three different kinds of e-mail on her desk while describing the virtues and technological challenges of synchronizing worldwide e-mail systems—not to mention the cost advantages! "For instance," Alana volunteers, "I can tell you that to send a one-page electronic message to New York, it costs sixteen cents. To send the same message by fax, it'll be $1.86, by telex $4.35." A true believer, no wonder she has been hired to proselytize for e-mail communication.

Alana says that at her previous job she increased e-mail usage from 48 percent of employees to 94 percent in about nine months—that is, she claims, before she was fired for trying to protect the system.

In March of 1989, Alana was hired as an e-mail administrator for Epson America, Inc., the American subsidiary of the giant Japanese electronics manufacturer. An e-mail system was already in place among the seven hundred employees at the company's Torrance, California, location. During Alana's tenure, the system was connected via MCI to other Epson subsidiaries as well as the 8 million other potential correspondents on the MCI Mail network.

According to Alana, the most important factor in increasing e-mail usage is ensuring confidentiality. She says employees will choose to use the system only if they believe that their communications are private, just like their traditional mail. Thus, ensuring confidentiality was a big part of Alana's job at Epson. In her e-mail training sessions, she instructed employees in the mechanics of selecting a password, the importance of not disclosing that password to anyone, and the procedure for changing the password if it no longer appeared to be secret. According to Alana, under directions from management—and often in the presence of her supervisor, Daniel R. Hilliard—she guaranteed her colleagues that the system was secure and that neither she nor anyone else at Epson had access to their passwords.

In the fall of 1989, Alana began to get a funny feeling about Daniel Hilliard. On a couple of occasions, she had walked into his office and noticed that e-mail messages were displayed on his terminal, only to have him, as she describes it, "hit a key real quick to clear it up or blank it out." Alana thought it was "kind of unusual" because, she says, "people don't usually do that unless they're trying to hide something." Also, she recalls that a few colleagues had questioned her about the security of the system, saying that in meetings Hilliard seemed to display "extra knowledge."

Shoars' suspicions peaked on December 20, 1989, when she walked into Hilliard's office to use the phone. She noticed a stack of computer messages on his desk—in fact, all the e-mail messages transmitted to or from the Torrance facility in August and September. Alana was not only horrified, she took it personally. She had no idea how Hilliard could have managed to get hold of what she understood to be confidential messages. She later learned that he had intercepted them as they passed through the electronic gateway between Epson's internal e-mail system and MCI Mail. Worried about what she might be getting into, she picked up a six-inch bundle of pages from the printout and took them with her.

Alana claims she told no one, fearing that e-mail usage among her coworkers would decline, but decided to confront Hilliard in the hope that he would stop. In brief, she says, "he became livid, told me it was none of my damn business what he did, and I'd better keep my mouth shut. He said I would leave the company before he did." Alana adds, "He was right." She also made an appointment with the CEO, who told her he would "take the matter under advisement."

Instead, according to Shoars, on January 25, 1990, Hilliard called her into another office, shoved an envelope at her, and said, "You're terminated immediately." She says he accused her of obtaining her own personal MCI Mail account against company policy, constituting gross insubordination—and he had two intercepted e-mail messages to prove it.

Alana claims that the accusation was a pretext. She explains that she had inquired via e-mail into the possibility of obtaining such an account directly from MCI for her home computer, and Hilliard had misread the message. She also claims that he misread a second message in which a colleague notified Alana that a trial account was in place on the system and she was eligible to test it.

On the other hand, Hilliard asserted that he had printed out and flipped through the electronic messages solely to make sure that the newly installed system was working properly, and to check on problems being reported by users.

Alana also believes that in order to intimidate her, Hilliard falsely told other Epson employees that she "had a gun and had threatened to come back and shoot people." Alana believes he had a phone call placed summoning the local police so that when she left the building she had to cross a phalanx of police officers to get to her car. "I was digging around in my purse for my keys, without my glasses, and the next thing I know these guys have their hands on their guns!"

Alana Shoars' next step was to find a lawyer. Attorney Noel Shipman filed two lawsuits against Epson: a personal suit for wrongful discharge (based on her termination for reporting what she believed to be wrongdoing) and slander (based upon the description of her as a deranged individual with a gun); and a class action suit for invasion of privacy under the California state constitution and California statutes. The privacy suit was filed on March 12, 1991, on behalf of Alana Shoars and seventy-seven other Epson employees at the Torrance facility whose e-mail had been intercepted between August 4 and September 29, 1989. Along with Alana's declaration, Shipman produced over 650 pages of hard copies of e-mail transmissions—the stack Alana had taken with her on December 20.

To Alana, the secret nature of Epson's monitoring was most offensive. What Hilliard had done was wrong, she says, as wrong as reading someone else's mail or listening in on their phone conversations—communications which are protected by law and custom. "I know I'm not supposed to go to somebody else's mailbox and read their mail," says Alana. "I've never seen that in print anywhere, but I know my mother told me that."

Both Alana and her lawyer would soon discover, however, that where e-mail is concerned, such homegrown values are murky at best. And so is the law. Shipman and Shoars were quite surprised to discover that there was no California law specifically covering e-mail. So Alana set out to make some. Quite unexpectedly, she found herself a pioneer in the no-man's-land where rapidly advancing technology has left the law behind.

In order to evaluate Alana's state constitutional claim, the California court had to answer the familiar question: Did Alana and the other Epson employees have an expectation of privacy in their e-mail? From Alana's point of view, the obvious answer was yes. "If there was no expectation of privacy, then we wouldn't have had any passwords," she says. Just like a PIN number on a bank account, the passwords were meant to keep uninvited "visitors" out.

At the heart of Epson's argument, on the other hand, was the idea that what happened to Epson e-mail was up to Epson's management. E-mail belonged to the provider of the service, they claimed, not to the employees who had sent it. Epson's attorney Rick Krantz explains: "Electronic mail is a business device used in a business environment for a business purpose. There is no other purpose for it. It's sitting on a table provided by the employer with the hardware and the software provided by an employer for only one reason, and that reason is to make the employee more efficient." In an increasingly competitive world with razor-thin margins of success, to expect an employer to provide hardware, software, and necessary technical support other than for its own use is simply "not rational," according to Epson's general counsel, Judy Bain.

Epson considered e-mail to be a new tool of business communication which, like the old tools—interoffice memos, business files, and equipment—belongs to the employer. They relied in part on a 1987 Supreme Court case, *O'Connor v. Ortega*, which upheld a supervisor's search of an employee's office, desk, and files in a public-sector workplace. The Court held that the employee did have an expectation of privacy in those areas, but that a search of them need only be "reasonable under all circumstances" to outweigh that expectation. No warrant or probable cause is required. Presumably, in a private company where employees do not have Fourth Amendment protection, the standard would be lower and the employer would have even more freedom to search an employee's files or desk. So why not e-mail as well?

Epson attorneys also point out that electronic monitoring is a valuable way for employers to discover wrongdoing by employees—for example, where there is reason to suspect theft or negligence, sexual harassment, or gambling. The most visible case involves a vice president for computer languages at Borland International, a large Silicon Valley software company. In September 1992, he defected to a rival company, Symantec Corporation. When suspicious Borland executives went to close down the man's office, they searched his e-mail box. They found messages he had sent to the Symantec CEO which Borland claims contained top-secret corporate data. They called in the police and filed a civil suit against the man and Symantec. His defense: privacy. Like Alana Shoars, the man claimed his e-mail was confidential and should not be read by his employer.

A further twist on the case shows just how far behind technology has left the law. The Santa Cruz County district attorney acknowledged that he didn't have the expertise to develop the case and allowed Borland to recommend a computer expert and cover $13,000 in prosecution costs. A judge then ordered the entire D.A.'s office removed from the case.

Even in a case of suspected wrongdoing, Noel Shipman remains unconvinced of the need to search employees' electronic files. "You can tell from the bill what they're doing, you can *ask* them what they're doing. I mean, sure, they're on your nickel and they're at the workplace, but there are limits!"

In the absence of any e-mail statute, Shipman argued that e-mail monitoring violated California's laws protecting older forms of communication, specifically telephone calls. California has a strict wiretapping law which provides that in order for anyone to listen in on a telephone conversation, *both* parties to the conversation must consent. The statute provides a $2,500 fine or up to one year in jail for "any unauthorized connection" with any "telegraph or telephone wire, line, or cable, without the consent of all parties, or any unauthorized attempt to learn the contents of any message report or communication while it is in transit over any wire line or cable." Shipman argued that although e-mail is not specifically mentioned, it is a communication captured in transit over a phone line and so the existing statute applied.

From Epson's point of view, technological times had changed. According to Judy Bain, "We have to break out of the paradigm of comparing old to new technology and examine this technology for what it is. It's new and it's different." Epson argued that the existing law applied only to telephone calls. The California legislature had not regulated e-mail; therefore, monitoring it could not be against the law.

The trial court agreed with Epson that e-mail was not covered by the California wiretapping statute. It was not the court's role to extend the law to cover e-mail; rather, the court suggested that the legislature should consider the issue. The court pointed out that the federal government, which began grappling with electronic issues in the Electronic and Communications Privacy Act of 1986, provided an exception for employers. Under ECPA, the provider of the service is not prohibited from examining it, which is just what Epson had argued in its case.

Then, on July 31, 1992, class action certification was denied in the privacy suit. The court found that Shipman failed to provide sufficient proof that Alana and the other Epson workers had an expectation of privacy in their e-mail. The court also found that the submitted e-mail messages were, "with few exceptions," business-related, and that the California state constitutional right of privacy covered only *"personal* information." The court found "no sufficient legal or factual basis for extending the right to privacy to cover business-oriented communications."

Alana was disappointed, but not surprised, by the judge's opinion. "You can tell he doesn't use electronic mail," she says. "Anybody who doesn't use it doesn't understand the [point of the] passwords." Alana took to signing her correspondence "Alana 'David v. Goliath' Shoars."

Perhaps the most important thing to come out of the case is a new appreciation for the importance of a clear company policy. As Rick Krantz himself says, "Despite the fact that Judy and I are representing corporate America . . . we are concerned like everyone else with our own privacy, our own rights. What we try to do is evolve a policy that makes sense for *us*. We're the ones who have to live with it, and it makes sense to me if I know my limits. . . . No, we don't check our privacy at the corporate door, but at some point we have to draw a line. It is easier in the e-mail context to draw a very bright line than it is to draw a shade."

Noel Shipman accepts the value of the policy approach, but for him it raises a new set of problems. Why should the employer, who already calls the shots, get to draw the line wherever it decides? Shipman is concerned that employees will be asked to give up their privacy rights when they are hired—and that most people will do so, in exchange for a job. "If you sign a waiver saying, 'I agree you can spy on me,' and you exchange that for a salary, you're working for a Nazi, but there you go. You've *sold* your right to privacy," says Shipman. The problem is compounded by the fact that often workers have no real choice and are not compensated for the rights they sign away.

At present, neither companies nor their workers really know what the limits are. The few rulings in the area seem to be going the employers' way, but even that trend is not sure to hold. In the electronic workplace, according to Noel Shipman, "When a worker like Alana Shoars asks, 'Do I have an expectation of privacy in the workplace?' 'Well, maybe' is the answer."

The problem of electronic privacy is growing. The number of e-mail users ballooned from 1 million in 1984 to an estimated 20 million in 1995, according to the Electronic Messaging Association and the consulting firm Arthur D. Little. The evidence suggests that electronic monitoring in general is also on the rise, by computer, by telephone, and even by hidden video cameras. A 1993 survey in *Macworld* magazine reported that 22 percent of companies engaged in searches of employee computer files, voice mail, e-mail, or other networking communications. In companies with one thousand or more employees, the figure rose to 30 percent. Based on survey results, the magazine estimated that 20 million Americans may be subject to computer monitoring on the job. It would appear that while the legality of monitoring is still somewhat unclear, companies are taking advantage of the uncertainty. Only 18 percent have any written policy regarding electronic privacy.

The loudest objections to electronic monitoring come from such workers as airline reservations clerks, customer service personnel, or telephone operators, where automation and a high degree of repetition can result in an increasingly dehumanized environment. Keystroke monitoring (where the computer counts the number of keystrokes per minute), telephone call accounting monitoring (where the number of phone calls per hour and the length of each call are recorded), as well as service observation (where supervisors listen in on calls) and keeping track of unplugged time (measuring time spent away from the computer) are all becoming commonplace.

Women interviewed by 9 to 5, Working Women Education Fund describe the stress caused by excessive monitoring. "The monitoring makes you feel like less than a child, less than a thinking human being. . . . You have to stop and think from time to time that your ancestors did not cross the ocean in steerage and come through Ellis Island to be treated like this," says Maxine O., a customer service representative for a New Jersey telephone company. Olivia L., the voice on the other end of a Georgia computer manufacturer's technical hot line, describes the monitoring in her office as a combination of phone, computer, and video camera. She says that establishing quotas for phone calls, measuring the time between calls, number of calls, and time on and off the computer system, along with video surveillance in the workroom and lunchroom have all combined to create "the feeling that Big Brother is counting us, listening to us, and filming us all the time."

Office workers are not the only ones who feel they are being shadowed. Already, global positioning systems allow truck drivers to be reached on the road, but can also monitor the length of their rest stops. Cellular phone systems can locate anyone using a phone in their car. And there's more to come. Olivetti and Xerox are developing the "active badge," a device which allows workers to be tracked around the company premises. The badge reveals its wearer's location by emitting an infrared signal every fifteen seconds to a network of wall-mounted sensors around the building. The information provided— including the name and location of the badge-wearer, the number of other badge-wearers in the room, the length of time they have been there, and the nearest telephone extension—are all displayed and updated on a central computer screen. So far, the badge is worn only by a few hundred workers in research centers, but the company plans to introduce it widely in the next couple of years.

In the face of such ominous devices, workplace privacy advocates take some comfort from the hope that eventually employers will discover that excessive monitoring is bad for business. They often cite the example of Federal Express, which pursued a "people first" approach to office automation and downplayed quantitative measurements. Worker productivity and performance increased above what it had been under electronic monitoring.

As far as Alana Shoars is concerned, something good may have come out of her experience. Her personal lawsuit against Epson for slander was settled in 1994 for an undisclosed sum. Although her e-mail class action privacy suit went nowhere and she lost her suit for wrongful discharge, her case raised awareness among both workers and management that electronic monitoring could no longer remain secret.

Passing Judgments

ELECTRONIC SURVEILLANCE

IN December 1994, voice mail entered the fray. In what appears to be the first voice-mail privacy case, a McDonald's manager in Elmira, New York, sued the franchise owner.

The manager had been a McDonald's employee for nearly twenty years when, in 1993, he began having an affair with an assistant manager at the McDonald's in nearby Binghamton. The couple often left romantic messages on each other's voice-mail boxes, which belonged to a voice-mail system linking a dozen McDonald's outlets. Though the manager claims he was told that only he knew the code to retrieve his messages, he believes that at some point another employee began retrieving the messages—and passing them on to the owner. According to the manager, in late 1993 the owner ordered the other employee to play the messages for the manager's wife.

The manager filed suit against the owner for $2 million. The suit is pending.

"$2 M Suit in Sweet Nuthin' Eavesdrop," *New York Newsday*, January 20, 1995.

WHEN Oliver North was fired after the Iran-Contra scandal came to light in 1986, he emptied his e-mail box before leaving the White House. Though he successfully deleted recent e-mail, little did he know that White House computers saved all messages on a long-term backup system. Prosecutors rushed to obtain the records, hoping to find the "smoking gun" enabling them to win a conviction. However, North's defense attorneys believe that e-mail turned out to be crucial evidence for them, enabling North to win acquittal on nine of the twelve counts with which he was charged.

In a related case that began in the final days of the Bush administration, a federal judge ruled that the government must provide the same level of protection to electronic records as it does to paper ones. Now, messages like North's 1986 memo to aide Ronald Sable will be preserved for future scholars: "Oh Lord, I lost the slip and broke one of the high heels. Forgive please. Will return the wig on Monday."

U.S. v. North, Washington, D.C. 1991

Armstrong v. Executive Office of the President, Washington, D.C. 1995

———

IN 1990, an inspector with the U.S. Postal Service received two anonymous letters alleging that gambling was taking place in the downtown post office in Lahaina, Maui. The letters were turned over to the police, who installed four video cameras in the ceiling and smoke detectors of the break room at the post office. A switcher and recorder were hidden in a yellow box on top of a vending machine. No warrant was obtained.

The images from the cameras were transmitted to a van parked outside the post office. Two police officers watched the activity in the break room during working hours for an entire year. When new tapes were required, the police officer on the case changed them at 3 a.m. to preserve secrecy. The police accumulated fifty videotapes containing twelve hundred hours of footage. The officers testified that only a minute fraction reflected any gambling.

The Supreme Court of Hawaii found that the employees had a reasonable expectation of privacy in their break room and that their employer could not "consent" to a search on their behalf. The court found that the search violated the Hawaii state constitution, and said the tapes could not be used against the postal workers.

State v. Bonnell, Hawaii, 1993

———

IN 1989, workers at telephone equipment manufacturer Northern Telecom, Inc.'s Nashville plant discovered that their employer had been eavesdropping on them. For thirteen years, the company had secretly intercepted and recorded personal telephone calls made by employees from the cafeteria, conference room, and guard station. Eight hundred and thirty-four employees sued the company for violating federal and state laws, including invasion of privacy. The judge ordered all original tape recordings of private conversations filed with the court, and prohibited disclosure of their contents except for those involved in the litigation.

The case was settled in June 1992. Northern Telecom agreed to pay $200,000 into a fund. The 8 plaintiffs whose voices could be identified on tapes of outgoing calls made from the cafeteria telephones each received $901.92. The 47 plaintiffs whose voices could be positively identified on tapes of other phone calls each received $450.96. The 761 remaining plaintiffs who could present adequate evidence that they had used the telephones each received $225.48.

Parish et al. v. Northern Telecom, Tennessee 1992

———

A "right-to-life" organization called the Family Life League brought an action seeking to require the Illinois Department of Public Aid to provide a list of physicians, hospitals, and other service providers who had furnished abortions under the state Medicaid program from 1978 to 1986. The league claimed that it was entitled to the information under the State Records Act. The department refused to create the requested "special abortion" list on the grounds that it would invade the providers' privacy and would place them at risk of harm. The Illinois State Supreme Court rejected the department's argument, holding that the disclosure of the list would not be an invasion of privacy and that there was no evidence that the information would be used in an unlawful manner.

Family Life League v. Dept. of Public Aid, Illinois 1986

Privacy and Information

Privacy and Information

PERHAPS the scariest threat to privacy comes in the area known as "informational privacy." Information about all of us is now collected not only by the old standbys, the IRS and FBI, but also by the MVB, MIB, NCOA, and NCIC, as well as credit bureaus, credit unions, and credit card companies. We now have cellular phones, which are different from cordless phones, which are different from what we used to think of as phones. We worry about e-mail, voice mail, and junk mail. And something with the perky name Clipper Chip—developed specifically to allow governmental eavesdropping on coded electronic communications—is apparently the biggest threat of all.

One hundred years ago, in arguing for a right to privacy, Louis D. Brandeis and Samuel D. Warren warned, "Numerous mechanical devices threaten to make good the prediction that 'what is whispered in the closet shall be proclaimed from the housetops.'" The device that has outstripped all other threats to privacy is the computer. Some say the computer is heralding no less than a new phase of civilization. Whether computers will alter our notion of the human condition is in dispute, but what is inarguable is that we will have to change the way we think about keeping certain information private.

Actually, we have always offered up all sorts of personal information about ourselves, whether when filing a tax return, applying for insurance, opening a bank account, or going to the doctor's office. Before computers, personal information about us was out there in the world, but it was relatively secure because a system based on pieces of paper is so unwieldy. Anyone wanting to obtain information would have to physically comb through file cabinets, perhaps at many different locations. And if the documents were not of recent vintage, they may well have been destroyed or banished to the "dead files," which was essentially the same thing.

The computer has changed all that. Given each tiny chip's staggering storage capacity, far more information about us can be stored for far longer periods of time. The kinds of data that can be collected are endless. So, apparently, is the number of places in which the information can be stored. Your medical history alone is likely to be in the data banks of your doctor (or doctors), any hospital or clinic that treated you, any laboratory that performed tests on you, your pharmacy, your insurance company (and any company where you applied for insurance), and possibly in the Medical Information Bureau (MIB), which collects medical data on some 15 million Americans and makes it available to insurance companies.

And as if we do not volunteer enough personal information already, new technology can generate more. Point-of-sale scanning at your grocery store can create a data profile revealing your taste in everything from soft drinks to supermarket tabloids. "Smart roads" have toll booths that pick up radio signals from small electronic cards placed on windshields. Tolls are then deducted from the driver's prepaid account. You get to whiz through a toll booth without stopping, but there is also a record of where you were at a particular time.

Advances in DNA research indicate that it is only a matter of time before a complete genetic profile can be created on each of us. A finding that you are genetically predisposed to a certain illness may be of great importance to you, but it may also be of interest to potential insurers, employers, even spouses or would-be spouses. And someday soon, the whole universe of information about you—credit report, insurance records, medical history, you-name-it—may be recorded on that little "smart card" that fits in your wallet.

Most important, computers assure that whatever information is out there is *accessible*. No more roaming door-to-door, file-to-file. A kid with a keyboard can get in to access your information. What's more, because the information exists in cyberspace rather than real space, it can be "stolen" (copied) without your even knowing it. For instance:

- In 1991 the FBI uncovered a nationwide group of "infobrokers," people who illegally obtained and sold information on individuals stored in government data banks. One company advertised its services: Criminal histories commanded the top fee of $100, followed by employment histories for $75. An individual's driving record cost $15, whereas credit reports went for a mere $10.

- A journalist set out to show how easy it was for just about anyone to get private information about just about anyone else. He did so convincingly when with one phone call, a $50 fee, and a home computer, he obtained Vice President Dan Quayle's credit report. After meeting with a member of the spooky information underground, he also obtained Dan Rather's credit report. The reporter said it was easy.

Total strangers can obtain even more personal information about you legally:

- In 1989, the actress Rebecca Schaeffer was shot to death in the doorway of her apartment building by an obsessed fan. The man had been stalking Schaeffer for two years. He finally obtained her home address when he hired a private investigator who simply requested the address from the California Department of Motor Vehicles. As in many states, California DMV records were available to the public for a fee. Schaeffer's killing prompted new restrictions on the release of such records in California, but many more states continued to make DMV records available, even selling the entire registration file for the cost of copying. In 1994, Congress finally stepped in and passed a law—to take effect in 1997—limiting disclosure of individuals' driving and registration records.

- It's not just the Motor Vehicle Bureau. When you fill out a change-of-address card, the U.S. Post Office adds the information to its National Change of Address (NCOA) database. The Post Office then helpfully passes on the NCOA to list brokers, who license the information to certain direct marketers. The Post Office says the process saves millions of dollars, as addresses are automatically updated on mail that would otherwise have to be forwarded. A note on the change-of-address form warns that the information may be passed on, but if you want your mail forwarded when you move, you have to fill out the card.

Other information can be tampered with or bungled:

- The National Crime Information Center (NCIC) database contains over 23 million records identifying, among other things, people and vehicles sought by the police. NCIC information is available by computer to approximately 71,000 local, state, and federal agencies across the country. In 1982, the Los Angeles Police Department entered an arrest warrant for one T. D. Rogan, suspected of robbery, into the NCIC computer. However, the entry was a mistake; the actual suspect was only *impersonating* Rogan. The LAPD failed to include a physical description with the warrant (which would have cleared Rogan), and even after the error became apparent, it was not corrected. Over a two-year period, based on the erroneous information in the NCIC, Mr. Rogan was arrested four times—three times at gunpoint—after stops for minor traffic violations.

- The people of Norwich, Vermont, entered the information age with a bang when, seemingly overnight, residents of the small New England village began to have problems with their credit cards and loan applications. A town clerk traced the problem to TRW, one of the nation's giant credit bureaus. TRW had hired a Georgia firm to collect information, and that company, in turn, had hired a Vermont housewife to check on delinquent taxpayers in Norwich. The woman went to the town hall and dutifully copied fourteen hundred names from tax records. The problem was, those records belonged to people who had paid their taxes, not tax delinquents. The information went into the TRW database and hence out into the world. The credit bureau corrected the error.

The so-called information superhighway, a global network of databases, will only make more information *more* accessible to more people. Even if you don't cruise the superhighway, your personal profile will. A portrait of you in 1's and 0's, the language of computers, will exist in cyberspace. The profile could be so complete that it will be like having another self living in a parallel dimension; it is a self you cannot see, but one that affects your life just the same. Even if you do not own a personal computer and never intend to, you are part of the revolution.

From a privacy point of view, we are in the midst of the most unsettling period in this revolution. For many, the technology itself is unfamiliar and frightening. Most important, the privacy problems posed are so different from those that have come before, there is no framework to deal with them. Technology is fast. The law, whether formed in tiny increments by individual cases or by the cumbersome legislative process, is *slow*. As a result, there is simply no comprehensive body of law established to deal with all of the privacy concerns arising in the digital age.

Rather, the response thus far has been a mishmash of protection from federal and state statutes, public pressure, self-help, and, yes, technology. Some high-tech intrusions have high-tech solutions. For instance, telephone companies introduced Caller ID as a means of tracing obscene calls and screening other unwanted phone calls. But privacy advocates expressed concern. In particular, shelters for battered women said their members needed to be able to call home from un-identifiable locations. Enter per-line or per-call blocking, now offered in many states to customers who want their telephone numbers to remain confidential when making a call.

Those well-versed in computers already protect their own electronic communications by encryption—a method of scrambling computerized information so that it appears to be gibberish to anyone who does not know the code. Many corporations do the same. But in the topsy-turvy world of high technology, this means of securing privacy has already generated another way to invade it.

If a rival company or computer hacker cannot decode encrypted electronic communications, then neither can the government. The problem with that is that law enforcement agents have always been able to tap into traditional telephone conversations if they have a warrant to do so. The government says this is more than a convenience, it is a crucial tool not only in capturing criminals but in preventing terrible crimes in the first place. Wiretaps figure prominently in combating organized crime, drug cartels, and terrorists. However, if these criminals begin communicating electronically and scrambling their messages, police cannot just tap in.

The government's solution was to come up with its own method of encryption, which government agents could decode with a warrant, and then make the method standard in the industry. The technology would be stored in a tamperproof chip known as Clipper. Decoding any message scrambled by the Clipper Chip would require the simultaneous use of two "keys" which would be stored by two separate organizations. Government agents would need a warrant to get the keys to unscramble any given communication. The government says that the Clipper Chip ensures the privacy of electronic communications while maintaining law enforcement's ability to tap in with a warrant.

Clipper was greeted with strong opposition from privacy advocates, civil libertarians, software corporations, and assorted "digerati." Because Clipper is classified, software companies and individual users would have no way of verifying the security of the system. (Indeed, as soon as the Clipper Chip was announced, computer professionals set about trying to crack the code, with some already claiming success.) Some also fear that the government has built a "back door" into the code so that police can tap in even without a warrant. Others think the plan ill-conceived from the start because criminals can hardly be expected to use a secret code to which the police hold the key.

Law enforcement officials concede that the Clipper Chip will not allow them to capture the most technologically skilled lawbreakers. However, they point out that some of the nation's biggest crimes have been solved when the perpetrators made stupendous blunders (think of the World Trade Center bomber who was captured when he returned to the car rental agency where he'd rented the van used in the crime). Still, opposition to the Clipper Chip was so strong, and the specter of a nationwide surveillance network so alarming, the government has at least temporarily backed away from the idea.

However, even if electronic communication can be made secure, mountains of information will continue to be collected into myriad data banks around the globe. In this area, some are taking matters into their own hands. You cannot opt out of the digital world, but you may be able to opt out of a piece of it. A surprising amount of the information we offer up is actually voluntary (check the warranty cards you fill out), so some of the data flow *can* be stopped at the source. Also, those who care to can have their names removed from many telephone solicitation and direct mail lists.

Old-fashioned public outrage has had an effect, too. In 1987, when Robert H. Bork was a nominee for the U.S. Supreme Court, a Washington, D.C., weekly published a list of the videotapes Bork had rented. People were appalled—not at the kinds of videos the nominee had watched, but that such information was there for the asking. The next year, Congress passed the Video Privacy Protection Act, which prohibits retailers from selling or disclosing video rental records without the customer's consent or a court order.

In 1990, Lotus Development Corporation announced a new product called Marketplace: Households. With information supplied by Equifax, one of the big three credit bureaus, Lotus had compiled information about 120 million Americans on software designed for personal computers. Now everyone could have access to the kind of databases previously available only to large corporations. Thousands of letters of protest and public condemnation by privacy advocates prompted Lotus to shelve the product.

Indeed, some see the Lotus episode as offering a solution to the proliferation of personal information. As consumers become more aware of how their personal profiles are bartered, they will become more insistent on certain protections. If you do not like what American Express did with your credit information, switch to VISA. In this way, the argument goes, market forces will pressure companies to respect consumers' privacy.

In fact, some predict that the model of the marketplace will be taken even further. If so much data about us is not only collected and stored but also bought and sold, then such information clearly has value in and of itself. That includes not just highly sensitive information about our medical or financial status but even our simple name and address. Thus at the most basic level, some propose that we be compensated for the use of personal information.

One proposal is to set up a royalty pool for the use of certain information, such as a change of address. Marketers would not have to get your permission to obtain your change of address, but they would have to pay into a pool each time they accessed the information. Individuals would then be compensated based on how often their information was used. The idea of a royalty pool, however, does not address privacy concerns.

Another view is that not only should we be compensated for use of our personal information, but such information should be considered our property. We own and control it. Marketers who want to know our names and addresses or buying habits would have to bargain or contract with us for that information. This more extreme proposal is unlikely to take effect in the near future, however, as it runs counter to the free flow of information so essential to our democracy. The idea that one can "own" a name or other basic identifying information raises serious First Amendment concerns.

Whether in the form of consumer pressure or the more ambitious compensation scheme, those who favor letting market forces do the job say that regulation by statute is too costly and inflexible an approach. First, privacy is such a personal issue that people will naturally differ on how much they are willing to give up for certain services. Some customers like it when they order by phone and the retailer has their previous purchasing history on file. Others want to receive all sorts of catalogues which they did not think to ask for. Simply banning certain uses of personal information does not accommodate individuals' needs.

Second, ever more state and federal regulations will only drive up the cost of services as companies are forced to comply with the multitude of rules and the bureaucracy that goes with them. Indeed, proponents of the market approach say that fear of regulation may do more than anything else to push corporations who traffic in our personal lives to come up with ways to maintain privacy.

On the other hand, privacy advocates argue that trusting corporations to sit on mounds of valuable personal information is naïve. Furthermore, even if leaving privacy protection to market forces makes sense in certain areas, it makes no sense where consumers have no choice, as in dealing with their state Motor Vehicle Bureau or the I.R.S. Then, privacy advocates say, we need tough new laws to secure personal information.

There are already several federal statutes aimed at protecting our privacy in some way. For example, in addition to the statute protecting video rental records, there is also a law protecting cable television subscribers' records. The Driver's Privacy Protection Act limits disclosure of motor vehicle records, and the Fair Credit Reporting Act limits disclosure of credit files. The Telephone Consumer Protection Act regulates telephone solicitations. And there is even something called the Privacy Act, which bars federal agencies from disclosing information for purposes other than the reason it was collected.

But privacy advocates complain that most of these statutes contain exceptions that gut the protection. For instance, the Privacy Act contains an exception for the "routine use" of information, and the Fair Credit Reporting Act allows disclosure of credit information to anyone with a "legitimate business need," terms which can be very liberally construed. In addition, at least some privacy advocates say that penalties for violating the statutes, and enforcement in general, are so weak that in the end, the laws do not protect much at all.

Perhaps the biggest problem with the statutory scheme is that there is no overall privacy policy behind it. As even a partial list of privacy laws indicates, they address a hodgepodge of individual concerns. The federal statutory scheme most resembles a jigsaw puzzle in which the pieces do not fit. That is because the scheme was put together backwards. Rather than coming up with an overall picture and then breaking it up into smaller pieces that mesh together, Congress has been sporadically creating individual pieces of legislation that not only do not mesh neatly but also leave gaping holes.

For example, the so-called Bork bill prohibits the disclosure of video rental lists, but there is no comparable protection for books, magazines, and other periodicals. For that matter, there is no general federal protection for some of the most sensitive information of all—our medical histories. It is difficult to understand the logic behind the fact that video records are accorded special protection in a federal statute, but our medical records are not. There is a limited constitutional interest in avoiding disclosure of certain sensitive medical information, but that right is often outweighed by other societal interests.

In some areas, state laws take up the slack. But privacy advocates argue that such statutes, too, are incomplete. Furthermore, state-to-state variations in protection only add to the haphazard approach to privacy in the United States. In any event, state laws may ultimately make even less sense in this area than others because there are no state lines in cyberspace.

Furthermore, an animating principle of cyberspace is the free flow of information. It is the ultimate democracy, where principles of open records and unfettered speech prevail. As a practical matter, the digital world is extremely difficult to police. In addition, courts are only beginning to consider how First Amendment freedoms will apply.

Thus, while the digital society is coming of age, laws designed to deal with it are still in their infancy. As in the other areas of privacy law, the answer will come at least in part by balancing the competing interests at stake. With all of the Big Brother imagery, it is important to remember that these invasive devices also provide a service, one we often very much want. Many of us appreciate the convenience of credit cards, automatic teller machines, catalogue shopping, and cellular phones. Even the scary-sounding "smart roads" and "smart cards" may become things we cannot do without. Many will happily let the world know which toll booth they passed through if it means they do not have to sit in traffic jams created by the current system. And if you collapse on vacation thousands of miles from home, having your complete medical history on a "smart card" may be more than handy. It could save your life.

Having these services and conveniences means that there will, as always, be a trade-off. The Fourth Amendment protects our privacy, but in the interests of law enforcement, there are times when the police may search our pockets or homes. The First Amendment guarantees a free press, but that means that your photograph may appear on the cover of a magazine without your consent. So, too, we will have all of the conveniences offered by computers, but we can never again expect that our personal papers and communications can simply be locked away from prying eyes and ears.

In some instances, simply knowing that privacy is not to be expected is safeguard enough. When the public first realized that cellular phone conversations, unlike traditional phone calls, could be snatched out of the air, there was an uproar. It turned out that when we spoke into a cellular phone, we really were shouting from the housetops. Now, although we may not like it, many have simply accepted that a stranger can pick up part of a cellular call. And if people have truly sensitive information to convey (for instance, certain government workers), they will not use a cellular phone to make the call.

In other instances, we are already learning to bargain for privacy—every time we read the fine print on products we buy or services we request. The cellular phone company tells us that a call may not be secure and the cable company sends us a notice detailing its privacy protections. We can sign up or not. Normally, we do not consider privacy protections in making such decisions, but we will have to begin to do so in the brave new digital world. E-mail is not the U.S. mail; a cellular phone is not a traditional phone; and our financial, medical, and other records are no longer stored in filing cabinets. If we want to secure our communications and personal profiles, we will have to become more vigilant.

Even so, there will still be some intrusions beyond the control of contract, legislation, or technology. Then we will have to alter our expectations.

This combination of education and altered expectations may hold the key to privacy protection in the future. There is a growing consensus that if the jumble of state and federal statutes, consumer pressure, and self-help is to be unified into meaningful privacy protection in the digital age, then we will have to do more than pass a law. The law in general, and each of us in particular, will have to make some fundamental adjustments in the way we think of personal information and electronic communication. In doing so, we will ultimately have to change our idea of what we can reasonably expect to keep private. With so much information available at a keystroke, it is now inescapable that there will be times when what is whispered in the closet will indeed be shouted from the housetops.

Afterword to the Vintage Edition

An Update

Notes

Bibliography

Index

Afterword to the Vintage Edition

IN THE YEAR since this book was published, we have had an opportunity to see and hear firsthand about the state of the right to privacy in America. We traveled extensively, appeared on call-in radio and television programs, and spoke to audiences around the country. What we heard was very interesting.

There is no doubt in our minds that awareness of privacy issues is growing. Many of the issues we cover in the book that were just emerging during the period of our research have become full-blown front-page national concerns: medical confidentiality, the accessibility of adoption records, physician-assisted suicide, privacy on the information super highway. In these and other areas, people are realizing that they are vulnerable to invasions of privacy; there also seems to be a growing willingness to disregard it, or trade it for other important interests.

In the older areas of privacy law, such as the Fourth Amendment, we heard new horror stories. In many of the cities we visited, an alarming number of people came up to tell us about their own experiences being strip-searched by the police. Drug testing programs in the workplace are now routine, and are even becoming commonplace in schools, although concerns remain about what *other* kinds of information—such as information about pregnancy or prescription medication—can be collected through urinalysis and how that data can be safeguarded. In addition, technology continues to change the entire landscape of law enforcement and, for the most part, receives an enthusiastic welcome. Cities such as Baltimore are installing closed-circuit video surveillance cameras in downtown neighborhoods in an effort to deter crime. High-tech scanners and instant access to motorist records are increasing the police's ability to apprehend suspects in the field. And in the wake of a series of heinous terrorist attacks, privacy may have to give way to the FBI's request for a broad range of new surveillance measures.

In the area of Privacy v. The Press, members of the media continue to expose private lives with the law on their side in the form of the First Amendment. However, we have seen an erosion of public support for such practices and recent cases indicate that the First Amendment may not provide the same degree of protection in the area of news *gathering*, especially when it involves surreptitious monitoring, hidden cameras, and confrontational behavior.

In the area of Privacy and Your Self, abortion remains a bitterly contested national issue. Last year, for the first time, Congress criminalized a medical procedure when it banned a form of late-term abortion. But two federal appeals courts have upheld the Freedom of Access to Clinics Act. And, as always, abortion played a major role in yet another Presidential campaign.

But in this area, the explosive new focus of controversy has shifted to the "right to die," and to receive assistance in doing so. Two federal appeals courts have upheld physician-assisted suicide, albeit for different reasons, and Dr. Kevorkian continues to keep the issue on the front page. The privacy arguments are familiar: Some argue that it is abortion revisited, with the courts overstepping their bounds and creating a right where none exists. Others argue that the courts must recognize individual autonomy and place certain fundamental rights beyond organized pressure groups and even state legislatures.

The erosion of medical confidentiality has also become a source of national concern. The transformation of the health care system, the increasingly large data banks that support it, and the vast amounts of information that are collected and disseminated have created privacy implications that are just beginning to be reckoned with. Many people are surprised to find that there is a federal law protecting the confidentiality of the videos they rent, but that there is no federal law protecting the confidentiality of our medical records.

The need for protection of genetic information is the undisputed issue of the future in this area, yet little has been done to set up a framework by which we may receive the benefits of genetic information, while preventing discrimination based upon it. Only eleven states have laws protecting genetic testing and information, and these vary widely in the degree of protection they afford.

Genetic information is just one example of what is far and away the biggest threat to privacy today, and the one individuals are most powerless against: the increasing technical ability to gather and disseminate all kinds of personal information about each and every one of us. Both government and the private sector are exponentially increasing their ability to track, monitor, and profile us. The FBI announced a plan to be able to wiretap 1 in every 100 telephones by the year 2000, up from the current of 1 in 175,000. The Defense Department is developing a DNA data bank for all service members that will be the largest in the world. The Human Genome Project is years ahead of schedule. By the year 2002 it will be possible to create a complete genetic profile of each of us. The private sector can already link our financial, medical, telephone, cable, and computer information to create profiles of our habits, behavior, and interests, as well as of diseases we have and those we are likely to get.

There is no doubt that we can benefit enormously from the use and convenience of all this information. However, we have seen time and time again that when information is collected, particularly sensitive personal information, it is often abused.

We recognize that in each of these areas where we are vulnerable to intrusions, there are other important interests at stake—law enforcement, a free press, free enterprise. But all of these other interests, whether government, media or big business, are powerful and well-represented. The only voice for privacy—the right to be let alone—is each one of us.

Ellen Alderman
Caroline Kennedy

An Update

In the case of Quill v. Koppell *(The Right to Die), which we discuss on pages 127 to 136, there were important developments over the past year.*

IN A STUNNING one-two punch, in the spring of 1996, the full Court of Appeals for the Ninth Circuit and a three-judge panel of the Second Circuit declared that physician-assisted suicide *is* protected by the Constitution. However, each court came to its conclusion for different reasons.

In Washington, the full panel of Ninth Circuit judges held that the "right to die" was protected under the concept of "liberty" in the Fourteenth Amendment. The court said that the right to die joined the right to terminate pregnancy, to use contraceptives, to marry whom one chooses, and other fundamental rights that the Supreme Court has declared are constitutionally protected even though they are not specifically listed. The Ninth Circuit said the earlier court's focus on the history of assisted suicide was too narrow. First, the court determined, the history of laws and attitudes relating to suicide was not so clear-cut. More important, history was only one criterion for determining whether a right is so fundamental that it must be protected by the Constitution.

Instead, the Ninth Circuit followed the reasoning in *Casey*, the Supreme Court's most recent abortion case, and *Cruzan*, the Court's only right-to-die case. The Ninth Circuit relied on the "compelling similarities" between the abortion and right-to-die cases. Like abortion, the right to die involved "the most intimate and personal choices a person may make in a lifetime, choices central to personal dignity and autonomy [which] are central to the liberty protected by the Fourteenth Amendment." That, coupled with the Court's recognition in *Cruzan* of an individual's constitutional right to refuse medical treatment, even if that refusal meant certain death, made the right to die a constitutionally protected right as well.

Balancing the right to die against the state's interest, the Ninth Circuit agreed that the state has a crucial interest in preserving life. But the court said that that interest diminished as life neared its end. The court also agreed that the state had an interest in protecting vulnerable citizens from abuse, but held that safeguards and regulation could protect against such abuses. All of the state's interest combined did not outweigh "the terminally ill individual's interest in deciding whether to end his agony and suffering ... with medication prescribed by his physician."

The court declared, "Under our constitutional system, neither the state nor the majority of the people in a state [through the legislature] can impose its will upon the individual in a matter so highly central to personal dignity and autonomy. Those who believe strongly that death must come without physicians' assistance are free to follow that creed, be they doctors or patients. They are not free, however, to force their views, their religious convictions, or their philosophies on all the other members of a democratic society, and to compel those whose values differ with theirs to die painful, protracted, and agonizing deaths."

Just a month later, in April 1996, the Second Circuit (in New York) agreed, but for a completely different reason. Taking Dr. Quill and his colleagues' appeal, the Second Circuit reversed the district court opinion and declared that New York's law banning physician-assisted suicide was unconstitutional. But the court specifically declined to follow the Ninth Circuit's lead.

The Second Circuit noted the confusion and controversy surrounding abortion and the general practice of using the notion of "liberty" to protect fundamental rights that are not specifically listed in the Constitution. It is also noted that the Supreme Court has been extremely reluctant to expand that list of rights. Therefore, the Second Circuit decided that if the right to die is to be added to the list of fundamental constitutional rights implicit in the notion of liberty, such a decision could only come from the Supreme Court.

However, the Second Circuit agreed with Dr. Quill that New

York's ban on physician-assisted suicide did violate the Equal Protection clause of the Constitution. Here the court agreed that the Supreme Court in *Cruzan* had essentially decided that there is a constitutional right to refuse medical treatment, even if that refusal meant hastening one's own death. Therefore, the Second Circuit reasoned, if a person could bring his own death by removing life support, then he should be able to do the same by self-administering prescription drugs from a doctor. The appellate court rejected the distinction made by the district court between refusing life support and "letting nature take is course" on the one hand and self-administering drugs on the other. First, the court said, there is nothing "natural" about the death resulting from the removal of life support. More important, the court said, the cause of death in both instances is identical: the patient's desire to put an end to his agony.

The Second Circuit then agreed with the Ninth Circuit in assessing the state's interest. Concerns about abuse could and should be addressed by proper regulation. And while the state has an important interest in preserving life, that interest diminishes to the vanishing point on the eve of the end of life. The court asked: "What business is it of the state to require the continuation of agony when the result is imminent and inevitable?"

Even with such strong pronouncements from two influential circuit courts, the right to die is hardly secure. In both cases, on both coasts, the states vowed to take the battle to the Supreme Court. And in between, across the country, the fight continues in hospitals, hospices, and homes. But with the two circuit court opinions, for the moment at least, there has been a seismic shift in the terrain on which the battle is being fought.

The United States Supreme Court has agreed to hear both cases.

Notes

All quoted remarks are from interviews with the authors unless otherwise noted.

INTRODUCTION

xiv Justice Brandeis' quote is from his dissenting opinion in *Olmstead v. United States*, 277 U.S. 438, 478, 1928 U.S. LEXIS 694 (1928).

PRIVACY V. LAW ENFORCEMENT
Joan W. v. City of Chicago

4–5 The description of the strip search of Joan W. is from *Joan W. v. City of Chicago*, 771 F.2d 1020 (7th Cir. 1985); Appellees' and Appellant's Briefs, *Joan W.*, 771 F.2d 1020 (No. 83 C 327); as well as interviews with the authors.

5–6 The description of the strip search of Mary T. is from *Levka v. City of Chicago*, 748 F.2d 214, 425 (7th Cir. 1984); as well as interviews with the authors.

6 The general description of the Chicago strip search policy is from *MaryBeth G. v. City of Chicago*, 723 F.2d 1263, 1266 (7th Cir. 1983), *aff'g Jane Does v. City of Chicago*, No. 79 C 789 (N.D.Ill. Jan. 12, 1982).

7 The general description of the manner in which the Chicago strip search policy distinguished between men and women is from *MaryBeth G.*, 723 F.2d at 1268.

7–8 The description of the strip searches of Carol D. and Diane H. is from *Carol D. v. City of Chicago*, No. 83 C 1000 (N.D.Ill. filed Aug. 31, 1983), and *Diane H. v. City of Chicago*, No. 83 C 999 (N.D.Ill. filed Aug. 31, 1983); Deposition of Carol D., *Carol D.* (March 23, 1984); Plaintiffs' Complaints, *Carol D.* and *Diane H.*; Defendant's Answers to Complaints, *Carol D.* and *Diane H.*; and interviews with the authors.

9 The description of the incidents prior to MaryAnn T.'s strip search is from *MaryAnn T. v. City of Chicago*, 687 F.2d 175 (7th Cir. 1982).

9 MaryAnn T.'s lawsuit filed by Ted Stein is *MaryAnn T.*, 687 F.2d 175.

10 The class action suit filed by the ACLU is *Jane Does v. City of Chicago*, No. 79 C 789 (N.D.Ill. Jan. 12, 1982), *aff'd sub nom. MaryBeth G. v. City of Chicago*, 723 F.2d 1263 (7th Cir. 1983).

10 The Illinois law prohibiting strip searches of people arrested for nonthreatening misdemeanors is Ill.Rev.Stat. ch. 38, para. 103-1(c) (1979).

10 The city of Chicago's position on the constitutionality of their strip search policy is explained further in *Jane Does*, slip op. at 7.

10 The Supreme Court's declaration that the Fourth Amendment protects an individual's right to privacy is from *Katz. v. United States*, 389 U.S. 347, 350, 1967 U.S. LEXIS 2 (1967). Justice Potter Stewart, in delivering the majority opinion of the Court, held that the "Amendment protects individual privacy against certain kinds of governmental intrusions." *Id.* In an oft cited concurring opinion, Justice John Marshall Harlan elaborated the point, stating that "a person has a constitutionally protected reasonable expectation of privacy." *Id.* at 360.

11 James Otis, Jr.'s quote is from William Tudor, *Life of James Otis* 66 (1823), cited in *Frank v. Maryland*, 359 U.S. 360, 364, 1959 U.S. LEXIS 1085 (1959), and *Boyd v. United States*, 116 U.S. 616, 625 (1885).

11 A more detailed description of the warrant and probable cause requirements of the Fourth Amendment can be found in Wayne R. LaFave and Jerold H. Israel, *Criminal Procedure*, 2d ed., 138 (St. Paul, Minn.: West Publishing, 1992).

11 The leading Supreme Court "hot pursuit" case is *Warden v. Hayden*, 387 U.S. 294, 1967 U.S. LEXIS 2753 (1967). In *Warden*, the officers pursued a fleeing robbery suspect into his house. In the course of looking for him, the officers searched the house and found incriminating evidence. The Court held that the warrantless search of the house was justified because the officers were in hot pursuit of the suspect.

An example of an application of the "plain view doctrine" is the oft cited Supreme Court case *Harris v. United States*, 390 U.S. 234, 1968 U.S. LEXIS 2283 (1968). In *Harris*, a robbery suspect's car was impounded as evidence of the robbery. A police officer opened the car door in order to roll up the windows to protect the car's interior from the rain. In doing so, the officer spotted an article belonging to the robbery victim. The Court allowed the incriminating evidence to be admitted even though the officer did not have a warrant, because the evidence was in "plain view" and the officer legally had a right to be in a position of viewing it. In order for the plain view doctrine to be applied, the officer must legally be in a position to view the item; thus, if an officer illegally searches a house, whatever may be in plain view is irrelevant because the initial search was illegal. S. Saltzburg, D. Capra, and C. Hancock, *Basic Criminal Procedure*, Black Letter Series, 167–74 (St. Paul, Minn.: West Publishing, 1994) (hereinafter Saltzburg, *Basic Criminal Procedure*).

11 The exception to the warrant requirement in which an officer may search people who are under arrest without a warrant is known as the Arrest Power Rule or Search Incident to Arrest. Saltzburg, *Basic Criminal Procedure*, 282. In emphasizing the need for such an exception to the warrant requirement, the Supreme Court held that "[t]here is ample justification . . . for a search of the arrestee's person and the area 'within his immediate control'—construing that phrase to mean the area from within which he might gain possession of a weapon or destructible evidence." *Chimel v. California*, 395 U.S. 752, 763, 1969 U.S. LEXIS 1166 (1969).

11 The Supreme Court's Fourth Amendment reasonableness standard is set forth in *Bell v. Wolfish*, 441 U.S. 520, 1979 U.S. LEXIS 100 (1979), among other cases. In *Bell*, Justice William Rehnquist held that the test for reasonableness under the Fourth Amendment "requires a balancing of the need for the particular search against the invasion of personal rights that the search entails." *Id.* at 559.

12 The Supreme Court case upon which the city of Chicago relied is *Bell*, 441 U.S. 520. *Bell* involved visual body-cavity searches of federal pretrial detainees at a correctional center in New York City. The searches occurred every time a detainee made contact with an outside visitor. The Supreme Court held that the searches were reasonable in light of the "serious security dangers" at a detention facility and that the strip search policy was an effective deterrent to the smuggling of weapons and contraband into the facility. *Bell*, 441 U.S. at 560.

12 The description of the city of Chicago's strip search policy is taken from *MaryBeth G. v. City of Chicago*, 723 F.2d 1263, 1267 (7th Cir. 1983).

12 The district court's decision that the strip search policy was unconstitutional is from *Jane Does*, slip op. at 8, 9. The district court distinguished the Supreme Court case *Bell* on the grounds that *Bell* involved detainees awaiting trial on serious federal charges after having failed to make bond and only after having contact with outside visitors. *Jane Does*, slip op. at 6, 7.

13 The district court's decision that the strip search policy violated the Equal Protection Clause is from *id.* at 3–5.

13 The city of Chicago's appeal to the United States Court of Appeals for the Seventh Circuit is *MaryBeth G.*, 723 F.2d 1263.

13 The district court's order that each case be tried separately to determine the appropriate amount of damages is from *Jane Does*, slip op. at 9.

14–15 Joan W's district court action is *Joan W. v. City of Chicago*, No. 83 C 327 (N.D.Ill. May 27, 1984).

15 The jury awards for MaryAnn T., MaryBeth G., and Sharon N. are listed in *MaryAnn T. v. City of Chicago*, 687 F.2d 175, 177 (7th Cir. 1982); *MaryBeth G.*, 723 F.2d at 1266.

15 The amount of Mary T.'s jury award is listed in *Levka v. City of Chicago*, 748 F.2d 421, 424–25 (7th Cir. 1984); her settlement amount is from interviews with the authors.

16 The Seventh Circuit Court of Appeals opinion is *MaryBeth G.*, 723 F.2d 1263. The court's declaration that the searches were unreasonable and in violation of the Equal Protection Clause under the Fourteenth Amendment is from *id.* at 1268–1274.

16–17 Joan W.'s jury award and Judge Getzendanner's opinion are from *Joan W. v. City of Chicago*, No. 83 C 327 (N.D.Ill. May 27, 1984).

17 The city of Chicago's appeal to the Seventh Circuit in Joan W.'s action is *Joan W. v. City of Chicago*, 771 F.2d 1020 (7th Cir. 1985). The court's opinion that her jury award of $112,000 was extravagant is from *id.* at 1025.

18 The Calumet City case is *Doe v. Calumet City*, 754 F.Supp. 1211, 1990 U.S.Dist. LEXIS 17257 (N.D.Ill. 1990).

PASSING JUDGMENTS

19 The case involving a Denver man who was strip-searched is *Hill v. Bogans*, 735 F.2d 391 (10th Cir. 1984).

20 The case about the multiple strip searches in Hastings, Minnesota, is *Doe v. Boyd*, 613 F.Supp. 1514 (D.Minn. 1985).

20–1 The case involving the strip search of an Upstate New York woman is *Weber v. Dell*, 630 F.Supp. 255 (W.D.N.Y. 1980), *rev'd by* 804 F.2d 796 (2d Cir. 1986), *cert. denied sub nom. County of Monroe v. Weber*, 483 U.S. 1020 (1987).

21–2 The 1980s case involving the Maryland woman who was strip-searched is *Smith v. Montgomery County*, 643 F.Supp. 435 (D.Md. 1986). The similar case occurring in the 1990s is *Roth v. Parries*, 872 F.Supp. 1439, 1995 U.S.Dist. LEXIS 174 (D.Md. 1995).

22 The case about the New Jersey man who was strip-searched is *Moctezuma v. Township of Montclair*, No. 93-3494 (D.N.J. 1993).

Is It a Search?

23 The 1960s Supreme Court case involving a wiretap is *Katz v. United States*, 389 U.S. 347, 1967 U.S. LEXIS 2 (1967). The Court's holding that the Fourth Amendment protects people, not places, is from *id.* at 351. The declaration that the Fourth Amendment protects a person's "reasonable expectation of privacy" is from Justice John Marshall Harlan's concurring opinion at *id.* at 360–61.

23 The case in which the Court held that extracting a person's blood for analysis is a search is *Schmerber v. California*, 384 U.S. 757, 767, 1966 U.S. LEXIS 1129 (1966). The Court held that "compulsory administration of a blood test . . . plainly involves the broadly conceived reach of a search and seizure under the Fourth Amendment." *Id.*

23–4   The Supreme Court case on voice sampling is *United States v. Dionisio*, 410 U.S. 1, 1973 U.S. LEXIS 110 (1973). The court's holding that there is no expectation of privacy in what a "person knowingly exposes to the public" is from *id.* at 14 (quoting *Katz*, 389 U.S. at 351). The Court's holding that voice sampling was not a search under the Fourth Amendment is from *id.* at 16. The Court's statement that "[n]o person can have a reasonable expectation that others will not know the sound of his voice" is from *id.* at 14.

24   In a companion case to *Dionisio*, the Supreme Court held that, like taking a voice sample, taking a handwriting sample is not a search or seizure under the Fourth Amendment in that both are "repeatedly shown to the public." *United States v. Mara*, 410 U.S. 19, 21, 1973 U.S. LEXIS 111 (1973). In *Mara*, the Court held that "there is no more expectation of privacy in the physical characteristics of a person's script than there is in the tone of his voice." *Id.*

24   The Supreme Court case that addresses the issue of fingerprints is *Davis v. Mississippi*, 394 U.S. 721, 1969 U.S. LEXIS 1869 (1969). *Davis*, however, dealt with an initial unlawful seizure of rape suspects. While the suspects were being unlawfully detained (without probable cause), they were fingerprinted. The Supreme Court held that the fingerprints were not admissible because they were obtained in the course of an illegal seizure. *Id.* at 724.

       In regard to whether fingerprinting itself is a search, the Court stated in dictum that "[f]ingerprinting involves none of the probing into an individual's private life and thoughts that marks an interrogation or search." *Id.* at 727. In a subsequent case, the Supreme Court categorized fingerprinting with voice exemplars and handwriting exemplars as such "physical characteristics . . . constantly exposed to the public." *Cupp v. Murphy*, 412 U.S. 291, 295, 1973 U.S. LEXIS 63 (1973).

24   The Supreme Court's holding and quote that fingernail scrapings are a search subject to Fourth Amendment scrutiny is from *Cupp*, 412 U.S. at 295.

24   The Supreme Court case involving the bullet in the robbery suspect's chest is *Winston v. Lee*, 470 U.S. 753, 1985 U.S. LEXIS 76 (1985). The Court's holding that the intrusion into the suspect's privacy would be "severe" and unreasonable under the Fourth Amendment is from *id.* at 766. The Court of Appeals quote regarding the drugging of a citizen, not yet convicted, with barbiturates is from 717 F.2d 888, 901 (4th Cir. 1983). The Supreme Court rejected the Commonwealth of Virginia's request to retrieve the bullet because the severe intrusion was not justified, especially in that the Commonwealth had other evidence linking the suspect to the robbery. 470 U.S. at 765.

24–5   The Supreme Court case in which the Federal Railroad Administration wanted to test railway employees' blood, breath, and urine for evidence of drug and alcohol use is *Skinner v. Railway Labor Executives' Ass'n*, 489 U.S. 602, 1989 U.S. LEXIS 1568 (1989). The Court's holding that the collection of "deep-lung" breath for chemical analysis is a search is at *id.* at 616–17. The Court's holding that the collection of urine for urinalysis is also a search is at *id.*

In a companion case, the Supreme Court upheld suspicionless drug testing of U.S. Customs employees who were applying for positions directly involving the interdiction of illegal drugs or the carrying of firearms; such testing was held to be reasonable under the Fourth Amendment. See *Nat'l Treasury Employees Union v. Von Raab,* 489 U.S. 656, 1989 U.S. LEXIS 1570 (1989).

25 William Pitt's plea for the inviolability of the home is quoted in *United States v. Sansusi,* 813 F.Supp. 149, 1992 U.S.Dist. LEXIS 17741 (E.D.N.Y. 1992).

25 The Supreme Court defines curtilage as the "area [that] harbors the intimate activity associated with the sanctity of a man's home and the privacy of life." *United States v. Dunn,* 480 U.S. 294, 300, 1987 U.S. LEXIS 1057 (1987).

The *Dunn* Court suggested four factors that should be considered in determining what constitutes curtilage:

1. the proximity of the area to the home;
2. whether the area is within an enclosure surrounding the home;
3. the nature of the uses to which the area is put; and
4. the steps taken by the resident to protect the area from observation by people passing by the area

Id. at 301.

25–6 The Supreme Court case upholding the search of the Kentucky man's farm is *Oliver v. United States,* 466 U.S. 170, 1984 U.S. LEXIS 55 (1984). The Court's quote regarding what an individual can legitimately demand as a zone of privacy is from *id.* at 178. The Court held that "[t]here is no societal interest in protecting the privacy of those activities, such as the cultivation of crops, that occur in open fields." *Id.* at 179.

26 The case in which the Supreme Court held that a barn sixty yards from a farmhouse was not within the curtilage is *United States v. Dunn,* 480 U.S. at 294.

26 The Supreme Court case holding that aerial surveillance of a California man's backyard did not constitute a Fourth Amendment search is *California v. Ciraolo,* 476 U.S. 207, 1986 U.S. LEXIS 154 (1986). The Court's determination that it is unreasonable to protect one's garden from aerial observation is from *id.* at 213–14.

Three years after *Ciraolo,* police acting on an anonymous tip flew a helicopter four hundred feet over a greenhouse in order to observe a marijuana crop. The Supreme Court held that *Ciraolo* was controlling and that there was no significant difference between a plane at one thousand feet and a helicopter at four hundred feet. Neither was held to be a search. *Florida v. Riley,* 488 U.S. 445, 450–51, 1989 U.S. LEXIS 580 (1989).

26   The case involving EPA investigators using a "precision aerial mapping camera" is *Dow Chemical Co. v. United States*, 476 U.S. 227, U.S. LEXIS 155 (1986). The Supreme Court's holding that the enhancement of human vision (as enhanced in *Dow*) did not constitute a search under the Fourth Amendment is from *id.* at 238. Reiterating how the Court's holding applied only to the type of mapping camera used in this case, the Court held that "[a]n electronic device to penetrate walls or windows so as to hear and record confidential discussions of chemical formulae or other trade secrets would raise very different and far more serious questions." *Id.* at 239.

27   The Supreme Court case involving the government's search of Mr. Miller's bank statements is *United States v. Miller*, 425 U.S. 435, 1976 U.S. LEXIS 148 (1976). The Court's holding that Mr. Miller had no legitimate expectation of privacy in his bank records because he voluntarily conveyed them to the bank is from *id.* at 442. The Court's quote that depositors take a risk that information will be conveyed to the government is from *id.* at 443.

       Two years following *Miller*, the United States Congress enacted the Right to Financial Privacy Act of 1978, 12 U.S.C.A. §3401 et seq. (1978). The Act was intended to protect customers of financial institutions from unwarranted intrusion into their records, while at the same time permitting legitimate law enforcement activity. H.R.Rep. No. 1383, 95th Cong., 2d Sess., at 33, 34 (1978), *reprinted in* 1978 U.S.C.C.A.N. 9305–9306. The legislative history states that "while the Supreme Court found no constitutional right of privacy in financial records, it is clear that Congress may provide protection of individual rights beyond that afforded in the Constitution." *Id.*

27–8   The case involving a pen register is *Smith v. Maryland*, 442 U.S. 735, 1979 U.S. LEXIS 134 (1979). The Court held that a man could not have expected the numbers he dialed on his telephone to be private is from *id.* at 742. The Court's comparison of the telephone numbers to the bank records in *Miller* is from *id.* at 744.

28   The case involving the search of a California man's trash is *California v. Greenwood*, 486 U.S. 35, 1988 U.S. LEXIS 2279 (1988). The Court's holding that trash placed out for collection is not protected by the Fourth Amendment is from *id.* at 39–43. The Court's declaration that individuals knowingly expose their trash to the public and voluntarily turn it over to third parties is from *id.* at 41 (quoting *Katz*, 389 U.S. at 351; *Smith*, 442 U.S. at 743–44).

28   The case in which a man unsuccessfully attempted to retain privacy in his garbage by shredding it is *United States v. Scott*, 975 F.2d 927, 1992 U.S.App. LEXIS 22877 (1st Cir. 1992), *rev'g* 776 F.Supp. 629, 1991 U.S.Dist. LEXIS 15953 (D.Mass. 1991). The Court of Appeals holding that the shredded documents were nonetheless "trash" and not protected by the Fourth Amendment is from *id.* at 928–29. The court held that the "mere fact that appellant shredded his garbage before he placed it outside of his

home does not create a reasonable heightened expectation of privacy under the Fourth Amendment." *Id.* at 930.

A Warrantless Search: Is It Reasonable?

29 Previously cited examples of exceptions to the warrant requirement are the "hot pursuit" exception and the "plain view doctrine." See *supra* note, p. 336.

29 The Supreme Court has frequently referred to warrants as a "preference" rather than a "requirement." Justice William Rehnquist, in a dissenting opinion, held that "[i]t is often forgotten that nothing in the Fourth Amendment itself requires that searches be conducted pursuant to warrants." *Robbins v. California*, 453 U.S. 420, 438, 1981 U.S. LEXIS 132 (1981). In another opinion, the Supreme Court reiterated that although "the Court has expressed a preference for the use of arrest warrants when feasible . . . it has never invalidated an arrest warrant supported by probable cause solely because the officers failed to secure a warrant." *Gerstein v. Pugh*, 420 U.S. 103, 113, 1975 U.S. LEXIS 29 (1975).

29 The legal standard that police officers, if they do not obtain a warrant, must have enough information "to warrant a man of reasonable caution" believing a crime has occurred is from *Terry v. Ohio*, 392 U.S. 1, 21–22, 1968 U.S. LEXIS 1345 (1968). The example of the warrantless blood test in *Schmerber*, and the Court's holding that the blood test was constitutional, are from *Schmerber v. California*, 384 U.S. 757, 770–72, 1966 U.S. LEXIS 1129 (1966).

29 The Court upheld warrantless fingernail scrapings in *Cupp v. Murphy*, 412 U.S. 291, 296, 1973 U.S. LEXIS 63 (1973). The Court held that the police were justified "in subjecting [Mr. Murphy] to the very limited search necessary to preserve the highly evanescent evidence they found under his fingernails." *Id.*

29 The "reasonable suspicion" standard was first laid out by the Supreme Court in *Terry*, 392 U.S. 1. In *Terry*, the Court declared that the legal reasoning to be applied by police officers prior to conducting a warrantless search is "whether a reasonably prudent man in the circumstances would be warranted in the belief that his safety or that of others was in danger." *Id.* at 27.

30 The Court's holding that the testing of railway employees for drug and alcohol use was constitutional is from *Skinner v. Railway Labor Executives' Ass'n*, 489 U.S. 602, 633, 1989 U.S. LEXIS 1568 (1989). The Court balanced the privacy rights of the workers against the importance of public safety and held that "the toxicological testing contemplated by the regulations is not an undue infringement on the justifiable expectations of privacy of covered employees, [and that] the Government's compelling interests outweigh privacy concerns." *Id.*

30 For a discussion of the inadequacy of the balancing test and the diminished power of the Fourth Amendment, see, e.g., *T.L.O. v. New Jersey*, 469

U.S. 325, 354–68, 1985 U.S. LEXIS 41 (1985) (William Brennan, dissenting, joined by Thurgood Marshall).

30   The two additional levels of suspicion that New York police officers must meet prior to asking a citizen a question are "objective credible reason" and "founded suspicion." These levels of suspicion are triggered on the basis of whether the police officer is simply requesting information and whether the request for information is a "common-law inquiry." See *People v. Hollman*, 590 N.E.2d 204, 206, 581 N.Y.S.2d 619, 620–21, 1992 N.Y. LEXIS 203 (N.Y. 1992).

People of New York v. Hollman

31   The statistics on the number of passengers entering New York's Port Authority Bus Terminal are taken from 1994 Fact Sheet, Port Authority of New York and New Jersey.

32   The New York Court of Appeals' four-tiered method for evaluating the propriety of encounters initiated by police officers is from *Hollman*, 590 N.E.2d at 205–6 (citing *People v. DeBour*, 352 N.E.2d 562, 386, N.Y.S.2d 375 (N.Y. 1976).

32–3   The two cases involving the searches at the Port Authority Bus Terminal were combined into one New York Court of Appeals opinion. See *Hollman*, 590 N.E.2d 204 (N.Y. 1992). The case in which the officer noticed a suspicious man in the boarding area is *People v. Saunders*. The case in which the police observed a man carrying an orange bag up and down an escalator is *People v. Hollman*.

33–4   The New York Court of Appeals holding in *Hollman* that the search and common-law inquiry were constitutional because the officer had a "founded suspicion that criminality was afoot" is from *Hollman*, 590 N.E.2d at 211. In *Saunders*, the court held that the officer's search of the bag was unconstitutional because "the defendant's consent was a product of the improper police inquiry." *Id.* The Court's declaration that the tone and politeness of the officer are irrelevant when requesting to search one's bag is from *id.* at 210.

34   The United States Supreme Court case in which the Court held that police officers may approach a citizen so long as they do not "convey a message that compliance with their requests is required" is *Florida v. Bostick*, 501 U.S. 429, 437, 1991 U.S. LEXIS 3625 (1991). The Court's holding that refusal to cooperate with the police does not justify detention or seizure is at *id.*

   Although the Court held that a search or a seizure does not occur when one's consent is requested to search one's luggage, "so long as the officers do not convey a message that compliance with their requests is required," the Court refrained from deciding whether a search or a seizure had occurred in this instance because the trial court made no express findings of fact. The Court stated that the lower court based its decision solely on the fact that Bostick was on a bus. The Court remanded the case back to the lower court to determine, based upon the totality of the circumstances, whether an unlawful encounter had taken place.

On remand, the Supreme Court of Florida held that the officers' search of Bostick's bag did not violate the Fourth Amendment. *Bostick v. State*, 593 So.2d 494, 1992 Fla. LEXIS 9 (Fla. 1992).

34 Justice Thurgood Marshall's quotes from the dissent are from *Bostick*, 501 U.S. at 445, 447.

New Jersey v. T.L.O.

36 The 1985 case in which the Supreme Court held that the Fourth Amendment applies to public school officials is *T.L.O. v. New Jersey*, 469 U.S. 325, 1985 U.S. LEXIS 41 (1985).

37–8 Vice Principal Choplick's description of the opening of T.L.O.'s purse is from Brief for Respondent at 3, *T.L.O. v. New Jersey*, 469 U.S. 325 (1985) (No. 83–712), as well as interviews with the authors.

39 T.L.O.'s action against the Board of Education contesting her suspension is *T.L.O. v. Piscataway Bd. of Educ.*, No. C2865–79 (N.J.Super. Ct.Ch.Div., Mar. 31, 1980). T.L.O.'s action in juvenile court is *State ex rel. T.L.O.*, 428 A.2d 1327 (N.J.Juv.Ct. 1980).

39 The Supreme Court's declaration that students do not "shed their Constitutional rights . . . at the schoolhouse gate" is from *Tinker v. Des Moines Indep. Community School Dist.*, 393 U.S. 503, 506, 1969 U.S. LEXIS 2443 (1969).

39 The 1943 case in which the Supreme Court emphasized the importance of teaching citizenship in the schools is *W. Va. State Bd. of Educ. v. Barnette*, 319 U.S. 624, 637, 1943 U.S. LEXIS 490 (1943).

40 Although the exclusionary rule is not specifically set out in the Constitution, the Supreme Court held that it was "an essential part of both the Fourth and Fourteenth Amendments and the only effective remedy for the protection of rights under the Fourth Amendment." *Linkletter v. Walker*, 381 U.S. 618, 634, 1965 U.S. LEXIS 2283 (1965).

Justice Benjamin Cardozo's quote about the exclusionary rule is from *People v. Defore*, 150 N.E. 585, 587, 242 N.Y. 13, 21 (N.Y. 1926).

40–1 T.L.O. first brought an action in the state chancery court against the Board of Education contesting her suspension. The chancery court quashed T.L.O.'s suspension, holding that the search violated the Fourth Amendment. See *T.L.O. v. Piscataway Bd. of Educ.*, No. C2865–79 (N.J.Super.Ct.Ch.Div., Mar. 31, 1980). In her action in juvenile court, T.L.O. attempted to rely on the chancery court's holding, but the court denied her motion to suppress the evidence found in her purse. See *State ex rel. T.L.O.*, 428 A.2d 1327 (N.J.Juv.Ct. 1980). The juvenile court's holding was affirmed by the appellate court, which held that there was no violation of the Fourth Amendment. See *State ex rel. T.L.O.*, 448 A.2d 493 (N.J.Super.Ct.App.Div. 1982). T.L.O. then appealed to the Supreme Court of New Jersey, which reversed the lower courts' rulings and ordered the evidence found in her purse suppressed. See *State ex rel. T.L.O.*, 463 A.2d 934 (N.J. 1983).

41 The Supreme Court of New Jersey's application of the "reasonable" standard is from *State ex rel. T.L.O.*, 463 A.2d at 941. The court's holding that Vice Principal Choplick was unreasonable is from *id.* at 942. The court's description of Choplick's search as "wholesale rummaging" is from *id.* at 943. The court's holding that the exclusionary rule applied in the school setting is from *id.* at 944. In applying the exclusionary rule, the court held that "evidence otherwise obtained as a result of a warrantless search is illegally obtained and is inadmissible in criminal proceedings against students." *Id.*

42–3 The original petition for certiorari raised only the question of whether the exclusionary rule applied to school officials. See *T.L.O. v. New Jersey*, 464 U.S. 991 (1983). The Supreme Court extended their review of *T.L.O.* to consider whether the Fourth Amendment applied to the activities of school authorities. See *T.L.O.*, 469 U.S. at 331–32. The Court's acknowledgment of the recent disorder in schools is from *id.* at 339. The Court's holding that the situation in the schools is not so dire as to warrant depriving the students of a legitimate expectation of privacy is from *id.* at 338. The Court's holding that teachers do not have to be trained in the "niceties" of probable cause but that they should act reasonably under the circumstances is from *id.* at 341–43. The Court's holding that Mr. Choplick's search was "in no sense unreasonable" is from *id.* at 343. The Court's reasoning that T.L.O.'s purse was the logical place to find cigarettes is from *id.* at 346. Once Mr. Choplick saw the E-Z Wider cigarette papers, the Court held, he was justified in looking further. *Id.* at 347.

43 Justice William Brennan's dissenting opinion that Mr. Choplick's search was a "serious intrusion" of T.L.O.'s privacy is from *id.* at 355. Justice John Paul Stevens, in a separate dissenting opinion, held that "[t]he search of a young woman's purse by a school administrator is a serious invasion of her legitimate expectations of privacy." *Id.* at 375. Justice Brennan's opinion that the new standard set forth by the majority was ambiguous is from *id.* at 354. The dissent's prediction that school administrators "would be hopelessly adrift . . ." under the new standard set forth by the majority is from *id.* at 365.

PASSING JUDGMENTS

44 The California case in which a student's wallet was searched after he was found in the boys' room without a pass is *In re Bobby B.*, 218 Cal.Rptr.253 (Cal.Ct.App. 1985).

44 The Arizona case in which a student was instructed to empty his pockets

after he was found on the bleachers outside the school is *In re Appeal in Pima County Juvenile Action No. 80484-1*, 733 P.2d 316 (Ariz.Ct.App. 1987).

45 The Ohio case in which a high school teacher smelled marijuana permeating from a student is *Widener v. Frye*, 809 F.Supp. 35, 1992 Dist. LEXIS 19934 (S.D. Ohio 1992).

45-6 The Alaska case in which school officials searched a student's car after the student appeared to be intoxicated is *Shamberg v. State*, 762 P.2d 488, 1988 Alas.App. LEXIS 101 (Alaska Ct.App. 1988).

46-7 The Texas case in which a student was searched after attempting to skip school is *Coronado v. State*, 835 S.W.2d 636, 1992 Tex.Crim.App. LEXIS 164 (Tex.Crim.App. 1992).

T.L.O. Revisited

48-9 The 1995 Supreme Court case upholding random drug testing of high school athletes is *Vernonia Sch. Dist. v. Acton*, 63 U.S.L.W. 4653, 1995 U.S. LEXIS 4275 (1995). The Court's declaration that the intrusion upon the students' privacy was "negligible" is from 63 U.S.L.W. at 4656. The Court's statement that the drug problem was fueled by the "role model effect of athletes' drug use" is from *id.* at 4658.

  The dissent's holding that the drug testing was "particularly destructive of privacy and offensive to personal dignity" is from *id.* at 4660. The dissent noted the "great irony" in the case at *id.* at 4662. In noting James Acton's explanation, Justice Sandra Day O'Connor wrote, "It is hard to think of [an] explanation that resonates more intensely in our Fourth Amendment tradition than this." See *id.* at 4664. Her fear that all school children will now be subject to random intrusive bodily searches is from *id.* at 4659.

PRIVACY AND YOUR SELF

54 The 1986 United States Supreme Court case that rejected the argument that homosexual behavior is constitutionally protected is *Bowers v. Hardwick*, 478 U.S. 186, 1986 U.S. LEXIS 123 (1986).

From Griswold to Casey

55 The quotes stating that liberty protects rights "deeply rooted . . ." and "implicit in the concept of ordered liberty . . ." are from *Bowers v. Hardwick*, 478 U.S. 186, 191, 1986 U.S. LEXIS 123 (1986).

55 The 1923 Supreme Court case in which the Court held that "liberty" included a parent's right to decide whether his or her child should study a foreign language is *Meyer v. Nebraska*, 262 U.S. 390 (1923). Two years later, the Court held that "liberty" also included a parent's right to send his or her child to private school. *Pierce v. Society of Sisters*, 268 U.S. 510, 1925 U.S. LEXIS 589 (1925).

55–6 The 1967 Supreme Court case striking down a law forbidding interracial marriage is *Loving v. Virginia*, 388 U.S. 1, 1967 U.S. LEXIS 1082 (1967).

57 The 1965 Supreme Court case involving the use of contraceptives by married people is *Griswold v. Connecticut*, 381 U.S. 479, 1965 U.S. LEXIS 2282 (1965).

57–8 Justice William O. Douglas' opinion for the Court in *Griswold* begins on *id*. at 480. The quotation regarding the right to marital privacy is from *id*. at 486. His point that freedom of association is a protected right even though it is not specifically mentioned in the Constitution is at *id*. at 483. The "zones of privacy" are referred to at *id*. at 485. The quotation about police searching private bedrooms for contraceptives is at *id*.

58 Justice Hugo Black's dissent begins at *id*. at 507. The quotation is at *id*. at 510.

58 Justice Potter Stewart's dissent begins at *id*. at 527. His statement that although the Connecticut law is "silly," the law does not violate the Constitution is from *id*. at 527. Justice Stewart's statement that he cannot find a general right of privacy in the Bill of Rights is from *id*. at 530.

58 The 1972 Supreme Court case involving contraceptives and unmarried people is *Eisenstadt v. Baird*, 405 U.S. 438, 1972 U.S. LEXIS 145 (1972). The quotation from Justice William Brennan's opinion is from *id*. at 453.

58 The 1973 Supreme Court case upholding the right to an abortion is *Roe v. Wade*, 410 U.S. 113, 1973 U.S. LEXIS 159 (1973).

58–60 Justice Harry Blackmun's opinion begins at *id*. at 116. The quotation regarding the beginning of life is at *id*. at 159. The Court's recognition of the diversity of opinions and sensitivity surrounding the abortion issue is from *id*. at 116, 158–61. The Court's conclusion regarding the legal status of the unborn is from *id*. at 158–62. Justice Blackmun's historical discussion of the laws regarding abortion is from *id*. at 129–41. The Court's recognition that modern-day medical advances have made abortion relatively safer than childbirth is from *id*. at 148–49. The Court noted that many of the states had loosened their restrictions on abortion. See *id*. at 147–48 n. 41. The Court's discussion of the constitutional right to privacy can be found at *id*. at 152–53. The Court's holding that the right to privacy encompasses a woman's decision as to whether to terminate her pregnancy is from *id*. at 153. The discussion of the state interests and the trimester framework can be found at *id*. at 162–65.

60 Justice William Rehnquist's dissent begins at *id*. at 171. His statement that abortion is not a fundamental right is from *id*. at 174. Justice Rehnquist's attack on the Court's trimester framework is from *id*. His statement that the Court has further confused the law is from *id*. at 173.

60–1 The Court struck down spousal consent in *Planned Parenthood of Central Missouri v. Danforth*, 428 U.S. 52, 1976 U.S. LEXIS 13 (1976); a twenty-four-hour waiting period in *Akron v. Akron Center for Reproductive Health*, 462 U.S. 416, 1983 U.S. LEXIS 63 (1983); and hospitalization for all second-trimester abortions in *Planned Parenthood Ass'n of Kansas City, Missouri, Inc. v. Ashcroft*, 462 U.S. 476, 1983 U.S. LEXIS 64 (1983).

The Court upheld the withdrawal of federal funding for abortion in *Harris v. McRae*, 448 U.S. 297, 1980 U.S. LEXIS 145 (1980); the requirement that all second-trimester abortions be performed in a licensed clinic in *Simopoulos v. Virginia*, 462 U.S. 506, 1983 U.S. LEXIS 65 (1983); and a requirement that a second physician be present during abortions performed after viability in *Planned Parenthood Ass'n of Kansas City, Missouri, Inc. v. Ashcroft*, 462 U.S. 476, 1983 U.S. LEXIS 64 (1983).

61   The 1976 case that struck down a parental consent requirement is *Danforth*, 428 U.S. 52. The 1981 case upholding a law that parents must be notified "if possible" is *H.L. v. Matheson*, 450 U.S. 398, 1981 U.S. LEXIS 81 (1981). The 1983 case in which the Court upheld a parental consent law with a judicial bypass provision is *Ashcroft*, 462 U.S. 476.

61–2 The 1989 Supreme Court case upholding restrictions on abortion is *Webster v. Reproductive Health Servs.*, 492 U.S. 490, 1989 U.S. LEXIS 3290 (1989). Chief Justice Rehnquist wrote the opinion for the Court, in which four other justices joined in the holding. However, the reasoning in portions of the opinion were joined by only two justices; thus, these parts are referred to as a *plurality* opinion and not a *majority* opinion. The plurality's statement that the Missouri law was designed to encourage childbirth over abortion is from *id.* at 519–20. The determination that viability occurs at an estimated twenty-four weeks is from the plurality opinion. *Id.* at 515–16. Justice Antonin Scalia's concurring opinion begins at *id.* at 532. In his concurring opinion, Justice Scalia stated that he would explicitly overrule *Roe v. Wade. Id.* at 532. The plurality opinion begins at *id.* at 512. In the plurality opinion, Chief Justice Rehnquist and Justices Byron White and Anthony Kennedy stated that the *Roe* trimester framework was "unsound in principle and unworkable in practice." *Id.* at 518. Justice Sandra Day O'Connor's concurring opinion begins at *id.* at 522. Justice O'Connor's refusal to revisit *Roe* is from *id.* at 525. Chief Justice Rehnquist's statement that the Court had turned into an "ex officio medical board" is from *id.* at 519. Chief Justice Rehnquist then questioned "why the state's interest in protecting potential human life should come into existence only at the point of viability." He said, "[The] State has compelling interests in ensuring maternal health and in protecting potential human life, and these interests exist throughout pregnancy." *Id.* (citation omitted). Chief Justice Rehnquist's statement that abortion is not a fundamental right, but rather "a liberty interest protected by the Due Process Clause" which can be regulated but not outlawed by the states, is from *id.* at 520.

62–3 Justice Blackmun's dissent begins at *id.* at 537. His quotations criticizing the plurality can be found at *id.* at 538, 546–47. Justice Blackmun's discussion of the constitutional right to privacy and related quotations in the text can be found at *id.* at 548–49. Justice Blackmun's defense of the trimester framework and viability standard is from *id.* at 549–54. Justice Blackmun's defense of *Roe* is from *id.* at 557 n. 11.

63   Another case demonstrating the division amongst the justices is the 1991 Supreme Court case in which the Court upheld what has been called the "gag rule." *Rust v. Sullivan*, 500 U.S. 173, 1991 U.S. LEXIS 2908 (1991). The "gag rule" is a federal regulation that prohibits staff or doctors in federally funded clinics or hospitals from counseling patients on abortion. Shortly thereafter, Congress passed legislation overturning the regulations. President George Bush first vetoed the legislation but then approved a modification exempting doctors from the ban on counseling. A federal district court in Washington, D.C., invalidated the modification on procedural grounds, thus the entire ban on abortion counseling could not be put into effect. *Nat'l Family Planning & Reprod. Health Ass'n v. Sullivan*, No. 92-935(CRR), 1992 U.S.Dist. LEXIS 7043 (D.D.C. May 28, 1992). Several months following the district court's decision, President Bill Clinton was voted into office, and on the twentieth anniversary of *Roe v. Wade*, by means of an executive order, the ban on counseling was repealed altogether. See Tamar Lewin, "Court Says U.S. Violated Law on Abortion Advice," *N.Y. Times*, May 29, 1992, at A13; and Robin Toner, "Clinics Free to Advise—Anniversary of Ruling Marked by Protest," *N.Y. Times*, Jan. 23, 1993, at A1.

63–5 The 1992 Supreme Court case reaffirming *Roe v. Wade* and setting forth the "undue burden" standard is *Planned Parenthood v. Casey*, 112 S.Ct. 2791, 1992 U.S. LEXIS 4751 (1992). The Court's declaration that "liberty finds no refuge in a jurisprudence of doubt" is from *id.* at 2803. Writing for the Court, Justice Sandra Day O'Connor reaffirmed the three parts of the essential holding of *Roe. Id.* at 2804. Justice O'Connor's defense of substantive due process and the right to privacy is from *id.* at 2804–2808. The Court's holding that "there is a realm of personal liberty which the government may not enter" is from *id.* at 2805. The Court's statement describing what is "at the heart of liberty" is from *id.* at 2807. The Court's discussion of *stare decisis* and the cost of overruling *Roe* is from *id.* at 2808–2813. The Court's holding that the trimester framework undervalued the state's interest in potential life is from *id.* at 2818. The Court's description of an *undue burden* as a "substantial obstacle" in the path of a woman seeking an abortion is from *id.* at 2820. The spousal notification provision is discussed at *id.* at 2829–2833. The Court upheld the other provisions in the Pennsylvania statute at *id.* at 2822–2826.

65   Justice Blackmun's argument that the trimester framework should be retained is at *id.* at 2847–2848. His compliment to the three justices who wrote the joint opinion as showing "personal courage and constitutional principle" is from *id.* at 2844. Justice Blackmun's criticism of the dissent as having a "stunted conception of individual liberty" and a disregard for previous decisions is from *id.* at 2853.

65–6 The dissent's declaration that *Roe* should be overruled is at *id.* at 2855. The distinction between abortion and other protected liberties is from *id.* at 2859. The dissent's criticism of the "undue burden" standard as unworkable and likely to encourage judges to instill their personal views is from *id.* at 2866. Justice Scalia's quotes criticizing the Court are from *id.* at 2875–2876, 2877 n. 4, and 2885. Justice Blackmun's quote is from *id.* at 2844.

PASSING JUDGMENTS

67   The case upholding the Mississippi two-parent consent statute with a judicial bypass is *Barnes v. State of Mississippi*, 992 F.2d 1335, 1993 U.S.App. LEXIS 12319 (5th Cir. 1993), *cert. denied*, 114 S.Ct. 468, 1993 U.S. LEXIS 7166 (1993).

67   The Eighth Circuit case upholding the North Dakota statute requiring abortion counseling and a waiting period is *Fargo Women's Health Org. v. Schafer*, 18 F.3d 526, 1994 U.S.App. LEXIS 2141 (8th Cir. 1994).

68   The case striking down the Louisiana abortion statute is *Sojourner T. v. Edwards*, 974 F.2d 27, 1992 U.S.App. LEXIS 22853 (5th Cir. 1992), *cert. denied*, 113 S.Ct. 1414, 1993 U.S. LEXIS 1984 (1993).

68–9   The Supreme Court case involving the antiabortion picketers in front of a Wisconsin doctor's home is *Frisby v. Schultz*, 487 U.S. 474, 1988 U.S. LEXIS 3026 (1988). The Court upheld the ban on picketing in front of a particular home, in that "individuals are not required to welcome unwanted speech into their own homes and that the government may protect this freedom." *Id.* at 485. The Court's statement that there is "no right to force speech into the home of an unwilling listener" is from *id.* The Court held that it was the singling out of one particular home that was the problem, whereas general marching through a residential neighborhood would be permissible. *Id.* at 483.

69–70   The 1994 Supreme Court case involving the antiabortion picketing in Florida is *Madsen v. Women's Health Center, Inc.*, 114 S.Ct. 2516, 1994 U.S. LEXIS 5087 (1994). The Court upheld the thirty-six-foot buffer zone around the clinic as well as the noise restrictions. *Id.* at 2526–2529. The Court's statement that patients should not have to undertake "Herculean efforts" is from *id.* at 2528. The Court's striking down of the thirty-six-foot buffer zone around the adjoining property, the ban on observable images, and the three-hundred-foot no-approach zone around the clinic and residences is at *id.* at 2528–2530.

In regard to residential picketing, the Court held that restrictions less burdensome than a three-hundred-foot buffer could have been implemented. *Id.* at 2530. The Court's statement that the government could require the protesters to turn down the volume if they overwhelmed the neighborhood is from *id.* at 2529.

70   In response to the nationwide spread of violence at abortion facilities, on May 26, 1994, President Clinton signed the Freedom of Access to Clinic Entrances Act of 1994 (commonly referred to as "F.A.C.E."). See 18 U.S.C. §248 (1994). F.A.C.E. makes it a federal crime to use force, threats, or violence to obstruct abortion clinics or to intimidate or interfere with patients or doctors.

F.A.C.E. was immediately challenged as unconstitutional. The Fourth Circuit recently heard two cases brought by two different antiabortion groups; factually, the cases were almost identical, but they were tried as separate cases. In both instances, the Fourth Circuit upheld F.A.C.E. as constitutional. See *Am. Life League, Inc. v. Reno*, 47 F.3d 642, 1995 U.S.App. LEXIS 2596 (4th Cir. 1995); *Woodall v. Reno*, 47 F.3d 656, 1995 U.S.App. LEXIS 2594 (4th Cir. 1995). Following the Fourth Circuit's decisions, both groups sought appeals to the United States Supreme Court. On June 19, 1995, the Supreme Court refused to hear the *Woodall* case, thus letting stand the Fourth Circuit's decision. See *Woodall*, 63 U.S.L.W. 3890, 1995 U.S. LEXIS 4096 (1995).

Several days after the Supreme Court denied certiorari in *Woodall*, the Eleventh Circuit also upheld the constitutionality of F.A.C.E. *Cheffer v. Reno*, 1995 U.S.App. LEXIS 15577 (11th Cir. June 23, 1995).

Davis v. Davis

The quoted remarks are from the Trial Transcripts, *Davis v. Davis*, No. E-14496 (Tenn.Cir.Ct. Aug. 7–10, 1989); as well as interviews with the authors.

77–8   The trial round of litigation in the Davises' battle over the frozen embryos took place in the Tennessee Circuit Court. *Davis v. Davis*, No. E-14496, 1989 Tenn.App. LEXIS 641 (Tenn.Cir.Ct. Sept. 21, 1989).

78   The 1976 United States Supreme Court case that struck down a law requiring a woman to obtain the consent of her husband prior to an abortion is *Planned Parenthood of Central Missouri v. Danforth*, 428 U.S. 52, 1976 U.S. LEXIS 13 (1976). The 1992 Supreme Court decision holding that spousal notification is also unconstitutional is *Planned Parenthood v. Casey*, 112 S.Ct. 2791, 1992 U.S. LEXIS 4751 (1992).

84   Judge Young's conclusions that life begins at conception and that the frozen cells were "children in vitro" is from *Davis*, slip op. at 2. His holding that it would be in the best interests of the children to be born and thus that custody should go to the mother, Mary Sue, is from *id.*

85   The decision of the Tennessee Court of Appeals is *Davis v. Davis*, No. 180, 1990 Tenn.App. LEXIS 642 (Tenn.Ct.App. Sept. 13, 1990).

85   The 1989 United States Supreme Court case upholding strict regulations on abortion is *Webster v. Reproductive Health Servs.*, 492 U.S. 490, 1989 U.S. LEXIS 3290 (1989).

85   Justice Blackmun's statement from his dissent is from *id.* at 560.

86   The Supreme Court's statement that it need not resolve the issue of when life begins is from *Roe v. Wade*, 410 U.S. 113, 159, 1973 U.S. LEXIS 159 (1973).

86–9   The Tennessee Supreme Court decision in the Davises' case is *Davis v. Davis*, 842 S.W.2d 588, 1992 Tenn. LEXIS 400 (Tenn. 1992). The Tennessee

Supreme Court's conclusion that the term "pre-embryo" was a proper scientific term is from *id.* at 594. The court's comments on Dr. LeJeune's testimony are from *id.* at 593. The court's conclusion that the embryos were neither persons nor property but were to be assigned to a special interim category is from *id.* at 594–97. The court's discussion of contract law and its conclusion that Junior Davis never intended to pursue reproduction outside his marriage is from *id.* at 597–98. The court's analysis of the rights of privacy and procreation under the Tennessee constitution is from *id.* at 598–603. The court's holding that under the Tennessee constitution the right to procreate is part of the right to privacy is from *id.* at 600. The court's statement that procreational autonomy is composed of two conflicting rights is from *id.* at 601. The court's statements regarding the tension between the two interests are from *id.* The court's balancing of the potential burdens on Junior and Mary Sue is from *id.* at 603. The court's conclusion that allowing Mary Sue to proceed with the donation would be extremely unjust to Junior is from *id.* at 604. The court's comment on the fact that Mary Sue could still become a parent without the frozen embryos is from *id.*

89 The United States Supreme Court refused to hear the Davises' case. See *Stowe v. Davis*, 113 S.Ct. 1259, 1993 U.S. LEXIS 1148.

89 The Tennessee Supreme Court's direction to Dr. King's clinic to dispose of the embryos is from *Davis*, 842 S.W.2d at 605.

89 The six-month "cooling-off" period was granted by Judge Young in *Davis v. Davis*, No. E-14496 (Tenn.Cir.Ct. May 24, 1993).

89 The June 7, 1993, Tennessee Supreme Court opinion overruling the cooling-off period is *Davis v. Davis*, No. 03 S01-9305 CV30 (Tenn. June 7, 1993).

PASSING JUDGMENTS

92 The New York case that directly contradicted *Davis v. Davis* is *Kass v. Kass*, N.Y.L.J., Jan. 23, 1995, at 34 (N.Y.Sup.Ct. Jan. 23, 1995). In an interview with the authors the husband's attorney confirmed his plans to appeal the trial court's decision.

92–3 The case in which the California attorney deposited fifteen vials of his sperm in a local sperm bank prior to his suicide is *Hecht v. Superior Ct.*, 20 Cal.Rptr.2d 275, 1993 Cal.App. LEXIS 638 (Cal.Ct.App. 1993), *review denied*, 1993 Cal. LEXIS 4768 (Cal. 1993).

93 The Louisiana case in which a widow sought survivor's benefits for a daughter born after her father's death is *In the Matter of J. C. Hart*, Dept. of Health and Human Servs., A.L.J. Elving L. Torres, May 27, 1995.

94 The New York case in which a gay man donated his sperm to a lesbian couple and then wanted to establish his paternity rights for the child is *Thomas S. v. Robin Y.*, 599 N.Y.S.2d 377, 1993 N.Y.Misc. LEXIS 217 (N.Y. Fam.Ct. 1993), *rev'd and remanded*, 618 N.Y.S.2d 356, 1994 N.Y.App.Div.

LEXIS 11385 (N.Y.App.Div. 1994), *stay granted*, No. 361, 1995 N.Y. LEXIS 1240 (N.Y. Apr. 4, 1995). According to the women's lawyer, following the New York Court of Appeals' stay in this action, the man withdrew his action.

94   The case involving the death row inmates' suit over their right to preserve their sperm for artificial insemination is *Anderson v. Vasquez*, No. 92-16631, 1994 U.S.App. LEXIS 17200 (9th Cir. July 13, 1994), *on remand, claim dismissed*, No. C-91-4540-VRW, 1995 U.S.Dist. LEXIS 1985 (N.D.Cal. Feb. 13, 1995).

In re A.C.

Except as indicated, the quoted remarks in this chapter are based on Angela C.'s "diary"; interviews with the authors; and the depositions of Rick C., Dr. Maureen Edwards, Dr. Lewis Hamner, Dr. Laurence Lessin, Dr. Jeffrey Moscow, Dan Stoner, and Nettie Stoner, taken in *Stoner v. George Washington Univ. Hosp.*, Civ. No. 88-05433 (D.C.Super.Ct.).

103   The Supreme Court's holding that the state's interest in potential life becomes compelling at the point of viability is from *Roe v. Wade*, 410 U.S. 113, 163, 1973 U.S. LEXIS 159 (1973).

104   The case involving the pregnant Muslim woman who refused a Cesarean section is *In re Madyun*, 114 Daily Wash.L.Rptr. 2233 (D.C.Super.Ct. July 26, 1986). The opinion is also reprinted in the District of Columbia Court of Appeals opinion *In re A.C.*, 573 A.2d 1235, 1259–1264, 1990 D.C.App. LEXIS 90 (D.C. 1990).

105–15   The testimony quoted is from the Hearing Transcript, *In re Angela* [C.], No. 87-609 (D.C.Super.Ct. June 16, 1987, 1 p.m.) (hereinafter Hearing Transcript, 1 p.m.).

111   The reference made by Robert Sylvester regarding the Supreme Court's abortion decisions and the fact that the Court does not permit a trade-off between a woman's health and fetal survival is based upon the Court's decision in *Colautti v. Franklin*, 439 U.S. 379, 400, 1979 U.S. LEXIS 51 (1978).

112   The opinion issued in the hospital by the D.C. Superior Court judge, Emmet G. Sullivan, on June 16, 1987, is *In re Angela* [C.], No. 87-609 (D.C.Super.Ct. June 16, 1987).

114–15   The three-member D.C. Court of Appeals opinion denying a stay of the Superior Court's order was argued and decided over the telephone on June 16, 1987. The account in the text is based on the Hearing Transcript, *In re A.C.*, 533 A.2d 611 (D.C. June 16, 1987, 6 p.m.) (hereinafter Hearing Transcript, 6 p.m.). The court's opinion was not filed and published until November 10, 1987. See *In re A.C.*, 533 A.2d 611 (D.C. 1987). The court explained that the opinion was written after the fact for the purpose of assisting others and to establish precedent.

    The court's acknowledgment that this was a case of first impression is from *id.* at 614. The court's comparison of A.C.'s case to cases in which adults refuse medical treatment for themselves is from *id.* at 615–16. The court's discussion of cases in which parents refuse medical treatment for their children is from *id.* at 616–17. The court's conclusion that the trial judge was correct in ordering the Cesarean section, and its appreciation of the work of the trial judge and counsel, are from *id.* at 617.

116–17   Robert Sylvester's appeal for a rehearing before the full D.C. Court of Appeals is *In re A.C.*, 539 A.2d 203, 1988 D.C.App. LEXIS 142 (D.C. 1988). The account in the text is based on the Hearing Transcript, *In re A.C.*, 539 A.2d 203 (D.C. 1988).

117   The Stoners' lawsuit against George Washington University Hospital for wrongful death and malpractice is *Stoner v. George Washington Univ. Hosp.*, Civ. No. 88-05433 (D.C.Super.Ct.).

118–20   The April 26, 1990, D.C. Court of Appeals opinion is *In re A.C.*, 573 A.2d 1235, 1990 D.C.App. LEXIS 90 (D.C. 1990). The court's finding that there were two issues to decide—first, who has the right to decide the course of medical treatment, and second, by what process should the decision be made—is from *id.* at 1237. The court's holding that "in virtually all cases" the decision should be the patient's is from *id.* The court's discussion of the informed-consent doctrine is from *id.* at 1243–1248. The court's finding that the right to accept or forgo medical treatment is of constitutional magnitude is from *id.* at 1244.

   The court's discussion of the duty to rescue, and its assertion that "courts do not compel one person to permit a significant intrusion upon his or her bodily integrity for the benefit of another person's health," are from *id.* at 1243–1244. The court cites as an example a case in which a man did not have to donate bone marrow to save the life of his cousin. See *McFall v. Shimp*, 10 Pa.D. & C.3d 90 (Allegheny County Ct. 1978), cited in 573 A.2d at 1244. The court's holding that the right to bodily integrity is not extinguished simply because a life-or-death situation exists is from *id.* at 1247. The court's statement that the fetus cannot have rights superior to those of someone who has already been born is from *id.* at 1244.

   The court's reliance on the arguments that court intervention erodes trust in the medical profession and that the emergency nature of the proceedings did not allow the parties adequate time to communicate is from *id.* at 1248. The court's discussion of substituted judgment is from *id.* at 1249.

   The court set aside the trial judge's order because he had not applied the substituted judgment procedure. See *id.* at 1251–1252. The court's language as to when a conflicting state interest would override a patient's wishes is from *id.* at 1252. The court's refusal to speculate as to what decision Angela C. would have made is from *id.*

   While the D.C. Court of Appeals was deciding *In re A.C.*, the D.C. legislature passed the Health-Care Decisions Act (the "Act"). D.C. Code §21-2201 et seq. (1995). The purpose of the Act is to address situations in which doctors, family members, and the courts may be required to make treatment decisions on behalf of a patient who has become unable to decide such matters for himself or herself. The Act contains a procedural hierarchy setting forth the order in which various family members should be given decision-making authority over health care decisions.

120 The Stoners' lawsuit against the hospital was settled for an undisclosed amount. See *Stoner v. George Washington Univ. Hosp.*, Civ. No. 88-05433 (D.C.Super.Ct. Nov. 21, 1990). The modifications in G.W.'s policies of informed consent and refusal of treatment are set forth in the Settlement Agreement, *Stoner v. George Washington Univ. Hosp.*, Civ. No. 88-05433 (D.C.Super.Ct. Nov. 21, 1990).

120 In December 1993, a twenty-three-year-old Chicago woman, eight months pregnant, was advised by her doctors that her baby was not receiving enough oxygen and nutrients from the placenta. The doctors said that inducing labor or performing an emergency Cesarean was the only way to prevent mental retardation or neurological damage. But the mother refused, preferring to trust the Lord rather than medical science. She and her husband were Pentecostal Christians, who objected on religious grounds to a Cesarean. The hospital, St. Joseph's, called the state's attorney, who took the couple to court.

On December 11, 1993, a juvenile court judge said he found no precedent for compelling a woman to undergo surgery to save a fetus. On December 14, in a unanimous decision, the Illinois appellate court affirmed the decision. See *In re Baby Boy Doe*, 632 N.E.2d 326, 1994 Ill.App. LEXIS 501 (Ill.App.Ct. 1994). The Cook County public guardian, representing the fetus, appealed to the U.S. Supreme Court, which refused to hear the case. See *Doe v. Doe*, 114 S.Ct. 1198, 1994 U.S. LEXIS 1988 (1994).

On December 29, a baby boy was born, weighing only four pounds twelve ounces but apparently healthy. He celebrated his first birthday in December 1994. See Maureen O'Donnell, "Anti-Caesarean Parents Celebrate Boy's 1st Birthday," *Chi. Sun-Times*, Dec. 23, 1994, at 3.

PASSING JUDGMENTS

121 The case involving the pregnant Long Island woman who was in a coma is *In re Klein*, 538 N.Y.S.2d 274, 1989 N.Y.App.Div. LEXIS 1613 (N.Y.App.Div. 1989), *appeal denied*, 536 N.E.2d 627, 73 N.Y.2d 705, 1989 N.Y. LEXIS 143 (N.Y. 1989), *stay denied*, *Short v. Klein*, 489 U.S. 1003, 1989 U.S. LEXIS 822 (1989).

121–2 The case in which the Florida woman was prosecuted for "delivering" cocaine through her umbilical cord to her baby is *Johnson v. Florida*, 602 So.2d 1288, 1992 Fla. LEXIS 1296 (Fla. 1992). See Mark Hansen, "Courts Side with Moms in Drug Cases," A.B.A.J., Nov. 1992, at 18.

122 The Connecticut case in which a woman shot up with cocaine after her water broke is *In re Valerie D.*, 613 A.2d 748, 1992 Conn. LEXIS 274 (Conn. 1992). See Kirk Johnson, "Child Abuse Is Ruled Out in Birth Case," *N.Y. Times*, Aug. 18, 1992, at B1; Kirk Johnson, "Hard Logic on Drugs Before Birth," *N.Y. Times*, Aug. 19, 1992, at B5.

123   The federal civil case brought on behalf of the pregnant women who
       were tested for illegal drug use in South Carolina is *Ferguson v. City of
       Charleston*, C-A No. 2:93-2624-2. See Philip J. Hilts, "Hospital Sought Out
       Prenatal Drug Abuse," *N.Y. Times*, Jan. 21, 1994, at A12; Philip J. Hilts,
       "Hospital Is Object of Rights Inquiry," *N.Y. Times*, Feb. 6, 1994, at A29;
       "60 Minutes," CBS News, "Cracking Down," Nov. 20, 1994.

123–5 The case about the Santa Cruz woman who was convicted of child en-
       dangerment is *People v. Pointer*, 199 Cal.Rptr. 357 (Cal.Ct.App. 1984). The
       facts regarding the woman's second conviction for child endangerment
       are from Steve Perez, "Pointer Ordered into Mental Ward," *Sentinel*, May
       1, 1993, at A1.

125–6 The case in which a California woman was sentenced to probation on
       the condition that she enter a drug treatment program and that she not
       become pregnant for five years is *People v. Zaring*, 10 Cal.Rptr.2d 263, 1992
       Cal.App. LEXIS 933 (Cal.Ct.App. 1992). The Court of Appeals' statement
       that judges must refrain from imposing their personal views is from *id.*
       at 269.

Quill v. Koppell

       The facts and personal statements relating to Diane's battle with leuke-
       mia and her treatment by Dr. Timothy Quill are from Timothy Quill,
       "Death and Dignity: A Case of Individualized Decision Making," 324 *New
       England J. Med.* 691–94 (1991); and interviews with the authors.

129–30 Information regarding Dr. Quill's grand jury hearing is from Lawrence K.
       Altman, "Jury Declines to Indict a Doctor Who Said He Aided in a Su-
       icide," *N.Y. Times*, July 27, 1991, at A1.

130   The New York State Health Department's inquiry into Dr. Quill's con-
       duct was never published, but a summary of its decision was reported in
       Lisa W. Foderaro, "New York Will Not Discipline Doctor for His Role in
       Suicide," *N.Y. Times*, Aug. 17, 1991, at A25.

130   The 1992 best-seller on suicide is Derek Humphry, *Final Exit* (Eugene,
       Or.: Hemlock Society, 1991).

130   The physician-assisted suicide referenda that were defeated in the states
       of Washington and California are discussed in the following articles: Pe-
       ter Steinfels, "Help for the Helping Hands in Death," *N.Y. Times*, Feb. 14,
       1993, at D4; Peter Steinfels, "Beliefs: California Considers a Bold Course
       on Euthanasia but Leaves Some Paths Unexplored," *N.Y. Times*, Oct. 10,
       1992, at A7; James Podgers, "Matters of Life and Death; Debate Grows
       Over Euthanasia," A.B.A.J., May 1992, at 60.
           The physician-assisted suicide law known as Measure 16, which was
       approved by the Oregon voters in November 1994, was challenged by a
       group of doctors and terminally ill patients as unconstitutional. The fed-
       eral district court in Oregon held that the law was unconstitutional and
       permanently enjoined the law from being implemented. See *Lee v. Ore-*

gon, No. 94-6467-HO (D.Or. Aug. 3, 1995). See also Robert A. Burt, "Death Made Too Easy," *N.Y. Times*, Nov. 16, 1994, at A19.

130   The article written by Dr. Quill and his colleagues proposing clinical criteria by which to evaluate dying patients' requests for help is Timothy E. Quill, Christine K. Callel, and Diane E. Meier, "Care of the Hopelessly Ill—Proposed Criteria for Physician-Assisted Suicide," 327 *New England J. Med.* 1380–1384 (1992).

130   Criticism of physician-assisted suicide is summarized in *Compassion in Dying v. Washington*, 49 F.3d 586, 1995 U.S.App. LEXIS 4589 (9th Cir. 1995); and *Lee v. Oregon*, 869 F.Supp. 1491, 1994 U.S.Dist. LEXIS 19867 (D.Or. 1994), *aff'd* No. 94-6467-HO (D.Or. Aug. 3, 1995).

131   The 1993 lawsuit filed by the ACLU challenging a Michigan law prohibiting assisted suicide is discussed in Isabel Wilkerson, "Suicide Law Struck Down, for Now," *N.Y. Times*, May 20 1993, at B9. The trial court held that the law criminalizing assisted suicide violated the Constitution and that individuals have a constitutional right to commit suicide. See *id.* and *Hobbins v. A.G.*, 518 N.W.2d 487, 492, 1994 Mich.App. LEXIS 232 (Mich.Ct.App. 1994) (discussing the trial court's holding). After several appeals, on December 13, 1994, the Michigan Supreme Court ultimately reversed the trial court's ruling and held that the law did not violate the Constitution and that there is no constitutional right to commit suicide. *State v. Kevorkian*, 527 N.W.2d 714, 1994 Mich. LEXIS 3033 (Mich. 1994), *cert. denied sub nom. Hobbins v. Kelley*, 115 S.Ct. 1795, 1995 U.S. LEXIS 2903 (1995).

131   Dr. Jack Kevorkian's May 1994 jury acquittal is described in David Margolick, "Kevorkian's Trial Has Come to End but Debate on Assisted Suicide Hasn't," *N.Y. Times*, May 4, 1994, at A16.

131   Dr. Quill's July 1994 article proposing the legalization of physician-assisted suicide is Franklin G. Miller, Timothy E. Quill, Howard Brody, John L. Fletcher, Lawrence O. Gostin, and Diane E. Meier, "Regulating Physician-Assisted Death," 331 *New England J. Med.* 119–23 (1994).

133   Dr. Quill's July 20, 1994, lawsuit, filed in the federal district court of New York, is *Quill v. Koppell*, 870 F.Supp. 78, 1994 U.S.Dist. LEXIS 17965 (S.D.N.Y. 1994). The plaintiff's reliance on *Planned Parenthood v. Casey*, 112 S.Ct. 2791, 1992 U.S. LEXIS 4751 (1992), and *Cruzan v. Director, Missouri Dept. of Health*, 497 U.S. 261, 1990 U.S. LEXIS 3301 (1990), is from *Quill*, 870 F.Supp. at 82.

133–4   The Supreme Court's 1990 "right-to-die" decision is *Cruzan*, 497 U.S. 261. The Court upheld the Missouri Supreme Court holding that the testimony did not "clearly and convincingly" establish that Cruzan would choose to die under these circumstances. See *id.* at 285. The Court's assumption that a competent person has a constitutional right to refuse life-saving medical treatment is from *id.* at 279. The Court's statement that family members could not simply step in and make life-ending decisions is from *id.* at 286–87. The Court's holding that nothing in the

Constitution prohibits a state from requiring that certain precautions be taken in such life-and-death situations is from *id.* at 280–83. The Court's conclusion that the "clear and convincing" standard was not too high is from *id.* at 284.

134 Dr. Quill's argument that the law banning physician-assisted suicide violated the constitutional guarantee of Equal Protection is from *Quill v. Koppell*, 870 F.Supp at 84–85. Dr. Quill's quote from the Supreme Court's opinion in *Casey* is at *id.* at 82 (quoting *Casey*, 112 S.Ct. at 2807). Dr. Quill's argument that the right to assisted suicide is a fundamental right equal to the right to abortion is from *id.* at 83.

135 The Seattle federal district court case that struck down Washington's ban on assisted suicide is *Compassion in Dying v. Washington*, 850 F.Supp. 1454, 1994 U.S.Dist. LEXIS 5831 (W.D.Wash. 1994), *reversed by* 49 F.3d 586, 1995 U.S.App. LEXIS 4589 (9th Cir. 1995).

135 The Michigan Supreme Court decision that upheld the state's law banning assisted suicide is *State v. Kevorkian*, 527 N.W.2d 714, 1994 Mich. LEXIS 3033 (Mich. 1994). The federal district court case in which an Oregon law allowing physician-assisted suicide was enjoined is *Lee v. Oregon*, 869 F.Supp. 1491, 1994 U.S.Dist. LEXIS 19867 (D.Or. 1994), *aff'd* No. 94-6467-HO (D.Or. Aug. 3, 1995).

135–6 The federal district court's holding that the New York law banning assisted suicide did not violate the Constitution is from *Quill v. Koppell*, 870 F.Supp. 78, 85, 1994 U.S.Dist. LEXIS 17965 (S.D.N.Y. 1994). The court's holding that the abortion analysis could not be applied to other situations is from *id.* at 83. The court's holding that the logic should follow the Supreme Court's decision in *Bowers v. Hardwick*, 478 U.S. 186, 1986 U.S. LEXIS 123 (1986) is from *id.* The court cites the Supreme Court's analysis in *Bowers* at *id.* (quoting *Bowers*, 478 U.S. at 191–92). The court's reference to thirteenth-century England is from *id.* at 84. The court's rejection of the Equal Protection claim and its statement regarding the severity of an "artificial death-producing device" is from *id.* The court's conclusion that resolution of the issue should be left to the democratic process is from *id.* at 85.

136 The March 1995 Ninth Circuit Court of Appeals decision is *Compassion in Dying v. Washington*, 49 F.3d 586, 1995 U.S.App. LEXIS 4589 (9th Cir. 1995). The Ninth Circuit's quotes are from *id.* at 1995 U.S.App. LEXIS 4589 at 14.

PASSING JUDGMENTS

137 The case about the Massachusetts woman who became comatose and died is *Gilgunn v. Massachusetts Gen. Hosp.*, No. 92-4820-H, jury decision (Mass.Super.Ct. Apr. 21, 1995). See Gina Kolata, "Court Ruling Limits Rights of Patients," *N.Y. Times*, Apr. 22, 1995, at A6.

138 The 1986 New York case in which a woman remained in a vegetative state despite her husband's wishes is *Grace Plaza of Great Neck, Inc. v. Elbaum*, 623 N.E.2d 513, 82 N.Y.2d 10, 1993 N.Y. LEXIS 3265 (N.Y. 1993). See

Kevin Sack, "Court Upholds Payment for Life-Sustaining Care for Woman in Right-to-Die Dispute," *N.Y. Times*, Oct. 15, 1993, at B3; Lisa Belkin, "In Right-to-Die Fight, Court Finds Family Liable for Care," *N.Y. Times*, Sept. 24, 1992, at B6.

138   The Pennsylvania case about the man involved in a motorcycle accident is *In re Fiori*, 652 A.2d 1350, 1995 Pa.Super. LEXIS 70 (Pa.Super.Ct. 1995).

138–9   The case in which a father was forbidden to order the removal of his comatose daughter's feeding tube is *In re Busalacchi*, No. 73677, 1991 Mo. LEXIS 107 (Mo. Oct. 16, 1991). See Tamar Lewin, "Man Is Allowed to Let Daughter Die," *N.Y. Times*, Jan. 27, 1993, at A12.

139   The case about the California man who was diagnosed with an inoperable brain tumor is *Donaldson v. Lungren*, 4 Cal.Rptr.2d 59, 1992 Cal.App. LEXIS 104 (Cal.Ct.App. 1992).

Doe v. City of New York

140   Information regarding John Doe's lawsuit against the city of New York and his settlement with Delta Airlines is from *Doe v. City of New York*, 15 F.3d 264, 1994 U.S. App. LEXIS 1459 (2d Cir. 1994); News Release, N.Y.C. Comm. on Human Rights, Aug. 6, 1992; as well as an interview with his attorney.

141–2   The 1977 Supreme Court decision relied upon by John Doe is *Whalen v. Roe*, 429 U.S. 589, 1977 U.S. LEXIS 42 (1977). The Court's declaration that the Constitution protects two types of privacy is from *id.* at 599–600. The Court recognized that disclosing certain medical information could implicate privacy rights; however, the Court held that the New York statute did not, on its face, "pose a sufficiently grievous threat to either interest to establish a constitutional violation." *Id.* at 600. The Court's statement that such disclosure was not "meaningfully distinguishable" from other invasions of privacy is from *id.* at 602. The Court's recognition of the safeguards put in place is from *id.* at 594. The Court's acknowledgment that the state already requires other medical information to be reported is from *id.* at 602 n. 29. The Court's statement regarding the possible threat to privacy brought about by the computer era is from *id.* at 605.

142   Several years following *Whalen*, the Third Circuit Court of Appeals upheld a government request for employee medical records in order to study whether workers had been exposed to toxic chemicals on the job. *U.S. v. Westinghouse Elec. Corp.*, 638 F.2d 570 (3d Cir. 1980). Their employer, on behalf of the employees, objected that disclosure of the records would violate their privacy. The court set forth a number of factors to be considered, including: the type of record requested, the information it contains, the potential for harm in any later disclosure, and the adequacy of safeguards to prevent unauthorized disclosure. *Id.* at 578. On the other hand, the court considered the government's need for access and the public interest, as well as any policy or statute supporting access. *Id.* at 579.

    The court found that there was a strong public interest in facilitating workplace safety research, which justified this minimal intrusion. *Id.* at 580. The court also held that employees would be permitted to object to the release of any particularly sensitive information in their files. A court could then rule on whether the disputed information should be disclosed. *Id.* at 581–82.

142–3   John Doe's appeal to the Second Circuit is *Doe v. City of New York*, 15 F.3d 264, 1994 U.S.App. LEXIS 1459 (2d Cir. 1994). The Second Circuit's holding that "individuals who are infected with the HIV virus clearly possess a constitutional right to privacy regarding their condition" is from *id.* at 267. The court's statement that the right to confidentiality extends to personal medical information is from *id.* The court's language regarding the sensitivity of one's HIV status is from *id.* The court's recognition of the city's need to disseminate certain information regarding settlements is from *id.* at 269. The court remanded the case to the district court to balance Doe's right to privacy against the public's right to know. See *id.* at 269–70.

143   The New York and California statutes prohibiting the disclosure of HIV test results without the consent of the patient are N.Y. Pub. Health Law sect. 27-F §2780 et seq. (Consol. 1994); Cal. Health and Safety Code §199.20 (Deering 1995). The Colorado statute that requires the reporting of the names of all people testing positive for HIV is Colo. Rev.Stat. §25-4-1402 (1994).

143   The Americans with Disabilities Act of 1990 prohibits discrimination based upon AIDS. See 42 U.S.C.S. §12101 et seq. (Law.Co-op. 1990).

PASSING JUDGMENTS

144   The case in which Mr. Doe's HIV status was revealed to his neighbors by a police officer is *Doe v. Borough of Barrington*, 729 F.Supp. 376, 1990 U.S. Dist. LEXIS 1059 (D.N.J. 1990).

145   The facts and holding of the case in which a New York woman was segregated in prison because of her HIV-positive status is *Nolley v. County of Erie*, 776 F.Supp. 715, 1991 U.S.Dist. LEXIS 15771 (W.D.N.Y. 1991). The district court's holding that the prison's policy was not "reasonably related to legitimate penological interests" is from *id.* at 733. The court's reference to an Alabama case in which segregation of HIV-positive prisoners was upheld is *Harris v. Thigpen*, 941 F.2d 1495, 1991 U.S.App. LEXIS 21811 (11th Cir. 1991). The court's holding that the segregation policy was an "exaggerated response" and violated the woman's constitutional right to privacy as well as New York law is from *Nolley*, 776 F.Supp. at 734, 736.

145–6   The case in which a doctor's HIV status was disclosed is *In re Milton S. Hershey Med. Ctr.*, 595 A.2d 1290, 1991 Pa.Super. LEXIS 2178 (Pa.Super.Ct. 1991), *aff'd*, 634 A.2d 159, 1993 Pa. LEXIS 276 (Pa. 1993).

146–7   The case in which a Florida man was unable to receive information regarding his previous blood transfusion is *Rasmussen v. S. Florida Blood Servs.*, 500 So.2d 533 (Fla. 1987). The court's quote regarding the social stigma attached to AIDS is from *id.* at 537. The court's concern about depleting blood supplies is from *id.* at 537–38. The court's conclusive balancing of Rasmussen's interests versus the blood donors' privacy interests is from *id.* at 538.

147   In 1995, the Third Circuit Court of Appeals permitted a plaintiff to obtain information about an HIV-positive blood donor is *Marcella v. Brandywine Hosp.*, 47 F.3d 618, 1995 U.S.App. LEXIS 2837 (3d Cir. 1995). In holding that information about the blood donor was admissible, the court relied upon the Pennsylvania Supreme Court case *Stenger v. Lehigh Valley Hosp. Ctr.*, 609 A.2d 796, 1992 Pa. LEXIS 344 (Pa. 1992).

     Some hospitals have adopted "look-back" programs under which a recipient of tainted blood can and should be notified. These programs are commonly referred to as "look-back" programs because the hospital and blood center actually "look back" through the donor and transfusion records to see where the contaminated blood came from and which patients received it. Once this is determined, the patients are then notified that they have received tainted blood. See Stuart Schlesinger and David Turret, "Transfused Tainted Blood," N.Y.L.J., May 17, 1995, at 3; *Chambarry v. Mt. Sinai Hosp.*, 615 N.Y.S2d 830, 1994 N.Y.Misc. LEXIS 338 (N.Y.Sup.Ct. 1994) (permitting the amendment of a complaint to include allegations that the hospital was negligent in not including plaintiff in its "look-back" program).

PRIVACY V. THE PRESS

154   The analogy between the press and a wild animal is expressed in Zechariah Chafee, *The Press Under Pressure* (Nieman Reports, 1948).

The Right to Be Let Alone

154   The quotation expressing outrage at the press is from Samuel D. Warren and Louis D. Brandeis, "The Right to Privacy," 4 Harv.L.Rev. 193 (1890).

154   For a discussion of the events that sparked Warren's outrage at the press, see, e.g., Diane L. Zimmerman, "Requiem for a Heavyweight: A Farewell to Warren and Brandeis's Privacy Tort," 68 Cornell L.Rev. 291, 295–96 (1983).

154–5   Warren and Brandeis' comments concerning emotional harm are from *id.* at 195.

155   The four privacy torts were introduced in an article by Dean William Prosser, "Privacy," 48 Cal.L.Rev. 383, 389 (1960).

155–6   The definitions of the four privacy torts are from the Restatement (Second) of Torts, §§ 652A–E (1977).

156   The "somewhat uncharted" language is from *The Florida Star v. B.J.F.*, 491 U.S. 524, 529 n. 5, 1989 U.S. LEXIS 3120 (1989).

157   The "exquisite pain" quotation is from Edwin L. Godkin, "Libel and Its Legal Remedy," 12 J.Soc.Sci. 69 (1880).

157   For a discussion of the privacy torts, see generally W. Page Keeton et al., *Prosser and Keeton on the Law of Torts* 5th ed. (St. Paul, Minn.: West Publishing, 1984) §117, at 849; David A. Elder, *The Law of Privacy* (New York: Clark Boardman, 1991); Bruce W. Sanford, *Libel and Privacy: The Prevention and Defense of Litigation* (New York: Prentice-Hall, 1987); Diane L. Zimmerman, "Requiem for a Heavyweight: A Farewell to Warren and Brandeis's Privacy Tort," 68 Cornell L.Rev. 291 (1983); Harvey L. Zuckman, "Invasion of Privacy: Some Communicative Torts Whose Time Has Gone," 47 Wash. & Lee L.Rev. 253 (1990); "Symposium: The Right to Privacy One Hundred Years Later," 41 Case W.Res.L.Rev. 643 (1991) (discussing the four privacy torts on the one hundredth anniversary of the Warren and Brandeis article).

Hall v. Post

158–9   The quotations from Mary Hall discussing the autumn of 1967 and child care are taken from the Deposition of Mary H. Hall at 13, *Hall v. Post*, No. 85-CVS-267 (N.C.Super.Ct. Apr. 21, 1986).

160–3   The articles at issue in the *Hall* case are: Rose Post, "Ex-Carny Seeks Baby Abandoned 17 Years Ago," *Salisbury Post*, July 18, 1984, at 1; and Rose Post, "Daughter Found; Mom Hopes for Reunion," *Salisbury Post*, July 20, 1984, at 1.

165   The case holding that a television station could not be sued for broadcasting the name of a rape-murder victim which the station had obtained from public court documents is *Cox Broadcasting Corp. v. Cohn*, 420 U.S. 469, 1975 U.S. LEXIS 139 (1975).

165   The cases holding that newspapers could not be sued for printing the names of juvenile offenders when the papers had obtained the names from public officials or from attending public proceedings are *Oklahoma Publishing Co. v. Oklahoma County Dist. Ct.*, 430 U.S. 308, 1977 U.S. LEXIS 58 (1977) (concerning an eleven-year-old boy accused of second-degree murder); and *Smith v. Daily Mail Publishing Co.*, 443 U.S. 97, 1979 U.S. LEXIS 139 (1979) (concerning a fifteen-year-old offender).

165–6   The case upholding a newspaper's right to publish a rape victim's identity obtained from the police press room is *Florida Star v. B.J.F.*, 491 U.S. 524, 1989 U.S. LEXIS 3120 (1989). The quotation concerning truthful publication is taken from *id.* at 541.

166   For a discussion of the constitutionality of the Private Facts tort, see, e.g., Anita L. Allen, "The Power of Private Facts," 41 Case W.Res.L.Rev. 757 (1991); Frederick Schauer, "Reflections on the Value of Truth," 41 Case W.Res. L.Rev. 699 (1991); Diane L. Zimmerman, "Requiem for a Heavyweight: A Farewell to Warren and Brandeis's Privacy Tort," 68 Cornell L.Rev. 291, 306 (1983) (hereinafter Zimmerman).

166   For a discussion of defamation law and truth as a defense, see, e.g., *Cox Broadcasting Corp.*, 420 U.S. at 490 (1975). In fact, in defamation law, even some false information is protected by the First Amendment. For instance, if a newspaper publishes a falsehood about a public official, the paper will not be held liable for defamation unless the paper *knew* the information was false or was *recklessly indifferent* as to its veracity.

166   At least thirty-six jurisdictions appear to recognize a private facts tort, while at least five have expressly rejected it. For a list of states' rulings considering a cause of action based on the publication of private facts, see Zimmerman at Appendix.

166   Many courts and commentators have adopted a definition of "news" that seems to beg the question: "The line is to be drawn when the publicity ceases to be the giving of information to which the public is entitled, and becomes morbid and sensational prying into private lives for its own sake, with which a reasonable member of the public with decent standards, would say he has no concern." *Virgil v. Time, Inc.*, 527 F.2d 1122, 1129 (9th Cir. 1975).

166–7   The case discussing the child mathematics whiz W. J. Sidis is *Sidis v. F-R Publishing Corp.*, 113 F.2d 806, 807, 809 (2d Cir. 1940).

167   The case discussing the woman photographed with her skirt blown up is *Daily Times Democrat v. Graham*, 162 So.2d 474 (Ala. 1964).

167   The case of the fan photographed with his fly unzipped is *Neff v. Time, Inc.*, 406 F.Supp. 858 (W.D.Pa. 1976).

167   The case concerning a photograph of a high school soccer player is *McNamara v. Freedom Newspapers*, 802 S.W.2d 901, 1991 Tex.App. LEXIS 195 (Tex. 1991).

167   The case involving a man leaving a portable toilet is *Livingston v. The Kentucky Post*, 14 Media L.Rep. 2076 (Ky. 1987).

167   The case of O. W. Sipple is *Sipple v. Chronicle Publishing Co.*, 201 Cal.Rptr. 665 (1984).

167–8   The case involving Rikki Diaz is *Diaz v. Oakland Tribune, Inc.*, 188 Cal.Rptr 762 (1983).

168   The case discussing the bodysurfer is *Virgil v. Time, Inc.*, 527 F.2d 1122 (9th Cir. 1975).

169   The appeals court decision in the Halls' case is *Hall v. Post*, 355 S.E.2d 819 (N.C.App. 1987).

170   The North Carolina Supreme Court holding is *Hall v. Post*, 323 N.C. 259, 269, 1988 N.C. LEXIS 611 (N.C. 1988).

170   Under the tort "intentional infliction of emotional distress," one can recover damages against another whose "extreme and outrageous conduct" either intentionally or recklessly caused one severe emotional distress.

It should be noted, however, that in 1988 the United States Supreme Court decided *Hustler v. Falwell*, 485 U.S. 46, 1988 U.S. LEXIS 941 (1988). That case cast doubt on the North Carolina court's reasoning that because the Private Facts tort overlaps with the already existing tort of intentional infliction of emotional distress, it is not necessary. In *Hustler*, Jerry Falwell, a nationally known minister and commentator on politics and public affairs, filed suit against *Hustler*, a nationally circulated magazine, and its publisher to recover damages for invasion of privacy, libel, and intentional infliction of emotional distress. The claim arose when, in November 1983, *Hustler* magazine featured a "parody" of an advertisement for Campari liqueur that contained the name and picture of Falwell and was captioned "Jerry Falwell talks about his first time." The ad continued with an alleged "interview" with Falwell in which he stated that his "first time" was during a drunken, incestuous rendezvous with his mother in an outhouse. In small print at the bottom of the page, the ad contained the disclaimer, "Ad parody—not to be taken seriously."

The Supreme Court held that public figures and public officials may not recover for the tort of intentional infliction of emotional distress based on publications such as the one at issue without showing that the publication contains a false statement of fact which was made with "actual malice," i.e., with knowledge that the statement was false or with reckless disregard as to whether it was true. In other words, unlike a Private Facts claim, which focuses on the publication of true information, a claim of intentional infliction of emotional distress made by a public figure could succeed only if the material was, in fact, false. The Court agreed with the lower court that the article was clearly a parody and not meant to be taken as fact. It is unclear whether this ruling applies in cases brought by private figures as well as public ones, such as Mr. Falwell.

170 The court's comment regarding punishing the media for telling the truth is from *Hall*, 323 N.C. at 269–70.

PASSING JUDGMENTS

171 The case discussing the forced sterilization of women is *Howard v. Des Moines Register*, 283 N.W.2d 289 (1979).

171 The case concerning the photograph of an escaping kidnapping victim is *Cape Publications, Inc. v. Bridges*, 423 So.2d 426 (Fla. 1982).

172 The case of the New Jersey couple who purchased a new home is *Bisbee v. Conover*, 452 A.2d 689 (N.J.Super.Ct. 1982).

172 The case discussing the father of an "illegitimate" child is *Hawkins v. Multimedia, Inc.*, 344 S.E.2d 145 (S.C. 1986).

172–3 Photographs of a recovered dead body are the focus of *Waters v. Fleetwood*, 91 S.E.2d 344 (Ga. 1956).

173–4 The television broadcast of a little girl's skull is discussed in *Armstrong v. H&C Communications*, 575 So.2d 280, 1991 Fla.App. LEXIS 1401 (Fla. 1991).

174-5   The case involving the videotape of a teenage girl being raped is *People v. Colon and Cardona*, N.Y.L.J., June 30, 1992, at 21 (N.Y.Sup.Ct. 1992).

Miller v. NBC

177-8   The statements of Marlene Belloni are from the Deposition of Marlene Belloni, *Miller v. Nat'l Broadcasting Co.*, No. C 324 427 (Cal.Super.Ct. June 15, 1983); as well as interviews with the authors.

179-81   Ruben Norte's conclusion that the heart attack victim was not identifiable is recalled in *Miller v. Nat'l Broadcasting Co.*, 187 Cal.App.3d 1463, 1476 (Cal.Ct.App. 1986). Ruben Norte's recollection of "a woman in the hallway" is from *id.* at 1475 n. 4.

183   Further to the notion that the home is sacrosanct under the law: The adage that "a man's house is his castle" has frequently and zealously been quoted. For example, in *Miller v. United States*, 357 U.S. 301, 306, 1958 U.S. LEXIS 753 (1958), the United States Supreme Court notes the remarks attributed to William Pitt, Earl of Chatham: "The poorest man may in his cottage bid defiance to all the forces of the Crown. It may be frail—its roof may shake—the wind may blow through it—the storm may enter—the rain may enter—but the King of England cannot enter—all his force dares not cross the threshold of the ruined tenement!" See also *United States v. Sansusi*, 813 F.Supp. 149, 1992 U.S.Dist. LEXIS 17741 (E.D.N.Y. 1992). Similarly, this sentiment was expressed in a concurring opinion by Justice W. O. Douglas which stated, "[T]he Bill of Rights, as applied to the States through the Due Process Clause of the Fourteenth Amendment, casts its weight on the side of the privacy of homes. The Third Amendment with its ban on the quartering of soldiers in private homes radiates that philosophy. The Fourth Amendment, while concerned with the official invasions of privacy through searches and seizures, is eloquent testimony of the sanctity of private premises." *Lombard v. Louisiana*, 373 U.S. 267, 274, 1963 U.S. LEXIS 1551 (1963).

183   Under intrusion, private facts, and false light, the right of privacy is considered personal in nature. The Restatement (Second) of Torts provides that:

> Except for the appropriation of one's name or likeness, an action for invasion of privacy can be maintained only by a living individual whose privacy is invaded.
> Comment
> a. The right protected by the action for invasion of privacy is a personal right, peculiar to the individual whose privacy is invaded. The cause of action is not assignable, and it cannot be maintained by other persons such as members of the individual's family, unless their own privacy is invaded along with his.
> Restatement (Second) of Torts §652I (1977).

See, e.g., *Young v. That Was the Week That Was*, 423 F.2d 265 (6th Cir. 1970); *Cordell v. Detective Publications, Inc.*, 419 F.2d 989 (6th Cir. 1969);

Santiesteban v. Goodyear Tire and Rubber Co., 306 F.2d 9 (5th Cir. 1962); *Lambert v. Garlo*, 484 N.E.2d 260 (Ohio 1985); *Loft v. Fuller*, 408 So.2d 619 (Fla.Dist.Ct.App. 1981); *Justice v. Belo Broadcasting Corp.*, 472 F.Supp. 145 (N.D.Tex. 1979).

184   The case involving the children who suffocated in the refrigerator is *Costlow v. Cusimano*, 312 N.Y.S.2d 92 (N.Y.Sup.Ct. 1970).

184   "Improperly circulated" photographs of a dead woman's body were discussed in *Smith v. City of Artesia*, 772 P.2d 373, 1989 N.M.App. LEXIS 16 (N.M.Ct.App. 1989), *cert. denied*, 772 P.2d 352, 1989 N.M. LEXIS 76 (N.M. 1989).

184   The case concerning the videotaped autopsy is *Williams v. City of Minneola*, 575 So.2d 683, 1991 Fla.App. LEXIS 711 (Fla.Dist.Ct.App. 1991), *aff'd*, 619 So.2d 983, 1993 Fla.App. LEXIS 4684 (Fla. 1993).

184   For an example of a case holding that a broadcast alone does not constitute an invasion of privacy, see, e.g., *Desnick v. Capital Cities/ABC, Inc.*, 851 F.Supp 303, 307, 1994 U.S.Dist. LEXIS 4029 (N.D.Ill. 1994) ("where the alleged offensive conduct and subsequent harm result from the defendant's act of publication, not from the act of prying, the plaintiff has not stated a claim for intrusion into seclusion"), *aff'd in relevant part*, 1995 U.S.App. LEXIS 454 (7th Cir. 1995).

185   Further to the relation between intrusion and trespass: In *Magenis v. Fisher Broadcasting Co.*, 798 P.2d 1106, 1110, 1990 Or.App. LEXIS 1324 (Or.Ct.App. 1990), the court held that proof of an unlawful trespass by the reporters, in and of itself, was insufficient to prove intrusion. Trespass was just one of the factors to be considered in deciding whether an invasion of privacy had occurred.

185   Actionable intrusion need not be a physical invasion into the private affairs of another. Courts have held that actions such as harassing telephone calls and intrusive and coercive sexual demands, as well as the unauthorized bugging of a dwelling or tapping of a telephone, are invasions of privacy. See, e.g., *Fowler v. Southern Bell Telephone & Telegraph Co.*, 343 F.2d 150, 156 (5th Cir. 1965); *Rogers v. Loews L'Enfant Plaza Hotel*, 526 F.Supp. 523, 528 (D.C. 1981); *Phillips v. Smalley Maintenance Servs.*, 435 So.2d 705, 710 (Ala. 1983); *Hamberger v. Eastman*, 206 A.2d 239, 241 (N.H. 1964).

185   The trial court's decision that Brownie Miller had suffered no "actual harm" is noted in *Miller v. Nat'l Broadcasting Co.*, 187 Cal.App.3d 1463, 1473–1474 (Cal.Ct.App. 1986).

185–6 Mitch Ezer's arguments are set forth in Appellant's Briefs, *Miller v. Nat'l Broadcasting Co.*, 187 Cal.App.3d 1463 (Cal.Ct.App. 1986) (No. C 324 427).

186   KNBC's response is set forth in Appellee's Briefs, *Miller v. Nat'l Broadcasting Co.*, 187 Cal.App.3d 1463 (Cal.Ct.App. 1986) (No. C 324 427).

186–7 The quotations from the court of appeals decision are from *Miller*, 187 Cal.App.3d at 1483, 1486, 1488, 1484, and 1493, respectively. In its opinion, the court noted that although the broadcast alone could not be grounds for a privacy claim, it could enhance the amount of damages awarded in the event that the plaintiffs prevailed.

PASSING JUDGMENTS

189 The case concluding that there was no trespass or invasion of privacy when the media entered a burned-out home is *Florida Publishing Co. v. Fletcher*, 340 So.2d 914 (Fla. 1976), *cert. denied*, 431 U.S. 930 (1977).

189 The New York case that expressly rejected the idea that media entry into private property was customary where newsworthy events were taking place is *Anderson v. WROC-TV*, 441 N.Y.S.2d 220, 223 (N.Y.Sup.Ct. 1981).

190 The case involving a television crew's filming of a police search in a private home is *Magenis v. Fisher Broadcasting, Inc.*, 798 P.2d 1106 (Or. 1990).

190 The case stating that "CBS had no greater right than that of a thief to be in the home" is *Ayeni v. CBS, Inc.*, 848 F.Supp. 362, 368 (E.D.N.Y. 1994), *aff'd*, 35 F.3d 680 (2d Cir. 1994).

Braun v. Flynt

192–3 Quotations about Jeannie Braun's reaction to her photo in *Chic* magazine are from the Fifth Circuit's opinion in *Braun v. Flynt*, 726 F.2d 245, 247–48 (1984), *cert. denied*, 469 U.S. 883 (1984).

193 Segments of "Chic Thrills" are taken from *Chic* 2, no. 2 (Dec. 1977).

193 The court's quotation describing *Chic* magazine is from the Fifth Circuit's opinion in *Braun*, at 247.

193–4 Henry Nuwer's account of how Jeannie Braun's photograph ended up in *Chic* magazine is from the Petition for Writ of Certiorari to the Court of Appeals for the Fifth Circuit, *Chic Magazine v. Braun*, Apr. 21, 1982, at 4–9; and *Braun*, at 247–48.

195 The description of the "privacy" protected under false light as protecting a person's "image of himself" is from *Easter Seal Soc'y v. Playboy Enterprises, Inc.*, 530 So.2d 643, 1988 La.App. LEXIS 1700 (La.Ct.App. 4th Cir. 1988).

195 Although both defamation and false light invasion of privacy involve publication, the nature of the interests protected by each action differs. A defamation action compensates damage to reputation or good name caused by the publication of false information. *Time, Inc. v. Hill*, 385 U.S. 374, 384, 1967 U.S. LEXIS 2991 (1967). To be defamatory, a publication must be false and must bring the defamed person into disrepute, contempt, or ridicule, or must impeach the person's honesty, integrity, virtue, or reputation. Privacy, on the other hand, does not protect reputation but protects mental and emotional interests. Under this theory, a plaintiff may recover even in the absence of reputational damage,

as long as the publicity is unreasonably offensive and attributes false characteristics.

The scopes of the torts differ with respect to the level of publicity required for the cause of action to arise. False light requires significantly broader publication than does defamation. Defamation only requires publication to a single individual; false light requires widespread dissemination. See, e.g., *Moore v. Big Picture Co.*, 828 F.2d 270, 273, 1987 U.S.App. LEXIS 12792 (5th Cir. 1987) (noting that false light requires widespread publicity); *Crump v. Beckley Newspapers, Inc.*, 320 S.E.2d 70, 87–88 (W. Va. 1983).

195   For a discussion of the constitutionality of the false light tort, see, e.g., Gary T. Schwartz, "Explaining and Justifying a Limited Tort of False Light Invasion of Privacy," 41 Case W.Res.L.Rev. 885 (1991); Diane L. Zimmerman, "False Light Invasion of Privacy: The Light That Failed," 64 N.Y.U.L.Rev. 364 (1989).

195   The North Carolina Supreme Court rejected the tort of false light in the case *Renwick v. News & Observer Publishing Co.*, 312 S.E.2d 405 (N.C. 1984), *cert. denied*, 469 U.S. 858, 1984 U.S. LEXIS 3614 (1984). For other jurisdictions that have questioned the validity of false light invasion of privacy, see, e.g., *Mitchell v. Random House, Inc.*, 865 F.2d 664, 672, 1989 U.S.App. LEXIS 1670 (5th Cir. 1989) ("We accordingly decline to adopt for Mississippi Mitchell's false light theory"); *Elm Medical Lab., Inc. v. RKO Gen., Inc.*, 532 N.E.2d 675, 681, 1989 Mass. LEXIS 19 (Mass. 1989) ("The only invasion of privacy the plaintiffs assert is 'putting plaintiffs in a false light.' This court has not recognized that tort and does not choose to do so now"); *Sullivan v. Pulitzer Broadcasting Co.*, 709 S.W.2d 475, 480–81 (Mo. 1986) (refusing to recognize the tort of false light based on a fact pattern that presents nothing more than a defamation claim); *Yeager v. Local Union 20*, 453 N.E.2d 666, 669–70 (Ohio 1983) ("Under the facts of the instant case, we find no rationale which compels us to adopt the 'false light' theory of recovery in Ohio at this time"); *Falwell v. Penthouse Int'l, Ltd.*, 521 F.Supp. 1204, 1206 (W.D.Va. 1981) ("The courts of Virginia simply do not recognize such a common law cause of action"); *Hoppe v. Hearst Corp.*, 770 P.2d 203, 208 n. 5, 1989 Wash.App. LEXIS 67 (Wash.Ct.App. 1989) ("We note that the trial court could have properly dismissed Hoppe's false light claim on the basis that thus far, Washington has not recognized the tort"); *Zinda v. Louisiana Pac. Corp.*, 440 N.W.2d 548, 555, 1989 Wisc. LEXIS 65 (Wisc. 1989) (stating that Wisconsin's privacy statute "does not provide a cause of action for placing a person in a false light in the public eye").

195–6 There are communications that, based on their content, are not defamatory but may be false light violations of privacy because they are highly offensive. See, e.g., *Hill*, 385 U.S. at 384–85 n. 9 (1967); *Crump*, 320 S.E.2d at 87 (W. Va. 1983).

196   The case involving the baseball star's action for invasion of privacy is *Spahn v. Julian Messner, Inc.*, 250 N.Y.S.2d 529 (N.Y.Sup.Ct. 1964).

196   The most famous of the so-called flattering false light cases was taken all the way to the Supreme Court by a young widow. Her husband was killed along with forty-three other people when a bridge across the Ohio River collapsed. A reporter for the *Cleveland Plain Dealer* visited her home and wrote a sympathetic story about the family, describing their economic hardship and proud bearing in the face of tragedy. The reporter wrote: "[She] . . . wears the same mask of non-expression she wore at her husband's funeral. She is a proud woman. . . . She says that after it happened, the people in town offered to help them out with money and they refused to take it." The only problem was, the reporter never saw or spoke with the widow. She was not even home when he came to her house. Although the newspaper story about her was not disparaging, it was not true. The widow argued that the story created a highly offensive false impression of her, making her the subject of pity and ridicule. She won a jury trial, and the Supreme Court upheld the verdict. *Cantrell v. Forest City Publishing Co.*, 419 U.S. 245 (1974).

196   Further to allowing the media some room for error: The Supreme Court has stated: "We create a grave risk of serious impairment of the indispensable service of a free press if we saddle the press with the impossible burden of verifying to a certainty the facts associated in news articles with a person's name, picture or portrait." *Hill*, 385 U.S. at 489 (1967).

197   The Supreme Court, in the first of its two false light cases, held that a private plaintiff in a matter of public interest must prove that the material was published with "actual malice." *Hill*, 385 U.S. 374 (1967). In the second case, however, shortly after deciding *Gertz v. Robert Welch, Inc.*, 418 U.S. 323, 1974 U.S. LEXIS 88 (1974) (which allowed a lesser standard than "actual malice" for private libel plaintiffs), the Supreme Court left undecided the question of whether the "actual malice" standard still applied to private false light plaintiffs. *Cantrell*, 419 U.S. 245 (1974).

197   The case in which the Oklahoma Supreme Court held that to prevail in a false light action, a private person must prove the higher standard of a reckless or intentional act rather than mere negligence is *Colbert v. World Pub. Co.*, 747 P.2d 286 (Okla. 1987).

197   The case holding that the mistaken publication of an obituary is not an invasion of privacy is *Thomason v. Times-Journal, Inc.*, 379 S.E.2d 551, 1989 Ga.App. LEXIS 381 (Ga.Ct.App. 1989).

197   The Michigan Court of Appeals case about a hairdresser's "blowtorch technique" is *Morganroth v. Whitall*, 411 N.W.2d 859 (Mich.Ct.App. 1987).

197–8   The case holding that the photograph and caption in *Forbes* magazine depicting Latin tourists were not highly offensive to a reasonable person is *Fogel v. Forbes, Inc.*, 500 F.Supp. 1081 (E.D.Pa. 1980).

198   The consensus that publishing a previously unpublished nude photograph of someone without their consent is "highly offensive to a reasonable person" comes from such cases as *Douglass v. Hustler Magazine, Inc.*, 769 F.2d 1128 (7th Cir. 1985), *cert. denied*, 475 U.S. 1094 (1986); *Wood v. Hus-*

tler Magazine, Inc., 736 F.2d 1084 (5th Cir. 1984), *cert. denied*, 469 U.S. 1107 (1985); *Gallon v. Hustler Magazine, Inc.*, 732 F.Supp. 322 (N.D.N.Y. 1990), 1990 U.S.Dist. LEXIS 3197.

199   The case involving photographs of the actress Ann-Margret is *Ann-Margret v. High Soc'y Magazine, Inc.*, 498 F.Supp. 401 (S.D.N.Y. 1980).

199   Braun's statement as to her level of embarrassment is taken from the Fifth Circuit opinion in *Braun* at 248.

200   The quotation stating that people are more likely to sue Larry Flynt and not Mr. Rogers is from Steven Helle, "Whither the Public's Right (Not) to Know?," 1991 U.Ill.L.Rev. 1077 (1991).

201   The Fifth Circuit's holding that Mrs. Braun's picture in *Chic* magazine was "fully capable of creating a false impression of Mrs. Braun" is from *Braun*, at 253. The court's opinion of the content of *Chic* magazine is from *id.* at 247, 256. The court's statement regarding the clientele of *Chic* is from *id.* at 248 n. 1.

202   One case that followed the Ann-Margret case was *Brewer v. Hustler Magazine, Inc.*, 749 F.2d 527 (9th Cir. 1984). In *Brewer*, the Ninth Circuit held directly opposite from the court in *Braun*, dismissing the argument that the photograph was reprinted in a sexually explicit magazine as "without merit because [plaintiff] had no right to choose the forum in which his photograph was displayed." *Brewer*, at 530.

202   The Texas Supreme Court case deciding not to recognize the false light tort is *Cain v. Hearst*, 878 S.W.2d 577, 1994 LEXIS 122 (Tex. 1994).

PASSING JUDGMENTS

203   The case about the "body" on the patio is *Grossman v. News Group Pub., Inc.*, 9 Med.L.Rep. 2014 (N.Y.Sup.Ct. 1983).

203–4   The case involving the model in the Viceroy cigarette advertisement is *Byrd v. Hustler Magazine, Inc.*, 433 So.2d 593 (Fla.Dist.Ct.App. 4th Dist. 1983).

204   The case about the high school teacher's photograph is *Salek v. Passaic Collegiate Sch.*, 605 A.2d 276, 1992 N.J.Super. LEXIS 132 (N.J.Super.Ct. 1992).

204–5   The case about the grandmother with a paper route who sued the *Sun* for defamation and false light is *Peoples Bank & Trust Co. v. Globe Int'l Pub., Inc.*, 978 F.2d 1065, 1992 U.S.App. LEXIS 28479 (8th Cir. Ark. 1992), *cert. denied*, 114 S.Ct. 343 (1993). For additional facts, see "Tabloid Journalism 101," *Harper's*, Dec. 1992, at 26; "Photographer's Guide to Privacy," *The News Media and the Law*, Summer 1994, Reporters' Committee for Freedom of the Press, at 2.

206–7   The cases involving actions against *Penthouse* magazine for its "Hard Times" features are *Grimsley v. Guccione*, 703 F.Supp. 903, 1988 U.S.Dist. LEXIS 15314 (M.D.Ala. 1988); and *Fudge v. Penthouse Int'l, Ltd.*, 840 F.2d

1012, 1988 U.S.App. LEXIS 2432 (1st Cir. 1988), *cert. denied*, 488 U.S. 821, 1988 U.S. LEXIS 3861 (1988).

207   With respect to the issue of opinions, see *Milkovich v. Lorain Journal Co.*, 497 U.S. 1, 1990 U.S. LEXIS 3296 (1990), in which the Supreme Court discusses statements of opinion on matters of public concern.

207   The case about the police officer pictured in the college sociology textbook is *Cibenko v. Worth Publishers, Inc.*, 510 F.Supp. 761 (D.N.J. 1981).

207–8   The Ninth Circuit case brought by the anti-pornography activist against *Hustler* magazine is *Ault v. Hustler Magazine, Inc.*, 860 F.2d 877, 884, 1988 U.S.App. LEXIS 14391 (9th Cir. 1988), *cert. denied*, 489 U.S. 1080, 1989 U.S. LEXIS 1393 (1989).

208   The Connecticut case about the "Berate the Bride" radio show is *Murray v. Schlosser*, 574 A.2d 1339, 1341, 1990 Conn.Super. LEXIS 1 (1990).

Arrington v. The New York Times Company

210   The quotation indicating that the photographer did not request permission from his subjects is from the Affidavit of Gianfranco Gorgoni in Support of Motion to Dismiss, *Arrington v. New York Times Co.* (Sept. 14, 1979).

210–11   The *New York Times Magazine* article at issue in this case is William Brashler, "The Black Middle Class: Making It," *N.Y. Times Mag.*, Dec. 3, 1978, at 34.

213   The quotation from the *New York Amsterdam News* is from an editorial, *N.Y. Amsterdam News*, Dec. 9, 1978.

213   The New York statute protecting the right to privacy is N.Y. Civ. Rights Law §§50–51 (McKinney 1992).

213   The case involving Christie Brinkley is *Brinkley v. Casablancas*, 438 N.Y.S. 2d 1004 (N.Y.App.Div. 1981).

213–14   The case concerning the photograph of a young girl used to advertise flour in which New York's highest court refused to find a common-law right to privacy, is *Robertson v. Rochester Folding Box Co.*, 64 N.E. 442, 171 N.Y. 538 (N.Y. 1902).

214   The New York privacy statute was enacted as ch. 132, Laws of 1903.

214   Many states have recognized all four categories of the tort of invasion of privacy. See, e.g., *Norris v. Moskin Stores, Inc.*, 132 So.2d 321, 322 (Ala. 1961); *Continental Optical Co. v. Reed*, 86 N.E.2d 306, 308 (Ind. 1949); *McCormack v. Oklahoma Publishing Co.*, 613 P.2d 737, 740 (Okla. 1980); *Crump v. Beckley Newspapers, Inc.*, 320 S.E.2d 70, 85 (W. Va. 1983).

214   New York courts have long held that although a newspaper or magazine may be published for profit, that does not mean that use of a person's name or picture in such a publication is for "purpose of trade" under the

statute. See, e.g., *Goelet v. Confidential, Inc.*, 171 N.Y.S.2d 223 (N.Y.App.Div. 1958); *Binns v. Vitgraph Co.*, 103 N.E. 1108, 1111, 210 N.Y. 51 (N.Y. 1913).

214–15   The quotation justifying the press's use of photographs taken in public is from the Memorandum of Defendant in Support of Its Motion to Dismiss the Complaint, *Arrington v. New York Times Co.* (Sept. 6, 1979).

215–16   The case involving the man dressed in Irish garb is *Murray v. New York Magazine Co.*, 267 N.E.2d 256, 318 N.Y.S.2d 474 (N.Y. 1971).

216   The Hindu musician who sued to protest the use of his photo is discussed in *Lahiri v. Daily Mirror, Inc.*, 295 N.Y.S. 382 (N.Y.Sup.Ct. 1937).

216   The case concerning the photograph of a man eyeing a woman passerby at a construction site is *Bourgeau v. New York News*, 5 Media L.Rep. 1799 (N.Y.Sup.Ct. 1979).

216   The case discussing a photograph of three boys used to illustrate an article on a neighborhood beating is *Metzger v. Dell Publishing Co.*, 136 N.Y.S.2d 888 (N.Y.Sup.Ct. 1955).

216   A photo used on the cover of a book about applying to colleges is discussed in *Spellman v. Simon & Schuster*, 3 Media L.Rep. 2406 (N.Y.Civ.Ct. 1978).

216   The trial court ruling in Arrington's case is *Arrington v. New York Times Co.* (N.Y.Sup.Ct. 1980). The trial judge reluctantly agreed with *The New York Times* that under existing New York law, use of Clarence Arrington's photo was "reasonably related to an article of public interest" and therefore not a violation of the statute. However, the court said that the *Times'* use of Arrington's photo was a "gross misuse of the concept of freedom of the press." Therefore, Arrington should be allowed to go forward with a claim that *The New York Times* had invaded his constitutional right to privacy.

216   The intermediate court's holding is *Arrington v. New York Times Co.*, 433 N.Y.S.2d 164 (N.Y.App.Div. 1980). The intermediate court reversed the lower court and threw out Arrington's claim altogether. Regarding the argument that Arrington could claim a violation of his constitutional right to privacy, the court curtly reminded the parties that the Constitution protects individuals against the government only. There is no constitutional cause of action against a private company such as *The New York Times*. It may well be, the intermediate court said, that the state's highest court, the Court of Appeals, should overrule the earlier cases and find a right to privacy in the common law of New York. But such a change can be made only by that highest-level court.

216–17   The New York Court of Appeals decision is *Arrington v. New York Times Co.*, 434 N.E.2d 1319, 449 N.Y.S.2d 941 (N.Y. 1982), *cert. denied*, 459 U.S. 1146, 1983 U.S. LEXIS 3098 (1983). The quotations from the Court of Appeals decision are at *id.* at 1320, 1322–1323.

217   As a result of the Court of Appeals opinion in *Arrington*, the legislature

changed the Privacy Statute. See N.Y. Civ. Rights Law §51, 1983 amends. L. 1983, c. 280, eff. June 13, 1983.

PASSING JUDGMENTS

218   The case concerning the use of a toddler's photograph in a children's book is *McWhir v. Krementz*, 15 Media L.Rep. 1367 (N.Y.Sup.Ct. 1980).

218–19   The case involving the couple photographed nude on the beach is *Creel v. Crown Publishers*, 496 N.Y.S.2d 219 (N.Y.App.Div. 1985).

219   The photograph of Hedda Nussbaum taken while she was at a psychiatric facility is discussed in *Howell v. New York Post Co.*, 612 N.E.2d 699, 596 N.Y.S.2d 350, 1993 N.Y. LEXIS 658 (N.Y. 1993).

219–20   The case concerning the article on caffeine-aided fertilization is *Finger v. Omni Publications Int'l, Ltd.*, 566 N.E.2d 141, 564 N.Y.S.2d 1014, 1990 LEXIS 4464 (N.Y. 1990).

220   The case discussing the broadcast entitled "Couples in Love in New York" is *Degregorio v. CBS, Inc.*, 473 N.Y.S.2d 922 (N.Y.Sup.Ct. 1984).

The Right of Publicity

221   The "Here's Johnny" portable toilets are discussed in *Carson v. Here's Johnny Portable Toilets*, 698 F.2d 831 (6th Cir. 1983), *aff'd after remand*, 810 F.2d 104, 1987 U.S.App. LEXIS 1297 (6th Cir. 1987).

221   Bette Midler's voice is the focus of *Midler v. Ford Motor Co.*, 849 F.2d 460, 1988 U.S.App. LEXIS 8424 (9th Cir. 1988), *cert. denied sub nom., Young & Rubicam, Inc. v. Midler*, 503 U.S. 951, 1992 U.S. LEXIS 1931 (1992).

221–2   The case involving a space-age Vanna White is *White v. Samsung Electronics America, Inc.*, 971 F.2d 1395, 1992 U.S. LEXIS 17205 (9th Cir. 1992), *cert. denied*, 113 S.Ct. 2443, 1993 U.S. LEXIS 3764 (1993).

PRIVACY V. THE VOYEUR
Cooper v. Anderson

227–40   Quoted remarks are from the Trial Transcript, *Cooper v. Anderson*, No. 86–29876 (D.Ct. Harris County, Texas, May 1989); as well as interviews with the authors.

235   Debbie Anderson originally claimed both negligence and intentional invasion of privacy, but later dropped the negligence claim.

240–1   Some states require a two-pronged analysis in establishing the validity of an intentional act exclusion provision in a homeowner's policy. The first prong questions whether the act causing the loss was intentional; the second, whether the results of the act were intended. For example, in *Vermont Mutual Insurance Co. v. Singleton*, 446 S.E.2d 417, 1994 S.C. LEXIS 144 (S.C. 1994), the Supreme Court of South Carolina held that the policy's intentional act exclusion could not be used to exclude coverage for eye injuries inflicted by the insured during a fight, because although the act of hitting was intentional, the specific resulting injury was not. Similarly, a New Jersey court held that a homeowner's policy did not provide coverage for an insured's harassing telephone calls after finding that the alleged actions could only have been intentional in both purpose and result. *Mroz v. Smith*, 617 A.2d 1259, 1992 N.J.Super. LEXIS 443 (N.J. 1992). In certain cases, intent may be inferred as a matter of law. For example, a Texas Court of Appeals, citing the majority rule nationwide, recently held that regardless of any subjective intent to injure, an adult's sexual molestation of a child is excluded from insurance coverage as a matter of law because the "act" is the "harm." Since there cannot be one without the other, the "intent to molest is, by itself, the same as the intent to harm." *Allen v. Automobile Ins. Co.*, 1994 Tex.App. LEXIS 3171 (Houston 14th Dist. 1994), citing *J.C. Penney Casualty Ins. Co. v. M.K.*, 804 P.2d 689, 278 Cal.Rptr. 64, 1991 Cal. LEXIS 354 (Cal. 1991); see also *Lehmann v. Metzger*, 355 N.W.2d 425, 426 (Minn. 1984).

241   The photographer who sued his insurance company for not covering the costs awarded in damages to a model is discussed in *Snakenberg v. Hartford Casualty*, 383 S.E.2d 2, 1989 S.C.App. LEXIS 103 (S.C.Ct.App. 1989).

241   The case concerning the man who was sued for child molestation who insisted that his insurance company pay the damages is *Allstate Ins. Co. v. Mugavero*, 589 N.E.2d 365, 581 N.Y.S.2d 142, 1992 N.Y. LEXIS 204 (N.Y. 1992).

241   The case where the parties argued that the insurance company should pay the cost of damages resulting from a rape was reported in the *Portland Press Herald*, Mar. 26, 1994, at 1B.

242   The Texas case that recognized a cause of action for the intentional infliction of emotional distress is *St. Elizabeth Hospital v. Garrard*, 730 S.W.2d 649 (Tex. 1987) (overruled in *Cooper v. Anderson*).

244–5 The first Supreme Court of Texas opinion is *Cooper v. Anderson*, 855 S.W.2d 593, 1992 Tex. LEXIS 154 (Tex. 1992), opinion withdrawn and replaced.

246–7 The second opinion of the Texas Supreme Court is *Cooper v. Anderson*, 855 S.W.2d 593, 1993 Tex. LEXIS 58 (Tex. 1993). The quotation from the concurring opinion is from *id.* at 604. The quotations from the dissent are from *id.* at 605, 606, and 610, respectively.

McCall v. The Sherwood Inn

249–63 Quoted remarks are from the Trial Transcript, *McCall v. The Sherwood Inn*, No. 52879 (Iowa Dist.Ct. June 25, 1992), as well as interviews with the authors.

254   The quotation discussing Pete's discomfort with mirrors in public places is from the Deposition of Pete McCall at 45–46, *McCall v. The Sherwood Inn*, No. 52879 (Iowa Dist.Ct.). Pete's tendency to associate his engagement night with the mirror incident is from *id.*

255   In addition to the Sherwood Inn, the hotel's parent company, Best Western, was also named as a defendant but was eventually dropped from the suit.

256   The Holiday Inn cases are discussed in an article by David Margolick, "At the Bar," *N.Y. Times*, Oct. 16, 1992, at B18.

262–3   The statements concerning the content of closing arguments are based on the recollections of the attorneys in interviews with the authors.

263   The verdict is stated in Special Verdicts Nos. 1 and 3, *McCall v. The Sherwood Inn*, No. 52879 (Iowa Dist.Ct. June 25, 1992).

264   Under Iowa's rules of civil procedure, an aggrieved party may, on motion, have an adverse verdict, decision, or report (or some portion thereof) vacated and a new trial granted where excessive or inadequate damages appearing to have been influenced by passion or prejudice have been awarded. Iowa Civ.P. §244 (1994).

264   Iowa law concerning the allocation of punitive damages states: If the conduct of the defendant was not directed specifically at the claimant, or at the person from which the claimant's claim is derived, "after payment of all applicable costs and fees, an amount not to exceed twenty-five percent of the punitive damages or exemplary damages awarded may be ordered paid to the claimant, with the remainder of the award to be ordered to be paid into a civil reparations trust fund." Iowa Code §688A.1 (1994).

PASSING JUDGMENTS

266   The case of the California man videotaping sexual activity is *People v. Gibbons*, 263 Cal.Rptr. 905, 1989 Cal.App. LEXIS 1186 (4th Dist. 1989).

266–7   The Kansas photographer who photographed women changing through a two-way mirror is discussed in *State v. Martin*, 658 P.2d 1024 (Kan. 1983).

267   The case concerning four women who received an unauthorized physical exam is *Turner v. State*, 494 So.2d 1292 (La.Ct.App. 1986).

267–8   The case involving a woman who was spied on through a bathroom mirror is *New Summit Associates v. Nistle*, 533 A.2d 1350 (Md.Ct.App. 1987).

268   The case involving the New Hampshire couple who found a hidden microphone in their bedroom is *Hamberger v. Eastman*, 206 A.2d 239 (N.H. 1964).

269   The off-duty security guard who was watched in a dressing room is discussed in *Lewis v. Dayton Hudson Corp.*, 339 N.W.2d 857 (Mich.Ct.App. 1983).

269   The case discussing see-through panels in the rest room of a roller-skating rink is *Harkey v. Abate*, 346 N.W.2d 74 (Mich.Ct.App. 1983).

270   A rest room used for homosexual activity is discussed in *Elmore v. Atlantic Zayre, Inc.*, 341 S.E.2d 905 (Ga. 1986).

270–1 The case discussing the surveillance of rest rooms at Mills Park in Carson City, Nevada, is *Young v. Nevada*, 849 P.2d 336, 1993 Nev. LEXIS 35 (Nev. 1993).

271–2 The cases of rest-room surveillance in Oregon are *Oregon v. Owczarzak*, 766 P.2d 399, 1988 Or.App. LEXIS 2231 (Or.Ct.App. 1988); and *Oregon v. Casconi*, 766 P.2d 397, 1988 Or.App. LEXIS 2237 (Or.Ct.App. 1988).

PRIVACY IN THE WORKPLACE

275   The national scandals involving child abuse led to the enactment of the National Child Protection Act of 1993. See 42 U.S.C. §5119 et seq. (hereinafter the Act). The Act requires employers at day care facilities to conduct background checks on all job applicants. President Clinton signed the Act on Dec. 20, 1993. Entertainer Oprah Winfrey was instrumental in establishing the Act, as she had been an abused child and is a leader in children's rights. Due to Oprah's involvement and association with the Act, the press has often referred to it as "Oprah's law." *Federal News Service, White House Briefing—President Bill Clinton signs the N.C.P.A.*, The White House, Washington, D.C., Dec. 20, 1993.

Soroka v. Dayton Hudson Corp.

282   The Bureau of National Affairs' estimate of the amount of money lost by U.S. retail businesses due to employee theft is taken from Ira Michael Shepard and Robert L. Duston, BNA, *Thieves at Work: An Employer's Guide to Combating Workplace Dishonesty* (1988).

282   The case involving an action for negligent hiring brought by the parents of a child who was sexually assaulted on the premises of a hotel is *Pittard v. Four Seasons Motor Inn, Inc.*, 688 P.2d 333 (N.M.Ct.App. 1984). The Minnesota Supreme Court case in which a tenant successfully sued an apartment complex owner for negligent hiring is *Ponticas v. K.M.S. Investments*, 331 N.W.2d 907 (Minn. 1983).

285   Examples of courts upholding pre-employment drug testing include such cases as *Int'l Brotherhood of Teamsters v. Dept. of Transportation*, 932 F.2d 1292, 1307, 1991 U.S.App. LEXIS 7352 (9th Cir. 1991) (pre-employment drug testing of bus and truck drivers upheld); *Willner v. Thornburgh*, 928 F.2d 1185, 1193, 1991, U.S.App. LEXIS 4934 (D.C.Cir. 1991), *cert. denied*, 112 S.Ct. 669, 1991 U.S. LEXIS 7232 (1991) (court upheld drug testing of applicants for positions as attorneys at the Justice Department); *Wilkinson v. Times Mirror Corp.*, 264, Cal.Rptr. 194, 204, 1989 Cal.App. LEXIS 1168 (Cal. Ct.App. 1st Dist. 1989), *review denied*, 1990 Cal. LEXIS 1284 (court upheld

pre-employment drug testing of all applicants at a publishing firm, asserting that applicants have a lesser expectation of privacy).

285   The California constitution explicitly protects the right to privacy as an inalienable right. "All people are by nature free and independent and have inalienable rights. Among these are enjoying and defending life and liberty, acquiring, possessing, and protecting property, and pursuing and obtaining safety, happiness, and privacy." Cal. Const., art. I, sect. 1.

285   The ballot-argument sections referred to are from the official ballot pamphlet section dealing with the Privacy Initiative. *Ballot Pamp., Proposed Amends. to Cal. Const. with arguments for voters, Gen. Elec.* (Nov. 7, 1972) 26–27 (hereinafter *Ballot Arguments*).

285–6   In support of its argument that applicants do not enjoy the same privacy rights as employees, Target relied on *Wilkinson v. Times Mirror Corp.*, 264 Cal.Rptr. 194, 204, 1989 Cal.App. LEXIS 1168 (Cal.Ct.App. 1st Dist. 1989), *review denied*, 1990 Cal. LEXIS 1284. *Wilkinson* involved job applicants at a legal publishing company, Matthew Bender, who had refused to submit to a urine test for drugs and alcohol as part of a regular pre-employment physical exam. They were not hired, and challenged the drug screening as an invasion of California's right to privacy. The court gave great weight to the distinction between applicants and employees, holding that "applicants for jobs . . . have a choice, they may consent to the limited invasion of their privacy resulting from the testing, or may decline both the test and conditional offer of employment." *Id.* at 204.

    In arguing that the use of the Psychscreen was reasonable, Target also relied upon *Wilkinson*. In *Wilkinson*, the court applied a reasonableness standard, balanced the employer's interest in a drug-free workplace against the individual's right to privacy, and upheld the drug testing program.

286   Soroka's argument that the California state constitution was intended to protect all individuals is taken from his appellate brief. In the brief, he cites page 27 of the *Ballot Arguments*, which specifically refers to the privacy rights of job applicants. *Brief for Appellant* at 9, 10.

286   Soroka's argument that Target must demonstrate a "compelling interest" for administering the Psychscreen is based upon his reliance on the California Court of Appeals case *Luck v. Southern Pac. Transp. Co.*, 267 Cal.Rptr. 618, 1990 Cal.App. LEXIS 152 (Cal.Ct.App. 1st Dist. 1990), *review denied*, 1990 Cal. LEXIS 2391 (Cal. 1990), *cert. denied*, 498 U.S. 939, 1990 U.S. LEXIS 5389 (1990). In this case, a computer programmer at Southern Pacific Railroad was fired after six and a half years for refusing to provide a urine sample as part of an unannounced drug test. A jury awarded her $485,042. The court of appeals upheld the verdict. The court found that urinalysis intrudes upon reasonable expectations of privacy and that losing a job placed a substantial burden on the programmer's right to privacy and must be justified by a compelling interest on the part of the railroad. The court then analyzed her duties to determine whether she performed a safety-sensitive job. When it found that she did not, the

court, applying the "compelling interest test," ruled that Southern Pacific had not shown a compelling interest in intruding upon her right to privacy. The court distinguished *Wilkinson*'s "reasonableness test" as applying to applicants only. *Id.* at 629 n. 13.

287 The quotation from the ACLU brief is from *Brief of Amicus Curiae, The ACLU of Northern California in Support of Appellants* at 11.

287 The unpublished trial court opinion in *Soroka v. Dayton Hudson, Corp.* was entered on November 8, 1990, in the Superior Court for Alameda County, California. The trial court denied Soroka's motion for class certification. The trial court also refused to permanently enjoin Target from administering the Psychscreen, but it did prohibit Target from giving the test to applicants who had already failed the initial threshold test—the Target Screening Inventory.

287 Following the trial court's order in favor of Dayton Hudson, Corp., Soroka appealed to the California Court of Appeals. The California Court of Appeals entered an opinion in 1991. *Soroka v. Dayton Hudson, Corp.*, 1 Cal.Rptr.2d 77, 1991 Cal.App. LEXIS 1241 (Cal.Ct.App. 1st Dist. 1991).

287–8 Target appealed the court of appeals decision, and the California Supreme Court granted review. 822P.2d 1327, 4 Cal.Rptr.2d 180, 1992 Cal. LEXIS 2895 (Cal. 1992). In granting review, the California Supreme Court depublished the court of appeals opinion for the purposes of official use. The California Supreme Court joined the *Soroka* case with the case *Hill v. Nat'l Collegiate Athletic Ass'n*, 273 Cal.Rptr. 402, 1990 Cal.App. LEXIS 1012 (Cal.Ct.App. 6th Dist. 1990).

288 The section of the Americans with Disabilities Act of 1990 which places restrictions on pre-employment medical examinations is 42 U.S.C. §12112 d(3).

288–9 The terms of the settlement agreement are from the *Consent Decree* at 6, 7, 10–12, *Soroka*, (No. H-143579-3).

290 The California Supreme Court's opinion in *Hill* overturned the lower court in holding that there was no invasion of privacy. The California Supreme Court opinion is 865 P.2d 633, 1994, Cal. LEXIS 9 (Cal. 1994).

289–90 The quotation from the California Supreme Court opinion in *Hill* explaining when the "compelling interest" test should be applied is from *id.* at 653. The court held that "[w]here the case involves an obvious invasion of interest fundamental to personal autonomy," e.g., freedom from involuntary sterilization or the freedom to pursue "consensual familial relationships," a "compelling interest" must be present to override the vital privacy interest. In contrast, if the privacy interest in less central, general balancing tests are employed. *Id.*

 The California Supreme Court in *Hill* held that in cases involving informational or autonomy privacy, a balancing test should be applied. *Id* at 654. The court defined informational privacy as the interest in precluding the dissemination or misuse of sensitive and confidential information. *Id.* The court defined autonomy privacy as the interest in making intimate personal decisions or conducting personal activities without observation, intrusion, or interference. *Id.*

Regarding private-sector drug testing, the court indicated that more than a drug-free workplace would be required to justify testing without reasonable suspicion, since workers' expectations of privacy would not be reduced like those of the athletes in *Hill.* However, lest anyone think that the *Hill* opinion resolved the issue, the court went out of its way to state, "We intimate no views about the legality of blanket or random drug testing conducted by employers, whether of current employees, or applicants for employment, or by other kinds of entities." *Id.* at 667.

291   The first of the two 1989 United States Supreme Court cases that dealt with drug testing is *Skinner v. Railway Labor Executives' Ass'n,* 489 U.S. 602, 1989 U.S. LEXIS 1568 (1989). The Court applied the "special needs" exception that was created in *New Jersey v. T.L.O.,* 469 U.S. 325, 340, 1985 U.S. LEXIS 41 (1985). In relying on *T.L.O.,* the *Skinner* Court held that if there are "special needs" as set forth in *T.L.O.,* suspicion of wrongdoing prior to a search is not required and the search may be reasonable despite the absence of such suspicion. *Skinner* at 624. See *supra* at 343 and 346 for a discussion of the Fourth Amendment relating to *Skinner.*

The second of the two 1989 United States Supreme Court cases involving drug testing is *Nat'l Treasury Employees Union v. Von Raab,* 489 U.S. 656, 1989 U.S. LEXIS 1570 (1989). The Court held that drug tests were reasonable for employees carrying firearms and involved in drug interdiction. *Id.* at 670–72. The Court held that "employees who are directly involved in the interdiction of illegal drugs or who are required to carry firearms in the line of duty likewise have a diminished expectation of privacy in respect to the intrusions occasioned by a urine test." *Id.*

291   Examples of cases upholding drug testing of government workers in public safety jobs include: *Int'l Brotherhood of Teamsters, etc. v. Dept. of Transp.,* 932 F.2d 1292, 1991 U.S.App. LEXIS 7352 (9th Cir. 1991) (testing of bus and truck drivers); *Bluestein v. Skinner,* 908 F.2d 451, 1990 U.S.App. LEXIS 11371 (9th Cir. 1990), *cert. denied,* 498 U.S. 1083, 1991 U.S. LEXIS 943 (1991) (testing of flight crew, pilots, and air traffic controllers); *Rushton v. Nebraska Pub. Power Dist.,* 844 F.2d, 562, 1988 U.S.App. LEXIS 4825 (8th Cir. Neb. 1988) (testing of nuclear power plant engineers); *Guiney v. Roache,* 873 F.2d 1557, 1989 U.S.App. LEXIS 6623 (1st Cir. Mass. 1989), *cert. denied,* 493 U.S. 963, 1989 U.S. LEXIS 5423 (1989) (testing of police officers).

291   Examples of cases prohibiting drug testing of administrative or clerical workers include: *Am. Fed'n of Gov't Employees, Local 1533 v. Cheney,* 754 F.Supp. 1409, 1422–23 (N.D. Cal. 1990), *aff'd,* 944 F.2d 503, 1991 U.S.App. LEXIS 20928 (9th Cir. 1991) (court denied blanket drug testing of employees with clerical positions, such as pathologists and dental hygienists); *Transp. Inst. v. U.S. Coast Guard,* 727 F.Supp. 648, 1989 U.S. Dist. LEXIS

15409 (D.C. Cir. 1989) (court denied drug testing of Coast Guard cooks, messmen, and cleaners); *Nat'l Fed'n of Fed. Employees v. Cheney*, 884 F.2d 603, 1989 U.S.App. LEXIS 12963 (D.C. Cir. 1989), *cert. denied*, 493 U.S. 1056, 1990 U.S. LEXIS 604 (1990) (D.C. Circuit Court held that the Army cannot test laboratory workers but it can test employees who occupy positions in the aviation, police, or guard departments); *Taylor v. O'Grady*, 888 F.2d 1189, 1989 U.S.App. LEXIS 16581 (7th Cir. Ill. 1989) (court upheld the drug testing of gun-carrying prison guards but did not permit the testing of administrative personnel); *Connelly v. Horner*, 753 F.Supp. 293, 1990 U.S.Dist. LEXIS 4528 (N.D.Cal. 1990) (district court held that blanket post-accident drug testing of employees is not permitted unless there is reasonable suspicion).

291   The American Management Association figures concerning the trend in drug testing is from its *1995 Survey: Workplace Drug Testing and Drug Abuse Policies*. According to the Institute for a Drug Free Workplace, as of 1994, thirty-six states, the District of Columbia, and Puerto Rico had no restrictions on workplace drug testing. Of these thirty-six states, none place restrictions on the type of drug testing permitted; however, twelve of these states have procedural restrictions in effect. Examples of such procedural restrictions on workplace drug testing include: providing employees with a written drug policy (Florida), implementing a "neutral selection" basis for random drug testing (Mississippi), requiring that all tests be analyzed at a state-licensed laboratory (Oregon), and requiring that chain-of-custody procedures be maintained (Nebraska). This 1994 figure on the number of states with no restrictions on workplace drug testing is from Marc A. deBernado et al., *1994 Guide to State Drug Testing Laws* (Washington, D.C.: Inst. for a Drug Free Workplace, 1994).

291   The Indiana woman's action against the Ford Meter Box Company was filed on January 15, 1991, in the Indiana Circuit Court, *Bone v. Ford Meter Box Co.*, No. 85C01–9101–CP-28. The opinion was not published, but the case led to the passing of Indiana state legislation that prohibits discrimination based on an employee's off-duty use of tobacco. Title 22, article 5, chapter 4 of the Indiana Code states as follows:

Employment or discrimination based on employee's off duty use of tobacco prohibited. An employer may not:
(1)   Require, as a condition of employment, an employee or prospective employee to refrain from using; or
(2)   Discriminate against an employee with respect to:
      (a) The employee's compensation and benefits; or
      (b) Terms and conditions of employment, based on the employee's use of tobacco products outside the course of the employee's or prospective employee's employment.

292   The Colorado clerk's action for invasion of privacy is *Mares v. Conagra Poultry Co., Inc.*, 773 F.Supp. 248, 199 U.S.Dist. LEXIS 13467 (D.Colo. 1991), *aff'd*, 971 F.2d 492, 1992 U.S.App. LEXIS 19806 (10th Cir. 1992).

292   The 1987 figure on polygraph tests and the percentage of tests given to

job applicants is taken from Ira M. Shepard, Robert L. Duston, and Karen S. Russell, *Workplace Privacy: Employee Testing, Surveillance, Wrongful Discharge, and Other Areas of Vulnerability* 91 (Washington, D.C.: BNA, 1989).

292   The polygraph questions listed are from the California Supreme Court opinion *Long Beach City Employees Ass'n v. City of Long Beach*, 719 P.2d 660, 665, n. 11 (Cal. 1986).

293   The First Circuit case involving an employee's action against Papa Gino's is *O'Brien v. Papa Gino's of Am., Inc.*, 780 F.2d 1067 (1st Cir. 1986).

293   The Employee Polygraph Protection Act of 1988 is found at 29 U.S.C.S. §2001 et seq. (1994).

Shahar v. Bowers

297–8 Robin Shahar's lawsuit against Michael Bowers is *Shahar v. Bowers*, 836 F.Supp. 859, 1993 U.S.Dist. LEXIS 14206 (N.D.Ga. 1993).

298   The 1986 Supreme Court case about homosexual sodomy argued by Michael Bowers is *Bowers v. Hardwick*, 478 U.S. 186, 1986 U.S. LEXIS 123 (1986). In *Hardwick*, the Supreme Court refused to recognize a "fundamental right to engage in homosexual sodomy." *Id.* at 191. Justice Harry Blackmun's quote in the dissenting opinion is found at *id.* at 206, 214.

298   Two of the more recent battles over gays in the military litigated under the Equal Protection Clause are *Meinhold v. U.S. Dept. of Defense*, 34 F.3d 1469, 1994 U.S.App. LEXIS 23705 (9th Cir. 1994); and *Steffan v. Perry*, 41 F.3d 677, 1994 U.S.App. LEXIS 33045 (D.C.Cir. 1994). The regulations banning gays in the military that were challenged are DOD Directive 1332.14, 32 C.F.R. pt. 41, app. A (1981), and Naval Military Personnel Manual 3630400(1) (1992). These regulations were replaced by the Don't Ask/ Don't Tell policy implemented by the Clinton administration in February 1994. See 10 U.S.C. §654 (1994). A federal district court held that the Don't Ask/Don't Tell policy was unconstitutional under the First Amendment. See *Able v. United States*, No. 94 CV 0974, 1995 U.S Dist. LEXIS 3928, at 6 (E.D.N.Y. Mar. 30, 1995).

299   The traditional intimate relationships that have been granted constitutional protection include: marriage—*Zablocki v. Redhail*, 434 U.S. 374, 383–86, 1978 U.S. LEXIS 57 (1978); the bearing of children—*Carey v. Population Servs. Int'l*, 431 U.S. 678, 684–86, 1977 U.S. LEXIS 104 (1977); and cohabitation with relatives—*Moore v. East Cleveland*, 431 U.S. 494, 503–4, 1977 U.S. LEXIS 17 (1977).

300   Bowers' statement regarding the natural consequences of marriage is taken from pages 80–81 of his deposition as cited in *Plaintiff's Memoranda of Law in Opposition to Summary Judgment* at 29.

301   Courts have established three standards of review for discrimination actions: strict scrutiny, heightened scrutiny, and rational basis review.

Courts have traditionally applied the highest standard of review, legally referred to as "strict scrutiny" or "compelling reason," to discrimination cases involving the "suspect" classes of race, ethnic origin, and alienage. A defendant must show that the challenged discriminatory action in question serves a "compelling" state interest and is narrowly tailored to serve that interest. Courts have also developed an intermediate level of review referred to as "heightened scrutiny" for the "quasi-suspect" classes of gender and illegitimacy. In the "heightened scrutiny" test, the law must be substantially related to a sufficiently important governmental interest in order to survive accusations of discrimination. In cases involving sexual-orientation discrimination, defendants are held to the lowest standard of review, legally referred to as "rational basis scrutiny." Under the rational basis test, the court considers only whether the government has a rational basis for its action. Courts are therefore more likely to uphold a challenged government action in the area of sexual orientation than one involving racial or gender discrimination.

In *Woodward v. United States*, 871 F.2d 1068, 1076, 1989 U.S.App. LEXIS 3882 (Fed.Cir. 1989), *cert. denied*, 494 U.S. 1003, 1990 U.S. LEXIS 1156 (1990), the court held that the only classes deserving a higher level of scrutiny are: racial status, ethnic origin, alienage, gender, and illegitimacy. In *High Tech Gays v. Defense Indus. Sec. Clearance Office*, 895 F.2d 563, 573, 1990 U.S. LEXIS 1329 (9th Cir. 1990), the court applied "rational basis scrutiny" in holding that "[h]omosexuality is not an immutable characteristic; it is behavioral and hence is fundamentally different from traits such as race, gender, or alienage."

In 1994, however, a trial court applied an intermediate level of review to sexual-orientation discrimination. In *Equality Found. v. Cincinnati*, 860 F.Supp. 417, 436, 1994 U.S.Dist. LEXIS 11444 (S.D. Ohio 1994), the district court held that "sexual orientation is a quasi-suspect classification. . . . Therefore laws drawing a distinction based on that characteristic must be substantially related [versus "rationally related"] to a sufficiently important governmental purpose."

301   Bowers' contention that an employee's interests should be balanced against the government's interests as an employer is based upon the Supreme Court test laid out in *Pickering v. Bd. of Educ.*, 391 U.S. 563, 1968 U.S. LEXIS 1471 (1968). In *Pickering*, a teacher was fired for writing a letter to a newspaper criticizing the school board. The Supreme Court held that there must be a "balance between the interests of the teacher, as a citizen, in commenting upon matters of public concern and the interest of the State, as an employer, in promoting the efficiency of the public services it performs through its employees." *Id*. at 568. In that case, the Supreme Court held that the teacher's fundamental right to freedom of speech outweighed the state's interests, and reinstated the teacher.

301–2 The federal district court opinion is the previously cited case of *Shahar v. Bowers*, 836 F.Supp. 859, 1993 U.S.Dist. LEXIS 14206 (N.D.Ga. 1993). In potentially significant language, the district court wrote that "[t]he court need not resolve the parties' debate over the definition of 'family' to determine whether [Shahar's] relationship with her female partner constitutes a protected association. Family or quasi-family relationships 'exemplify' the considerations which underlie the constitutional protection extended to intimate association. Family and quasi-family relationships do not, however, constitute the only relationships protected by the right to intimate association." *Id.* at 863. The court found that Shahar's public wedding ceremony could undermine the department's operations. *Id.* at 865. The court also granted summary judgment for Bowers on the Equal Protection claim. It found that Shahar had not made a sufficient showing of discriminatory intent and that although Bowers was aware of Shahar's sexual orientation, his action was based not solely on her sexual orientation but on her sexual orientation plus conduct (her same-sex marriage), viewed by Bowers as inconsistent with state law. The court's quote that continuation of Shahar's employment could undermine the operation of the department is from *id.* at 865. The court's quote regarding the "unique circumstances of this case" is from *id.*

PASSING JUDGMENTS

303 The facts about the case against Rohr Industries are taken from the Respondents' Brief, *Bingham and Everett v. Rohr Indus., Inc.,* Civ. No. D017408 (Cal.Ct.App.); Lorie Hearn, "Couple Fired by Rohr to Receive Millions," *San Diego Union Trib.*, Nov. 17, 1992, at A1; as well as an interview with Sue Everett's attorney.

303–4 The romantically involved employees brought an action against Wal-Mart for wrongful termination. The New York state attorney general's office also filed an action in state court against Wal-Mart for violating New York Labor Law sec. 201(d). The employees' action against Wal-Mart was scheduled to be argued in federal court, but was voluntarily dismissed by the employees in the hopes that the action brought by the New York state attorney general would provide them with the relief they are seeking. The dismissed federal action is cited as *Allen v. Wal-Mart Stores,* 1994 U.S. Dist. LEXIS 10514 (N.D.N.Y. 1994). In the New York state action, the trial court held that the attorney general's cause of action could proceed to trial, and denied Wal-Mart's motion to dismiss. Wal-Mart appealed, and in January 1995, the Third Department Appellate Division issued a decision in favor of Wal-Mart. *State v. Wal-Mart Stores,* No. 70609, (N.Y.App.Div. 1995), 1995 N.Y.App.Div. LEXIS 17. The Third Department held that "dating" is not a "recreational activity" protected under New York Labor Law sec. 201(d); thus, Wal-Mart was not at fault in firing the employees. The attorney general's office has decided not to appeal this decision.

 Information about this case is taken from Jacques Steinberg, "Fraternization and Friction in Store Aisles; New York Challenges Wal-Mart Over Dismissal of Two Who Dated Against the Rules," *N.Y. Times,* July 14, 1993, at B1; documents filed in the case; and interviews with Assistant Attorney General Jim Williams. Wal-Mart attorneys refused to speak with the authors.

304   The case of the administrative assistant who sued her company after being demoted is *Pasch v. Katz Media Corp.*, No. 94-Civ-8554 RPP, 1995 U.S. Dist. LEXIS 11153 (S.D.N.Y. Aug. 7, 1995).

304–5   The action against the Best Lock Company brought by an employee who was fired for off-duty drinking is *Best Lock Corp. v. Review Bd. of Dept. of Employment & Training Services*, 572 N.E.2d 520 (Ind.Ct.App. 1991).

305–6   The Texas Court of Appeals decision holding that the city of Dallas had violated Mica England's right to privacy under the Texas state constitution is *Dallas v. England*, 846 S.W.2d 957, 1993 Tex.App. LEXIS 451 (Tex. Ct.App. 1993). At the time Mica England was bringing her action against the city of Dallas, there was another important case being heard in the Texas court system regarding the constitutionality of the Texas sodomy statute, *State v. Morales*, 826 S.W.2d 201, 1992 Tex.App. LEXIS 643 (Tex.Ct.App. 1992), *rev'd*, 869 S.W.2d 941, 1994 Tex. LEXIS 17 (Tex. 1994). In *Morales*, the Texas Court of Appeals held that the sodomy law violated the Texas state constitutional right to privacy. On January 12, 1994, the Texas Supreme Court reversed the court of appeals decision on the procedural ground that the issue was not ripe for review in that there was only a hypothetical controversy. In procedurally reversing the appellate decision, the Texas Supreme Court declined to make a substantive decision as to whether the sodomy statute violated the state constitution. Information is taken from the court papers, as well as interviews with Mica England and LAMBDA attorney Evan Wolfson.

306–7   The California police applicant's action against the city of El Segundo is *Thorne v. El Segundo*, 726 F.2d 456 (9th Cir. 1983), *cert. denied*, 469 U.S. 979 (1984). The court's holding on the privacy claim is found at *id.* at 468.

307–8   The case about the police officers who were having relationships with prostitutes is *Fugate v. Phoenix Civil Service Bd.*, 791 F.2d 736 (9th Cir. 1986). The court's holding and reference to *Thorne* is found at *id.* at 741.

308   The case against the North Muskegon Police Department is *Briggs v. North Muskegon Police Dept.*, 536 F.Supp. 585 (W.D.Mich. 1983), *aff'd*, 746 F.2d 1475 (6th Cir. 1984), *cert. denied*, 473 U.S. 909 (1985).

308–9   The case against the Amarillo police chief is *Shawgo v. Spradlin*, 701 F.2d 470 (5th Cir. 1983), *cert. denied*, 464 U.S. 965 (1983).

Shoars v. Epson America, Inc.

312   Alana Shoars' personal suit for wrongful termination and slander is *Shoars v. Epson Am., Inc.*, No. SWC 112749 (Cal.Super.Ct. Dec. 8, 1992), *aff'd*, No. B073234 (Cal.Ct.App. Apr. 14, 1994), 1994 Cal. LEXIS 3670. The class action suit for invasion of privacy is *Flanagan et al. v. Epson Am., Inc.*, No. BC 007-036 (Cal.Super.Ct. Aug. 3, 1992).

313   The 1987 United States Supreme Court case relied upon by Epson is

O'Connor v. Ortega, 480 U.S. 709, 1987 U.S. LEXIS 1507, *remanded*, No. C-82-4045-JPV (N.D.Cal. Mar. 23, 1993), 1993 U.S.Dist. LEXIS 3882. The case involves an action brought by a physician and psychiatrist with Napa State Hospital. In 1981, the hospital's executive director became concerned about possible improprieties on the part of the doctor and told him to take paid leave while he investigated the matter. While the doctor was away, hospital officials searched his office, including his desk and file cabinets. The hospital officials seized some of the doctor's personal items as well as billing records for one of his private patients.

The doctor claimed that the search violated the Fourth Amendment. The case went to the United States Supreme Court. In a 5-to-4 decision, the Supreme Court held that he had a reasonable expectation of privacy in his office, and in his desk and file cabinets. Justice Sandra Day O'Connor led the majority in holding that "public employer intrusions . . . should be judged by the standard of reasonableness." *Id.* at 725–26.

The Court remanded the case to the trial court to determine whether the search in *Ortega* met the new test. On remand, the district court applied the Supreme Court's "reasonable standard" and granted judgment for the defendants. The court held that the "search clearly was reasonable in its scope, and the Fourth Amendment was not violated by defendants' conduct." Slip op. at 6.

313–14   The facts of the Borland V.P.'s case are from Stephen Kreider Yoder, "Silicon Valley Days: High-Tech Firm Cries Trade-Secret Theft, Gets Scant Sympathy," *Wall St. J.*, Oct. 8, 1992, at A1; Charles Piller, "Bosses with X-Ray Eyes," *MacWorld*, July 1993 (hereinafter Piller).

314   The facts surrounding the district attorney's recusal in the *Borland* case are from Bill Kisliuk, "One Person's Bribe Is Another's Efficient Government," *American Lawyer Media, The Recorder*, Sept. 7, 1994, at 2.

314   The California wiretapping law is Cal. Penal Code §631. The summary in the text has been abbreviated.

315   The court's January 4, 1991, ruling on whether e-mail is covered by the California wiretapping statute is *Flanagan et al. v. Epson Am., Inc.*, No. BC 0070036 (Cal.Super.Ct. Jan. 4, 1991). The court ruled that "extension [of electronic communications] to Penal Code §631 . . . is the proper province of the Legislature, which is better equipped than a court to determine the precise nature of such an extension." *Id.* slip op. at 4.

315   The court's reference to the Electronic and Communications Privacy Act of 1986 is at *id.*

The Electronic and Communications Privacy Act was an amendment to the Omnibus Crime Control and Safe Streets Act of 1968. 18 U.S.C.A. §2510 et seq. The original statute, enacted in 1968, covered only the interception of oral and wire communications. The statute was enacted as a legislative response to two 1967 United States Supreme Court cases.

The first of the two United States Supreme Court cases that extended Fourth Amendment protection to communications in the electronic era is *Katz v. United States*, 389 U.S. 347, 1967 U.S. LEXIS 2 (1967).

Katz involved the electronic eavesdropping of a public telephone booth. The Court held that the Fourth Amendment protects people and not places. *Id.* at 351.

Several months prior to *Katz*, the Supreme Court ruled on a case involving electronic eavesdropping, commonly known as "bugging." In *Berger v. New York*, the Court declared unconstitutional the New York state statute that authorized electronic eavesdropping by law enforcement officers during criminal investigations. *Berger v. New York*, 388 U.S. 41, 1967 U.S. LEXIS 2964 (1967).

In an effort to conform with the Supreme Court's guidelines set forth in *Berger* and *Katz*, the legislature drafted the Omnibus Crime Control and Safe Streets Act of 1968, which placed restrictions on wiretapping and eavesdropping surveillance. S.Rep. No. 1097, 10th Cong., 2d Sess., at 156 (1968). In 1986, the legislature amended the 1968 Act to include electronic communications, commonly referred to as the Electronic and Communications Privacy Act of 1968. 18 U.S.C.A. §2510 et seq.

Under the ECPA, the provider of the services is not prohibited from monitoring the electronic communications. Section 2511(2)(a)(I) of the statute states that "[i]t shall not be unlawful under this chapter for an operator of a switchboard or an officer, employee, or agent of a provider of wire or electronic communication service, whose facilities are used in the transmission of a wire communication, to intercept, disclose, or use that communication." 18 U.S.C.A. §2511(2)(a)(I).

315 The July 31, 1992, court ruling denying class certification is *Flanagan et al. v. Epson Am., Inc.*, No. BC 0070036 (Cal.Super.Ct. July 31, 1992). The court's ruling that the e-mail statements were mostly business-related, and thus not protected by California's right to privacy, is from *id.* slip op. at 6, 7. Plaintiffs withdrew their appeal in exchange for $2,500.

316 The statistic on the increase in the number of e-mail users is from Ilana DeBare, "E-Mail—Electronic, Easy and Often Embarrassing," *Sacramento Bee*, Nov. 14, 1993, at A1.

316 The facts and figures are taken from a survey reported in the July 1993 issue of *MacWorld* magazine.

316–17 The stories of the women interviewed by 9 to 5, Working Women Education Fund are from *Stories of Mistrust and Manipulation: The Electronic Monitoring of the American Workforce*, 9 to 5, Working Women Educ. Fund, Feb. 1990, at 17, 29 (hereinafter *Stories of Mistrust*).

317 The facts about the development and application of the "active badge" are from Peter Coy, "Big Brother, Pinned to Your Chest," *Business Week*, Aug. 17, 1992, at 38; Leonard Sloane, "Orwellian Dream Come True: A Badge That Pinpoints You," *N.Y. Times*, Sept. 12, 1992, at 11.

317 The example of Federal Express' "people first" approach is taken from *Stories of Mistrust*, at 7.

317 In a December 8, 1992, order, the California State Superior Court awarded summary judgment in favor of Epson; Alana Shoars appealed.

On appeal, the California State Court of Appeal affirmed summary judgment on the wrongful discharge cause of action but reversed on the slander claim. *Shoars v. Epson Am., Inc.*, No. B0732234 (Cal.Ct.App. Apr. 14, 1994), 1994 Cal. LEXIS 3670. Following that ruling, a settlement was reached and the case was dismissed.

PASSING JUDGMENTS

318 The facts of the voice-mail case involving the McDonald's manager is from Pamela Mendels, "$2M Suit in Sweet Nuthin' Eavesdrop," *Newsday*, Jan. 20, 1995, at A4; Ben Dubbin, "Federal Suit Questions Worker Privacy Rights; Courts Case Will Weigh What Protections Employers Are Entitled To, as Well as How Far Employers Can Go in Monitoring Staff," *L.A. Times*, Jan. 25, 1995, at D7.

318–19 The quotation from Oliver North's memo is from "So You Thought That Computer Note Was Private," *N.Y. Times*, Feb. 7, 1993, at 32. Although North was acquitted on nine counts, he appealed the three counts on which he was found guilty. *U.S. v. North*, 910 F.2d 843, 1990 U.S.App. LEXIS 12106 (1990), *cert. denied*, 500 U.S. 941, 1991 U.S. LEXIS 2936 (1991). The Court of Appeals vacated the guilty verdict. On September 16, 1991, Oliver North's case was dismissed.

The federal case in which the court ruled that the government must keep all electronic records regardless of whether there is a paper backup is *Armstrong v. Executive Officer of the President*, 810 F.Supp. 335, 1993 U.S.Dist. LEXIS 95 (D.D.C. 1993), *aff'd*, 1 F.3d 1274, 1993 U.S.App. LEXIS 20527 (D.C.Cir. 1995). In *Armstrong*, private parties brought an action to prohibit the destruction of materials stored on the National Security Council's computer system. The parties bringing the action claimed that under the Federal Records Act, the NCS had an obligation to keep all computer records. The NSC argued that if the records were transcribed onto paper, the computer records could be deleted. The Court of Appeals for the D.C. Circuit held that paper copies of the records did not satisfy the Federal Records Act and that the computer records had to be properly preserved.

In a case related to *Armstrong*, a federal district court in *American Historical Ass'n v. Peterson*, Civ. No. 94-2671 (CRR), 1995 U.S. Dist. LEXIS 2407, held that all presidential records, including computer records, are subject to the Presidential Records Act, 44 U.S.C. §2201 et seq.

319 The case involving the illegal surveillance of the Hawaii post office workers is *State v. Bonnell*, 856 P.2d 1265, 1993 Haw. LEXIS 34 (1993).

320 The facts of the case involving the Northern Telecom workers are taken from documents in the case and interviews with both parties' attorneys. The federal court order prohibiting public disclosure of the tapes is *Jesse Parrish et al. v. Northern Telecom, Inc.*, No. 3:90–0790 (M.D.Tenn. Oct. 24, 1990).

320 The facts and holding of the Family Life League case are from *Family Life League v. Dept. of Public Aid*, 493 N.E.2d 1054 (Ill. 1986).

PRIVACY AND INFORMATION

323   Louis Brandeis and Samuel Warren's quote about mechanical devices threatening privacy is from Samuel D. Warren and Louis D. Brandeis, "The Right to Privacy," 4 Harv.L.Rev. 193, 195 (1890).

324–5   The story about "infobrokers" is from "For Sale: Data About You," *Harper's*, Mar. 1992, at 26; and authors' interviews with the U.S. Attorney's Office, District of New Jersey, Newark, New Jersey.

325   For further information about the journalist who obtained Dan Quayle's credit report, see Jeffrey Rothfeder, *Privacy for Sale* (New York: Simon & Schuster, 1992).

325   Rebecca Schaeffer's story is from Eric Malnic, "Man Who Killed T.V. Actress Gets Life Without Parole," *L.A. Times*, Dec. 21, 1991, at B3.

325   For further information regarding the NCOA and the U.S. Post Office, see Anne Wells Branscomb, *Who Owns Information?* (New York: Basic Books, 1994).

325–6   Rogan's case regarding the NCIC is *Rogan v. City of Los Angeles*, 668 F.Supp. 1384, 1987 U.S.Dist. LEXIS 10456 (D.Cal. 1987).

326   The story about the people of Norwich, Vermont, is from "TRW Will Pay Vermont Residents Hurt by Firm's Credit-Report Errors in 1991," *Wall St. J.*, Dec. 23, 1992, at B4.

328   The Video Privacy Protection Act of 1988 is cited at 18 U.S.C.S. §2710 (Law.Co-op. 1994).

330   The Cable Television Consumer Protection and Competition Act of 1992 is cited at 47 U.S.C.S. §551 (Law.Co-op. 1994).

330   The Driver's Privacy Protection Act of 1994 is cited at 18 U.S.C.S. §2721 et seq. (Law.Co-op. 1994).

330   The Fair Credit Reporting Act is cited at 15 U.S.C.S. §1681 et seq. (Law.Co-op. 1994).

330   The Telephone Consumer Protection Act of 1991 is cited at 47 U.S.C.S. §227 (Law.Co-op. 1994).

330   The Privacy Act of 1974 is cited at 5 U.S.C.S. §552a (Law.Co-op. 1994).

Some other sources for this chapter include:

Edmund L. Andrews, "U.S. Plans to Push Giving FBI Access in Computer Codes," *N.Y. Times*, Feb. 4, 1994, at A1

Barbara Everitt Bryant and William Dunn, "Census and Privacy," *Am. Dem.*, May 1995, at 48

Nathan Cobb, "The End of Privacy," *B. Globe Mag.*, Apr. 26, 1992, at 17

William G. Flanagan and Brigid McMenamin, "The Playground Bullies Are Learning How to Type," *Forbes*, Dec. 21, 1992, at 184–89

Notes

David Gelernter, "Wiretaps for a Wireless Age," *N.Y. Times*, May 8, 1994, at A17

Mitchell Kapor, "Where Is the Digital Highway Really Heading?," *Wired*, July/Aug. 1993, at 3

Richard Lacayo, "Nowhere to Hide," *Time*, Nov. 11, 1991, at 34

John Markoff, "Gore Shifts Stance on Chip Code," *N.Y. Times*, July 21, 1994, at D1

John Markoff, "A Push for Surveillance Software," *N.Y. Times*, Feb. 28, 1994, at D1

John Markoff, "U.S. Code Agency Is Jostling for Civilian Turf," *N.Y. Times*, Jan. 24, 1994, at D1

John Markoff, "Big Brother and the Computer Age," *N.Y. Times*, May 6, 1993, at D1

John Markoff, "Electronics Plan Aims to Balance Government Access With Privacy," *N.Y. Times*, Apr. 15, 1993, at A1

John Markoff, "A Public Battle Over Secret Codes," *N.Y. Times*, May 7, 1992, at D1

Brock N. Meeks, "Privacy Is My Life," *Wired*, July/Aug. 1993, at 40

Anthony Ramirez, "The F.B.I.'s Latest Idea: Make Wiretapping Easier," *N.Y. Times*, Apr. 19, 1992, at A2

John Schwartz, "How Did They Get My Name?," *Newsweek*, June 3, 1991, at 40

Jacob Sullum, "For Sale," *Reason*, Apr. 1992, at 29–35

Mary B. W. Tabor and Anthony Ramirez, "Computer Savvy, With an Attitude," *N.Y. Times*, July 23, 1992, at B7

Larry Tye, "No Private Lives" (four-part series), *B. Globe*, Sept. 5–8, 1993

Judith Waldrop, "The Business of Privacy," *Am. Dem*, Oct. 1994, at 46

Paul Wallich, "Make, Model and . . . : Privacy Advocate Puts License Plates on the Line," *Sci. Am.*, May 1993, at 30

"Is Computer Hacking a Crime?," *Harper's*, Mar. 1990, at 45–57

and conversations with:

John Perry Barlow, Electronic Frontier Foundation

Jerry Berman, Center for Democracy and Technology

Jan Lori Goldman, Center for Democracy and Technology

Evan Hendricks, *Privacy Times*

Eli Noam, Columbia University School of Business

Marc Rotenberg, Electronic Privacy Information Center

Robert Ellis Smith, *Privacy Journal*

AFTERWORD

337 The full panel opinion from the Ninth Circuit is *Compassion in Dying v. Washington*, 79 F.3d 790 (9th Cir. 1996) (en blanc). The Second Circuit opinion is *Quill v. Vaco*, 80 F.3d 716 (2d Cir. 1996.)

Bibliography

American Law Institute. *Restatement of the Law. Second Torts.* St. Paul, Minn.: American Law Institute, 1965.

Andrews, Lori B., Neil A. Holtzman, and Arno G. Motulsky, eds. *Assessing Genetic Risks: Implications for Health and Social Policy.* Washington, D.C.: National Academy Press, 1994.

Branscomb, Anne Wells. *Who Owns Information?* New York: Basic Books, 1994.

Brill, Alida. *Nobody's Business.* Reading, Pa.: Addison-Wesley, 1990.

Califano, Joseph A., Jr. *Radical Surgery: What's New for America's Health Care.* New York: Times Books, 1994.

Cornish, Craig M. *Drugs and Alcohol in the Workplace: Testing and Privacy.* Wilmette, Ill.: Callaghan & Co., 1988.

Decker, Kurt H. *Employer Privacy Law and Practice.* New York: Wiley Law Publications, 1987.

DeMaio, Harry B. *Information Protection and Other Unnatural Acts: Every Manager's Guide to Keeping Vital Data Safe and Sound.* New York: American Management Association, 1992.

Dworkin, Ronald. *Life's Dominion: An Argument About Abortion, Euthanasia, and Individual Freedom.* New York: Alfred A. Knopf, 1993.

Elder, David A. *The Law of Privacy.* New York: Clark Boardman, 1991.

Elkouri, Frank, and Edna Asper. *Resolving Drug Issues.* Washington, D.C.: Bureau of National Affairs, 1993.

Flaherty, David H. *Privacy in Colonial New England.* Richmond: University of Virginia Press, 1972.

Garrow, David J. *Liberty and Sexuality.* New York: Macmillan, 1994.

Glendon, Mary Ann. *Abortion and Divorce in Western Law.* Cambridge: Harvard University Press, 1987.

———. *Rights Talk: The Impoverishment of Political Discourse.* New York: Free Press, 1991.

Goode, Stephen. *The Right to Privacy.* New York: Franklin Watts, 1983.

Hendricks, Evan, Trudy Hayden, and Jack D. Novik. *Your Right to Privacy: A Basic Guide to Legal Rights in an Information Society.* 2d ed. Carbondale and Edwardsville: Southern Illinois University Press, 1990.

Hill, Marvin F., Jr., and James A. Wright. *Employee Lifestyle and Off-Duty Conduct Regulation.* Washington, D.C.: Bureau of National Affairs, 1993.

Hixson, Richard F. *Privacy in a Public Society.* New York: Oxford University Press, 1987.

London, Martin, and Barbara Dill. *At What Price? Libel Law and Freedom of the Press.* New York: Twentieth Century Fund Press, 1993.

Loomis, Lloyd. *Drug Testing: A Workplace Guide to Designing Practical Policies and Winning Arbitrations.* Washington, D.C.: Bureau of National Affairs, 1990.

McAffee, John, and Colin Haynes. *Computer Viruses, Worms, Data Diddlers, Killer Programs, and Other Threats to Your System: What They Are, How They Work, and How to Defend Your PC, Mac, or Mainframe.* New York: St. Martin's Press, 1989.

Mayer, Michael F. *The Libel Revolution: A New Look at Defamation and Privacy.* New York: Law Arts Publishers, 1987.

Mensch, Elizabeth, and Alan Freeman. *The Politics of Virtue: Is Abortion Debatable?* Durham, N.C.: Duke University Press, 1993.

Neumann, Peter G. *Computer-Related Risks.* New York: Addison-Wesley, 1995.

O'Brien, David M. *Privacy, Law, and Public Policy.* New York: Praeger, 1979.

Player, Mack A. *Employment Discrimination Law.* St. Paul, Minn.: West Publishing, 1988.

Prosser, William L., and W. Page Keeton. *Prosser and Keaton on the Law of Torts.* St. Paul, Minn.: West Publishing, 1984.

Rosenblatt, Roger. *Life Itself: Abortion in the American Mind.* New York: Random House, 1992.

Rothfeder, Jeffrey. *Privacy for Sale.* New York: Simon & Schuster, 1992.

Rule, James M. *The Politics of Privacy.* New York: Elsevier North Holland, 1980.

Sanford, Bruce W. *Libel and Privacy: The Prevention and Defense of Litigation.* New York: Prentice-Hall, 1987.

Seipp, David J. *The Right to Privacy in American History.* Cambridge: Harvard University Press, 1987.

Shepard, Ira M., Robert L. Duston, and Karen S. Russell. *Workplace Privacy: Employee Testing, Surveillance, Wrongful Discharge, and Other Areas of Vulnerability.* Washington, D.C.: Bureau of National Affairs, 1989.

Smith, Robert Ellis. *Privacy: How to Protect What's Left of It.* New York: Anchor Press, 1979.

———. *Workrights.* New York: E. P. Dutton, 1983.

Tribe, Laurence H. *Abortion: The Clash of Absolutes.* New York: W. W. Norton, 1990.

Index

abortion, xiv, xvi, 53, 55–70; in case of coma, 121; federal funding for, 60; history of, 59; parental consent to, 61, 67; spousal consent to, 60, 78; spousal notification of, 64, 78; waiting period for, 60; *see also Roe v. Wade*

active badge, 317

Acton, James, 48–9

adoption, revealed, 160–7, 170–2

advertisements, 224–5

aerial surveillance, 26

AIDS, 54, 142, 143–7, 285

alcohol: testing for, 23–4, 29; use, 304–5

Allen, Laural, 303–4

Amarillo Police Department, 308–9

American Civil Liberties Union (ACLU), 115, 281, 286–7; Lesbian and Gay Rights Project, 299; and strip-search cases, 9–10, 14

American College of Obstetricians and Gynecologists, 116

American Fertility Society, 79, 87

American Management Association, 291

American Medical Association (AMA), 116, 117

Americans with Disabilities Act (ADA), 143, 288

Anderson, Debbie (sex tape case), 227–48

Anderson, Faye, 231–33, 237

Anderson, Sally, 232

Anderson, Walt, 231–33, 237

Anderson v. Vasquez, 94

Anderson v. WROC-TV, 189

Ann-Margret (actress), 199

antiabortion protests, 68–70

appropriation cases, 209–22; and right to publicity, 220–2

appropriation tort, 155, 156, 213–14

Aquarena Springs amusement park, 191–5, 199, 201

Armstrong v. Executive Office of the President, 319

Armstrong v. H&C Communications, 173–4

Arrington, Clarence, 209–17, 221

Arrington, Lloyd, 210

Arrington v. The New York Times Company, 209–17

Asbury Park Press, 172

association, freedom of, 57, 299–301, 306–7

Atlantic Zayre stores, 270

attorneys: contingency-fee, 234, 242, 255, 256; personal injury, 255

Ault v. Hustler Magazine, Inc., 207–8

automatic teller machines (ATMs), 331

Ayeni v. CBS, Inc. et al., 190

background checks, 275, 289, 306
Backus, Barbara, 192
baggage searches, 31–5
Bain, Judy, 313–14
Baker, Ken, 235, 236, 238, 240
Baker, Kevin, 228, 229, 235, 236, 238, 240
bank records, 27; *see also* credit
bankruptcy, 241, 246
Barnes v. Mississippi, 67
Belloni, Marlene, 176–86
Belloni, Tom, 176–85
Best Lock v. Review Board, 304–5
Bill of Rights (U.S. Constitution), 2, 55, 56, 58, 63, 152; *see also* First Amendment; Fourteenth Amendment; Fourth Amendment
Bingham, Ken, 303
Bingham and Everett v. Rohr Industries, Inc., 303
birth control, *see* contraception
Bisbee v. Conover, 172
Black, Hugo, 58
black middle class, 209–17
Blackmun, Harry, 59–60, 62–3, 65, 66, 85, 298
blood: donors, 146, 147; testing, 23, 24–5, 29; transfusions, 146–7
body-cavity searches, 5, 6, 7, 12, 16
Bone v. Ford Meter Box, 291
books, 152, 218–19; and false light cases, 204, 207
Bork, Robert H., 328
Borland International, 314
Bouser, Steve, 164, 170
Bowers, Michael, 294–302
Bowers v. Hardwick, 135–6
Brandeis, Louis D., xiv, 154–5, 323
Brashler, William, 209
Braun, Ed, 194
Braun, Jeannie, 191–5, 198–202
Braun v. Flynt, 191–5, 198–202
breath testing, 24–5, 29
Brennan, William, 43, 58
Breyer, Stephen, 66
Briggs v. North Muskegon Police Dept., 308
Brinkley, Christie, 213
Brown, Lucy, 232, 233, 235
Brown, Robin, *see* Shahar, Robin

Bryan, William Jennings, 78
Brzeczek, Richard, 7, 8–9
Burch, Ken, 234, 236
Bureau of National Affairs, 282
Burke, Vincent, 104–7, 112, 117
Bush administration, 319
Byrd v. Hustler Magazine, Inc., 203–4

C., Angela, 95–120
C., Rick, 97–103, 109–15, 117
cable television records, 330, 332
California: eavesdropping statute, 266; and physician-assisted suicide, 130, 131; state constitution, 285, 286, 287, 292, 312, 313, 315; wiretapping law, 314, 315
California Department of Motor Vehicles, 325
California Personality Inventory (CPI), 284, 288
California Supreme Court, 187, 287, 289, 292
Caller ID, 327
Calumet City, Illinois, 18
Cape Publications, Inc. v. Bridges, 171
Capra, Tom, 180, 182, 183, 185, 186, 188
Cardozo, Benjamin, 40
Carey, Peter, 14–15, 17
Carol D. v. City of Chicago, 7–8, 9, 10, 14, 15
car searches, 46, 47
Carson, Johnny, 177, 221
Carson v. Here's Johnny Portable Toilets, 221
catalogue shopping, 329, 331
cause, probable, 29, 32, 42
CBS, 174, 190, 220
celebrities, 151–2; and appropriation cases, 218–20; and defamation of, 196, 198
Celebrity Skin magazine, 199
cellular phones, 323, 331
Center for Reproductive Law and Policy, 122
cesarean section: forced, 95–120; postmortem, 103–5
Chafee, Zechariah, 153
change-of-address card, 325

Chasnoff, Barry, 242–3, 247
Chicago Police Department, 3–18
Chic magazine, 192–5, 198–201
child(ren): education, 54, 55, 57, 59; endangerment, 124–6; of lesbian couples, 94; rearing, 59
Choplick, Theodore, 37–43
Christenberry, Jay, 76–8, 82
Cibenko v. Worth Publishers, Inc., 207
Clifford, Charles, 76, 78, 82, 83–4, 89, 91
Clipper Chip, 323, 327–8
Coleman, Bob, 296
coma, 137–9
common law, 118, 214, 217; defined, 155
computer(s), 323–4; hackers, 327; monitoring, 275, 316, 317; records, 285; *see also* electronic monitoring; e-mail; workplace
Conagra Poultry Company, 292
Connecticut Supreme Court, 122
Constitution, *see* U.S. Constitution
contingency-fee attorneys, 234, 242, 255, 256
contraception, xvi, 56–9, 65, 298; forced, 123–6
Cooper, Jeff (sex tape case), 227–48
Cooper v. Anderson (sex tape case), 227–48
Coronado v. State, 46–7
Court of Appeals, *see* U.S. Court of Appeals
creation v. evolution dispute, 78
credible reason, 32
credit: bureaus, 323, 326, 328; card companies, 323, 326; checks, 275; reports, 325, 330; unions, 323
Creel v. Crown Publishers, 218–19
crime, xiii, 327
criminal: history, 324–5; records checks, 289
Cruzan, Nancy, 133–4
Cruzan v. Director Missouri Department of Health, 133–4, 136, 138, 340, 341
cryogenic suspension, 139
cryopreservation, 74, 80, 82, 83; frozen embryo case, 71–92
curtilage, 25–6
cyberspace, xiii, xvi, 324, 326, 331

Daily News Tribune, The (Georgia), 172
Dallas Police Department, 305–6
Dallas v. England, 305–6
Darrow, Clarence, 78
dating, of co-workers, 303–4, 308–9
Davis, Brenda, 85, 89
Davis, J.R. (Junior), 71–91
Davis, Margaret, 114
Davis, Mary Sue (Mary Stowe), 71–91
Davis v. Davis, 71–91
death: double effect, 128; televised, 176–88; *see also* right-to-die
death row inmates, and sperm preservation, 94
deceased persons; photographs of, 172–4, 184; publications about, 186
defamation; cases, 194–6, 200, 204, 205, 207; overlap with false light, 195–6, 202
defamation tort, 155–7, 166, 195
DeGregorio v. CBS, Inc., 220
DeJulio, Lois, 41
Delta Airlines, 140, 143
democratic process, 56
Denver, Colorado, 19
depression, 130, 132
Des Moines Register, 171
Diane H. v. City of Chicago, 7–8, 15
direct mail lists, 328
direct marketing, 325
disabilities, 143, 275
discrimination: against gays, 143, 298, 299; based on disability, 143; gender, 275, 306; job, 288; laws prohibiting, 275
DNA research, 324
documents, 26–7; shredding, 28; *see also* informational privacy
Doe v. Borough of Barrington, 144
Doe v. Boyd, 19–20
Doe v. City of New York, 140–3
"Donahue"(television program), 244
Donaldson v. Lungren, 139
double effect death, 128
Douglas, William O., 57
dressing room surveillance, 269
Driver's Privacy Protection Act, 330
driving records, 325, 330
drug(s), 25–6; cartels, 327; couriers,

drug(s) *(continued)*
31–5; interdiction cases, 31–5; off-
and on-duty use of, 304–5; use
during pregnancy, 121–3; war on, 291
drug testing, 24–5, 29; of government
workers in public safety jobs, 291;
of pregnant women, 123; of
students, 36, 47–9; of student
athletes, 287, 289–90; in workplace,
275, 285, 287, 289–90, 291–2
Due Process Clause (Fourteenth
Amendment), 55, 56

eavesdropping, 185, 186, 266, 267, 320;
see also electronic monitoring;
wiretapping
education of children, and parental
rights, 54, 55, 57
Edwards, Maureen, 103, 104, 107, 112,
117
Eisenstadt v. Baird, 58
Electronic and Communications
Privacy Act (ECPA), 315
electronic communications,
encrypted, 327
Electronic Messaging Association, 313
electronic monitoring, 310–11; active
badge, 317; computer, 275, 316, 317;
e-mail, 310–17; telephone, 314–17;
video, 275, 316, 317, 319
Elmore v. Atlantic Zayre, Inc., 270
El Segundo, California, 306–7
e-mail, 310–17
embryos; frozen, 71–92; as persons or
property, 86–7
emotional distress, infliction of, 157,
184, 186, 234, 240–6, 255
employee: gambling, 313, 319;
negligence, 313; sexual
harrassment, 313; theft, 278, 283,
292, 313; *see also* employer;
workplace
Employee Polygraph Protection Act
(EPPA), 293
employer, xiv, xv, xvi; liability, 276;
negligent hiring and retention, 276,
282; *see also* employee; workplace
employment history, 324–5
encryption, 327

England, Mica, 305–6
English common law, 59, 60, 136
Epson America, Inc., 310–17
Equal Protection Clause (Fourteenth
Amendment), 10, 13, 16, 58, 134, 136,
298
Equifax (credit bureau), 328
euthanasia, voluntary active, 132; *see
also* right-to-die
Everett, Sue, 303
exclusionary rule (Fourth
Amendment), 40–3
Ezer, Mitch, 185–6, 188

Fair Credit Reporting Act, 330
false light cases, 203–8; *Braun v. Flynt*,
191–5, 198–202; flattering, 196; and
statements of opinion, 207–8
false light tort, 155–7, 195; overlap
with defamation, 195–6, 201
*Family Life League v. Dept. of Public
Aid*, 320
Farfalla, Frank, 31, 32, 35
*Fargo Women's Health Organization v.
Schafer*, 67
father; legal, 93; natural, 93
Federal Bureau of Investigation (FBI),
323, 324–5, 336, 337
Federal Express, 317
Federal Railroad Administration
(FRA), 24
Ferguson v. City of Charleston, 123
fetus: appointed guardian for, 121;
viability of, 61, 62, 64, 68, 86, 103,
107, 110–12, 119, 134, 121; *see also*
abortion
Final Exit (Humphry), 130
financial status, 27; *see also* credit
fingernail scrapings, 24, 25, 29
fingerprints, 24, 25
Finger v. Omni Publishing, 219–20
First Amendment (U.S. Constitution),
xvi; and protection of truthful
publications, 165–6, 170; right to
free speech, 57, 68–70, 152, 166; *see
also* press; speech, freedom of
Fowler, Ray, 252, 253
Fisher Broadcasting, Inc., 190
Fitzpatrick, Dave, 259–62

Florida Publishing Company v. Fletcher, 189

Florida Supreme Court, 122, 146, 189

Flynt, Larry, 193, 194, 198–201

Forbes magazine, 198

Ford, Gerald, 151, 167

Ford, Henry, 276

Ford Meter Box Company, 291

Ford Motor Company, 221

founded suspicion, 32, 33

Founding Fathers, 10, 30, 152–3

Fourteenth Amendment (U.S. Constitution): Due Process Clause, 55, 56; Equal Protection Clause, 10, 12, 16, 58, 134, 136, 298; liberty in, 55, 57

Fourth Amendment (U.S. Constitution), xv, 2, 10; determination of reasonableness, 29–30; drafted, 25; exclusionary rule, 40–3; protection and new technology, 23; protection triggered, 23; reasonable expectation of privacy, 10; and searches and seizures, xv, 2, 9, 10, 11, 12, 16, 18; *see also* searches

fraternization, *see* dating

Freedom of Access to Clinics Act, 336

free society, 166, 217

Frisby v. Schultz, 68–9

frozen embryo cases, 71–92

Fudge v. Penthouse, 206–7

Fugate v. Phoenix Civil Service Bd., 307–8

Fulton, Janet, 259–63

Fulton, Kirt, 258–9

gambling, 313, 319

Gammon, Gail, 230, 235, 237

Gannett Suburban Newspapers, 174

garbage, 28

gay rights movement, 301; *see also* homosexuals; lesbians

gender, 275, 306

genetic: profiles, 324; testing, 285

George Washington University Hospital, 99–120

Georgia, sodomy law, 270, 298, 300

Gershon, Rita, 257, 261

Getzendanner, Susan, 17

Gilgunn v. Massachusetts General Hospital, 137

Ginsberg, Ruth Bader, 66

Gordon, Ann and Bob, 161–4, 168

Gorgoni, Gianfranco, 209, 210, 213

gossip, xv, 154

government: eavesdropping, 323, 327–8; employee lifestyle and off-duty behavior, 294–309

Grabow, Karen, 283, 284

Grace Plaza of Great Neck, Inc. v. Elbaum, 137–8

Greenfield, Francine, 294–96, 297, 300, 301

Grimsley v. Guccione, 206–7

Griswold v. Connecticut, 57, 63

Grossman v. News Group Publications, 203

hair testing, 285

Haley, Harold, 35

Hall, Earle, 158–62, 165, 168–70

Hall, Mary, 158–65, 168–70, 221

Hall, Susie Jean, 158–65, 168–70, 221

Hall v. Post, 158–65, 168–70

Hamberger v. Eastman, 268

Hamner, Lewis, 99–106, 110, 113, 114

handwriting samples, 24

Hardwick, Michael, 298

Harkey v. Abate, 269

Harlow, Ruth, 299

harrassment: sexual, 313; telephone, 185, 186

Hart v. Shalala, 93

Harvard Law Review, 154

Hastings, Minnesota, 20

Hawaii Supreme Court, 319

Hawkins v. Multimedia, Inc., 172

health insurance, xvi, 276

Hecht v. Superior Court, 92–3

Hershey Medical Center, Pennsylvania, 145–6

Hilliard, Daniel R., 311, 312

Hill v. Bogans, 19

Hill v. NCAA, 287, 289

HIV, 140–7

Holiday Inns, peephole cases, 256

Hollman, T., 33

home: as man's castle and domain, 152; privacy in, xiii, xiv, 68–70; searches of, 25–6

homeowner's insurance, and negligent infliction of emotional distress cases, 240–1, 241, 242, 246

homosexuals, 54, 140, 270–2; lifestyle and off-duty behavior, 294–302, 305–6; in military, 301; sexual practices, 135, 136, 270, 298–301, 305–6; sperm donation by, 94; *see also* AIDS; HIV; lesbians

honesty testing, 285

Howard v. Des Moines Register, 171

Howell v. New York Post Co., 219

Human Genome Project, 337

Humane Society of Rochester, New York, 189

human interest stories, 166

Hustler magazine, 193, 198, 202, 203–4, 207–8

identity, appropriation of, 213, 220–2

Illinois, 18; Department of Public Aid, 320; State Records Act, 320

Illinois Supreme Court, 320

infobrokers, 324–5

information: age, 151–2; royalty pools for, 329; superhighway, 326

informational privacy, 286, 323–32; *see also* workplace

informed consent, 119

in loco parentis, 39–40

In re A. C., 95–120

In re Appeal in Pima County Juvenile Action No. 80484–1, 44

In re Bobby B., 44

In re Busalacchi, 138–9

In re Fiori, 138

In re Klein, 121

In re Milton S. Hershey Medical Center, 145–6

In re Valerie D., 122

"Inside Edition" (television program), 244

insurance: business policies, 255, 264; company records, 324; health, xvi, 276; homeowners, 240–2, 247; premiums, 242

intentional infliction of emotional distress (cause of action), 157, 255; *see also* emotional distress

Internal Revenue Service (IRS), 28, 323, 330

intrusion: cases, 176–90; nonphysical, 186; televised death, 176–88; theory, 255; upon seclusion, 263

intrusion tort, 155, 157, 185, 187, 226

invasion of privacy: appropriation tort, 155–7, 213–14; creation of right to sue for, 155; false light tort, 155–7, 195; intrusion tort, 155, 157, 185, 187, 226; private facts tort, 155–7, 165–8, 170, 196; torts defined, 155–7

in vitro fertilization (IVF), 72–4, 79, 88

Iowa, punitive damage laws, 264

Joan W. v. City of Chicago, 3–5, 8, 13, 14, 15, 16–18

job(s): discrimination, 288; safety-sensitive, 283; *see also* employee; employer; workplace

Johnson, Cal, 258

Johnson, Samuel, 303–4

Johnson v. Florida, 121–2

judicial bypass, 61, 67

Kansas, eavesdropping statute, 267

Kansas v. Martin, 266–7

Kass v. Kass, 92

Katherine Goes to Nursery School (Krementz), 218

Katz Media Corp., 304

Kennedy, Anthony, 61, 65

Kevorkian, Jack, 130–5, 336

kidnapping, 151, 174–5

King, I. Ray, 71–6, 79, 85, 89

Kirkley, Dorothy, 300

Kirkpatrick, Bill, 283

Klein, Edward, 209–10, 212, 215

KNBC, Los Angeles, 176–88

Krantz, Rick, 313, 315

Krementz, Jill, 218

Krist, Ronnie, 234–9, 242–4, 247

Ku Klux Klan, 166

Kuralt, Charles, 192

"Larry King Live" (television program), 244

law enforcement, xiv, xv, 3–49, 305–9; drug cases, 31–5, 44, 46; school searches, 36–49; searches, 23–30; strip-searches, 3–22; surveillance, 274–6

LeJeune, Jerome, 82–4

Lesbian and Gay Rights Project (of ACLU), 299

lesbians, 294–302, 305–6; *see also* homosexuals

Lessin, Laurence, 100, 101, 108

Levka v. City of Chicago (Mary T.), 5–6

Lewis v. Dayton Hudson Corp., 269

liberty: interpreted by U.S. Supreme Court, 55–7, 63, 133–4; in U.S. Constitution, xvi, 53

lie detector testing, *see* polygraph testing

life, beginning of, 58, 86; *see also* fetus

lifestyle and off-duty behavior: monitoring, 294–302; private sector, 303–5; public sector, 305–9

life support, termination of, 138–40; *see also* medical treatment

listening devices, 23, 185, 268, 327

Long Beach City Employees Ass'n. v. City of Long Beach, 292

Los Angeles, emergency medical services, 176–8, 180–1, 182

Los Angeles Police Department, 326

Lotus Development Corporation, 328–9

Lou Gehrig's Disease (ALS), 132

Louisiana, abortion statutes, 68

Louisiana National Guard, 267

Love, Richard, 104, 111

MacWorld magazine, 316

Madsen v. Women's Health Center, 69–70

magazines, 152, 168, 219–20; and defamation cases, 194, 195, 198; and false light cases, 191–5, 198–202, 203, 206–7; *see also* press *and specific names*

Magenis v. Fisher Broadcasting, Inc., 190

Manis, Stephanie, 296

Mares v. Conagra Co. Inc., 292

marijuana, 25–6

Marketplace: Households (software), 328

marriage, 53, 59, 64, 65; homosexual, 295–7, 299; interracial, 55

Marshall, Thurgood, 34, 43

Martin, Chuck, 161

Martin-McAllister (consultants), 278, 283, 284

MaryAnn T. v. City of Chicago 9, 15

MaryBeth G. v. City of Chicago, 15

Maryland, strip-search cases, 21–2

Maryland Casualty Company, 255–6

McCall, Peter, 249–65

McCall v. The Sherwood Inn, 249–65

McCarter, Debbie, 75

McDonalds, 318

McWhir v. Krementz, 218

media, 151–3; First Amendment protection, 152, 196; and protection of truthful publication, 165–6, 170; ride-alongs, 181, 188; and torts, 157; *see also* press; speech, freedom of; television

medical exams, testing in the workplace, 275, 284–5, 286, 287–92

medical information: disclosure of, 140–7; doctor-patient relationship, 143; histories and records, 28, 54, 123, 324, 331, 332; and public health, 141, 142, 143, 145, 146; routine disclosure to medical community and insurance companies, 141; *see also* medical treatment

Medical Information Bureau (MIB), 324

medical treatment: parents' right to refuse for children, 115; refusal of, xiv, 54, 115, 127–8, 133–4; and substituted judgment, 118; withdrawal of, 133–4, 137–9; *see also* medical information

metal detectors, 36

Meyer, Sister Jane, 236–7, 244

Michigan: and physician-assisted suicide, 131

Michigan Supreme Court, 135

microphones, hidden, 268; *see also* listening devices; wiretapping

Midler, Bette, 221
Midler v. Ford Motor Company, 221
military, gays in, 298
Miller, Brownie, 176–88
Miller, Dave, 176–7; televised death of, 178–88
Miller, M., 27–8
Miller, Norm, 176, 177
Miller v. NBC, 176–88
Millsaps, Joe, 165, 169–70
Mills Park, Carson City, 270–1
Minnesota Multiphasic Personality Inventory (MMPI), 284, 288
Minnesota Supreme Court, 282
Minogue, Dr., 110
minorities, 130
Miranda warnings, 38
mirrors, two-way, 229; *see also McCall v. The Sherwood Inn*
Mishkin, Barbara, 104–12, 117
Mississippi, abortion regulations, 67
Missouri: abortion laws, 61; and withdrawal of medical treatment, 133, 138–9
Moctezuma v. Township of Montclair, 22
Montgomery County Detention Center (MCDC), 21–2
Morrison, Dick, 234, 235, 236, 238, 242
Moscow, Jeffrey, 99–102, 119
Motor Vehicle Bureau (MVB), 325, 330
motor vehicle records, 327, 330
Murray v. Schlosser, 208

National Change of Address (NCOA) database, 323, 325
National Collegiate Athletic Association (NCAA), 287, 289
National Crime Information Center (NCIC), 323, 325–6
National Institutes of Health (NIH), 95, 96, 97, 101
NBC, 174; KNBC Los Angeles, 176–88
negligence tort, 155; hiring and retention, 276, 282
Nelson, Terry, 249–65
Nevada Supreme Court, 271
New Jersey v. T.L.O., 36–43, 47
newsletters, 152
New Summit Associates v. Nistle, 267–8

newspapers, 151–2, 204–5, 219; *see also* press
newsworthiness, 166, 168, 169, 220; defining, 166–7
New York: common law, 214, 216, 217; Court of Appeals, 216–17, 217, 220; Department of Health, 130, 141; law banning assisted suicide, 135; and physician-assisted suicide, 133, 135, 136; and police encounters with citizens, 30, 32; public health law, 145; statute on right to privacy, 213–14, 216, 217
New York Amsterdam News, 212–13
New York City Human Rights Commission, 140, 142
New Yorker, The, 167
New York Post, The, 203, 219
New York Times Magazine, The, cover photo, 209–17
nexus requirement, 286, 287
9 to 5, Working Women Education Fund, 316
Nodes, Alan, 41
Nolley v. County of Erie, 145
Norte, Ruben, 176, 179–83, 186, 187
North, Oliver, 318–19
North Carolina: adoption law, 160, 169; and private facts tort, 170
North Carolina Supreme Court, 169–70
North Dakota, abortion regulations, 67
Northern Telecom, 320
Nussbaum, Hedda, 219
Nuwer, Henry, 193–4

Oakland Tribune, 168
O'Brien v. Papa Gino's of America, Inc., 293
O'Connor, Sandra Day, 48–9, 61, 63, 64, 65
O'Connor v. Ortega, 313
off-duty behavior, *see* lifestyle and off-duty behavior
offensive to reasonable person, 168, 169, 187, 195, 197, 226
Olivetti, 317
Omni magazine, 219–20

opinion, statement of, 207–8
"Oprah" law, 276
Oregon, and physician-assisted
  suicide, 131, 135
Oregon v. Casconi, 271–2
Oregon v. Owczarzak, 271–2
organized crime, 327
Otis, James, Jr., 10

Paltrow, Lynn, 116
Papa Gino's, 293
papers, privacy of, 26, 27–8; shredding
  of, 28; *see also* informational privacy
parent(s): conduct of, 122; education
  of children, 54, 55, 57, 59;
  endangerment of children, 124–6;
  homosexual, 94; termination of
  rights of, 122
Parish et al. v. Northern Telecom, 320
Pasch v. Katz Media Corp., 304
paternity and visitation suits, 94
patient, competence of, 133–4
Paulo, Judy, 229, 230, 232
peephole cases, 249–65, 266–69; *see
  also* voyeurism
Pennsylvania: abortion regulations,
  63–5; and termination of life-
  support, 138
pen register, 27
Penthouse magazine, 206–7
People of New York v. Hollman, 31–5
*Peoples Bank & Trust Co. v. Globe
  International Publishing, Inc.*, 204–5
People v. Colon and Cardona, 174–5
People v. Gibbons, 266
People v. Pointer, 124–5
People v. Zaring, 125–6
personal injury attorneys, 255
Phoenix, Arizona, 307–8
phone, *see* cellular phones; telephone
photographs: and appropriation
  cases, 209–22; of deceased, 172–4,
  184; and false light cases, 198, 199,
  203, 204, 206–7; nude, 198, 199,
  266–7; publication of private, 151,
  167, 171, 172–3
physical agility testing, 306
physician-assisted suicide, 128–9,
  130–6, 139

Pitt, William, 25
Pittsburgh Steelers, 151, 167
Planned Parenthood, 57
Planned Parenthood v. Casey, 63, 66, 68,
  133, 134–5, 136
police, *see* law enforcement
political affiliation, 28
polygraph testing, 285, 292, 305, 306
pornography, 194, 198, 199, 201
Port Authority of New York and New
  Jersey, 31, 32
Post, Rose, 161–3
postmortem cesarean section, 103,
  104, 105
post-traumatic stress syndrome,
  238
precedent, lack of, 165
pre-embryos, 74, 75, 79, 87
pregnancy: court-ordered ban on,
  124–6; drug testing during, 123; and
  forced cesarean section, 95–120;
  prosecution for drug use during,
  121–3; teenage, 174
press, xiii, 151–222; appropriation
  cases, 209–22; and errors in
  publication, 196–7; and false light
  cases, 191–208; freedom of, xiv, xv,
  xvi, 152–3, 157, 196; and intrusion
  cases, 176–90; and newsworthiness,
  166–7, 168, 169; and private facts
  cases, 158–75; and right to be let
  alone, 154–7; and truthful
  publications, 165–6, 170; *see also*
  First Amendment; magazines;
  television
privacy: erosion of, xiv; not
  mentioned in U.S. Constitution,
  xiii, xv, 10, 53; reasonable
  expectation of, 10, 47
Privacy Act, 330
private citizens, xiv, 196
private facts, 158–75; adoption
  revealed, 158–65, 168–70; cases,
  171–5; and newsworthiness, 166–7,
  168, 169
private facts tort, 155–7, 165–8, 170,
  196, 213–14
probable cause, 29, 32, 42
pro-choice advocates, xiii; *see also*
  abortion

procreation, xvi; 59, 62, 65, 88, 124; *see also* abortion; contraception; embryos; fetus; pregnancy
property: right, 156; surveillance, 23, 26; *see also* home
Prosser, Dean William, 155–6
prostitution, 307–8
psychological testing, 277–89, 306
Psychscreen, 278–81, 284, 286, 287, 288, 289
public disclosure of private facts, *see* private facts tort
public figures, xiv, 151, 152, 196, 199; and defamation, 196–7; *see also* celebrities
public health interests, 54
publicity: right to, 220–1; unwanted, 184
public restrooms, surveillance of, 269–72

Quayle, Dan, 325
Quill, Timothy, 127–36
Quill v. Koppell, 127–30, 337, 339–41

race, 275; *see also* black middle class
radio, 151, 208
Ralph (swimming pig), *see Braun v. Flynt*
rape, 174–5
Rasmussen v. South Florida Blood Services, Inc., 146–7
Rather, Dan, 325
Reagan administration, 291
reason, credible, 32
reasonable person standard, 156, 187
reasonable suspicion, 29, 32
Rehnquist, William, 60, 61, 62, 65, 133
religion, freedom of, 275, 299, 301
residence, *see* home
restrooms, surveillance of, 269–72
right-to-die, 54; cases, 127–39; movement, 134
right to know, 157; *see also* press
right-to-life groups, *see* antiabortion protests
right to privacy, creation of, 154–5

"The Right to Privacy" (Warren, Brandeis), 154–5
right to publicity, 220–2
Riley, Tom, 255–64
Robertson, John, 79, 80, 87
Roe v. Wade, 57, 58–66, 85, 86, 103; trimester framework, 60, 61, 62, 64, 65; *see also* abortion
Rogan, T. D., 326
Rogers, King, 283, 289
Rohr Industries, 303
Romano, Stacey, 229, 230, 232, 234
Roth v. Parries et al., 21–2
royalty pools, 329

Sable, Ronald, 319
Salek v. Passaic Collegiate School, 204
Salisbury Post, 160–5, 168–70
Samsung Electronics, 222
San Francisco Chronicle, 167
Saunders, G., 32–4
Scalia, Antonin, 48, 61, 65, 66
Schaeffer, Rebecca, 325
Schmerber, Mr. (blood sample case), 23, 29
school search cases, 36–49
Scopes monkey trial, 78
searches: baggage, 31–5; based on consent, 35; car, 46, 47; defined, 23; of effects, 28; filmed, 191, 192; of homes, xiii, 26; of papers, 27–8; of persons, 23–5; reasonable, 11, 40–3; school, 36–49; strip, 3–22; warrantless, 29–30; *see also* Fourth Amendment
search warrants, 11, 29
Seligman, Brad, 281, 286
sex tape case, 227–48
sexual: activities and off-duty behavior, 305–9; discrimination, 307; harrassment, 313; orientation and lifestyle monitoring, 140, 151, 167, 276, 294–302; practices, 27; *see also* homosexuals; lesbians
Shahar, Robin (Brown), 294–302
Shahar v. Bowers, 294–302
Shamberg v. State, 45–6
Shawgo v. Spradlin, 308–9

Sherwood Inn (peephole case), 249–65

Shipman, Noel, 312, 314, 315–16

Shivers, Charles, 72, 73, 75, 80

Shoars, Alana, 310–7

Shoars v. Epson America, Inc., 310–17

shoplifting, 278, 283

shredding of documents, 28

Sidis, W. J., 166–7

Silver, Manny, 205

Simpson, Charles, 129

Sipple, O. W., 167, 168

slander, 312, 317

smart cards, 324, 331

smart roads, 324, 331

Smith, M. L., 27

Smith v. Montgomery County, 21–2

smoking, 291, 304

sodomy, 135–6, 270, 298, 300, 301, 306

software companies, 328

Sojourner T. v. Edwards, 68

Soroka, Sibi, 277–89

Soroka v. Dayton Hudson Corp., 277–89

Souter, David, 65

South Carolina Hospital, Medical University, 123

Spahn, Warren, 196

speech, freedom of, 57, 152, 166; and antiabortion protests, 68–70; hateful and harmful, 166; and press, 152–3, 157, 196; *see also* First Amendment

sperm: donation, 94; ownership, 92–3; preservation, 94

Sports Illustrated, 168

Standora, Leo, 203

Stanford University, 287

Stapleton, Keith, 256–64

stare decisis, 63

states: constitutions, xiv; protection of citizens' privacy, xiv, xvi, 30; and tort law, 155; *see also individual names*

State v. Bonnell, 319

State v. Wal-Mart Stores, 303–4

Stein, Ted, 9, 14, 15

Steinberg, Joel, 219

sterilization, forced, 171, 289–90

Stewart, Potter, 58

Stewart, Sheilah, 282, 283

Stoner, Dan, 96, 97, 100–5, 114, 115, 117, 120

Stoner, Nettie, 95–105, 109–10, 112, 114, 115, 117, 120

Stoner, Sherri, 102, 103

Stowe, Mary, *see* Davis, Mary Sue

strip-searches, 3–22; body-cavity, 5–6, 7, 12, 16; damage assessment, 13–15; gender discrimination in, 6, 8, 13

students: drug testing of, 36, 47–9; expectation of privacy, 47; searches of, 36–49

substantive due process, 55, 56, 57, 63

substituted judgment, 119

suicide, 128, 129; assisted, 54, 128, 129, 135; history of, 135; physician-assisted, 128–9, 130–6, 139; recipe for, 130

Sullivan, Emmett, 104

Sun (tabloid), 204–5

surveillance: aerial, 26; court sanctioned, 269–72; dressing room, 269; restroom, 269–72; *see also* electronic monitoring

suspicion: founded, 32, 33; reasonable, 29, 32

Sykes, Bob, 282, 289

Sylvester, Robert, 104–16

Symantec Corporation, 314

tabloid journalism, xiii, 204–5

TAD rule, 304–5

Talbot, J. R., 235, 236, 238, 240

Target Stores, 277–89

tax fraud, 28

Taylor, Ned, 253, 257–61

technology, raising new legal questions, 53, 276, 314, 326–7

Telephone Consumer Protection Act, 330

telephone(s): Caller ID, 327; cellular, 323, 331; company records, 27–8; harrassment, 185, 186; monitoring, 275, 314–17, 320; solicitation lists, 328, 330; wiretaps, 23, 185, 327

television, 152, 220; broadcast of death, 176–88; broadcast of private facts, 173–4; cable records, 330, 332;

television (*continued*)
   invasion of privacy cases, 189–90;
   ride-along coverage, 181, 188
Tennessee, state constitution, 87–8
Tennessee Supreme Court, 85–90, 92
terminal illness: competence of
   patient, 134; and physician-assisted
   suicide, 127–39
terrorism, xiii, 327
Texas: Court of Appeals, 306; sodomy
   law, 306; state constitution, 306
Texas Supreme Court: and emotional
   distress cases, 242, 244–6, 247; and
   false light tort, 202
Thomas, Clarence, 65
Thomas S. v. Robin Y., 94
Thorne v. El Segundo, 306–7
tort(s), 155–7; appropriation, 155–7,
   213–14; defined, 155; false light,
   155–7, 195; intrusion, 155, 157, 185,
   187, 226; invasion of privacy, 155–7,
   213–14; law, 155–7, 245; negligent
   hiring and retention, 276; private
   facts, 155–7, 165–8, 170, 196, 213–14;
   reform, 242; v. constitutional right,
   183
transsexuals, 151, 167–8
trespass, 185, 187, 189; tort, 155, 156
TRW (credit bureau), 326
Turner v. Louisiana and Sudduth, 267
"$2 M Suit in Sweet Nuthin
   Eavesdrop" (*New York Newsday*), 318
two-way mirrors, *see McCall v. The
   Sherwood Inn*

United States v. Miller, 27
urine testing, 24, 29; of students,
   47–9; in workplace, 275
USAA (insurance company), 241
U.S. Bill of Rights, *see* Bill of Rights
U.S. Constitution, xiv; framers of, 25,
   53; privacy not mentioned in, xiii,
   xv, 10, 53; right of intimate
   association, 301; rights not
   specifically mentioned in, 57; right
   v. tort, 183; *see also* Bill of Rights;
   First Amendment; Fourteenth
   Amendment; Fourth Amendment
U.S. Court of Appeals: First Circuit,

293; Second Circuit, 21, 142, 143, 337,
   341; Fifth Circuit, 67, 68, 201, 309;
   Sixth Circuit, 308; Seventh Circuit,
   13, 15, 16, 17; Eighth Circuit, 67;
   Ninth Circuit, 48, 94, 136, 307, 337,
   340, 341; Eleventh Circuit, 302
U.S. Department of Health and
   Human Services, 93
U.S. Office of Civil Rights, 123
U.S. Post Office, 319, 325
U.S. Secret Service, 190
U.S. Supreme Court, 12, 53–4;
   abortion issue, 53–66; and aerial
   surveillance, 26; and citizen
   encounters with police, 34;
   exceptions to warrant rule, 11;
   interpretation of Fourth
   Amendment, 10; interpretation of
   the law, 56; interpretation of
   liberty, 55–7, 63, 134–5; life service
   of justices, 56; and private facts
   cases, 165–6, 170; and right-to-die,
   134; and school searches, 42–3,
   47–9; and unwanted medical
   treatment, 133; and what
   constitutes a search, 23; *see also
   individual cases and issues; Roe v.
   Wade*
U.S. v. North, Washington, D.C., 318–19

vegetative state, 137–9
Veronia, Oregon, 47, 48
Video Privacy Protection Act, 328
video rental records, 328, 330, 331
video surveillance, 225, 266, 317;
   hidden, 316, 319; sex tape case,
   227–48; in workplace, 275, 316, 317;
   see also electronic monitoring
voice mail, 318
voice sample, 23–4, 25
voice stress analyzers, 293
voluntary active euthanasia, 132
voyeurism, 225–6; peephole cases,
   249–65, 266–9; sex tape case,
   227–48; surveillance cases, 270–2

Wal-Mart Stores, 303–4
warrantless searches, 29–30

warrants, search, 11, 29
Warren, Samuel D., 154-5, 323
Washington, D.C., Court of Appeals, 114-18
Washington State, and physician-assisted suicide, 130, 135, 136
Waters v. Fleetwood, 173-4
Weber v. Dell, 20-1
Webster v. Reproductive Health Services, 61, 85, 88
Weingold, Alan, 101, 103, 104, 106, 107, 110, 112-14, 118, 120
Whalen v. Roe, 140-1, 142
White, Byron, 61, 65, 66
White, Vanna, 222
White v. Samsung Electronics America, Inc., 222
Widener v. Frey, 45
Wilcox, Win, 235, 236, 240
wiretapping, 23, 185, 327; laws, 314, 315
workplace, 275-6; dating of co-workers, 303-4, 308-9; drug testing in, 275, 289-90, 291-2; electronic monitoring in, 310-20; job applicant rights v. worker rights, 285, 287; lifestyle monitoring, 294-302; nexus requirement, 286, 287; psychological testing, 277-90, 306; search of employee files and offices, 313
World Guide to Nude Beaches and Recreation, 218
World Trade Center, New York, 328
writs of assistance, 10, 16

Xerox, 317

Young, William Dale, 77, 84, 85, 86, 89
Young v. Nevada, 270-1